John Carroll

Case and his contempories; or, The Canadian itinerant's memorial: constituting a biographical history of Methodism in Canada, from its introduction into the province, till the death of the Rev. Wm. Case in 1855

Vol. V

John Carroll

Case and his contempories; or, The Canadian itinerant's memorial: constituting a biographical history of Methodism in Canada, from its introduction into the province, till the death of the Rev. Wm. Case in 1855
Vol. V

ISBN/EAN: 9783337207823

Printed in Europe, USA, Canada, Australia, Japan

Cover: Foto ©ninafisch / pixelio.de

More available books at **www.hansebooks.com**

CASE,

AND

HIS COTEMPORARIES;

OR,

THE CANADIAN ITINERANTS' MEMORIAL:

CONSTITUTING A

BIOGRAPHICAL HISTORY OF METHODISM IN CANADA

FROM ITS

INTRODUCTION INTO THE PROVINCE TILL THE DEATH OF THE
REV. WILLIAM CASE, IN 1855.

BY

JOHN CARROLL, D.D.

"Tell ye your children of it, and let your children tell their children, and their children another generation."—PROPHET JOEL.

VOLUME V.

TORONTO:
PUBLISHED AT THE METHODIST CONFERENCE OFFICE,
KING STREET EAST.
1877.

A FINAL WORD TO THE READER.

My long cherished desire and purpose are achieved at last. The unparalleled production of a history of sixty-four years course of operations, and a portraiture of the actors in its accomplishment combined, is before the reader. It is as if the "Nonconformist's Memorial," and "Baxter's Life and Times," or "The History of the Puritans," should be woven into one. I pretend not to say whether this is an excellence, or defect, but there it is. My original and fondest wish was to preserve a memorial of each of the itinerants who had labored in Canada from 1790 to 1855; next, I adopted the idea of presenting the public life, pre-eminently, of the most influential among them, and one who exercised his ministry fifty years; but in the accomplishment of these two objects, I accomplished a third, and more important one than either, the history of the Church as well as its ministry. If such things are of any importance, then I say that I have furnished the great Methodist Church (so far as it relates to "the two Canada's" especially) an account of its rise and progress and a memorial of all its ministers, something which no Church in existence possesses but herself, at least that I know of.

This work has been accomplished amid scores of disadvantages which are too painful to dwell upon. It has been conceived and carried on without one breath of endorsation, or encouragement, from any Conference or convocation in the world. It is true, the Book Committee of our Connexion so far countenanced it as to secure the copyright; and the Rev. Samuel Rose, the Book Steward, has not flinched from the outlay in its publication, notwithstanding the book was so much larger than was at first expected, and was so much more costly to print than nearly any other book, being very much crowded and full of matter, with no vacant places to eke out the book. So also among my encouragements, I must say, that one individual in a high official position,—I refer to the Rev. Dr. Wood,—has been an undeviating sympathizer, counsellor, and help from the first to the last.

The absence of Conferential endorsation has relieved me from one embarrassment: I have been preserved from the temptation to write in the interests of a party, as is characteristic of some histories I wot of; I have been enabled to preserve my own individuality and to keep to historic truthfulness, so far as I could discover the truth. I have not presented the Conference and Church as I might have wished them to appear, but as what they were.

For reasons I have stated in former Prefaces, this work is not perfect, but, in fact, is very imperfect: still, in the very nature of things, a first edition of a multifarious work of this kind must, almost inevitably, be so.

This volume has been delayed by many insuperable ob

stacles, principally by the crushing injury I received on the 8th day of August last, from which I barely escaped with my life. For many weeks I could not write at all, and to this hour, the posture to be taken in writing is most painful to assume. And now I have to hurry the work through press.

There is only one thing about which I am particularly anxious, namely :—*that my Publisher may be re-imbursed within a reasonable time.* I have submitted to the personal disagreeable of canvassing for my own work, principally to prevent this loss to him. But I do hope that the ministers and members of the Church will now aid me in this matter. There are many of them to whom I owe much in my humble endeavors in the past.

Some of the individuals mentioned, or who have a right to be mentioned, in a work of this kind, may not be altogether pleased. At this I am not surprised, for I have not been able to please myself. By inadvertency, in a few cases, while all the facts have been given, the *name* has been omitted. In some cases a temporary laborer has been overlooked altogether. And among those who have been named, some will think enough has not been said, or particulars of interest to them omitted; and some will wish that I had not been so minute, or particular, with regard to them; there may be truth in all this, but I have looked at the interest and information of the general reader; and I have been swayed by what I thought would be the general judgment of those who knew the parties.

This volume will have appended to it a *desideratum*, the need of which has been felt from the first, namely, an *Alphabetical Index*, and it will be for the former four volumes as well as this. This convenience I owe to the ability and painstaking of the Rev. GEORGE HENRY CORNISH, who excels in such matters. I had not time and strength to accomplish it: and I confess I have not the ability to do it as he has completed it. From this piece of industry and care it seems that no less than nearly thirteen hundred considerable persons connected with Canadian Methodism, lay and clerical, are referred to, and more or less fully described in these volumes.

I am rejoiced to know that although my biographical history leaves the last nineteen years of our Canadian Methodist history unnarrated—that is to say, from 1855 to 1874, when our present comprehensive organization went into effect—the recent published recollections of his public life, by the Rev. Dr. Green, who has been so conspicuously identified with Connexional matters, will go a great way towards supplying that lack.

Asking pardon for all my short-comings, and for all the offences, inadvertently, given to any one, I commend these volumes to the patronage of the Methodist Church of Canada and to the countenance and furtherance of Almighty God.

THE AUTHOR.

Don Mount, April, 1877.

ANALYTICAL INDEX TO VOL. V.

BOOK TWELFTH.

1847-48.

	PAGE
1. Meeting of Conference in 1847 and of the Canada Western District—President and Secretary	1
2. Dr. Alder, and Rev. Messrs. Wood and Harvard introduced	2
3. Union restored by vote of 88 to 8	2
4. Assumption of the chair by Dr. Alder—Congratulations and prayer	3
5. Articles of the re-constructed Union: embracing the relations of the English and Canada Conferences—Chapel property—President—Co-Delegate—Book of Discipline—Superintendent of Missions—Standing Board—Canadian Missionary Society—British Missionaries now in Canada—Trial of British Conference Members—Claims of such	3
6. Great augmentation of the ministerial ranks	7
7. Rev Dr. Richey co-Delegate and acting President through the year	8
8, 9, 10, and 11. Rev. Enoch Wood, Superintendent of Missions, &c	8
12. Five ministers in full standing never before connected with the Conference	9
13. Account of Rev. Robert Brooking	10
14. Rev. Samuel Dwight Rice	10
15. Three British and ten Canadians received into full connexion	11
16. Intermediate probationers from the British side	12
17. Three received on trial: Trickey, McGill, Nelles	12
18. McGill's previous history	12
19. Nelles's antecedents	13
20. No reduction of Conference excepting Butcher's location	13
21. Manner of providing for Circuits where there had been rival interests	14
22. Number of Districts and who were the Chairmen	15
23. Editor and Book Steward, Sanderson and Green—Dr. Ryerson	15
24. How Mr. Case was situated—W. Ames	16
25. No increase of Districts, but Chairmen to *travel* them for the ensuing year, and why	16
26. Their labors untiring	16
27. So with the rank and file—Particulars of several Districts	16
28. Number of members embarked in the Union from the two sides, but no increase on the first year, but apparent decrease	18
29. Papers opposed to the Connexion	18
30. Agitation because of the new University measure, with details thereof	18
31. Canada Eastern District Meeting—Cox and Dorey	20
32. Particulars of the two named	20
33. Amended Stations for Canada East, during 1847-48	21
34. Still further modifications—Cases of Rev. Messrs. Evans and Davidson	21
35 to 38. Extracts from Mr. Slight's Journal, illustrative of Lower Canada work	22
39. Remarks on Mr. Slight's opinions—Philip Embury	24
40. Slight decrease—Total number	24

1848-49.

	PAGE
41. Conference of 1848. Rev. Dr. Dixon, President	24
42 to 44. Further interesting particulars of President Dixon	52
45. Rev. Matthew Richey and his doctorate	28
46. Belleville Conference—Vanduse, Secretary—The six received into full connexion	29
47. Five received on trial—Their names	29
48. Particulars of John G. Laird	39
49. Case of James Gooderham	30
50. Particulars of John English	30
51. Some account of Noble Armstrong, and Lewis Morton	30
52. Rev. James Evans—His life and death	31
53. Three discontinued, on different several grounds, from the Conference roll—Snider—Connor	32
54. Robert Darlington's supernumeration and after labors	32
55. The Connexional staff at Toronto—Drs. Richey and Green, and Revs. Wood and Sanderson	32
56. Changes in the City of Toronto—Evans, Rice, and Davis	32
57. Supply of vacancies in Toronto District—Nottawasaga, Barrie, and Brock, with Reid, Smith, and Gundy	33
58. Three vacancies in the London District: Sarnia, St. Clair, Sydenham—Chase—Account of Edward White	33
59. Case of Gosfield and Amherstburg—Edwin Clement	34
60. Brantford District—Budge and Fish—Fish's labors and success—J. Jackson	35
61. Two vacancies in the Hamilton District—G. Smith—J. S. Evans	36
62. Cobourg District—Case in charge of a District again after twenty years	36
63. Bytown District—Budge and the town of Bytown—L'Original and John B. Armstrong—Squire, the Chairman of Kingston District, and Shepherd, of Bytown	37
64. Three who received appointments in Canada East: Lanton, Scott, Taylor—Botterell to P. E. Island	38
65. Sanderson, Editor; and A. Geeen a D.D	38
66. Work prosecuted with vigor, but disruption in London	39
67. Circuits favored with revivals—Letter from Rev. W. Case (note)	30
68. Missionary anniversaries and deputations	40
69. Literary Institutions of the denomination—A. McNabb, D.D	40
70. Gain on the year 1848-49—Total	41
71. District Meeting for Canada East—Dr. Richey and Mr. Jenkins	41
72. A history of Rev. John Jenkins	42
73. First appearance of one who proved a remarkable man: G. Douglas	42
74. Things cheering in that Province	43
75. Veritable Stations for the year	43
76. Messrs. Hutchinson and Graham—G. Douglas's intermediate occupation	44
77. Few sources of information about the labors of the year	44
78 and 79. Illustrations from Rev. B. Slight's MS. Journal	44
80. Causes of small numerical progress—Membership in the two sections	45

1849-50.

81. Hamilton Conference	46
82. Dr. Richey actual President, &c	46
83. Deliberations passed smoothly, with one exception	46
84. Six received into full connexion—A slight anticipation of their history	46
85. Intermediate probationers passed over—Eight formally received on trial—Those who had labored under a Chairman and those who had not	47
86. Byrne and Griffin	48
87. Particulars of A. S. Byrne	48
88. W. S. Griffin's previous history	49
89. A minister of fifty received—C. Byrne	50
90. The functionaries at the Publishing House	50
91. J. Ryerson's visit to England	50
92. Revs. J. Jenkins and J. G. Witted	50
93. *Hiati* in the Minutes to be supplied	51

		PAGE
94.	Toronto District: Nottagawasa and St. Vincent—Reid and Rice	51
95.	London District: Wardsville, Chatham, and St. Thomas Circuits—Peacock, Armstrong, and T. Stobbs	51
96.	Brantford District: Woodstock, &c.	53
97.	Hamilton District: Grimsby and Barber	53
98.	Scugog in the Cobourg District	53
99.	Case of Peter Jones, S. D. Rice, C. Lavell, L. Demorest, and D. Hardie	54
100.	Indian Industrial School at Muncey	54
101.	Sailing of the Representative	54
101.	President purposes to travel at large	54
102.	The "rank and file" struggle hard against the untoward prejudices of the times	55
103.	Camp-meetings in Vaughan—Among the Indians—Ingathering	55
104.	Good news from thirty-six several Circuits	56
105.	Goodly, but not great increase	56
106.	Methodism in Canada East—MS. Journal exhausted	56
107.	Stations of Canada Eastern District	57
108.	Four known to be authentic	57
109.	Long extracts from B. Slight's MS. Journal	57
110.	Records the Chairman's sudden death	59
111.	Circumstances of Rev. M. Lang's death—Numbers	59
112.	The above specimen labors	61

1850-51.

113.	Brockville Conference—Dr. Richey—A. Hurlburt, Secretary	61
114.	Fifteen received into full Connexion—Six afterwards Chairmen—Eminence of others	61
115.	Five recruits—Names and nationalities	62
116.	I. Barber's previous labors	62
117.	W. Burns' character and history	62
118.	R. M. Hammond's character and history	62
119.	Particulars of Andrew A. Smith	64
120.	Particulars of Joseph Hugill	65
121.	Old soldiers putting off the harness—Healy—Metcalf's obsequies	65
122.	The visit of Dr. Bangs and Rev. C. Churchill	66
123.	The particulars and pleasure of Dr. Bangs' visit, &c.	67
124.	Official Connexional appointments—Removals—Rice and Rose	67
125.	Dr. McNabb's resignation and provisions to supply his place—Nelles	68
126.	Dr. Ryerson, failing to reach the Session of British Conference, confided his duties to Dr. Alder	69
127.	The supplement to the Barrie District Stations: Muirhead, Clarke, Smith, Dean, B. Jones	69
128.	London District: Hutchinson and Strathroy	70
129.	Chatham and Joel Briggs	71
129.	No real vacancy at Amherstburg—Thomas Stobbs	72
130.	Brantford District—Error about Woodstock	72
131.	Glanford—G. Young to London—Haw in his place—W. Creighton	73
132.	Supply for Nanticoke—G. Washington, 1st	73
133.	Wm. Case's assistant at Alderville—G. McDougall	73
134.	Sidney Circuit—Fawcett, A. D. Miller	74
135.	Kingston District, Waterloo—J. W. McCollum and John Wesley German	75
136.	Osgoode: Shaler, S. Huntingdon *	75
137.	L. Taylor returned by C. E. with thanks, and Lavell asked for another year	76
138.	A testimonial to Rev. John Black	76
139.	Union Camp-meeting for Yonge Street, Newmarket, and Humber Circuits	76
140.	Good services of Burlington Academy	76
141.	Dr. Ryerson appointed to the Chief Superintendency of Schools	77

* There is an error here: Huntingdon spent that year on the *Clarendon* Circuit, and Mr. Shaler's assistant was *Andrew McAllister*.

		PAGE
142.	Missionary income augmented	77
143.	News from England of the appointment of Rev. Messrs. Wood and J. Ryerson to the two highest offices	77
144.	New church—145. Good augury for the College	77
146.	Revivals in two Circuits	77
147.	Letter from P. Jones—148. Wesley Church	77
149.	Owen Sound Camp-meeting—150. Do. Manning Settlement	78
151.	Revival on Napanee—152. Missionary Anniversary	78
153.	Saugeen—154. Letters from Rev. T. Bevitt	78
155.	Brick parsonage—156. Stratford, Brampton, St. Thomas, and Dundas Circuits	78
157.	Chippewa Chapel—158. Good news from Malahide, Peel, Norwood, Newboro', Bowmanville, Orillia, Glanford, Cornwall, &c.—Church at Cline's	79
159.	Gain of 1,170 souls in 1850-51	79
160.	C. E. District Meeting	79
161.	Particulars of the above Stations	79
162.	Whom we miss	80
163.	Shut up to Mr. Slight's Journal	80
164 to 172.	Transcript of interesting particulars	81
173.	Returns—Decrease—Totals	83

1851-52.

174.	Coincidence of the first year of President Wood with the 27th Session of Canada Conference—Satisfactory	84
175.	A layman's letter concerning this Conference	84
176.	Rev. James Musgrove, Secretary	85
177.	Brethren fully received: Webster, Osborn, McGill, and Henry Reid	85
178.	Nineteen candidates for admission	86
179.	Names of ten who had labored the year before	86
180.	Case of A. Campbell	86
181.	David Sawyer, an Indian preacher	87
182.	Thomas Crews' labors the year before—J. S. Evans	87
183.	McRitchie's antecedents	88
184.	Eight candidates and their nationality	88
185.	History of Richard Clarke	89
186.	History of James Preston	90
187.	Drummond G. Fletcher	90
188.	Wm. Sanderson—189. Robert Brewster	91
190.	McAllister—191. Robert Hobbs	91
192.	David Robertson	92
193.	A previous blunder corrected relating to the two brothers McDowell	92
194.	Death of Wilson, Ferguson, and Byrne	93
195.	Obituary of Rev. Jas. Wilson	93
196.	Obituary of Rev. G. Ferguson	93
197.	Byrne's obituary *in extenso*	94
198.	G. R. Sander's retirement and James Spencer's elevation to the Editorial Chair—Antithetical contrast	95
199.	Propose to inquire after supplies	97
200.	Supply for Humber—Wm. Richardson—Case of Nelson Circuit	97
201.	Mr. Warner and Barrie District—Beausoliel, &c.—S. James—G. McDougall and Bruce Mines	98
202.	Nottawasaga—J. M. Clarke—His Journal	98
203.	Clarke's entrance into the Ministry	99
204.	London District and change of Chairman—The four vacancies and supplies	99
205.	First pair—Early history and character—John Shaw	99
206.	Chatham and James Taylor	100
207.	Wallaceburg and St. Thomas; Harman, Hugill, E. H. Dewart	101
208.	Amherstburg—Whiting—W. Williams	102
209.	Brantford District; Ingersoll and Norwich	102
210.	Hamilton District; Nanticoke—Baxter and Tomblin	203

		PAGE
211.	Dunnville: J. Hunt and G. Washington	103
212.	S. Waldron and Elora—Edmund Cooke	103
213.	Peel: Rev. E. Adams and his son-in-law, Mr. Swann	104
214.	Three vacancies in the Cobourg District—Scugog—Alderville and T. Hurlburt—Metcalf and T. McMullen	104
215.	Good news from McMullen's Mission	105
216.	Belleville District: Picton and B. Jones—Sidney and H. Jones	105
217.	Newboro', in the Kingston District—M. Baxter and John Mills	106
218.	Hinchinbrooke unexplained	106
219.	Brockville and Bytown Districts: J. G. Witted	106
220.	A year of great Connexional activity	106
221.	Places where Camp-meetings were held	170
222.	New churches, &c.:—Bradford, Learn's, King, Janestown, Kizer's, Burford, Hamilton, Bytown, Vandusen's, Port Hope, Strathroy, North Port, Waterdown, Prince Albert, Mercea Street, Cookstown	107
223.	Good news from various Circuits	107
224.	From Bruce Mines and Garden River, Wellesley, Rawdon, Nelson, Hamilton, Madoc, Proton, Brockville District, St. Catharines and neighbouring Circuits, Glanford, Markham, Brighton, Chatham, Waterloo, Kingston, St. Thomas, Alderville, Rice Lake, St. Clair, Hurlburt, Alnwick, Mono, Port Hope, Green Bush, and Wardsville	108
225.	The greatest success in Toronto	109
226.	The Financial District Meeting satisfactory	109
227.	Lay suspicion about the Bill for incorporating Connexional Funds	109
228.	Re-opening of the Clergy Reserve Question	110
229.	Sunday-school Society and *S. S. Guardian*	110
230.	Deaths: C. Biggar, Esq., Mr. J. VanCamp	110
231.	Rev. J. Ryerson starts for St. Rupert's Land, *via* England	111
232.	Gain and total numbers for Canada West	111
233.	Scarce materials relative to Canada East	111
234 to 237.	Full account of the business and prospects of Lower Canada District, from the pen of Rev. J. Borland	111
238.	Stations for Canada East during 1851-52—Case of G. N. A. F. T. Dickson	113
239.	Note of encouragement from Mr. Brock	113
240.	Good news from Granby, per Rev. R. A. Flanders	114
241.	Letter from Rev. J. Borland	114
242.	Communication from a friendly Presbyterian—Leeds	114
243.	Making up totals	115

1852-53.

244.	The Conference for 1852 in Kingston—President, co-Delegate, Mr. Sanderson, Secretary—Harmonious and devout	115
245.	Names of ten admitted into full connexion—Three performed five years' labor	116
246.	Case of F. Berry peculiar	116
247.	The public reception, Messrs. Case and Carroll, and Dr. Ryerson	117
248.	Nine received on trial—Names	117
249.	Henry Jones described	117
250.	McAllister and Preston retire for want of health—Death of McAllister, &c.	118
251.	Rev. C. Turver visits England	118
252.	Fall of Jonathan Loverin	118
253.	Visit from Rev. James Brock	118
254.	Rev. J. Ryerson Representative to English Conference—Does not go to Hudson's Bay	119
255.	Speakers at the Conference Missionary Meeting	119
256.	Touching address and request of Mr. Case, who was released from responsibility—Mr. Musgrove, &c	119
257.	Rev. L. Taylor renewing his strength for a wider field	120
258.	Incumbents at the Book and Printing Establishment	120
259.	Toronto District: Humber and a young Irishman—McDonagh	120
260.	Bramton, Young, and Blackstock, and a nameless supply	122
261.	Georgetown and Jos. Messmore	122
262.	Nelson, McCollum, Hunt, Prindle, Washington	123

		PAGE
263.	Stouffville and Snake Island provided for by their neighbors	123
264.	Barrie and its extemporized supply—A comparison between Harris and Edwards	123
265.	St. Vincent and Derby, with their probable supplies	125
266.	Sandwich and Windsor—Ames	125
267.	Cayuga add Elora	126
268.	Scugog and Mud Lake—Antecedents and character of H. O. Ellsworth—Name omitted—Note concerning Woolsey, but in the wrong place	126
269.	Belleville: J. Ryerson and Preston—Case of Thomas D. Pearson	128
270.	Consecon and Witted—Allison	129
271.	Hungerford and John D. Pugh	129
272.	Kingston, Brockville, Bytown—M. Baxter—Hinchinbrooke, Keegan—Maitland, Peake—T. McMullen	129
273.	Great activity—*Guardian*—*S. S. Advocate*	130
274.	Rev. S. D. Rice, and efforts to redeem the College	130
275.	A Collegiate Church	131
276.	Professor Wright and Professor Wilson	131
277.	A church and parsonage building year—Instances	131
278.	Churches in Essa and Port Stanley	132
279.	Moraviantown Chapel	132
280.	New church in Reach, &c	132
281.	Hewitt's Church, Mono Road	132
282.	Richard Phelps and Morpeth, &c	132
283.	Carlisle and its new church	132
284.	New church in Galt—Eminent brothers	133
285.	Camp-meetings and their gear	133
286.	Camp-meetings at Brampton, Chatham, Mono, Woolwich	133
287.	Strathroy, Toronto West, Norwich, Jackson's S. H., Garden River	133
288.	Tuscarora Indians and A. Sickles	133
289.	Great revivals in Kingston and Hamilton, under Mr. Caughey	134
290.	The general gain on the year	134
291.	Canada East—Temporary Chairman	134
292.	Time and place of District Meeting	134
293.	Pleasing Session	134
294.	Tried, but preserved	135
295.	Ingathering of souls	135
296.	Three probationers—Two ordained for special purposes—Sermon by Mr. Davidson	135
297.	Anniversary Meeting of District Missionary Society	136
298.	Future position and relations of the District	136
299.	Rev. J. Brock Representative to Canada Conference	136
300.	Unmistakable indications of amalgamation	136
301.	List of Stations for 1852-53	136
302.	Quebec news, from Mr. Borland	137
303.	Sudden death of Rev. Wm. Squire	138
304.	Letter in the *Guardian* from a Montreal layman	138
305.	"G. H. D's" letter of encouragement	138
306.	Their doings estimated by results—Provincial and general totals	139

1853-54.

307.	Conference preceded by C. E. District	140
308.	Conference in McNab Street Church, Hamilton—Rev. E. Wood—I. B. Howard, Secretary	140
309.	Four in full connexion with Conference	140
310.	E. L. Koyle, from another body	141
311.	Seven candidates—Names—Who presented before	141
312.	S. E. Maudsley—Antecedents, &c	142
313.	Thomas Woolsey from London	142
314.	Edwin Peake—Last year with Rev. W. McGill	143
315.	Allen Salt, Indian preacher	143
316.	Richard John Forman and his history	144
317.	Staff officers unchanged	144
318.	Omissions of the Minutes to be supplemented	145

	PAGE
319. Brampton and Joseph E. Sanderson	145
320. Nelson and Robert Fowler, M.D.	146
321. Nauticoke and its two supplies : Ira B. Kilborn and John V. Wilson	146
322. Dunnville and Wm. Tomblin	147
323. Supply for Grand River—Surmise about Peter Jones—Norwich and Ingersoll—Case of Rev. Joseph Shepley and Paris, Aylmer, &c	147
324. White's assistant at Windsor, &c.—William Williams	148
325. New District—Two supplies of great promise—Elora and George Cochran	149
326. Mitchel and Lucius Adams	150
327. Mono, its preachers and successes	152
328. No response from Barrie	153
329. Lindsay and G. J. Dingman	153
330. Norwood and John Fawcett	153
331. Hungerford and an extraordinary supply—L. Houghton	153
332. Hinchinbrooke and Storrington—Newborough and William Bryers	154
333. No help for V. B. Howard at Cornwall	155
334. Lochaber and Richard Wilson	155
335. Clarendon and its supplies—Andrew Armstrong	155
336. Several specialties—A Miller's rest—E. Hurlburt and W. Andrews for Canada East	156
337. Case in the "Thames Country"	156
338. Original letter to Digman	157
339. Intense activity of a strong force	157
340. A summary digest	158
341. Statistics of the Hamilton revival	158
342. Impulse by Camp-meetings—Three named	159
343. More particularized	159
344. News of revivals from twenty Circuits and more	160
345. Importance of churches	160
346. The Collegiate Church, Cobourg	161
347. Revival and church at LaChute	161
348. Norwood, Garden River, and Percy Mill's Churches	161
349. Tosotoronto and Mono Circuit	161
350. Brighton and Frankford Church	161
351. McCullough and Perrytown Church	162
352. London and Bruce Mines Churches	162
353. Woodstock Church	162
354. Collection for Conference students	162
355. Clergy Reserve Question	162
356. Rev. S. D. Rice in the service of Victoria College	163
357. Heman Hurlburt and his biographer	163
358. Missionary meetings and deputations—Hurlburt and Herkimer—Advance.	163
359. How these chronicles may close	163
360. Numerical gains	164
361. Canada Eastern District	164
362. Rev. E. Wood and that District Meeting	164
363. Counselling with lay-officials	165
364. Harmony and interest	165
365. Case of Brethren Ingalls and John Douglas	165
366. Deputation to Canada Conference : Jenkins, Borland, and Brock	165
367. Stations as supplemented by an Upper Canada loan	
368. Cases of Dickson and E. Hurlburt, of Eaton and Graham—Vacan es at Durham, Brome, Sutten, Dudswell, Danville, and Gaspe	
369. Glimpses of labor and success	
370. News of British Conference concurrence	
371. Quebec and Rev. James Caughey	
372. New life-blood—Unusual increase—Totals	16

BOOK THIRTEENTH.

CASE AND HIS COTEMPORARIES AMALGAMATED INTO ONE HOMOGENOEUS WHOLE.

1854-55.

	PAGE
1. A short but final epoch in our history	169
2. Where and when the epochal Conference sat—The number of ministers—Deputation and visitor	169
3. President and co-Delegate—I. B. Howard, Secretary	169
4. No change in Connexional officers, excepting Dr. Green—G. R. Sanderson, Book Steward	170
5. Absence of a distinguished man from the central position	170
6. Important question of the class-meeting test of membership raised—Debate and debaters—Retirement of the mover for one year	170
7. Prevailing laxity—Advice	172
8. The proposal for amalgamation of the Eastern District endorsed	173
9. The progress of endowment by scholarships	173
10. Sixteen received into full connexion—Case, Green, and Borland speakers	174
11. The names of the fully admitted—The two from Lower Canada	174
12. The great number taken on trial—Their names	174
13. Some who had labored a year without credit	174
14. Mere surmises in some cases	174
15. Ashton Fletcher, the younger	175
16. Jay S. Youmans, and his history	175
17. John S. Clarke, and his history	176
18. John Wakefield—before and after	176
19. William Scales, history, character, size	177
20. Peter German, a married man, &c.	177
21. Wm. Braden, not Briden, comes out from Osnabruck	178
22. Samuel G. Philips—Canada East—St. Johns	178
23. George F. Richardson—More on a subsequent page	178
24. George Jaques, nationality, &c.—More to follow	178
25. Two who went to Episcopalianism—Davidson and Montgomery—Resemblances and contrasts	179
26. Those have finished their course	179
27. The first, George Poole—Obituary	179
28. Rev. James Booth—British Minutes	180
29. Silence on the Clergy Reserves	181
30. The number stationed this epochal year	181
31. An instalment of the Stations by Districts—Toronto District, &c.	181
32. Next in order—Hamilton District	182
33. Cases of Cainsville and Corson—Nanticoke and Wilson—Welland	183
34. Brantford District Stations, with note about Woodstock and Morgan	184
35. Revds. W. S. Griffin, and P. German's accounts of their Circuits, respectively	185
36. London District Stations—Note showing the exchange of Stobbs and Creighton	186
37. Assistant for Sarnia—Wm. Hawke	188
38. Warwick and John Wesley Savage	188
39. Stations of the Chatham District	189
40. Who will tell the vacancies, deaths, and falls—Hutchinson	189
41. Guelph District Stations	190
42. Elora and Guelph—Dyer and Clarke	190
43. Peel and Alexander R. Campbell	191
44. What, and how we find out about James Berry	192
45. Morris and Rev. A. Campbell—Note explanatory—John Hough	192
46. Stations in the Owen Sound District	193
47. Four supplies wanting—Wisdom of employing temporary laborers	193
48. Edmund Cooke—Peculiar, but true	194
Father Atkey"—Good life and happy death	195

INDEX.

		PAGE
50.	Case and antecedents of Wm. Shannon	195
51.	Some account of Peter Empy	195
52.	A young married laborer—W. K. Dyre	197
53.	Attempt to distribute and locate the four supplies	197
54.	Stations in the Barrie District	197
55.	Surmises about Beausoliel and Snake Island—Orillia—J. B. Keough	198
56.	Stations for the Cobourg District—Note on Mud Lake and its Supply	199
57.	No supply for Lindsay with Rev. Thos. Hanna	200
58.	Millbrook and Samuel Down—His characteristics	200
59.	A Chairman's supply for Metcalfe	201
60.	Norwood—Exchange between supplies	201
61.	Stations for the Bellevile District	201
62.	One vacancy, satisfactorily supplied—Sidney and David A. Johnson	201
63.	Kingston District and its stations	202
64.	Two of the four supplies ascertained—William Briden and Sheffield	203
65.	"Storrington" or Battersea supplied by James Thompson, his obituary	203
66.	Stations of the Brockville District	205
67.	Reserve the annotations and give the Bytown District Stations	205
68.	Four supplies required—Three ascertained—Cavignal and W. L. Hewett	206
69.	Osgoode, Pattyson, J. A. Dowler, supply	206
70.	Clarendon and L. Houghton—Grenville and James Roy	207
71.	Cases of Costello and Luke—Surmises about James Masson's Circuit—Character and capabilities	208
72.	Another for this category ; Richard Pinch and Blenheim	208
73.	Facts omitted by hurry	209
	(1) Data about Wm. Hawke	209
	(2) " " George Jaques	209
	(3) Dunnville and 1854-55 and '55-56	209
	(4) More facts about G. T. Richardson	210
	(5) " " " J. W. Savage	210
	(6) " " and connections of Wm. Scales	210
74.	Stations for Canada put all together—Six U. C. Canadians in the East	210
75.	Manifesto relative to that section of the work and the stations arranged in three Districts	211
76.	Montreal no vacancy—Quebec three—Stanstead one	213
77.	Point Levi and its supply—Edward Cragg's letter	213
78.	The "Ambassadors sent unto Heathens"—Names	213
79.	Four considerable men : J. Ryerson, S. Hurlburt, Brooking, and Salt—Account of Mr. Ryerson till then	214
80.	Hurlburt's labors and attainments	214
81.	Mr. Brooking and his missionary life	215
82.	None superior to Mr. Salt in his way	215
83.	The women and children in the missionary party—Mesdames Hurlburt, Brooking, and Salt—Gov. Simpson	215
84.	Mr. Salt the first located : "Rainy Lake"	216
85.	Red River striking the eye of Mr. Ryerson	216
86.	How their course thence tended	216
87.	Course of the party after leaving Mr. Hurlburt	217
88.	Mr. Brooking goes on past his station with Messrs. Ryerson and Steinhaur to York Factory	218
89.	Messrs. Ryerson and Steinhaur, after a short stay in England, recross the Atlantic to Canada	218
90.	History of Steinhaur from childhood till then	218
91.	Proceedings of this climacteric year	219
92.	Camp-meetings and in what places	219
93.	Revivals, however, arising	219
94.	An attempt to particularise the places and character of revivals	219
95.	Missionary and Anniversary now commingled	220
96.	Places where churches built and opened, &c.	220
97.	Dr. Green's account of a visit to the British Conference, and Peter Jones's visit to the Christian Union Convention	220
98.	Things sober and sad—Death of O'Loan	221
99.	Mixed Convention—Its rise	221
100.	The character and call of the "Joint Committee"	222

		PAGE
101.	Apprehensions, but needless	222
102.	Number of laymen appointed—Opening and organization of proceeding ..	223
103.	The gist of recommendations afterwards modified by the enactments of the Quarterly Meetings—[See note.]...	223
104.	Missionary Anniversary and Report—Progress	224
105.	Rising trouble in Montreal...	228
106.	Former relation of Montreal churches—An attempt to make three circuits by District Meeting...	228
107.	Both parties appealed to the Canadian authorities—Extraordinary meeting, and confirmation of the arrangement..................................	229
108.	Resignation of suburban officials—A plan for pacifying them by the chairman	230
109.	Reasons for a measure so bold..	231
110.	Letter to the President—Cautious answer—Executive disapproval—Measure set aside by co-Delegate	231
111.	Recalcitrant officials withdrew and seventy members lost................	232
112.	Lessons to be learned..	232
113.	Displacement and removal of the chairman—Slow return to favor........	233
114.	Reform Ministry bring in a Bill to alienate the Clergy Reserves wholly from religion—Action of laymen at Kingston.................................	233
115 to 120.	Elder Case's last year exhibited: letter to Rev. Dr. Bangs	234
121.	The results, or gains for the year..	237

1855.

THE BALANCE OF THE YEAR AND THE DEATH OF CASE.

122.	Effort to rise to the jubilation of this Conference.......................	237
123.	Place and composition of the Conference..	137
124.	Genial month and weather	238
125.	Conference officers and distinguished visitors..............................	238
126.	Comparison or contrast between the year 1805 and when Mr. Case entered the country and this year—Progress...	239
127.	Delivers his Jubilee Sermon...	239
128.	Modest and reverend character of his service	239
129.	Three young men—one middle-aged, and one aged passed away, Prindle.	240
130.	God burying His workmen, but carrying on His work.................	241
131.	Account of the Revs. Thomas Robson and Thomas Lawson.............	241
132.	Number of additional labors, and whole number stationed, &c..........	242
133.	Inability to be minute..	243
134.	Morden, Latimer, A. Fletcher, Sen., S. Tucker, Revs. M. H. Laird and Crane...	243
135.	Particulars of the first three, one Morden not to be confounded with 'another	243
136.	Latimer more at large	243
137.	Particulars of Mr. Fletcher, Sen...	244
138.	Crane and Tucker, &c...	244
139.	W. H. Laird and Russ contrasted somewhat..................................	244
140.	Some of the supplies, &c..	245
141.	Take them as they turn up: (1) Edward Ward, (2) Thomas Cobb, (3) Wm. Hansford, (4) Thomas S. Howard, (5) J. N. Lake, (6) Wm. Norton, (7) H. Fowler, (8) H. H. Perdue, (9) M. Short, (10) M. L. Scott, (11) Jas. Berry, (12) C. Stringfellow, (13) two married men, Davies, Atkinson, obituary, (14) E. E. Sweet, and B. Cole—Particulars of both, (15) A. Andrews, (16) S. Bond, (17) J. E. Betts............................	245
142.	Notable man—Account of Rev. A. Sutherland	253
143.	Conference addressed by Rev. Dr. Beecham..................................	255
144.	Close of Conference...	255
145.	Testimonials	256
146.	Glowing news in the *Guardian*...	256
147.	Victoria College—Moral Governor, S. D. Rice; Graduates, E. B. Ryckman, A. Carman, B. M. Britton, —— Parker's prelection, &c..............	256

148. Account of Autumn Session 257
149. Revival among Sunday-school children............................... 257
150. Triumph East and West.. 257
151. Case and his relation to the work —Letter from Steinhaur................ 258
152. Cheerful old man—Letter from Case..................................... 258
153. "Master to be taken from the head of the lesser prophets"—Cathey's letter 259
154. Intimation of Mr. Case's fall 260
155. Account of his death and burial.. 260
156. More particulars about his funeral—How so many ministers were there.. 261
157. Summary of his character... 262
158. Tablet to his memory in Belleville—Delay of the Conference memorial .. 263

REV. WILLIAM CASE,

AND

HIS COTEMPORARIES.

BOOK TWELFTH.

CASE RESTORED TO HIS CANADA BRETHREN FOR THE REST OF LIFE.

1847-48.

1. THE anxious year of negotiation and expectation ended its tardy moons at length, and the Conference of 1847 commenced its sittings in Toronto, on Monday, the third of June, with a full attendance of members, and proved a valuable and happy session. The meeting of the Canada Western District had been made to coincide with it in point of time and place, so far as the city was concerned. The Conference sat in the old Adelaide Street, Church and the the district meeting convened in the larger and newer British Wesleyan Church in Richmond Street. The Rev. Wm. Martin Harvard, A.M., was the chairman of the latter, and the Rev. Wm. Ryerson was elected the second time to preside over the former, and continued to do so until, the Union having been restored, he was superseded by the

President provided by the appointment of the British Conference. The Rev. James Musgrove, who had often served the Conference in a subordinate position of that kind, was appointed principal secretary, a man in every way qualified for the duties of the post and worthy of the honor.

2. As soon as the Conference was organized the Rev. Dr. Alder, the Rev. Enoch Wood, who had accompanied him from New Brunswick, and the Rev. Mr. Harvard were introduced to the Conference and invited to take part in its deliberations.

3. At an early stage of the proceedings, the report, both written and oral, of the late delegates to the British Conference, the Revs J. Ryerson and A. Green, was given to the Conference, accompanied by remarks confirmatory and explanatory from the Rev. Dr. Alder. The deliberations on this subject occupied the principal part of the first week of the Conference. The opponents of the measure wished to make the election of Chairman by the Conference, instead of being appointed by the President on the advice of his Advisory Council, and that the Chairman should be restricted to a circuit, on which he should be dependant for his support, instead of travelling through his district, conditional to the Union. At length a compromise was made by the British representative offering to accept the stationing proposition, on condition that the appointing power should remain where it was. This was eargerly caught at and accepted, and the Union measure carried by a majority of *eighty-eight,* against *eight* of a minority.

4. The ratification of this important measure was followed by the concession of the Presidential Chair on the part of the Rev. William Ryerson to the Rev. Dr. Alder, the appointee of the British Conference, and by the introduction of the members of the Western Canada District, who

expected to remain in the Province. Then followed a season of mutual congratulation and pleasing reminiscences of former days before the unhappy estrangement. Tears of tenderness and gratitude flowed from many eyes, in which the excellent and venerable Case was observably demonstrative. Next succeeded a time of earnest prayer, in which the re-united ranks of gospel-laborers renewedly consecrated themselves to their Divine Master and His work. Thus happily terminated seven years of fratricidal rivalry between those who were essentially one and should have been always organically so. This second union, although not carried in the Canada Conference with the same apparent unanimity as the first one, really proved vastly more harmonious and complete.

5. The principles, or articles of the re-constructed union, were as follows:—

(1) "The future relations of the English and Canadian Conferences shall be the same, as nearly as local circumstances will admit, as has heretofore been proposed by the Canada Conference.

1. "But that the Chapel and other Property now held in trust for the Wesleyan Methodist Church in Canada, remain exclusively under the control of the Conference known in Law as the 'Conference of the Wesleyan Methodist Church in Canada!' and that, in respect to those Chapels in Western Canada, the deeds of which require that the pulpits should be supplied by the British Conference, the appointments to them by the Canadian Conference be subject to the sanction of the English Conference.

2. "The English Conference (according to the former Articles of Union) shall annually appoint one of their number as President of the Canadian Conference; and, (as in Ireland) a Co-Delegate, who shall be associated as a Member of the Stationing Committee, and who may be either an

English or Canadian Minister, in full connexion with either Conference, as may, from time to time, be judged most convenient. If the appointed President cannot remain in Canada during the whole of his presidency, his Associate shall, for the remainder of the year, take his place in Canada, and superintend the work of God there.

3. " In accordance with the preceding Resolution, by which it is provided, that the future relation of the Canadian Conference to the English Conference, shall be, as nearly as may be, similar to that which is now sustained with the English Conference by the Conference in Ireland, (as is expressed in the Poll Deed prepared by Mr. Wesley) " all, and every, the acts, admissions, expulsions, and appointments, whatsoever," of the Canadian Conference, the same being put into writing, and signed by the President, or by the Minister appointed as his associate, and Co-Delegate, shall be annually laid before the ensuing English Conference, and, when confirmed by their vote, shall be deemed taken, and be, to all intents and purposes, valid and obligatory, from the respective times when the same shall have been ordered or done by the said Canadian Conference. *Provided always* that all appointments to Chapels in Canada, the Trusts of which require that the appointments of Ministers and Preachers shall be made by the Canadian Conference, shall be of sbsolute authority from the time of such appointment by that Conference.

4. " The existing Book of Discipline shall remain in force, with the exception of such clauses as may be affected by these proposals; but subject to any improvement which may, from time to time, be mutually agreed upon by the English and Canadian Conferences, in conformity with the laws of the second articles of the former Articles of Union in 1833; and the British practice, relating to the Chairman of Districts being stationed on Circuits be adopted, and that the Advisory

Committee associated with the President in the appointment of Chairman be chosen by the several District Meetings, one for each, either by nomination or by ballot, as they shall judge most suitable.

5. "The English Conference shall (in conformity with the former Articles of Union) appoint a General Superintendent of Missions, who shall be, *ex-officio*, a member of the Stationing Committee, as well as of the Canadian Conference.

6. "The Missions amongst the Indian Tribes and new settlers, which are now, or may be hereafter established in Canada West, shall be regarded as Missions of the English Wesleyan Missionary Society, under the following regulations, viz :—

(1) The Parent Committee in London shall determine the amount to be annually applied to the support and extension of Missions; and the sum granted shall be distributed by a Committee consisting of the President of the Conference, the Co-Delegate, Superintendent of Missions, the Chairman of Districts, and seven other persons to be appointed by the Canadian Conference. A standing Board or Committee, consisting of an equal number of Ministers and Laymen, shall also be appointed at every Conference, which during the year, shall have authority, in concurrence with the General Superintendent of Missions, to apply any means granted by the Parent Committee, and not distributed by the Conference, in the establishment of any new Missions amongst the heathen, and in otherwise promoting the Missionary work.

(2) The Methodist Missionary Society in Western Canada, under the sanction of the Canadian Conference, shall be auxiliary to the Wesleyan Missionary Society in London; and all sums which may be contributed to its funds shall be paid over to the Treasurers of the Parent Society.

(3) The Missionaries of the Parent Wesleyan Missionary

Society now in Canada, shall be stationed by the Cadadian Conference, in the same way as the other Ministers of that Conference.

(4) The trial of any Missionary sent out from England to Canada, in full connexion with the English Conference, who may at any time be accused of misconduct, or of any deviation from the doctrine or discipline of the Methodist Church, shall be left with the District Meetings to which such Missionaries may respectively belong, and subsequently to the Canadian Conference; but such Missionaries in full connexion with the English Conference, shall have the right of appeal to that Conference.

(5) The Missionaries who may now be in full connexion with the English Conference, or any other Missionaries hereafter to be sent, who may be in full connexion with that Conference, shall, notwithstanding the Union between the English and Canadian Conferences, so far retain their connection with the former, as not to loose any claims, privileges, or pecuniary advantages, which may belong to them by virtue of their relation to the English Conference.

7. "The foregoing articles constitute the basis of the settlement and Union, the following are the means by which the Wesleyan Missionary Committee in London are to aid in the promotion of the work of God in Canada: That work is of a twofold character. 1. It embraces purely missionary ground among the aborigines and others. 2. Circuits which contain within their limits new and destitute settlements. With a view of assisting these different classes, it is proposed, *First*, That in addition to the sum raised in Canada West by the Auxiliary Missionary Society, and to what may be received from other sources, the Parent Society in England make an annual grant to the Canadian Conference of One Thousand Pounds for missionary purposes. *Secondly*, That as a great number of Circuits include within their limits new and desti-

tute settlements inhabited by emigrants of so poor a class as to be unable to support their ministers, the sum of six hundred pounds be annually placed at the disposal of the Canadian Conference, for the purpose of carrying on the work of God in those sections of the country."

6. The ministerial ranks of the Canada Conference were greatly strengthened by the consolidation of the two sections of Wesleyan Methodism in Canada West. The Rev. Messrs. William Case, William Scott, Douse, Ephraim Evans, Thomas Fawcett, Byers, once of the Conference, came back into membership with the body, either temporarily or permanently. By this arrangement there was removed to England, and forever from the Provinces, one distinguished individual, who had occupied, in one or other of the two Provinces of Canada, very influential positions. This was the Rev. William Martin Harvard, A.M., and afterwards D.D., late Chairman of the Western Canada District. At this moment we have not the means of tracing his English appointments after his return, but we are sure they were very important, embracing the chairmanship of an important district, and afterwards, until his death, the Moral Governorship of the Connexional Theological Institution at Richmond, where he died December 15th, 1857, about ten years from the time of his leaving Canada. His English brethren say of him: "His character was distinguished by lowliness and sanctity—by 'whatsoever things are pure, whatsoever things are lovely.' He was faithful in the exercise of his ministry; 'gentle' among the churches, 'even as a nurse cherisheth her children;' esteemed and beloved by a multitude on both sides of the Atlantic, as well as by the students who composed his last and most interesting charge. The standard of his personal religion was a high one; and the affectionate courtesies which never failed to adorn his external deportment flowed

from supreme love to Christ, the Friend and Saviour of all. In the course of his affliction, deep heart-searchings wrought in him most affecting self-abasement before God; but, on the atonement, as he gratefully declared, he found 'firm footing.' He drew strong consolation from the truths he had long preached, and resigned himself, without a reluctant wish or care, into the Divine hands. In silent patience, and holy, tranquil hope, he still endured languor, weariness, and pain, till it pleased his Lord to give him rest."

7. The Rev. Matthew Richey, A.M., was appointed to fill the newly-constituted office of Co-Delegate, or Vice-President of the Conference; and as the President, the Rev. Robert Alder, D.D., was returning to England, Mr. Richey was the acting President throughout the year 1847-8, upon which we are entering, travelling at large throughout the Province.

8. And the Rev. ENOCH WOOD, who has been already referred to, entered the Conference as Superintendent of Missions, being thus the representative of British Conference interests in that department, and proving, in his accession, a great gain to the Canada Conference itself, on account of his wisdom, weight of character, and tendency to sympathize with colonial interests.

9. This gentleman, just then making his appearance in Canadian Methodist history, deserves a somewhat more extended notice. He was a native of England, born in Gainsborough, Lincolnshire, on the 12th of January, 1804—the year memorable for the formation of the British and Foreign Bible Society. He had gone out into the itinerant ministry so early as 1826, but had performed all his labors out of England. His first year's missionary labor was bestowed on the West Indies, in two several islands, Montserrat and St. Kitts; and the intermediate eighteen years between his West India services and his coming to Canada West, in the

Province of New Brunswick. Excepting Miramichi, where he was stationed two years, he alternated during the other sixteen years between the cities of Fredericton and St. Johns, in all which places he won the love and confidence of all who knew him. This was particularly true of his fellow-missionaries, who elected him, when comparatively a young man, upon an unexpected vacancy, to the chair of the district, in which office he was continued by the British Conference until his designation by the Wesleyan Missionary Committee in London to the office of Superintendent of Missions in connection with the Canada Conference.

10. As to personal appearance, even at the date when introduced among the Canada brethren, he is well represented, so far as facial looks are concerned, by his engraved portrait in the *Canada Methodist Magazine* for July, 1875. He was, even at that early period, stout, broad, and heavy, although well proportioned—unless it causes a large man to be out of proportion to have a massive head,—while, at the same time, he has a delicate hand and a small foot.

11. He impressed all his friends from the first with the average completeness of his talents for the pulpit and the platform, and the even balance of his character on all sides, combining, as he did, a vigorous intellect with an emotional nature—pastoral adaptation, with a capacity for connexional business. He was destined to be the originator, or to stand with others in the origination, of several measures of vast importance to Colonial Methodism, all of which come into notice in the course of this history.

12. Returning to the subject of the accession of laborers under the direction of the Canada Conference by the restoration of the union, the list will be observed to be lengthened by five other ministers in full standing, who had never before been connected with the Conference—at least directly

*1

—namely, the Revs. Edmund Botterell, James Booth (often mentioned), Henry Lanton, Robert Brooking, and Samuel Dwight Rice.

13. Of the first three of these the reader has been more or less informed, in one way or another; the two last must now receive some attention. *Robert Brooking* was by birth and education an Englishman, and went out into the ministry under the direction of the Wesleyan Conference and missionary authorities of England; but the whole of his effective labors had been expended in their foreign fields. Although naturally as strong and healthy as he was large, his health had been impaired by no less than six years' missionary labor in the most trying of all climates, Western Africa, namely, in the Cape Coast Castle, Accra, Ashanti, and Ananaboo stations. On discontinuing, for want of health, he came to Canada at his own instance, and was taken up by Western Canada District, and by that body introduced as an ordained minister to the Canada Conference. As all his previous active life had been devoted to missions among heathen, under the direction of the English Conference, so the balance of his after-life was destined to be devoted to similar work in connection with the Colonial Conference. But we must turn to one whose accession to the Conference was of as great significancy as the man of distinguished calibre placed in connection with that body by this union measure.

14. We are referring to the Rev. SAMUEL DWIGHT RICE. This minister of Christ, because of his essential worth and the distinguished position he was destined to win for himself in the Canada connection, first in its narrower and afterwards in its broader acceptation, deserves more space than the greater number. He, like his friend Mr. (now Dr.) Wood, came to us from New Brunswick. He was the son of a New England physician, in which

country Samuel himself was born; but as Dr. Rice settled in New Brunswick (Woodstock) while his children were yet young, this son grew up with British ideas very strongly ingrained within him; although the higher part of his education was obtained in an American institution. There is reason to believe that he pursued an optional course, and that whatever related to commerce enlisted the supreme interest of his eminently practical mind. Whatever may be said of his natural birth, British ground was the place of his spiritual birth. Fredericton, the capital of New Brunswick, was the spot, and if I have been rightly informed, his friend, the Rev. Arthur McNutt, was the instrument. This change occurred when he was about nineteen years of age. In two short years from the time of his conversion he was out in the itinerant work, proclaiming the gospel of the grace of God. His early ministry was bestowed on some of the most trying circuits in the Eastern Provinces, and that ministry was characterized by zeal, laboriousness, adventurous daring, and great success. His appointments before coming here had been as follows: Mirimachi, St. Johns South, Sackville Wesleyan Academy, and St. Johns West, in which last he remained four years; giving him, in all, ten years' ministerial experience before coming to Canada West. What mark he was destined to make in this Province the future pages of this history will show.

15. Brethren John Breden, William Andrews, and John Gundy were also from the British ranks, who were received into full connexion and ordained along with the following Canadian candidates for ministerial orders, namely: Abraham M. Sickles (Oneida Indian), John Goodfellow, William Ames, Noble Franklin English, Robert Lochead, Charles Taggart, James Greener, and Isaac Brock Aylsworth, M.D.,

albeit that Messrs. Greener and Aylsworth had been previously ordained for special purposes.

16. So, also, Samuel Fear, John Hunt, Charles Turver, probationers of the *third* year ; David Clappison, a *two*-years' man, and James C. Slater, in the *first* year of his probation, all were from the British section of Wesleyan Methodism.

17. The preachers admitted on trial were three, and all came out under the auspices of the Canadian section of Wesleyan Methodism. These were H. Trickey, W. McGill, and S. S. Nelles. *Henry Trickey* was personable, genteel, well connected, and apparently pious; but neither piety nor two years' training at Victoria College could supply the lack of what God had left out—an aptitude for preaching. If the published minutes are any guide in the inquiry, he was never more than a student at Cobourg, under the direction of the Conference.

18. *William McGill* was a young man of twenty-three years of age, having been born in 1824. He was a native of Cornwall, but of parents born in other lands—his father was from Ireland and his mother of Huguenot extraction, from the Island of Jersey. He was instrumentally brought to God and introduced into the Wesleyan Methodist Church by the Rev. Joseph Wesley McCollum, in the spring of 1844. The following year he received a license to exhort, signed by the presiding chairman of the district, the Rev. John Carroll. Part of the next Conference year he was employed as a chairman's supply, to assist the Revs. W. Haw and V. B. Howard on the extensive Waterloo Circuit. He had been very respectably educated in early life, and had followed the profession of school-teaching for several years, in which he gave general satisfaction. He was light-complexioned, sprightly in manners, and nearly up to medium size. His natural gifts and his assiduity in study combined

to make him more than an average preacher in point of ability.

19. *Samuel S. Nelles*, B.A., the last of the three candidates, was by no means the least. At the time of his reception on trial he was one year older than Mr. McGill, having been born October 17th, 1823. He was of worthy Methodist parents, and born at Mount Pleasant, near Brantford. His great natural abilities had received superior cultivation and exercise. He attended the Lewiston Academy, New York, in 1839-'40, of which the Rev. Reuben Close was principal, and J. G. Saxe, Esq., the poet, one of the tutors. The next year he removed to the Genesee Wesleyan Seminary, New York, where he was converted and joined the Methodist Church, of which, therefore, he had been a member some years when he was introduced as a probationer into the Canada Conference. Two years after, he matriculated at Victoria College (of which he was destined to be long the President), under the principalship of the Rev. Dr. Ryerson, where he remained two years, and was distinguished for two things—intellect and eloquence. For some reason he concluded to graduate at an older institution, and went to Middletown University, Connecticut, from which he received his degree in arts, in 1846. The intermediate year between his graduation and his entrance on the full ministry of the Word, he conducted the academy at Newburg, of this Province, and was recommended to the work of the ministry by the Napanee Quarterly Official Meeting, under the Superintendency of the Rev. George Goodson. We have reason to believe that he had exercised his preaching gifts the greater part of his religious life. In person Mr. Nelles was medium-sized, agile, and dark-complexioned. Had he been left in the pastorate, few ministers would have equalled him as a pulpit man.

20. There was no occurrence nor casualty to reduce the

number of Conference members, excepting one. Through the mercy of Almighty God, none had been called away by death, none had been expelled, and none had withdrawn; only George B. Butcher had "desisted from travelling," "on account of ill-health." This brother remained a Methodist preacher some years in a local sphere, and then accepted a call to the pastorship of a Congregational church, and after some years longer was called to his final account; but I am not furnished with the particulars of his history during the latter part of his career.

21. I shall not repeat the STATIONS—they are to be found in the General Minutes; but it may just be remarked that in most places where there had been two Wesleyan societies, a ministerial representation of the two reunited interests were stationed together, if it had been found possible to effect it. Thus, *London* had Messrs. Botterell and Goodfellow (albeit, as Mr. Goodfellow was ill and unable to take his work for the first half of the year, the two societies and congregations united as one in the British chapel). *Woodstock* had Messrs. Thomas Fawcett and Cawthorne; *Gosfield* and *Amherstburgh* had Messrs. Phelps and Fear; *Simcoe* had Messrs. Booth and Gray; *Sarnia* and *St. Clair* had Messrs. William Scott and Axtell; *Hamilton* had Messrs. Douse and Rattray; *Toronto* (two circuits), had Messrs. E. Evans and Rice in the West, and Messrs. Carroll and Joseph E. Ryerson in the East (albeit Mr. Ryerson discontinuing after some time, Mr. Goodfellow came in his place, instead of going to London); *Peterborough* had Messrs. McCullough and Slater; *Kingston* was to have Messrs. Lanton and I. B. Howard, and they were to labor in conjunction, but Mr. Squire came in the place of Mr. Lanton, and the congregation were not brought together during that year; *Bytown* had Messrs. Shepherd and Andrews, and *Adelaide* had Mr. Corson and Mr. Constable, a chairman's supply

from the British side of the house, who ultimately had the time allowed during which he had labored on circuits as a hired local preacher. *Newmarket* was similarly circumstanced, Mr. William Young being the Superintendent, and his colleague, a Mr. Sharp, being a chairman's supply from among the British employees. He, however, fell into immorality, and fled in the fall of 1847. His place was supplied for the balance of the year, Mr. Young says, "by William" (*Thomas*, I suspect) "Ross, a zealous and useful local preacher, who presided in the circuit." I saw this brother converted, and I am glad to give him a niche in our temple of fame. "The Revs. George McRichey and James Scott were among the hundreds converted that year." The supply for the "one wanted" for *Norwood* was a local preacher from Picton, a Mr. George Gillespie, who did not, however, permanently enter the work; and *Brock* received the appointment of Charles W. M. Gilbert and a Mr. Wm. Gundy, who had been laboring several years as a hired local preacher among the British missionaries, whom it would have been wise to ordain and retain in the united Connexion.

22. The number of districts was not increased by the increase of laborers, and each of the districts was placed in charge of a Canadian minister, who, the reader has been prepared to expect, for this year only, was to travel through his district, visiting each circuit and mission at least once a quarter. The brethren in charge of these districts were those of the preceding year: the Rev. William Ryerson, for the London District; the Rev. John Ryerson, for Hamilton; the Rev. Henry Wilkinson, for Toronto; the Rev. Richard Jones, for Cobourg; the Rev. Thomas Bevitt, for Kingston; and the Rev. James Musgrove, for Bytown.

23. The Rev. George R. Sanderson was continued in the editorship of the *Guardian*, and the Rev. Anson Green

continued as Book Steward; while the Rev. Egerton Ryerson, D.D., was still permitted by the Conference to occupy the position of Chief Superintendent of Schools.

24. The Rev. William Case, whose public life has been made the central channel of these biographical streams, was continued at Alderville, in charge of the Industrial School, having for his assistant, to look after the outlying appointments connected with this mission, a young Canadian preacher, William Ames by name, who has already come to view in the course of this work.

25. Although there was an increase in the number of laborers by the absorption of the members of the previously existing British Wesleyan District for Canada West, there was no augmentation of the number of districts within the bounds of the Conference, the Indian Missionary District, which existed during the first union, not being continued or resumed under the second. The chairmen were all Canada Conference men, and for the current year their itinerancy through their districts, by specific enactment of the Conference of 1847, continued as it had been up to that time, with a view to their bringing all the different materials, men, and usages into harmony under the newly-modified discipline. And I am of opinion that there are few men of experience in the body who, after a knowledge of all the facts of our subsequent history, and after mature reflection, are not of opinion that it would have conduced to the energy of the Connexion and to uniformity in its usage and disciplinary action, had the travelling of the chairmen, at least in a modified form, continued until the present time.

26. The labors of the above-named chairmen were most untiring, and very influential in promoting the prosperity of the Church.

27. So, likewise, the rank and file of this militant host in conflict with sin and error, in the several districts, were

equally indefatigable. They labored, not without instances of success, in various localities. This will appear by a very abbreviated summary of news, gleaned from communications sent to the *Christian Guardian* during the year: *Adelaide Mission* projected both a tea meeting and a camp meeting early in the Conference year—the first to promote friendliness, the latter a revival; and subsequent communications showed that their labor had not been in vain in the Lord. *Matilda Circuit* began the year with accessions to the Church. The Chairman of the *Bytown District*, at an early day in the year, reported peace and prosperity. News from the Rev. Richard Phelps showed that the union worked well in the *Gosfield Circuit.* There was good news from the *Coteau Landing.* The reunited officials on the *Sidney Circuit* worked well under the pacifying and devoted John Black, and conjointly they enjoyed prosperity, and had to call out a third preacher. An ingathering, after long years of sterility, took place in the *Hull Circuit*, under the usually successful George Young. The *Richmond Circuit* had reviving times. The *Napanee*, under the superintendency of the Rev. George Goodson, was favored with an outpouring. There were protracted meetings and revivals in the *Peterborough Circuit.* *Streetsville* erected a new church. After hard toiling, they were watered from on high in the *Shannonville* and *Tyendinaga Mission*. *Bellevue*, under Mr. Gemley, enjoyed a revival. There was good news from *Bath*, under Mr. Fawcett. A number of souls were converted in the *Goderich Circuit*. *Seventy* were added in the *Colborne Circuit*, under the laborious Morton. There were great prospects of good in the *Wardsville Mission.* Mr. Madden gave favorable reports from *St. Andrews Circuit.* *Kingston West* had conversions and accessions; and a good account was given of the *York Mission*, by its Superintendent, at the close of the year.

28. Still, after all these favorable communications, there was a decrease reported in the aggregate official returns at the end of the year, taking the return of members of the two sections of Wesleyan Methodism, who were understood to have embarked in the united Church. The return of the Canada Conference at the Session of 1847 was 21,749; that of the British Conference was 3,032; the two returns united were 24,781; and yet the whole return at the close of the year 1847-'48 was only 23,842, it being 900 less than the Connexion was supposed to have started with. Two causes may be assigned for the want of progress.

29. The first impediment the united Connexion suffered was from the hostility of the public press. Several of the so-called Liberal journals (this applies especially to the *Globe* and *Examiner*) were pleased to view the union measure as fraught with evil consequences to the cause of liberty and reform; and, consequently, poured contumely upon it, and endeavored to awaken suspicion among the membership and adherents of both sections of the denomination against its authorities—first, in the minds of the "Missionary" section, and afterwards in all—on the ground of what was represented as their Tory and Church and State leanings. These representations were not without their influence both on members of the Church and those without its pale, and went far to neutralize the labors of the devoted men who were striving to build the walls of the Methodist Zion in those troublous times.

30. But a public event, which occurred during the year, gave still greater occasion for complaining and agitation in the Province and Connexion :—This was an attempt on the part of the Conservative Government, then in power, to settle the long-agitated University question. The lands originally set apart for a university, colleges in different parts of the country, and a grammar school in every district,

had increased in value (although there had been an unwarranted exchange of some of the best of those lands for others of less value) so as to yield the sum of £10,000 ($40,000) a year. The Bill proposed to give £3,000 ($12,000) out of this revenue, with King's College grounds and buildings, to the Episcopal Church; and £1,500 ($6,000) to each of the following colleges, namely : Regiopolis (Roman Catholic), Queen's (Presbyterian), and Victoria (Wesleyan Methodist), funding what was expected to be an annually increasing overplus for any other colleges, denominational or otherwise, which might thereafter arise. A draft of the Bill was sent to all the parties concerned for their opinion thereon, and, among the rest, to the authorities of the Wesleyan Methodist Church. This was submitted by them to the Board of Victoria College, and the Conference Special Committee was called together and the measure was submitted to them. Both of these bodies accepted the proposal as tolerably fair, and as comprising probably the best terms that could ever be secured. The Special Committee of the Conference issued a circular, signed by the Acting President and the Secretary of the Conference, inviting concurrence on the part of the members and adherents of the Church throughout the Province. Upon this, attempts were made by the papers in opposition to arouse the laity of the Connexion against the measure (as one of Tory party politics and unjust), and against its promoters, especially the Conference and authorities of the Connexion. The Bill failed to command a majority of the Legislature, and an appeal was made to the country. A general election ensued, the Ministry was defeated, and the division scheme failed to carry. The papers referred to, and their upholders, boldly asserted that the action of the Conference authorities was due to their Tory and Church and State leanings, which went to prejudice ministerial influence among their flocks and congregations. Although these allegations were ably answered by the editor of the Connexional organ and his contributors, yet obstacles enough were created to greatly circumscribe the influence and progress of the Church, as a whole. This was, therefore, another instance of the incidental evils, at least, of public interference in public questions on the part of religious denominations in their Church capacity.

31. But we turn to a brief exhibit of affairs among the Wesleyan brethren in Lower Canada District. The District Meeting, held at the commencement of this ecclesiastical year, began Saturday, the 8th of May, 1847, in the City of Montreal. It was presided over by the Rev. Matthew Richey, A.M., and the Rev. Matthew Lang was elected Secretary. Eighteen brethren were present. Hugh Montgomery was unable to attend, through indisposition. In the list of preachers present at that meeting, we observe two names new to the North American work, namely, *Henry Cox* and *Gifford Dorey.*

32. So far as we can discern, they were both received on trial at the British Conference of 1846. "Hill's Alphabetical Arrangement" places the former at *Quebec* during the year 1846-'47, where "one was asked" at the beginning of the year. The latter, by the same authority, is placed at St. Johns, N. B.; but we have good reason for believing that appointment to have been changed, and that Mr. Dorey spent that year in Montreal. The probable reason for the change was the hope that, as this brother was a native of the Channel Islands, and his vernacular the French language, he would be useful among the French Canadians of the Eastern Province. But we have reason to believe that, what with obstructions to the commencement of the French work at that time, and Mr. Dorey's own predilections for the English department (for he was equally as good in the

English as French), that he never accomplished much, if anything, among the French Canadians. These two brethren are returned in the MS. Minutes of the District Meeting as having labored one year. They were men of promise— Dorey, perhaps, the more accurate and painstaking; but Cox had the more genius and extempore talent. His fine person and free manner in the pulpit, amounting to a sort of *abandon*, made him quite run after in some of the cities in which he was stationed.

33. The list of stations for the year 1847-'48, as amended from the prospective plan of the British Conference, was as follows:—

Montreal.—Matthew Richey, A.M., Charles Churchill, George H. Davis; Robert L. Lusher, supernumerary.

Quebec.—Ephraim Evans, Henry Cox.

Three Rivers.—Alexander McLeod.

Wesleyville.—Rufus A. Flanders.

St. Johns and Chambly.—James Brock, Gifford Dorey.

Russeltown.—Hugh Montgomery.

Odelltown.—Matthew Lang.

Clarenceville.—Thomas Campbell.

St. Armands.—William E. Shenstone.

Dunham.—John Tomkins.

Shefford.—Malcolm McDonald.

Stanstead.—Edmund S. Ingalls.

Compton and Hatley.—Benjamin Slight.

Sherbrooke.—John Douglas.

Melbourne.—John Borland.

New Ireland.—One wanted.

34. But even this modified list must have undergone still further modification after the Session of the Upper Canada Conference, at which the union was restored. At that Conference Mr. Evans was stationed in Toronto, instead of Quebec. If the list of printed stations is any clue, the

Rev. John C. Davidson was sent to Quebec, instead of Mr. Evans.

35. The only authentic information accessible to the writer relative to the labors of the year in this section of the work, is found in the MS. journal of the Rev. Benjamin Slight, appointed to Compton and Hatley. The extract about to be furnished is illustrative of the difficulties attending the endeavor to plant and establish Methodism in its integrity in Canada East, together with Mr. Slight's conscientious and painstaking endeavors to accomplish it— endeavors, it is to be feared, which had not characterized every one who preceded him. The excerpt is as follows :—

36. "June 13th, 1847 (Sunday).—This is my birthday. I am to-day forty-nine years of age. When I was twenty-one years of age (that falling also on Sunday), I was appointed on the printed plan to preach on the Bregg Circuit. I have been, therefore, twenty-eight years a preacher. Oh, how little have I done! How unprofitable I have been! Preached, including this day, three thousand five hundred and ninety-seven times.

37. "June 18th. I have marked the procedure of some of our most useful preachers and revivalists in England, and I have always found it to consist in stirring up the zeal and energies of the pious and working portion of the church; thus to engage all in co-operation, to have 'all at it, and always at it.' By this means something may be done to advantage. But where you can have no co-operation by the church, one man, however earnest and desirous to save the souls of men, can do but little. He visits a place once in two weeks, preaches, &c., and passes on to another, and without this co-operation, all the improvements he makes evaporates before he comes around again. Where we have efficient class-leaders, local preachers, and prayer-leaders, to engage in the work, they keep up the spirit, talk with, and invite those who may have

received any good impressions, and thus keep all that is gained, and bring them forward. I have been so impressed with this, that it has been a maxim with me not to stay on a circuit where the members are not disposed to work and help on the cause. On this account I left St. Johns at the end of two years. And on this account, I am beginning to think I did wrong in returning to this circuit a second year. Of all the circuits I have been on, surely this is the most deficient. Here we can have no regular church organization. We have scarcely any class-meetings, to which to invite any who are impressed with the necessity of working out their soul's salvation. I go around and preach, impressions I know are made ; but they are either lost again, or the subjects of them are picked up by the Baptists, who have twelve ministers operating within the space of country I alone occupy, and whose church members are ever ready to lay hold of any advantage they perceive. I feel I cannot, in twelve different directions, do anything ; I cannot induce any, or scarcely any, to help on the cause. I can only cry to God to take the matter into His own hands, and to try to be content to drag through the year without any efficiency."

38. May (1848). The following is a short abstract of the report I returned to the District Meeting concerning the state of this circuit :—

"This circuit has improved in several respects, the congregations are better. Some have manifested religious impressions, and a few have been gathered into the church. There have been eight removals from the circuit, and but two into it. The present number of members is ninety-nine, and one on trial. Last year the number was eighty-three, being an increase of sixteen. I have left twenty persons on the book, who are not returned in this number, as a reserve for better times ; if they should return to duty, and attendance on the ordinances of the church," well.

39. The opinions of Mr. Slight are worthy to be written in letters of gold. If our class-meetings and society organization are permitted to fall into decay; and if we fail to raise up a staff of lay and local workers to aid the minister and to stand in the gap in his absence, Methodism will be scarcely as efficient as many other forms of Protestant Christianity, as almost all have some other method of conserving the Church's life, corresponding to those we are suffering to fall into desuetude, without any compensating agency in their place. May all the watchmen on the walls of our Zion sound the alarm, and join hands in preserving the vital institutions of our heaven-originated Methodism. The journalist records one incident interesting to every lover of Methodist history, namely, the happy death of a Mr. Philip Embury, the grandson of the apostle of Methodism to New York and America in general.

40. After the most strenuous efforts of the Lower Canada Wesleyan ministers, of which, it is presumed, Mr. Slight's labors were an average example, no increase was reported at the end of the year, but a slight decrease of fourteen; and, unhappily, this was a second consecutive falling off for the Province. The total return of members stood at 3,909. The total for the two Canadas at 37,751.

1848-49.

41. The Conference of 1848 was noticeable for having been presided over, in the appointee of the British Conference, by one of the ablest who ever sat in its presidential chair, or indeed that of the English Conference either, which he had also filled seven years before. This was the venerable JAMES DIXON, D.D., an aged, white-haired gentleman of sixty years, who had been in the Wesleyan ministry thirty-six years. When he assumed the chair of the Canadian Conference he apprised that venerable body that he would need

their forbearance, as he "was not considered a business man in his own country." He was no doubt one of those book-loving, reflective men who do not fussily affect the details of himself, but who had a right judgment of all practical matters when brought before him. The Conference found him wise, deliberate, and capable; and although blunt, and sometimes a little wanting in patience, simple-minded, fair, and honest to a great degreee. As to his preaching, eschewing ll prettinesses, it was fresh, original, profound, unctious, and scintillated with the coruscations of true genius; also, gloriously independent of paltry pulpit conventionalisisms. But we must allow his brethren, who knew him best, to speak of him, as they do in his Conference obituary, which is found much fuller than is the wont of the British Conference in such cases, unless upon the character of very remarkable men. He was born in Castle Dornington, October 28th, 1788. We adopt the obituary account:—

42. "He became an earnest Methodist at the age of twenty, and after four years spent in the cultivation of his mind and the study of theology, was sent into the ministry by the Conference of 1812. It seemed likely at the first that his career would be that of a missionary, but a short trial in Gibraltar proved, to his deep regret, that his constitution was unsuitable to a foreign climate. Accordingly he returned to England, and was permitted, with almost unvarying health and vigor, to discharge, for more than fifty years, the duties of a Christian minister. To the sacred office he brought a remarkable combination of endowments. His devotion to the Saviour and the spread of His kingdom was of that strong and tranquil kind which is independent of external circumstances, and unaffected alike by prosperity or adversity. It was much and severely tried, but never failed. He gave to the service of the Gospel a vigorous mind, in the constitution of which the finest qualities were blended. His

reasoning power was great, his fancy was rich, and his faculty of utterance ready and copious beyond that of most men. The first determinate bent of his intellectual discipline had been theological, and in most branches of English theology he was well read. But the culture of his mind was not limited to his vocation; he was a general reader, and a diligent student of the course of human affairs and of the depths of the human mind. His earlier ministry, though useful and effective in its sphere, scarcely gave promise of his subsequent eminence. But in due time he became one of the most able preachers and speakers of the day. He was for many years a great power in the pulpit, where he handled with equal vigor and success the terrors of the convincing law, the promises of the Gospel, and the obligations of the regenerate life. He proclaimed the catholic, evangelical truth of the New Testament under all its aspects; he declared the whole counsel of God.' But he was emphatically a Methodist preacher; he exhibited in his ministry all those characteristics which honorably distinguish that class of men; and it was his happiness to rejoice in the success with which God had been pleased to crown their labors. Dr. Dixon was also extraordinarily effective on the platform, where his robust eloquence, inspired by such themes as the claims of the heathen world and the wrongs of the slave, and having at his command a voice of wonderful compass and delicacy, produced effects, upon a far wider public than his own community, which will not soon be forgotten. For a season he was, both in the pulpit and on the platform, one of the most prominent men in Methodism. By degrees he retired, however, from other spheres of usefulness and restricted himself to the ministry of the Word. Towards the close that ministry became more and more practical, and tender, and searching. His eloquence ceased from the swelling periods and broader effects, and became sententious, racy and epigrammatic ; to the last full of originality and fertility of conception, and rich in that quaint beauty which never fails to enchain the hearer. The pastoral outpourings of his later years were, in their own order, as memorable as the mighty appeals of his middle age!

43. Dr. Dixon had attended the American General Conference in the preceding May as the representative of the British Conference, along with the Rev. John Ryerson, who represented the Canada Conference, where the Doctor won golden opinions. He had made the acquaintance of Bishop Soule, when representing the American Church to the British Conference many years before, and although the Bishop was now severed from his Northern brethren and the Episcopos of a Church not officially recognised by either of the older bodies, he had made his English friends a visit at Philadelphia, the seat of the General Conference, and the two renewed the pleasing intercourse of other years. These two great men had evidently a great affinity for each other, and possessed many things in common. They were both strong, sizable, grave, dignified men, characterized by a sort of oracular utterance in private, and a stately, measured eloquence in the pulpit. Dr. Dixon published on his return to England a very interesting account of his American tour, in which he showed himself a shrewd observer.

44. The President returned to England soon after the Conference was over, and continued to serve the British Connexion in various ways, as he had done before. "He was at his post," says the obituary, "in the forefront of its great enterprises, entirely faithful to its constitutional principles, and at the same time ready to join any sound progressive movement." "Towards the end of his course, he was smitten with blindness, partial at first, but slowly and surely becoming total. During nine years he still preached and edified the people, both publicly and in his own house. His

mind retained its vigour to the last; and his interest in the affairs of his own community was unabated. In many ways he expressed his zeal for its welfare, losing no opportunity of urging on his successors in the ministry the necessity of holding firmly to their early principles. His end was peace. His long season of seclusion from the outer world was spent in communion with his Saviour, and preparation for his departure. "I sit here in my blindness," he said, "and they read parts of the Bible to me: the words seem to be raised and luminous. Dwelling much as I do alone, I have been enabled to obtain views of God such as I never had; of God in His unity, His fulness of divine perfection, God in the Trinity of Persons, in the relation of the Persons to each other, and also in their relations to the world and to me in the mediatorial scheme. Then as to original sin, I never saw its extent and loathsomeness as I have seen it in this arm-chair. And these two extremes—the Holy God and the fallen state of man—have prepared me to see the redemption wrought out by Christ in its aspect of imputation; on this ground alone I look for the mercy of God and hope to enter heaven." These sum up the labors of his life and his hope in death. His departure was sudden, when the time came "Sleep and death were literally one." "He died at Bradford, December 28th, 1871." "The Methodist community will always rank him as having been amongst its foremost men."

45. The *Rev. Mathew Richey*, who had received the degree of Doctor of Divinity during the preceding Conference year, was re-appointed co-delegate by the British Conference; and having to perform the duties of the Acting President for the prospective year, the Conference invited him to travel at large through the Connexion, which he proposed to do, purchasing a horse and chaise for that purpose; and if we may anticipate, his labors were truly apostolic and his

influence on the Connexion of a truely episcopal character. But we must return to the doings of the Conference.

46. The Conference sat in Belleville, and began its sessions on the 7th of June. The Rev. Conrad Vandusen was elected Secretary, and performed his duty efficiently. Six brethren were received into full connexion, three of whom had gone into the work under British auspices, and the others under Canadian: John Hunt, Charles Turner, and Samuel Fear were from the British side, and Abraham Dayman, John Howes, and Erastus Hurlburt from the Canadian.

47. Five were now received on trial, none of whom, although some of them may have labored under a chairman, have ever come under the notice of the reader before. These brethren were John G. Laird, James Gooderham, John English, Noble Armstrong, and Lewis Morton. The three last of them had each a brother in the ministry, whose ability and fidelity might have augured well for those now coming into the work. But three out of the five candidates were, from one cause and other, not destined to continue long in the itinerant ministry of the Canada Church. We notice them in the order in which they stand in the Minutes.

48. *John G. Laird* was a native of Ireland who had arrived in Canada during the preceding year. He was born in Fermanagh in 1823, so that at the time of his reception on trial he was about twenty-five years of age. He was sizable and comely enough. He was trained for the work of a National School teacher in the Normal School, Dublin, and followed the occupation of teaching in his native land. He was converted, and connected himself with Wesleyan Methodism, in his fourteenth year. He had filled the offices of leader, and local preacher for several years when he emigrated. No description would give any one an exact idea of

his preaching who had not heard him; but we might say it was richly scriptural, above mediocrity, and very satisfying to those who loved the truth. He was destined to make a faithful and successful laborer.

49. *James Gooderham* was the next. He was born in Scole, Norfolk, England, but came with his highly respectable parents to Toronto in very early life. They were of the Church of England, and otherwise than prepossessed in favor of Methodism; nevertheless, being converted about the age of seventeen, he united himself to the British Wesleyan Methodist Society, very much to the dissatisfaction of his friends, which, in many ways, became a source of trial to him. He remained faithful to his convictions, however; gave himself up to most assiduous study of every branch of knowledge that had immediate relation to the Christian ministry, and became a very acceptable and useful local preacher. His preparations for the pulpit were careful, and his ministrations most satisfactory. He received the suffrages of the Toronto West Quarterly Meeting, and was readily accepted by the Conference, at the age of twenty-three.

50. *John English* was nearly about the age of the two last brethren, the son of respectable, pious Methodist parents in the town, or city, of London. He was the subject of an early conversion, and exhibited a blameless course of Christian character thenceforward. Being persuaded that he was called to preach, he spent a considerable time at Victoria College in preparation for his work. Scarcely equal to his brother, Noble Franklin, in point of mind and scholarship, he was, perhaps, even more than his equal in zeal and tender feeling for souls. His pathos gave him persuasiveness.

51. The remaining two candidates, *Noble Armstrong* and *Lewis Morton*, may be disposed of together. They were both

of intelligently pious Irish parentage, Armstrong certainly born in Ireland,—perhaps Morton in Canada. They both came out from the neighborhood of the Ottawa River, Armstrong from Clarendon, Morton from Goulburn. From all we have learned, they were of average promise, but as they were both destined to leave the Canadian ministry before their probation was ended, we are not furnished, at this stage of our writing, with further particulars concerning them.

52. Fortunately none of the Conference proper had been summoned from their posts by death, but the Conference thought well to record in answer to the usual question, "Who have died?" a testimonial to the character and labors of the *Rev. James Evans*, whom the Canada Conference had lent to the British Conference eight years before, to introduce and superintend their missions within the Hudson Bay Territory, and who had died suddenly, November, 1846. The answer to the above question, from the Minutes of the British Conference, was as follows :—

"JAMES EVANS ; a missionary of remarkable ability and zeal, and of great usefulness among the North American Indians. His success among the aborigines of Canada led to his appointment as General Superintendent of the recently-formed missions in the Hudson Bay Territory. To his mental vigor and indomitable perseverance, the Indians are indebted for many advantages: among these is a written and printed character, suited to their language, of which Mr. Evans was the inventor. Many were the afflictions and trials he had to endure : these issued in a failure of health, which rendered his return home desirable, but the results were not favorable. He died suddenly at Keilby, in Lincolnshire, on the 23rd of November, 1846, at the house of a friend, after attending a missionary meeting, at which his statements had excited great interest. He entered upon the missionary work in 1834."

53. Three who had stood as efficient laborers in the list of appointments at the previous Conference were discontinued, and had their ministerial authority cancelled, at this Conference. One of these was "*excluded* from the Church for intemperance; another had become dissatisfied with the Church in its renewed relation to the British Conference; and the third, in a fit of despondency at a long move, with slender means to defray the expenses of it, had dropped out of the itinerant work. The fallen brother never regained his ministerial standing, although, I think I learned, he recovered himself from the habit into which he had fallen; the second became (and is now) a Congregational minister, and the third battled on in secular life for some years, and was drowned in some pioneering enterprise at the west. Our first case was that of poor *John Gundy;* the second, that of the *Rev. Solomon Snider*, who, I have no doubt, left very conscientiously; and the last, that of the once-laborious and much-regretted *Matthew Connor.*

54. For want of health at the time, an energetic and successful preacher, Bro. *Robert Darlington*, took a supernumerary relation at this Conference, which relation he sustains until this day. Since then, "his own hands have ministered to his necessities," while he has still, to a large extent, " preached the gospel of God," and preached it "freely."

55. The Connexional staff (not of the pastorate) in Toronto this year was the Rev. Dr. Richey, Co-Delegate; Rev. Enoch Wood, Superintendent of Missions; Rev. Anson Green, Book Steward; Rev. G. R. Sanderson, Editor, who also had the honor of being elected Secretary of the Conference.

56. We will not take up the reader's time in reproducing such information relative to the stations as he can find elsewhere, but simply run through them, and supplement the omissions of the Minutes. The list of stations in the *Toronto District* will show the reader that a name, with which he had

become acquainted in the Canada East District, has been transferred to the Canada Conference, and placed as the colleague of the Rev. S. D. Rice, among the late British Wesleyan people of the West Toronto Circuit, its last year's Superintendent, the Rev. Ephraim Evans, having been recalled by the British Conference, of which he was a member, and sent to Halifax to remain in the Eastern Provinces for ten or eleven years as pastor and chairman in two several districts, and as Governor and Chaplain of the Wesleyan Academy at Mount Allison. This was the Rev. G. H. Davis.

57. There were three vacancies to be accounted for in this district, thus: the preacher in charge of the Nottawasaga and St. Vincent Circuit, and the assistant preachers for Barrie and Brock Circuits. The first vacancy was supplied by Henry Reid; the next, it is believed, by George Smith; the third, by no one (the devoted missionary, L. O. Rice, took the fortnight's work of two laborers in three weeks, and went on through the year alone), and the fourth by William Gundy, who had exerted a good influence in bringing the British element into a good temper after the reunion measure went into effect.

58. There were three such vacancies to supply in the LONDON DISTRICT. *Sarnia* was in charge of the Rev. Thos. Fawcett, with "one to be sent;" but whether that one was really sent the author cannot now recollect, although he was the chairman of that district at the time. My present impression is, that the necessity for a supply was obviated by the preaching to the Indians at St. Clair by *Mr. Henry P. Chase*, who was an educated native and was recognised as a local preacher. *Sydenham* had the Rev. Edward Sallows for its Superintendent, and no indication from the Minutes that there was another preacher associated with him; but there was another, a man who afterwards performed a good work and became historic. This was no other

2*

than *Edward White*, a large, strong, dark young man, who, only then laboring under the chairman, had spent a part of the previous year in the Woodstock or Oxford Circuit, but who had desisted because of deep depression of mind. His age at that time was twenty-six. He was born in Pennsylvania, and transplanted, with his parents, to the swamps of Raleigh Township, at the tender age of three years. He had been convinced of sin in boyhood, and had found peace with God at the early age of sixteen, at a prayer meeting in his own father's house. His early educational opportunities had not been great, but his native preaching abilities and powers of mind were above the average. He was genial, zealous, and laborious, and had powers of voice, both for speaking and singing, which greatly aided him in his public functions.

59. On *Gosfield and Amherstburg* Circuit the second preacher was also "one to be sent," but it had been all arranged by the authorities of the Connexion before the year began. A young man, born in England (in Plymouth, I think), was converted early, and exercised some years as a local preacher, and felt that he was called to devote himself to the full ministry of the Word; but an early marriage, or an engagement to be married, prevented that in England. He went to the United States, and entered the ministry there, where he labored three years. His wife was related to some of the most influential people in the Wesleyan Connexion in England, both lay and clerical: those friends preferred the two to be identified with Methodism in the British dominions, and through their influence a way was opened for him to cross the lines and labor on a frontier circuit in Canada. He had received at least deacon's orders, so that after one year's travelling under the Conference direct, he was received into full connexion with the Conference in 1850. This was *Edwin Clement*, a man medium-

sized, with good preaching ability, studious, and very successful in his work.

60. The BRANTFORD DISTRICT had but one such vacancy, and that was most efficiently supplied. At the Conference in Belleville that summer, two young local preachers from England, seeking employment in the itinerancy in Canada, made their appearance. There had been an obstacle to their entering the ministry in the home Connexion, and yet they had been encouraged to come to Canada. The obstacle was, that they were married. One had a child or two, the other had none. One was tall, the other was short. The former was the more promising to look at, but the latter outweighed and transcended him, in the long run, immeasurably. They had both come from hot-beds of Methodist productiveness. The tall man was from Devonshire, the short one from Yorkshire (Selby). They both glowed with fervor demonstratively; the fervor of the Devonshire man, however, ultimately cooled, but that of the Yorkshire man burnt with ever-increasing flame, and has not burned itself out till this day. We are writing of Bro. *Charles Fish;* he it was who was "sent" as the assistant of the Rev. John Bredin in the Guelph Circuit. He was then twenty-six years old, but fair and fresh-looking, compact and heavy. He was converted at fourteen, and began to preach only a year later, thus giving him ten or eleven years' experience as a public speaker when he entered on circuit work. He was an easy, commanding speaker, and a born homilist. He had studied much that related to the ministry then, and this species of study he has vastly extended from that time to this, by which he has greatly compensated for any lack of academic training he may have had to mourn. He entered on his work under the pecuniary disadvantage of having only a single man's claim; but he found a Yorkshire friend in the Guelph Circuit who gave him house and home free of

charge. The name of Mr. John Jackson, on this account and many others, deserves to go down favorably to posterity. Conversions and revivals were the fruits of Mr. Fish's labors in that circuit, as also in all the others to which he has been appointed.

61. In the stations made for the HAMILTON DISTRICT at the Conference of 1848, there were two vacancies to be supplied by preachers not on the Conference roll, namely, the place of a second preacher at *Simcoe*, and the same at *Owen Sound*. The Superintendent of the former was the Rev. Thomas Cosford, and the Superintendent of the other the Rev. James Hutchinson. The colleague sent to assist, in each case, chanced to be an Irishman. A middle-aged brother, who has come to view before as a hired local preacher, was Mr. Hutchinson's assistant—we refer to pious *George Smith*. The colleague of Mr. Cosford at Seneca was a youth not quite a year out from the old country, yet one who had experience as a preacher, and was able in the pulpit. This was *John Swanton Evans*, perhaps twenty-four years of age, who had labored on a circuit two or three years in Ireland, in connection with the Primitive Wesleyans, otherwise known as "Clonites." He was tall and graceful in person, genteel and pleasing in manners, well-educated, thoughtful, if not studious, very intellectual, with a tendency to a metaphysical sort of reasoning. He was pious and amiable among the people, but it took him several years' experience in Canada, besides his old country experiment, to convince himself that he was called to preach. He was, however, the only one who doubted his ability and duty to preach the gospel.

62. The COBOURG DISTRICT had no vacancies such as we have been considering, and might have been passed over, excepting that the venerable Case, our principal subject, still remained within its bounds, in charge of his beloved Indians

at Alderville, erst of Grape Island, and in charge of the Manual Labor School, of which he had been the founder. But the principal reason for mentioning him in connection with the district is, that he was restored to the chair of the district, an office he had vacated twenty years before, when elected General Superintendent of the Connexion, at the memorable Ernestown Conference, and which office he was now to retain another three years. He was allowed an assistant on his mission, and went in and out among his brethren greatly respected.

63. We pass over Belleville, Kingston, and *Brockville* Districts, as requiring no annotation, and come to *Bytown*, which had two vacancies, although only one appears upon the Minutes. The first occurred at the head of the district. That vacancy was supplied by *Henry Budge*, the taller of the two young Englishmen already referred to. He had a commanding person and native talent for the pulpit, and, had he not been trammelled in one particular, might have been very useful. *L'Orignal*, it now appears, had a second preacher, in the person of *John B. Armstrong*, a native of Ireland, but spiritually born and raised up into the ministry in that hot-bed of ministerial candidates, Clarendon, in Canada East. He was very youthful, lithe, and graceful in person, with a good mind, and commanding elocution—perhaps we should say, also, native eloquence; and if two things had concurred in his favor, he would have been more distinguished than he has become, which is saying much:— we refer to his want of a strong constitution, and his being thwarted in his wish to get a more liberal training at Victoria College. The discontinuance of the travelling chairmanship necessitated the circumscribing of the boundaries and the increase of the number of the districts. The previous year there were only six districts; this year there were nine. All the chairmen had been in the office before except-

ing two—*William Squire*, the Chairman of the Kingston District, and *Edmund Shepherd*, the newly-appointed Chairman of Bytown, the district we have been considering.

64. Besides the Rev. E. Evans, whose transfer has been referred to, four others received appointments in the Eastern Provinces. Three of these were members of the British Conference, and came not under the jurisdiction of the Canada Conference until the Eastern Canada District was incorporated with it in 1854. These were *Edmund Botterell, Henry Lanton,* and *William Scott.* Indeed, Mr. Botterell, who went to Prince Edward Island, never became associated with his Upper Canada brethren again until the great unifying measure of 1874. The fourth brother removed was only temporarily lent to the Lower Canada District, for want of a suitable young man for Montreal. This was the genial and eloquent *Lachlin Taylor*, who continued that year at Montreal, and the next at Three Rivers, while he occasionally rendered service at Quebec, also.

65. The Rev. G. R. Sanderson was re-appointed Editor of the *Guardian*, and conducted it with great efficiency, the paper being enlarged through the year, and its circulation considerably augmented. The Rev. Anson Green continued in the office of Book Steward, and received the honorary degree of D.D. from an American University during the year.

66. Every department of Connexional work was prosecuted with unwonted vigor during the year. The diligence of the circuit preachers resulted in an upward tendency in nearly all the circuits, except in those where the union brought antagonistic elements together, which resulted in the invocation of outside agency. This last was the case in *London*, as the writer well remembers, to his sorrow and cost at the time, upon his going a stranger among them. A large disruption was the result, and the organization of a

strong New Connexion cause. How happily the present state of the unified body contrasts with the alienation and turmoil of that sorrowful time!

67. The following circuits were among the most favored with revivals during the year, some less and some in a marked degree for the greater part of the year: Richmond Street, Toronto; Hallowell, Kemptville, Oakville, Winchester, Oshawa, Stamford, Norwich, St. Thomas, St. Vincent's, Demorestville, Sherbrooke, Richmond, Bowmanville, Goderich, Peterborough, Seneca, Matilda, with several others.*

* Since the text for 1848- was made up, a letter from our principal subject, the Rev. William Case, the veteran missionary at Alderville, has been discovered, in which, after enumerating a number of very interesting particulars concerning their Manual Labor School, for which we have not room, gives a summary of his people's improvement under missionary teaching and example:—

"Twenty years ago this people were without house, or field, or cattle, roving in bands through the wilderness, under the influence of ardent spirits, wounding and murdering one another, and a terror to the white settlements. At the annual distribution of their presents and annuities, the whole were expended in revelry, leaving them in suffering the remainder of the year. Since their conversion, their presents and annuities have been saved, and applied for their comfort. They have now in a block three thousand six hundred acres of land, forty dwelling-houses, decent and comfortable, barns, saw-mill, oxen, cows, pigs, horses, farming implements—all purchased with annuities which once they would, in a few weeks, squander in drunken revelries. These advantages are contained in 'the promise of the life that now is.' And, further, a whole people renouncing paganism, attending religious worship, both in public and in their families; the Sabbath held sacred; their widows and aged provided for; the savage warriors become ministers of the gospel, some of whom are ordained and stationed in your missions, some teachers of schools and interpreters for the white missionary. When Dr. Alder was at Alderville, he inquired for the boys of the Grape Island School, whom he saw at Hallowell in 1832. Several of them are now laboring in the mission work as ministers or teachers; some have, after witnessing a good

68. The several missionary deputations were very able, and the missionary anniversaries held with great enthusiasm and with good monetary results. And the new Superintendent of Missions, the Rev. Enoch Wood, was enabled to make a very encouraging statement of the condition of the Indian missions for the missionary notices issued by the parent society.

69. The literary institutions of the denomination, both *quasi*-Connexional and those really such, were accomplishing a good work. In the first class was the Burlington Academy, conducted by the Rev. Daniel C. Van Norman, A.M., in Hamilton, and the Adelaide Academy, conducted by the Rev. Jesse Hurlbert, A.M., in Toronto. The former was the more efficiently prosecuted. The Connexional University, Victoria College, at Cobourg, also was favorably reported of. Its President, the Rev. Alexander McNabb, received the honorary degree of Doctor in Divinity from Union College, New York, during this year. Unhappily, however, the bestowment of this honor upon him by some *contretemps*, was made the occasion of an unseemly discussion in the Conference organ.

70. The result of the labors of the (say, one hundred and fifty laborers, besides, perhaps, another fifty) Connexional office-bearers, supernumeraries and superannuates, students, and the like, after a year of most assiduous toil, resulted in the moderate gain of four hundred and twenty-six members,

confession, died in great peace. One is the excellent teacher of this interesting Manual Labor School (just now at the Normal School in Toronto.) Twenty-two years ago he was following the trail of his drunken pagan parents through the woods, often, as he expresses it, 'cold and hungry.' This 'cold and hungry' pagan boy, reclaimed by Christianity and educated in your mission-schools, is now the intelligent Christian of courteous manners, and useful to hundreds of his nation. The youth of his school are preparing to follow his example of honor to religion and usefulness in the world."

making the whole membership for Canada West, at the close of the Conference year 1848-49, just twenty-four thousand two hundred and sixty-eight.

71. We turn to the *Canada East* section of Wesleyan Methodism. The District Meeting for 1848 commenced its sittings on Thursday, the 25th of May, in the City of Quebec. All the ministers of the district, except one supernumerary, were present. The Rev. Matthew Richey, D.D., presided, and the Rev. John Jenkins, the eloquent returned missionary from India, was chosen Secretary.

72. The name of this last-mentioned gentleman has never before appeared upon our pages, he having been sent from the British Conference during the previous Conference year to the City of Montreal. We think we have learned that he was a native of the south-west of England, probably some part of Devonshire or Cornwall. Certainly his country could not have been determined from his accent, for a man more purely English, or more correct and charming in the intonations of his fine and flexible voice, is seldom met with. In that respect he was like " one that can play skilfully upon the harp." He had enjoyed the benefit of the Theological Institution two years before being sent into the full ministerial work. These were the Conference years 1835-36 and 1836-37. Thence, like several of the most clever and erudite men of the old body, he was sent into the foreign missionary field. Goobee and Bangalore, in India, enjoyed between them the first five years of his full ministry—three years at the first place, and two in the second. Malta, the scene of St. Paul's shipwreck, in the classic and beautiful Mediterranean, claimed the next two years of his labors. Then he returned and labored in his native shire, n the important Penzance and Camborne Circuits, where his ability as a pulpit man became known to the Connexional authorities. And when the exigencies of the Upper Canada

Connexion called the Rev. Matthew Richey, M.A., from the great Central Methodist Church, in Montreal, the demand of its trustees for a minister of equal pulpit power led to the selection of Mr. Jenkins to supply his place. That short year's performances were of a character to so far earn the approval, not to say admiration, of his ministerial brethren as to lead them to place him in the secretariat of the district. At that period he seemed the able theologian, the attracting preacher, and the urbane Christian gentleman and minister. He was rather small than large in person, but exceedingly handsome and presentable—fair and florid in complexion was he.

73. At this meeting of the district a young man was brought forward for reception on trial, who has won so distinguished a place in Methodism, and, we might add, before the Christian public at large, as to make the entry in the District Minutes, anent his proposal as a candidate, of great interest as to every line : " Question 6th.—What persons are recommended to be admitted on trial into our ministry at the ensuing Conference ? Answer :—GEORGE DOUGLAS, of the Montreal Circuit, a young man of deep piety, ardent zeal, consistent Christian character, vigorous intellect, and studious habits. He has preached with much acceptance as a local preacher for the last two years, and has exercised the office of a leader with great spiritual profit to the members of his charge. He possesses religious and intellectual qualifications for the work of the ministry of no ordinary kind. He believes and teaches our doctrines as taught in Mr. Wesley's Sermons and Notes, and approves of our Discipline as set forth in our larger Minutes. He is twenty-two years of age, is out of debt, and has no matrimonial engagement. He was unanimously recommended by the March quarterly meeting, the members of which earnestly hope he may be permitted to enjoy the privileges of the Wesleyan

Theological Institution. He offers himself for the general work. Recommended by JOHN JENKINS, Superintendent" (whose autograph is here given).

"NOTE.—Bro. Douglas was subjected to a rigorous examination by the chairman. His replies to the questions proposed evinced an extensive acquaintance with theology, great doctrinal discrimination, and a sound judgment. The meeting is unanimous in adopting the recommendation of the Superintendent, both as to introduction into the probationary ministry and his reception into the Theological Institution, believing that such a step would lead to his extensive usefulness in the Christian Church and in the world."

74. Very refreshing religious services, an enthusiastic public missionary meeting, and the impressive laying of the corner-stone of the "new and elegant church edifice then being erected" in the City of Quebec, characterized this assembling of the ministers from the various parts of this extensive district.

75. We are happy that it is in our power to give the veritable stations which finally went into effect in the district, something so hard to record, in most years, with historical certainty. The places of the ministers, probationers, and hired local preachers were as follows :—

Montreal—John Jenkins, Charles De Wolfe, Lachlin Taylor.

Quebec—John C. Davidson, Charles Churchill.

Three Rivers—Henry Lanton.

Wesleyville—John Hutchinson.

St. Johns and Chambly—James Brock, Gifford Dorey.

Huntington and Russeltown—Hugh Montgomery, Robert Graham.

Odelltown and Hemmingford—Matthew Lang, John Douglas.

Clarenceville—Edmund S. Ingalls.
Dunham—John Tompkins.
Shefford—Malcolm Macdonald.
Stanstead—John Borland.
Compton—Thomas Campbell.
Sherbrooke—Henry Cox.
Melbourne—Benjamin Slight, G. Douglas.
New Ireland—Rufus A. Flanders.

76. A few remarks will be required relative to these names. Messrs. Hutchinson and Graham have already come before the reader as itinerant preachers from two of the smaller Conferences in Europe, whose standing as veritable ministers was acknowledged, but who were not properly members of the British Conference. They ultimately became members of the Canada Conference. Mr. George Douglas, some time between this District Meeting and his appointment to the Bermudas, in 1849, went to one of the theological institutions in England, but, at this writing, we are not informed how long he spent there, or what time, if any, he was employed on the Melbourne Circuit, with which his name stood connected.

77. All sources of information have been applied to in vain to illustrate the labors of the Lower Canada brethren during the course of this year (1848-49), excepting the journal of the Rev. Benjamin Slight, which may be quoted in part as setting forth the labors in the average rural circuits in that Province. It will be remembered that his name and that of the youth, George Douglas, stand for the *Melbourne* Circuit.

78. His circuit itself, and several incidents of the year, are described. "This circuit," said he, "is extensive. It will require the travelling of one hundred and sixty miles to go around it; seven times preaching per week, besides a class or two to meet. This is in its present state; but I

expect to have a colleague, who will take one corner and extend his sphere of labor in that direction. Then I shall take up a few places nearer home. The whole will save a sermon or two in the fortnight, and a few miles of travelling.

79. "September 3rd, 1848.—I was agreeably surprised, and, I trust, thankful to God, to see in the *Zion's Herald* that that respectable institution, the Wesleyan University, had conferred an honor upon me, thus expressed: '———— ———— and the Rev. Benjamin Slight, Canada East, were severally elected to the honorary degree of *Master of Arts!*' My heart has been led out in prayer for more of the manifestation of the Spirit—for more holiness, and that I might be enabled to consecrate all the influence I may acquire from this hour to the cause of God. The following are the remarks of the *Herald :* 'Our readers know that we do not estimate highly such titles as usually given. We are happy that the deserved severities we have from time to time uttered on the prodigality of American college honors are in no wise applicable to our own institution. Its cautious discrimination has won it high public respect. Its honors are really honorable.'"

80. The Protestant and English-speaking population of Canada East have shown a great desire and tendency to escape from their popish surroundings, and to go to Canada West or the United States. This may have been one of the causes why the District Meeting at the close of the ecclesiastical year had to report a decrease of 127 members, leaving the total number only 3,782. These, added to the membership under the care of the Upper Canada· Conference, which was 24,268, made the total strength of Wesleyan Methodism, in point of membership, in the two Canadas, just 28,050.

1849-50.

81. THE Conference which sat at the commencement of this ecclesiastical year began its deliberations in the Town of Hamilton, on the 6th of June, 1849, and continued them until the 14th of the same month.

82. The *Rev. Matthew Richey, D.D.*, was no longer the mere Vice-President, but the actual President of the Conference by appointment of the British Conference of the foregoing year. As this country was his home, it was thought unnecessary to appoint a Co-Delegate. Dr. Richey's ability ran rather in the line of scholarship, theological knowledge, and speaking ability than in that of legislation and debate. He pretended to no extra acquaintance with points of ecclesiastical law, especially the peculiarities of our Anglo-Canadian Methodist law and usages, or any very superior administrative ability; yet his good sense, good nature, and his quick observation carried him through—especially as he was not unwilling to learn from the pleadings on either side and from the advice and experience of those who had filled the presidential chair before him; and as he was evidently desirous to do what was fair and equitable, so he secured the support of the dispassionate majority of the Conference, who sustained his rulings.

83. The deliberations of the session passed rather smoothly except as it related to a discussion which grew out of some college affairs that had transpired through the year, which was rendered acrimonious by, perhaps, too much pertinacity on one side, and too much sensitiveness on the other. As it was, it was preparing the way for the withdrawal of one who had been considered very useful and very respectable for a good many years, a few months after.

84. Eight probationers were received into full ministerial standing with the Conference, four of whom yet continue in the active work, namely: *David Clappison, Richard Whiting,*

Robert Robinson, and *Thomas W. Constable*. Two "are not, for God took them" to himself, namely: *Francis Chapman* and *James Armstrong;* one, alas! after some time, forfeited his standing in the body, but it will be time enough to furnish his name when we are obliged to record his expulsion; and one is an enfeebled but honored superannuate, namely, Brother *Alexander T. Green.*

85. No object will be served by transcribing the names of those in the intermediate years of probation between the first and fourth: we come to those whose names appear as being received on trial for the ministry. Eight were of this class, six of whom had labored through the previous Conference year under the direction of chairmen of districts. Of these, *Edwin Clement, Edward White, Charles Fish, Henry Budge,* and *John Armstrong* (five in all) we have described already in connection with the account of last year's work. The sixth of the chairmen's supplies, *Richard Wilson*, was overlooked by not knowing his station, till now discovered through Mr. Cornish's invaluable Handbook. Young Wilson was of English (Yorkshire) parentage, both of them hearty, demonstrative Methodists of the old school, born also himself in England; for his parents came to this country about fifteen years before, and he could not have been certainly less than twenty when introduced to the Conference. We are morally certain that he was converted very early in life at an appointment of the Osgoode Circuit, known as Long Island Locks. He is remembered as a remarkably conscientious and religiously-minded boy, and through divine help he "never wickedly departed from the Lord." He was naturally gifted and eloquent, and his diligent private studies were all prosecuted in the direction of the Christian ministry. He evinced a readiness in writing, as well as speaking, which would have enabled him to excel in that respect had he chosen. Personally, he was stout and healthy-looking, which augured

more for his physical energy than some late derangements of his system have permitted to be fulfilled. From the authority above indicated, it appears he had spent the previous year (1848-49) under the direction of his chairman, on the St. Andrews Circuit, on the Lower Canada side of the Lower Ottawa, enjoying the instructive superintendency of that strict and efficient disciplinarian, the Rev. D. B. Madden.

86. The only two candidates who had not been mentioned before were really young men of great promise; these were *Alexander Sturgeon Byrne* and *William Smith Griffin*. Griffin was twenty-three years of age, Byrne was only seventeen. Each was of a good Methodist stock. Byrne was Irish, Griffin was Canadian. Both were well started on the road to a liberal education. Griffin had decided natural talents, but Byrne evinced genius of a superior order.

87. All who want full particulars of Mr. Byrne may consult the "Stripling Preacher," which preserves a memorial of his "Life and Remains." He was a grandson of the Rev. Alexander Sturgeon, for many years a leading member of the Irish Conference, after whom he was named, and immediate son of the Rev. Claudius Byrne, twenty-four years a member of the Irish Conference, and afterwards twenty-seven years a member of the Canada Conference. Alexander was born in the itinerancy at Dungannon, Ireland, June 20, 1832. Early dedicated to God and carefully trained up in accordance with his baptismal obligations, being carried to the class-meeting by his pious nurse from infancy, he seemed never to have sinned away prevenient grace. Yet in advance of all that, in his thirteenth year, after a livelong night of prayerful agony, he was brought into the assured liberty of the sons of God. This event took place about daybreak, on a Monday morning, in the month of February, in 1845, a little over four years before his being received as a Conference probationer. He developed in mind

and body several years earlier than is common to boys. When introduced to the Conference, he was not tall but stout and heavy, bearded like many at twenty-five, and apparently in good health. His cranium was a good deal beyond the average adult masculine head. He was led by a train of providences, almost immediately after his conversion, to exercise his gifts in public, which were of such an extraordinary character as to open his way, when not more than fifteen years of age, into many of the first pulpits of the Irish Connexion, from which he proclaimed the unsearchable riches of Christ to large congregations, brought together by the fame of his precocious talents. In the winter of 1848-49 his father and family emigrated to this country. Preaching in the City of New York, offers of a free collegiate training were made to detain him in the States, but declined. From the period of his arrival in Toronto until the Conference, he assisted the Rev. Lewis Warner on the Yonge Street Circuit, where he won golden opinions. A visit to London along with the President of the Conference, soon after his arrival, was accompanied with such a blessing and such marvellous indications of talent, as to lead to his appointment to that city at the Conference we are describing, as the colleague of the writer.

88. *Mr. Griffin* was the son of Mr. Ebenezer Griffin, of Waterdown, where William S. was born, and the grandson of the notable Smith Griffin, from whom he received his second name, a distinguished man in early Canadian Methodism, who came to view in the earlier volumes of this work, and of the end of whose career we shall give an account. Our subject was converted and joined the Church at the age of twenty. The history of our Canadian Methodist Church will have to chronicle his doings among the leaders of the Connexion. Griffin had the advantages of a fine person and good physique.

89. Besides those received into full connexion in a regular course of graduation, a matured minister of fifty, who had labored twenty four years in connection with the Irish Conference, during five of which he had been chairman of a district, was accepted by the Canada Conference, and appointed to the important Brantford Circuit, which he superintended with great care and success, as, indeed, he did all his circuits. This gentleman was low in stature, but stout and enduring. With all the native wit and vivacity of his country, he knew how to perform sacred duties in a serious manner; and in his intercourse with those to whom he owed respect, he was the well-bred gentleman. This was the *Rev. Claudius Byrne,* father of the young preacher of that patronymic of whose reception on trial we have just given an account.

90. The two functionaries at the Conference publishing-house in Toronto, were re-appointed by the ballot of their brethren for another year, namely: the REV. ANSON GREEN, as Book steward; and the Rev- George R. Sanderson as Editor of the *Guardian.*

91. Among the doings of this Conference was the appointment of the REV. JOHN RYERSON "to proceed to England as representative of the Conference to the English Conference, to be held in Manchester, on the 25th of July, 1849," ensuing.

92. Among the visitors at this Conference was the REV. JOHN JENKINS, of the Canada East District, whose fine talents and pleasing elocution came into play in the pulpit and on the platform at the public reception of the young ministers into full connexion, and at the Annual Conference Missionary Meeting. Another visitor was the *Rev. J. G. Witted,* an Englishman by birth, but member of the Genesee Annual Conference of the M. E. Church in the United States, Bethel Missionary at Buffalo, N.Y., whose addresses, interlarded as they were with sailor phrases, gratified the taste of some. This brother, who for a part of his life had been

a sailor, after some time, became a member of the Canada Conference; in consequence of which, he will come under review once more.

93. The stations of the brethren for the ensuing year, till June, 1850, may be seen by reference to the published Minutes, but a few *hiati* may be supplied by the historian from private sources of information :—

94. THE TORONTO DISTRICT had three places to be supplied, namely, first, the *Nottawasaga* and *St. Vincent* Missions. We have reason to believe that the latter was supplied by *Henry Reid*, whose name was not yet in the Minutes, but who was ultimately received into connexion with the Conference and his time allowed him. The Nottawasaga ground was taken into the Barrie Circuit, and although the "one to be sent" to the aid of the Rev. Luther O. Rice was never sent, yet that indefatigable brother took the whole ground, as he had done the year before, going to each preaching place once in three weeks. Here is the register of his work: "During the two years, I travelled rising of 14,000 miles, nearly two-thirds of which was performed on horseback.—L. O. R."

95. THE LONDON DISTRICT had three vacancies to be supplied, namely: the place of second preacher in the *Wardsville, Chatham,* and *St. Thomas Circuits*. In the first named circuit, the Rev. Edward Sallows was assisted by a young man of very considerable mind and education, of whose antecedents we are thus summarily informed in his Conference obituary : " *Thomas Peacock,* born A.D. 1817, in Yorkshire, England. He gave himself to God and joined the Wesleyan Church in the nineteenth year of his age. In 1839 he received license as an exhorter; in 1845 was recommended to the itinerant work, placed on the list of reserve, and appointed to a circuit the following year. At the close of the year he emigrated to America, and after two or three years

in the Methodist Episcopal Church, in the United States, he came and joined the Wesleyan" (Church) "in Canada." On the recommendation of the Rev. W. Pollard, the chairman appointed him to *Wardsville* for the year of which we write. He was a brother of sincere piety, but not marked by great impressiveness in the pulpit or uncommon zeal as a pastor. The *Chatham* Circuit had, along with the devoted Samuel Fear, for, perhaps, the first quarter of the year, a *Mr. Armstrong*, an Irishman by birth, who had been recognised as a minister in the Methodist New Connexion, in Canada; but despite a considerable amount of a peculiar sort of talent, he was not satisfactory with them, and did not prove satisfactory to the Wesleyan body, and after a short time, retired from among them also. His place was well supplied by a young man who had not had great previous advantages of mental training, and who had scarcely expected ever to enter the full ministry of the Word, yet who, when called upon, left his secular occupation without gainsaying and came in unclerical attire to the circuit. But he had been savingly converted a few years before in the north of England, where he had been afterwards appointed a local preacher, whence he had come out to a relative in one of the western townships of the Province not long before being employed. But then, he was naturally gifted—had a good voice—a warm heart—a commanding person—and a great zeal for God and souls. Need I say, that such a young man, under the direction of such a Superintendent as Samuel Fear, was well received and succeeded well among the fervent-minded Methodists of that circuit? This young man, with some of his probation spent at Victoria College, grew up to be our highly-respected ministerial brother, the *Rev. Thomas Stobbs*. The *St. Thomas Circuit* was supplied by a young man who has come into notice on two other circuits as a supply, but whose name, on account of his own hesitancy, does not appear in the Minutes for that year. This was our intellectual and able friend, *John S. Evans.*

96. THE BRANTFORD DISTRICT had but one vacancy, the second preacher's place on the *Woodstock* Circuit. The *Rev. Kennedy Creighton* was the Superintendent, and informs me that his colleague, during the first part of the year, was a *Mr. Frank Bottome*, not long from England. He was quite satisfactory,.but for some reason left and went to the United States, where a person of that name (whether he, or not) has attained some eminence in the Methodist Episcopal Church. The balance of the year was supplied by *John Wesley Cawthorn*, who had been employed and discontinued, and of whom, therefore, we obtain another glimpse. He had sincere piety and mind, and he made good sermons, but there were physical and other defects which neutralized the good which he might otherwise have done. He did, I believe, obtain a standing, for a time at least, after leaving Canada, in the Michigan Annual Conference, but further the memorial of him cannot be carried.

97. There was one vacancy in THE HAMILTON DISTRICT, namely, in the *Grimsby* Circuit, where " one was to be sent " to the assistance of the *Rev. Hamilton Biggar.* The supply was one of two preaching brothers, the sons of exemplary parents, at East Settlement, in the old Ottawa Circuit. His elder brother had been in the work about seven years. This one, with more natural ability and a better education, was just entering it. We are writing of *Isaac Barber*, a young man some twenty-two or twenty-three years of age.

98. *Scugog Mission*, in THE COBOURG DISTRICT, was supplied from some adjacent circuit. The only vacancy in the BELLEVILLE DISTRICT was the second preacher's place at *Napanee*, under the superintendency of the *Rev. Wm. McFadden*, who informs us that his colleague was *Thomas Cleghorn*, a young man of good connections (in fact, of a

talented family), good early opportunities, good mind, good physique, short, stout, and strongly built. He had also youth on his side ; and while he remained in the country, his career did not belie his early promise, rising early, as he did, to a chairman's place in the Connexion.

99. *Peter Jones*, the Indian evangelist, was designated to general missionary work, "under the direction of the Superintendent of Missions," the *Rev. S. D. Rice* having taken his place at the Muncey Mission. *Charles Lavell*, by the consent of the Conference, was sent to aid the brethren in Canada East, and stationed in Montreal. *Thomas Demorest*, the old itinerant, was appointed General Travelling Agent for the Book Room, and gave a good account of his specific work. *Wm. Haw* was allowed to visit England, and was absent for the year. *David Hardie*, by some oversight, was left without a station, but afterwards received an appointment at *Bath*, and gave good news from the circuit through the year.

100. During this Conference year the Indian Industrial School was erected and commenced, under the management of the Rev. S. D. (now Dr.) Rice, which was the beginning of his valuable connection with the educational efforts of the Canada Conference. The corner-stone was laid in the presence of the President of Conference, Superintendent of Missions, Chairman of the District, Editor of the *Guardian*, the Chiefs of the Ojibway nation of that vicinity, and a large concourse of persons, on the 17th of July, 1849.

101. Seven days before that event, the representative to the British Conference sailed from New York, and after a successful voyage, was received by the British Conference with great cordiality. His account of the successful working of the reconstructed union afforded great joy.

101. The President of the Conference procured a horse and chaise and prepared himself to inspect every part of his

extensive charge in person, and only for a lamented accident, sustained while driving through the streets of Toronto, which laid him up for a time, he would have gone far towards the realization of his purpose. Fortunately he rallied after some weeks, and resumed his episcopal oversight, although it may be well doubted whether he ever fully recovered from the effect of the shock he sustained.

102. The rank and file of this militant host, in the several positions assigned them, whether in front or rear, seem, as a whole, to have exerted themselves to their utmost for the extension of the moral conquests which they were prosecuting. The communications to the *Guardian* relative to their several labors and successes were frequent and voluminous; and were more or less fraught with encouraging news— despite the prejudice against *Wesleyanism* here, as well as in England, consequent upon the agitation and inflammatory publications which followed upon the expulsion of Messrs. Dunn, Everett, and Griffith from the British Wesleyan Conference; and despite the embittered discussion of the question of "denominational colleges" *versus* the "Godless Provincial University," the former side of which was taken by the leading influences of the Connexion and their organ, but which did not prove to be the more popular side.

103. A profitable camp-meeting was held in the Township of Vaughan soon after the Conference, attended by the President of the Conference and Editor of the *Guardian*, and sustained by such ministers as Warner, William Young, J. Baxter, Law, A. Campbell, and Slater, which was cheered by evidences of the divine presence, and gave one of the first impulses to the work for the year. An *Indian campmeeting*, which followed in the month of September, had a similar effect on that department of the work; *twenty-four* converts were reported. Even more powerful meetings took place before the summer was ended that were in no respect

behind these two. Before the winter had set in, conversions were reported from six to a dozen circuits in various numbers—from thirty souls to one hundred. This last number was gathered in on the Goderich Mission.

104. Minute accounts of successful Sunday-school, chapel, and missionary anniversaries, social tea-meetings, and revival services were sent in from many circuits, stations, and missions, ranging from the Ottawa to the St. Clair Rivers, including Bytown, Richmond, Perth, Winchester, Elizabethtown, Waterloo, Belleville, Sidney, Picton, Brighton, Cobourg, Norwood, Millbrook, Peterborough, Alderville, Scugog, Bowmanville, Oshawa, Markham, Hamilton, Niagara, St. Catharines, Dundas, Guelph, Brantford, Woodstock, London (town and township circuits), Blanchard, Stratford, Goderich, St. Thomas, Adelaide, Gosfield, Amherstburg, and Sarnia.

105. Considering the two forces counteracting each other, the evangelizing one and the repressive ones, which have been referred to, perhaps the medium result, shown in the goodly, but not great, number of 774, added to the membership of the societies in connection with the Canada Conference, was as many as could have been expected under the circumstances. One popular measure was enacted at the Conference and carried out through the year: that of the creation of the Financial District Meeting, which embraced an equal number of laymen to that of ministers.

106. Having disposed of the Canada West Connexion, I turn to see what can be made of the doings of Wesleyan Methodism in Canada East during this Conference year of 1849-50. But we are sorry to confess that, although so near the present time, we find less data than usual to guide us in our inquiries. Our MS. journal is exhausted, and we have sought in vain, in the *Christian Guardian* and *Wesleyan Magazine*, for the time, place, and transactions of the district

meetings which marked the end of the year 1848-49 and the beginning of 1849-50, of which we now write; or, indeed, for the occurrences which related to this part of the work throughout the year. We give the stations for Canada East as found in the General Minutes for that year, although, for reasons often assigned, we are sure that they are not perfectly reliable.

107. CANADA: EASTERN DISTRICT:—

Montreal—John Jenkins, Charles De Wolf, A.M., Chas. Lavell, Henry Cox.

Quebec—Charles Churchill, Lachlin Taylor.

Three Rivers—Malcolm McDonald.

Wesleyville—One wanted (John Hutchinson).

St. Johns and Chambly—Matthew Lang, John Douglas.

Huntingdon—James Brock.

Russeltown—Hugh Montgomery.

Odelltown and Hemmingford—John C. Davidson, Gifford Dorey.

Clarenceville—Edmund S. Ingalls.

St. Armands—William Scott.

Shefford—Rufus A. Flanders.

Stanstead—John Borland.

Compton—Thomas Campbell.

Sherbrooke—Henry Lanton.

Melbourne and Danville—Benjamin Slight, A.M.

Leeds—One wanted.

108. Four of the above we know to be authentic, namely, those for Montreal, Quebec, Melbourne, and Wesleyville, and feel almost morally certain all the rest were so.

109. In the absence of other sources of information, we make some extracts from the journal of the Rev. Benjamin Slight, A.M., in charge of the *Melbourne* Circuit, as a specimen of the manner and spirit in which the labors of the brethren were prosecuted in that section of the work:—

"June 25th, 1849.—Held our first quarterly meeting for this ecclesiastical year. We introduced many useful measures, such as new prayer meetings, appointed two or three exhorters, arranged for a new class-meeting, and also the holding of a Bible class at Melbourne.

"July.—Preached back in the woods. There was present a poor girl, about seventeen or eighteen years of age, who had never seen a meeting or heard a sermon in her life. On inquiry, I found her parents did not possess a Bible or a New Testament; so, perhaps, she knew almost as much of even nominal Christianity as a Hottentot.

"September 24th.—Yesterday and to-day together I have preached five sermons, renewed tickets to one class, buried a corpse, and travelled thirty-five miles. Last evening a young woman was under deep conviction.

"September 30th.—I am happy to reflect that we have had a few instances of conversion this year. Our congregations in most places are very good, and a good deal increased, and there is a most fixed and deep attention to the Word delivered. I would add, I have had uncommon liberty in preaching. I hope all these things are omens of good.

"October 7th.—Held our second quarterly meeting. An unusual influence attended the sermon, from Eph. iii. 8: "The unsearchable riches of Christ." At the love-feast there was much good feeling. Several said it was one of the best they had ever attended, and one who had been in several places declared it the very best he had attended in Canada.

"October 16th.—The last three days I have travelled seventy-five miles, preached five times, married three couples, and baptized two infants.

"January 1st, 1850.—Last night we held our watch-night in Melbourne Chapel. The Word appeared to take effect.

"January 18th.—Our missionary anniversaries this year

were among the most successful we have had. The speeches excellent. In every place there was an excellent degree of divine influence. The collections in every circuit more than those of last year—in some places more than double, and in one place more than three times the amount of last.

"February.—We have just concluded a series of special services at Melbourne. The congregations, owing to the state of the weather and other causes, were small. Five young persons came forward for prayers.

"March 21st.—The following item is in the *Watchman:* 'Walsingham.—This circuit is one of the largest and most toilsome in the nation, extending over an area of twenty-four by fifteen, under the care of *two* ministers.' Compare this with my present circuit. Melbourne Circuit, without touching Danville, is twenty-six miles by eighteen, and then such roads as take twice the length of time and fatigue to travel over them—and all for one preacher. So, then, the Walsingham preachers would travel over this area once a month, whereas the Melbourne preacher has to travel over his area once in two weeks."

110. Mr. Slight, under the date of "February, 1850," records an event which must have been a great blow to the district, in the sudden death of their respected chairman, who had been one of the most laborious and successful preachers the Canada Connexion had ever been favored with. This is the brief entry in Mr. Slight's journal in which he chronicles that solemn event: "Heard of the sudden death of the chairman of our district, the Rev. Matthew Lang. He had gone to the barracks at St. Johns to meet the military class, and died in about twenty minutes after his arrival there."

111. The reader of these volumes has been informed of Mr. Lang's birth, in the north of Ireland, in the year 1798; of his bringing up in Preston, Lancashire, England; his

conversion at the age of sixteen, and his entrance on the work of foreign missions at the age of twenty-five—that is to say, in 1823. It only remains for us to transcribe the testimony to his character, and the particulars of his death, to be found in his Conference obituary, in which his brethren say of him : "He maintained an unblemished character through the whole of his public course, and was eminently distinguished by fervor and uniformity of zeal in seeking the glory of Christ and the salvation of man. He yielded to none of his brethren in attachment to the doctrines and established economy of Methodism, or in the faithful enforcement of its discipline. He was 'in labors more abundant;' and his acceptable ministry was signally attended with the divine blessing. He sustained with honor and integrity some of the most important offices in his district, and was, at the time of his death, Chairman of the Eastern Canada District and General Superintendent of its missions. The oft-repeated desire of his soul, in his most devout frame, was that which is expressed in the words,—

> 'O that, without a lingering groan,
> I may the welcome word receive;
> My body with my charge lay down,
> And cease at once to work and live !'"

His end was in accordance with this wish. While engaged in the service of the Church, he was suddenly seized with sickness, which in twenty minutes terminated in death. His last utterance, and, indeed, the only one which he had power to articulate, was in perfect unison with his unvarying trust in the atonement of Christ, and his untiring zeal for God's glory : 'Sweet Jesus, help me to glorify Thee !' He died at St. Johns, on the 21st of February, 1850, in the fifty-second year of his age, and the twenty-seventh of his ministry."

112. Labors like those recorded by Mr. Slight, and laboriousness such as that ascribed to Mr. Lang, which, we have cause to believe, were generally characteristic of the brethren in that district, would have produced great results, under the divine blessing, only for the drawbacks with which Protestantism has hitherto had to contend in that Province, namely, a scattered population accessible to their labors, and the constant tendency of the Protestant population to emigrate to parts more congenial. Yet, with all these hindrances, about fifty souls ("forty-nine") were netted in their societies, making their whole number 3,849, and the whole net gain in Canada East and West, 813; and the total strength of Wesleyan Methodism, in the two Provinces, 28,891.

1850-51.

113. THE Conference of 1850 commenced its sessions on the 5th of June, and continued them until the 13th of the same month, in the beautiful Town of Brockville, under its last year's President, the Rev. Dr. Richey, who had been re-appointed at the request of the Canada Conference. There was a large attendance of members—ninety in number. A modest, but able and long-tried member of the Conference, the *Rev. Asahel Hurlbert*, was elected Secretary, who performed his duties with quiet dignity and efficiency.

114. No less than fifteen junior brethren were received into full connection with the Conference and ordained, all of whom afterwards rendered good service to the Church in one way or another; and the greater part of them may be said to have risen to Connexional eminence. Six of them afterwards became chairmen of districts, besides becoming otherwise conspicuous, namely, *James C. Slater*, *James Gray, Edwin Clement, John A. Williams, David C. McDowell*, and *Thomas Cleghorn*. Messrs. Gray and Williams

were severally afterwards secretaries of the old Canada Conference; and the latter the first President—and that for the space of two years, of the newly-constituted London Annual Conference. One of the fifteen brethren (and before that year was expired) was called to preside over the Connexional University at Cobourg—Victoria College—in which arduous and honorable position he continues until this day, more than a quarter of a century. Need any Methodist be told that we are writing of the *Rev. Samuel S. Nelles*, A.M., now Doctor of Divinity? One—*William Henry Poole*—has stood pre-eminent for years among the most laborious and successful city pastors. *George Case, Thomas Hanna,* and *William Pattyson* were destined to labor long and efficiently; and *Francis Chapman* to enter early and triumphantly into his rest.

115. Five young brethren offered themselves as recruits to the ranks of the Church's ministerial staff, and upon examination were found to answer the standard required, who were all in the vigor of early manhood, ranging from twenty to twenty-five years of age—none much below twenty, and certainly none much above twenty-five. These were *Isaac Barber, Joseph Hugill, Andrew A. Smith, Richard M. Hammond,* and *Wm. Burns.* All but one were from the lower portion of our Provincial work—a region which has been very fruitful of good preachers. Their nationalities were diversified. Barber was an Americo-Canadian, Burns and Hammond were Irish Canadians, Smith was a Scotch Canadian, and Hugill an Anglo-Canadian.

116. *Isaac Barber* was employed during the preceding year under a chairman of a district, and his early history and characteristics have been given in our account of the last year's operations.

117. *Wm. Burns*, we have said, was an Irish Canadian. Both his parents were from the North of Ireland; but his

father, who had been in the British army, and who was discharged in this country (to which he came in 1814) at the close of the war of 1812-15, who, drawing land in the Township of Goulbourn, remained in the one locality until the day of his death. William had the benefit of pious parents, whose eldest born he was. His mother had been converted in Ireland before her immigration in 1826; and his father was converted in this country soon after his marriage, which took place a few months after Miss Rutledge's (his wife's name) arrival. The training of a religious household predisposed the son, at the early age of sixteen, to accept the truth effectually from the lips of a young evangelist, Charles Taggart, newly come on his first circuit. The Rev. B. Nankivill, of whom many retain a pleasing memory, made him both leader and local preacher. His advanced education qualified him to teach school, in the prosecution of which useful profession he left the Richmond for Kemptville Circuit, where the discerning eye of the Rev. A. Hurlbert singled him out for the itinerant work. Through the Kemptville Quarterly Meeting and the Brockville District Meeting he was proposed to the Conference for reception on trial. He was only twenty-two years of age, yet, being dark-complexioned and heavily bearded, as also stocky and strong, he seemed several years older. His twenty-seven years of toil have not falsified the promise of his physical endurance. His sound average mind, more than medium preaching abilities, and unostentatious assiduity, have made him a blessing to all the circuits on which he has labored.

118. *Richard Metcalf Hammond* was of Irish Methodist parentage, born in the Township of Lanark, and received his second baptismal name in honor of the much-loved pioneer evangelist of those townships, to whom the people felt they were under such great religious obligations—the Rev. Mr. Metcalf. This young man was early converted, and brought

the best moral habits into his official life; and as he had enjoyed the advantages of Victoria College for a considerable time before going into the public ministry of the Word, his sound, active, good mind had received more development than was enjoyed by many candidates at that time. He had a native aptitude for clear, cogent, and pointed practical preaching. Such was the introduction of one of the most useful preachers of the body.

119. *Andrew A. Smith* was born in the vicinity of Perth, U. C., in December, 1824, of Scotch Presbyterian parents, but with a kindly estimate of Methodism. He was religiously brought up, and drew instruction and benefit from all contiguous sources. He attended the Methodist Sabbath-school in Perth superintended by the devoted McGrath, in which E. B. Harper was a teacher, and the Bible-class of the catholic-spirited Thomas C. Wilson, Kirk minister. His educational advantages comprised the Common School in Bathurst, the High School in Perth, two years, or more, at Victoria College, and a classical training under Rev. Robert Taylor, A.M., of Trinity College, Dublin (son of a Wesleyan minister in Peterboro'). His occupation during the intervals of his educational course, was school teaching; first in the County of Lanark, and afterwards in the Town of Peterborough. His conversion took place in Perth under the labors of a fellow-Scotsman, the Rev. James Currie, in the year 1841. The revival of which he was one of the happy subjects began in the Methodist church, but extended to the Presbyterian church under the pastoral care of the Rev. Mr. Wilson. Nevertheless, Andrew cast in his lot among the Methodists and was licensed to exhort while at Cobourg by the Rev. R. Jones, and authorized to preach in a local sphere at Peterboro' by the now sainted Goodson. I should have said, had I received the information sooner, that Mr. Smith

supplied Sabbath appointments almost all the previous Conference year—the year 1849-50,—and in the month of January, 1850, he moved within its boundaries and took his full share of circuit work until the end of the year. They had a prosperous time. He was low-set, stout and strong, with a clear, ringing voice, good elocution, good fancy, and good preaching ability.

120. We have said that *Joseph Hugill* was an Anglo-Canadian, but upon more minute inquiry, we find that he was born in Yorkshire, old England, although brought up in this Province, to which he came with his parents at the age of eight years. He was converted to God in March, 1844, at a protracted meeting held at Switzer's Church, on what is now called the Streetsville Circuit. He was a light-complexioned young man, of good manners, who had received a liberal education; and his official obituary pronounces him "a diligent student, a good preacher, a faithful, judicious pastor, a wise counsellor, and a warm and sincere friend." Thus constituted and thus qualified, he was destined to begin with an important circuit (the Dundas), and to give great satisfaction in his ministry of the very considerable length of nineteen years. He was about the age of twenty-two at this his setting out in the work.

121. While young soldiers were putting on their harness and mounting the ramparts, two old veterans were being laid to their rest, crowned with the honors of glorious, though bloodless warfare. The Canada Connexion owed them both to the neighboring Republic; but both had become naturalized and spent over thirty years in the service of the Canadian Church. Both were amiable, attracting men personally—both were above the average (one considerably more so) for ministerial attractiveness and efficiency—and both fell without an instant's warning, but fell in the maturity of

Christian excellence. Each died in the fields, abroad under the open canopy of heaven, and alone—one beneath the glorious rays of the noonday sun, and the other in the night season under the shimmering rays of the multitudinous stars. The mention of their names will recal to the reader two prominent actors in the heroic work of Canadian Methodist evangelism, the venerable and Reverends *Ezra Healey* and *Franklin Metcalf*. "They were lovely and pleasant in their lives, and in their death they were not (very) far divided." Healey had fallen dead on the night of December 27th, 1849, in the act of crossing a field to assist a neighboring family whose house was on fire; Metcalf died (no one knows) while on an errand, with horse and cart, to the back part of his farm, on the 10th day of June, 1850. The news reached the Conference while in sesssion, and soon the heads of all his "old companions in distress" were bowed in sorrow and tears. A service was held during the Conference to the honor of his memory. A solemn procession of his brethren was organized, and proceeded from the house of Mr. Amos Stearns with crape badges on their arms, which proceeded with "solemn steps and slow" to the church, where a sermon was preached by the President, the Rev. Dr. Richey, and a eulogy on his character pronounced by Elder Case. The Conference pronounced Healey "a man of amiable disposition, good pulpit abilities, an indefatigable pastor, and energetic in his work." Metcalf was said to have "filled most of the important stations in the work."

122. This session of Conference was enlivened and rendered interesting by the visit of two honored strangers from other sections of Methodism, both of whom have appeared in our pages before. The one a comparatively young man, who came, at his own instance, from the Eastern Canada District Meeting, and preached a 'truly evangelical sermon,

besides addressing the Conference; the other, an aged minister of Christ, who came as the authorized bearer of the salutations of the American Church, being delegated by the General Conference of that body. The first was the *Rev. Charles Churchill,* of *Montreal*; the other, the venerable and *Reverend Nathan Bangs, D.D.,* of *New York.*

123. It was interesting to have the company and to enjoy the conversation and the ministrations of this ripe old divine of seventy-two years; and that the rather, because he owed his conversion and introduction into the ministry to the instrumentality of Canadian influences. The first nine years of his half-century of ministerial life had been given to the two Provinces, beginning with the century and expiring with the first decade of this. His figure and appearance were most majestic: about six feet three inches in height, and proportionately sizable, still erect, and moderately active, with ample locks, white as the driven snow, falling upon his shoulders. His peculiar voice had lost none of its power, and his mind none of its activity. Besides his official address to the Conference, which abounded in reminiscences of the past and statements of Connexional progress, he spoke at the reception of the young ministers into full connexion, and took the President's place by preaching, with great power, the sermon at their ordination, on the following Sunday. Appropriate resolutions were passed, complimentary to both the strangers. The venerable delegate returned to his home, and in about twelve years after was gathered to his fathers, and thus passed from the field of our historic vision.

124. The official Connexional appointments were: The *Rev. John Ryerson* as the President's *Co-Delegate;* the *Rev. Anson Green* was re-elected Book-Steward; and the *Rev. G. R. Sanderson,* Editor. Some changes were made in lesser ap-

pointments. The *Rev. S. D. Rice* was removed from Mount Elgin to Kingston, where his business talents were made available in the erection of the much-needed Sydenham Street Church; and the wide-spread business reputation of the *Rev. Samuel Rose* led to his removal from Dundas to take charge of the *Industrial Institute* at *Munceytown*, a work in which, because of his adaptation, he was successful, perhaps, beyond the average.

125. We might anticipate another change which took place before that civil year was ended. About this time the *Rev. Alexander McNabb, D.D.*, resigned his connection with the Wesleyan ministry, and was returned "withdrawn" in this year's Minutes, which, of course, terminated his Principalship in the College, in which there was a vacancy when the stations were made out. *Rev. Conrad Vandusen* still continued Treasurer and Agent, a situation which he had held during the preceding year, as he did for another year after the one of which we are writing. When the College Board met to make arrangements for the ensuing year, the *Rev. Samuel S. Nelles, A.M.*, who was the writer's colleague at London, giving great satisfaction to his fellow-laborer and the people, was literally forced, much against his own preferences, to accept the office of Principal of the Connexional University, then in a most enfeebled and precarious state. For many reasons, which might be satisfactorily given, the London Circuit was one which just then required an efficient ministerial staff. The question was, who would make a satisfactory successor to Brother Nelles? The authorities cast about, and the following was the solution of the question:—The *Rev. George Young,* a very popular pastor, was removed from his Superintendency at *Glanford* to be Mr. Carroll's assistant at London; and the *Rev. Wm. Haw,* who had just returned from a year and a-half's

absence in Europe, was appointed Mr. Young's successor. The whole matter seemed providential : Mr. Haw needed a place, and an opening was provided for him : there was not another who would have answered as well for the College as Principal Nelles, as the history of his incumbency from that time to this attests ; and as for the London Circuit, no person could have been sent who would have done it more, if so much, service as Brother George Young. He was urbane and pleasing in manners, devout in spirit, diligent in pastoral duties, a painstaking student and able preacher, and a skilful and successful laborer in revival meetings. Every interest of the cause went forward, and there was a net augmentation in the membership of ninety-six at the close of the year.

126. The *Rev. Egerton Ryerson, D.D.*, who was about to proceed to Europe on some business connected with the Educational Department of the Province, was elected delegate to the next meeting of the British Conference, and sailed at an early day after the rise of the Canada Conference ; but having to proceed to the Continent at the time of the session of the Parent Conference, his functions as delegate were confided to the *Rev. Dr. Alder*, the Colonial Missionary Secretary.

127. The stations for the *Barrie District*, as they stand in the Minutes for 1850, leave a good deal to be supplemented. But, fortunately, an appeal to the then active Chairman, the *Rev. Lewis Warner*, enables me to supply the first four omissions : *Mr. Warner* called to his assistance for the first half of the year a young Scotchman named *Muirhead*, a local preacher, formerly of Carleton Place ; and when he sent him to open a new mission at Kincardine during the course of the year, he supplied his place, as his own colleague on the *Barrie Circuit*, with a young Irish-Canadian by the

name of *James M. Clarke*, whose journal is in my possession, of whom I will give an account under the history of the coming year. *Muirhead* did not remain permanently in the work. *Nottawasaga* was supplied by a hired local preacher, a Bro. *George Smith*, whose peculiar relation to the work has been already described. *Henry Reid*, whose relation was the same, but who was ultimately received into full connection with the Conference and ordained, efficiently worked up the *St. Vincent Circuit*. *Beausoliel Island* and *French River* were in charge of the *Rev. Horace Dean*, whose name was left off the Minutes for one year because of an involuntary mistake. I owe it to the painstaking researches of the Rev. G. H. Cornish, as recorded in his Hand-Book, that I am able to inform the reader that *Owen Sound* was supplied by the *Rev. Benjamin Jones*, who had been located during the three previous years, and who travelled this and the next year under a chairman, preparatory to his uniting again with the Conference for a time. He will come into view once more.

128. There were several vacancies to be provided for in the LONDON DISTRICT at the beginning of the year, as anyone will observe by casting his eye over the printed list of stations. The *Adelaide* Mission was the first. Although the appointee's name could not appear in the Minutes, according to Connexional usage, this case was arranged for in the Stationing Committee at the Conference: *John Hutchinson*, who had been a New Connexion missionary in Canada from 1838 to 1842, and then became a Wesleyan local preacher in the City of Montreal till 1845, was at that time employed by the Eastern Canada District authorities to supply, first on one circuit and then another, till the end of the year 1849-50, and his *ministerial* standing acknowledged, in which capacity he has come to view several times in these memorials, was recommended to the Stationing Committee

for a circuit by the Rev. Dr. Richey, and the Chairman of the London District agreed to accept him as a supply for the Adelaide Mission. After some little delay he arrived, and proved to be an able and original preacher, besides being otherwise approved of. He gave great satisfaction in his circuit; but, taking the fever and ague, he was forced to give up his circuit towards the end of the year, and retired to Hamilton, where he was very useful till 1857, when, we shall see, he was called out again.

129. The Minutes show the want of a second preacher for *Chatham*. The chairman knew of no supply at the Conference, but on his homeward-bound way he was informed by the venerable S. Waldron of a young local preacher teaching a school within his own charge, whom he could recommend. He was solicited to go, and consented to, so soon as he could disengage himself from his school. The following August he appeared at my door in London, mounted on a tall horse and accoutred for the itinerancy. This was *Joel Briggs*, then twenty-two years of age, but looking stout and enduring. The following is from his official obituary, the substance of which was compressed from an account of him by the present writer, published soon after his lamented death:—

"Bro. Briggs was the son of a pious mother, who was descended herself from some of the earliest Methodists in the Township of Ancaster. He was left without a father at the early age of eight years; the mother was taken from her family not long afterwards. Joel may be said to have been deprived of a parental home and to have lived among strangers until he had a home of his own.

"The circumstances in which he was placed exposed him to great hazard of soul and body during his early youth, from which he was rescued by a marked conversion at the age of eighteen. A sermon preached by a gifted blind man,

Mr. Dixon, was the means of his awakening; and the Revs. Messrs. Jeffers and Pollard are mentioned in his journal as being the instruments in leading him to Christ. But he placed marked emphasis on the good he received from the pious counsels of a Mrs. Sophrona Gilmour during that transition period.

"He immediately united with the Methodist church in Dundas, a connection destined to be severed only by death. He was characterized by conscientious fidelity, from the hour of his conversion devoting himself to prayer, fasting, Bible reading, and earnest efforts for the salvation of souls. His thoughts evidently ran on the Christian ministry from the time that he was brought to God.

"He had good business talents, and by the time he was twenty-one he had enough saved to enable him to procure an education, the last two years of which were spent at Victoria College, where he was distinguished as a diligent and successful student, and as being useful in the offices of leader and exhorter, and finally as local preacher, going about to country appointments and to camp-meetings, in which he always much delighted. He preached his first sermon in a church at a watch-night service which closed the year 1849 and introduced the year 1850. The next August he was employed on the Chatham Circuit by the Chairman of the London District."

Amherstburg seems to have a vacancy, but it was really supplied by the devoted *Thomas Stobbs*, who has been already introduced to the reader.

130. Only one circuit in the *Brantford District* requires any elucidation. The Minutes for the year assign the superintendency of *Woodstock* to the *Rev. Edwin Clement;* while it is certain that he was not there, it is also certain that the venerable and excellent *Matthew Whiting* occupied

that position, but the "one to be sent" to his assistance we cannot recall or learn.

131. We have seen, that although Glanford was placed under the superintendency of the Rev. George Young, he was removed to London during the year, and the Rev. Wm. Haw supplied his place. The Minutes leave "one to be sent" to that circuit. Fortunately a young man of some twenty-five or six years of age, less or more, newly from Ireland, well educated, who had experience of school teaching and preaching as a local preacher in his own country, very serious and devout, was procured, who entered upon the work with diligence and fidelity; and though his tall, dark person did not seem very strong he was destined to perform at least twenty years of active service in the itinerant field. We are presenting the *Rev. William Creighton* to our readers for the first time.

132. We have reason to believe that the "one to be sent," as assistant of the Rev. John Baxter, on the Nanticoke Circuit, was *George Washington*, a middle-aged preacher from Ireland, who had been an itinerant for several years among the "Primitive Wesleyans" in that country. He was a plain, sound preacher, lively and affectionate, whom the people liked. We hope to have more data concerning him ere his name recurs.

133. The *Rev. Wm. Case's* assistant at *Alderville* is the only one we require to have placed before us in the *Cobourg District*. From other sources than the Minutes, we learn that the venerable missionary had a man with him after his own heart, in the person of his junior colleague; a man who was destined to become distinguished in the Indian mission field, a work to which he was in some measure adapted by early intercourse with the Indians, and for which he was now seeking further preparation. It will, perhaps, be already surmised that we are referring to one whom we might now,

4

almost, denominate the *martyred George Macdougall*. He is believed to have been of Scottish, perhaps Highland, parentage, but brought up, if not born, in this country. He had been converted and introduced among the Methodists, some years before, in the neighborhood of Barrie, a mere youth; but he married early and had been in business some years. That he was married and had two or more children, was the objection urged by some members of the Conference to his being received on trial for the ministry; yet these very things constituted real recommendations for the Indian department of the work for which he offered himself. Though young, he had had several years' experience of business among the aborigines, which consisted in sailing a vessel upon Lakes Huron and Superior employed in the Indian trade. This had given him considerable acquaintance with their minds and manners, and some knowledge of their language. To perfect this lingual knowledge was one reason for his being sent, with the father of Canadian Missions, to this old mission station, preparatory for his distant and responsible labors in the future. His wife's excellent character, and his own physical strength and hardihood were also weights in the scale.

134. The Minutes account for the provision for all the circuit in the *Belleville District*, excepting how the second preacher's place was supplied in the old Sidney Circuit. The lively and laborious Michael Fawcett had been transferred from the charge of Bowmanville to the superintendency of this circuit, where he was well and favorably known, and which was the commencement of seven very successful years' labors around the head of Bay Quinte. The supply sent him was a young man small in stature and short-sighted, but of good stock, German-Irish, of good character, and of fair abilities. This was our well-conducted friend, *Aaron D. Miller*, who has continued in the work until this day.

135. The *Kingston District* makes neither call for, nor promise of assistance to the ministerial staff in any of the circuits. The large old *Waterloo* Circuit had but one name set down to perform the duties of its laborious pastorate. True, that was a man whom it is not too much to say did usually as much pastoral work, at least, as two ordinary preachers. This was the indefatigable *Joseph Wesley McCallum*, but even he seems to have required a colleague and to have received one ; and received it in the person of one *German*, by name if not by descent, who, moreover, bore the baptismal name of the founder of Methodism, *John Wesley*. *John Wesley German* was the son of that one of the two Peter Germans who did such good service about the Bay Quinte on Canal circuits, in the capacity of a hired local preacher. This (his son) was destined to be one of the most exact and successfully laborious preachers on the good average circuits to which he has usually been sent.

136. *Brockville* District had no vacancies, and *Bytown* had only one. That energetic old itinerant, *Henry Shaler*, needed an assistant at *Osgoode*, and received one, as large as he was small, in the person of *Silas Huntington*, a native Canadian, brought up near Kemptville, but converted amid the wilds of the Upper Ottawa only one year before his entrance on a circuit. He was naturally clever, and had received a fair commercial education. His gifts were so prominent from the first that a society-class for the neighborhood in which he lived, which coincided in its organization with his union with the Church, received him as its *practical* leader, while the *nominal* leadership devolved on an old professor, and a much older man, whose own talents were not sufficiently commanding. The development of young Huntington's abilities in prayer, counsel, exhortation, and preaching, within the short space of eleven months, led to his being selected as the chairman's supply for this defectively supplied circuit. We opine

that he had been chosen by Mr. Shaler himself as his helper from the knowledge he had possessed before of the young man. We have this brother's journal, and will draw on it to illustrate the work in coming years.

137. The Conference had received the thanks of the Canada East District Meeting for the services of the *Rev. Lachlin Taylor* during the previous two years, and craved the continuance of the *Rev. Charles Lavell* among them for a second year, which was accorded to them. Mr. Taylor's health being somewhat impaired, he received from the Conference, according to his request, a supernumerary relation for a year, and he retired to the parental home, near Cobourg, where it appeared, after a few months, that he was gathering physical strength and intellectual furniture for a more prominent position and a wider sphere of operation, namely, the General Agency of the Upper Canada Bible Society, of which more anon.

138. The humble-minded and amiable, but useful John Black, on going back from the Conference to Sidney, his previous three years' scene of labor, was sent to his new field, Napanee, with testimonials and presents.

139. The Union Camp-meeting for the Yonge Street, Newmarket, and Humber Circuits, concerted and carried out soon after Conference, held in the Township of Vaughan, and attended by Brethren Demorest, Law, Warner, Ker, and Wm. Young, was of a most delightful character, and followed by reviving influences.

140. The Burlington Ladies' Academy, still under the management of the Rev. Daniel C. Van Norman, skilled in that description of work, rendered great service to the country at large, and especially to the Methodist Church, being prosecuted with great vigor and success.

141. Under the date of July 27th, 1850, the Rev. Egerton Ryerson, D.D., a prominent member of the Wesleyan

Conference, was appointed by government proclamation to the "*Chief* Superintendency of Schools for Upper Canada, under the Act of the present session of Parliament, for the better establishment and management of schools in that Province."

142. It was one indication of prosperity during this period of our Church's history, that the augmentation of the missionary income enabled the General Missionary Committee to increase the grants to the laborers in certain needy cases. The Society was reported out of debt.

143. Authoritative news came from England, after the session of the British Conference, that the Rev. Enoch Wood was appointed President of the Canada Conference and the Rev. John Ryerson was appointed his Co-Delegate.

144. A new church was opened on the Fly Road, Township of Clinton, on Sabbath, September the eighth. And the noble Sydenham Street Church, in Kingston, was built during this Conference year.

145. The appointment of Mr. Nelles to the Principalship of Victoria College received the good augury of an increased number of students during the summer session.

146. A revival was reported on the Augusta Circuit as early as October; as also, in the same month, at Allenburgh, on the St. Catharines Circuit, likewise on several other circuits, the names of which have escaped us.

147. A very encouraging letter from the Rev. Peter Jones, Indian missionary, showing the progress of civilization and the large amount of material comfort and prosperity, as well as religious advancement which obtained among the people who composed that band, appeared in the *Guardian*.

148. Wesley Church, on the east bank of the Grand River, near the Village of Cayuga, was built during the summer, and dedicated in the autumn of 1850.

149. A very satisfactory camp-meeting, near Owen Sound, conducted by the Rev. Enoch Wood, took place during the time we have under consideration.

150. A very powerful meeting of the above description was held about this time in the Manning Settlement, within the Town of London Circuit, intended to accommodate the St. Thomas and Aylmer Circuits as well, which was attended by a large measure of sanctifying influence on preachers and people. It aroused, however, the hostility of some bad men, who revenged, for being restrained by the hand of civil authority, by their damaging a buggy and cutting a set of harness to pieces, which they supposed to belong to the writer, who had the meeting in charge. By the 13th of January, 1851, this circuit had netted a gain of fifty members in town and an increase in all the country appointments.

151. Brother John Black, whose transfer to Napanee we have considered, with his youthful colleague, Joseph Reynolds, was cheered by a most gracious revival on that important field of labor.

152. The missionary anniversaries were conducted with great enthusiasm throughout the Connexion, and a corresponding pecuniary and spiritual gain was realized.

153. The Saugeen Mission, which had been in a state of spiritual decline for some time, was greatly quickened during the course of this year.

154. About mid-winter, a glowing letter came from the aged Chairman of the *Brockville District*, Rev. Thomas Bevitt, a man not predisposed to paint things in rose color, giving a cheering account of the aspects of the cause, both local and Connexional, throughout his district.

155. A brick parsonage was erected on the Markham Circuit, and Connexional and local interests were prosperous.

156. The same may be said of the accounts received

from the Stratford, Brampton, St. Thomas, and Dundas Circuits.

157. The new chapel in the Village of Chippewa was opened during February, 1851. There was a marked revival on the Oshawa Circuit during this Conference year.

158. In fine, there was good news from Malahide, Peel Mission, Norwood, Newborough, Bowmanville, (where a new church was erected,) Rama, and Orillia, Glanford, Cornwall, Moulinette.—A new church was dedicated in Cline's neighborhood, on the Nelson Circuit, and Brampton had great prosperity.

159. We have followed the brethren in their efforts for Connexional advancement, in church building, education, Connexional funds, and missionary extension; but their direct efforts for the salvation of souls and the upbuilding of the societies must have been equally energetic and persistent, for there was, at least, the very respectable net gain of *one thousand one hundred and seventy souls* to the several societies of the Connexion during the year 1850-51, of which we write.

160. We turn now to see what can be made of the doings and successes of the *Wesleyan ministers and preachers in the Province of Eastern Canada* during the same period. The first item of information relating to this section of the work is found in the *Christian Guardian* for May 29th, 1850— it relates to the District Meeting with which the ecclesiastical year began, and is embraced in the next paragraph :—

161. "The Canada East District Meeting has closed its Annual Session. It will be recollected that the Rev. Matthew Lang, *Chairman* of the District, was recently summoned by the Great Head of the Church from the Church militant to the Church triumphant. Owing to his lamented death, the Rev. Dr. Richey, President of our Conference, proceeded to Quebec, and presided at the District Meeting.

Unanimity and peace prevailed. The following are the stations of the brethren in Canada East for 1850-51 :—

"*Montreal*—John Jenkins, Charles De Wolfe, A.M., and Charles Lavell.

"*Quebec*—Charles Churchill.

"*Three Rivers*—Thomas Campbell.

"*Wesleyville and Rawdon*—Henry Cox.

"*St. Johns*—George H. Davis.

"*Chambly*—John Douglas,

"*Huntingdon*—James Brock.

"*Russeltown*—Hugh Montgomery.

"*Odelltown and Hemmingford*—J. C. Davidson.

"*Clarenceville*—Edmund S. Ingalls.

"*St. Armands*—William Scott.

"*Dunham*—John Tomkins and John Armstrong.

"*Shefford*—R. A. Flanders.

"*Stanstead*—John Borland.

"*Compton*—Malcolm McDonald.

"*Sherbrooke*—Henry Lanton.

"*Melbourne*—Benjamin Slight, A.M.

"*Leeds*—Gifford Dorey."

162. There is not much in this brief entry which calls for or admits of remark. We discover that the meeting was held in the ancient capital somewhere about the middle of May, but the precise time of its beginning and ending we do not learn. We miss the laborious Chairman, who has gone to his rest, as also Brother George Douglas, who is abroad in the Bermudas, but no new names are observable: all the brethren whose names are given are persons with whose antecedents and character the reader has been made acquainted.

163. All the usual sources of information have been resorted to for details of the manner, and to see with what success the work was prosecuted during the year, and all have failed us but two. First, the *Guardian* informs us of

a glorious revival in the City of Montreal, during the year, aided by the presence and labors of the *Rev. James Caughey*, of revival celebrity, who had been made of signal service in that city before; secondly, the journal of the Rev. B. Slight, A.M., the entire of whose entries for the year we insert, as a probably fair specimen of the manner in which the Lower Canada brethren performed their work. It will be perceived that Mr. Slight was still at *Melbourne*. His record is as follows:—

164. "January 19th, 1851.—Finished our annual missionary tour.—Travelled two hundred and sixteen miles.—Preached three missionary sermons—ten or twelve missionary speeches. The congregations were generally large, and the meetings increasing in interest. On our own circuit the meetings were the best in the whole round. The tea-meeting at Durham was specially good. The number attending surprised us all. The clear proceeds were £7. 7s. 6d." ($25.50), "the largest sum ever realized on this circuit, except once when it was a few shillings above." Surely it could not have been a very productive circuit as it respected money. But Mr. B. resumes:—

165. "March.—This circuit has evidently been increasing in good feeling and attendance on the means. The truths of the Gospel are listened to with intense interest. I have usually, of late, had unusual liberty and power in preaching. All these things warrant me to hope for some good.

166. "A review of these circumstances encouraged me to hold some special services at Kingsey and Durham. I continued them six days at the former place. I never saw a congregation so unusually impressed. About twenty have promised to meet on probation. I hope many more will speedily decide to be on the Lord's side.

167. "March 21st.—I am not indisposed to acknowledge the labors of the ministers of other Churches. But when I

4*

see anything like display, it affords disgust. In a newspaper I lately met with an article setting forth the uncommon labors of a Congregational minister in Canada West, the evident *animus* is to be entitled to adopt as a motto, 'In labors more abundant.' It is as follows :—

168. "'Preached (1850) 153 sermons ; attended temperance, church, and prayer meetings, 42 ; visited, read, and prayed with 298 families, and baptized 14 children; preached 5 funeral sermons; received into the Church 32 new members; travelled 3,400 miles ; 114 days and nights from home !' Then he enumerates a few books, mostly of small importance, which he had read, amounting in number to about thirteen volumes, with sermons, comments, &c., and three newspapers.

169. "All these things appear to be noticed with care, for the purpose of effect. To be sure, it is far in advance of the generality of Congregational ministers in this country ; but let me recollect something of my own labors. Are not Methodist preachers in general considerably in advance?

170. "I preached in this circuit each year about 350 sermons ; special, church, and other meetings, from 130 to 150 ; pastoral visitations numerous ; funeral sermons, 8 or 10 ; marriages, 8 to 10 ; received on trial, about 30 to 40 ; travelled about 5,000 miles or more; about 150 nights from home, and about 300 days ; reading quite as voluminous, and writing extensive in many departments.

171. "God speaks to us by His word, and sometimes directs us to particular passages. One Monday morning lately, as I was reflecting rather sadly on the state of things and the many untoward circumstances which existed here when I entered on the circuit, I took up a New Testament and opened on the words, 'For this purpose I left thee in Crete, that thou shouldst set in order the things which are wanting.' From this I thought it might have been providential that I was appointed to this circuit. To rectify

wrong things, to exercise discipline, to set things on a proper footing, &c., &c., are things of moment. One Friday or Saturday morning lately I took up the Bible, after having been some time in prayer for direction to a proper subject for the ensuing Sabbath, and opened upon : ' Occupy till I come ; ' and opening again, immediately after, the first passage that struck my eye was, 'These things teach and exhort !' I took the passage for my text, and the sermon appeared to be attended with much power.

172. "May 26th, 1851.—Finished making up my returns for district meeting. On reviewing the last three years on this circuit, I find I have received on trial 59 persons—have had 29 removals, 12 deaths, and about 55 expelled and dropped. The present number of members is 270, and 4 on trial. The number when I entered was 262—8 increase. From the careless manner in which the returns were made by my predecessor, I have had to clear the lists of a large number of names that ought not to have been left on them, otherwise my total increase would have been much larger. Danville has been left without a supply for two years, and I have lost twenty in that portion of the country from want of pastoral oversight. Although I have had to give up all receipts on the Danville side of the circuit, yet, taking the Melbourne side of the circuit alone, 1 find our income is now £14 ($56) in advance of the year before my taking the charge, which was then receiving £10 ($40) from the Danville portion of the circuit. The spiritual state of the circuit, I have satisfaction in reporting, is much improved. There is much increase of unction and power attending the ministration of the Word and ordinances, and a deeply-fixed attention to them. I am thankful to leave the circuit better than I found it"—a pleasing reflection this with which to close a ministerial term of three years !

173. Taking this as a specimen of how and with what

anxiety the brethren toiled through the twelve months from June, 1850, to June, 1851, we feel anxious to know how it resulted, and turn to the Minutes of 1851 to ascertain; and lo! we find there is a *decrease* of eighty members! Their total was 3,769, which, added to the Canada Conference returns of 26,213, made scarcely *thirty thousand*—or 39,982 members in the two Provinces.

1851-52.

174. THE commencement of the first seven years of the uninterrupted presidency of the Rev. Enoch (afterwards Doctor) Wood coincided with the twenty-seventh session of the Canada Conference, which commenced in Adelaide Street Church, Toronto, whose sittings began on the 4th of June, 1851, and closed on the 13th of the same month, covering a period of nine days, including a Sabbath. Mr. Wood proved himself a very satisfactory presiding officer; naturally sage and overseer-like, he had enjoyed four years' acquaintance with Anglo-Canadian Methodism; this, with his peace-loving disposition and aptness to learn from the discussions themselves as they went forward, enabled him to conduct the business of Conference to a desirable issue and with reasonable despatch. At this Conference every Connexional fund was found to be in advance of former years.

175. A respectable and observing layman, long before identified with the interests of Methodism in the Province, who, after an absence from Upper Canada for several years, chanced to be called by the Government office which he held to sojourn in Toronto at the time of this Conference, expressed some thoughts in the *Guardian* relative to the character of that session, which, because of their justness, I will take the liberty of transferring to these pages. *Mr. Vaux* (for that was the gentleman's name) holds the following language: "One of the first and most pleasing features, as presented to my mind, was the harmony that dwelt

among the brethren; one heart seemed to pervade the whole. They had no *party* purposes to serve. The only purpose, and in which all joined, was evidently the building up and maintaining the kingdom of the Redeemer. * * * Being privileged to attend the Conference prayer-meetings and love-feast, it was matter of rejoicing to witness the spirit and simplicity which reigned throughout. * * * In reflecting upon and comparing the present state of the work under the care of the Wesleyan Methodist Church in this Province with the earliest period of which we have the Conference records (in 1824), I am sure every one having the extension of the Redeemer's kingdom at heart will praise Him who, verifying Mr. Wesley's assurance, has continued to be, and still is, 'with us.' In 1824 we find thirty-six of the Lord's laborers in the vineyard, and 7,150 in church-membership; now, in 1851, there are 200 laborers and 26,213 members. * * * I expect shortly again to leave this part of the Province. May God bless the labors and strengthen the hands of His servants, and sanctify the Church wholly!"

176. After many years' service as Journal Secretary, the Conference conferred the honor of the principal Secretaryship on the *Rev. James Musgrove,* who was eminently qualified for its duties, and who had earned this expression of confidence by twenty years of faithful ministerial labor, embracing several official responsibilities. He also performed the duties of this new position with dignity and despatch.

177. Three brethren, after the usual four years' probation with the Conference, were received into full connexion and ordained. These were *John Webster, John C. Osborne,* and *William McGill,* with all of whom the reader has been made acquainted. There was also an exceptional case. Brother Henry Reid—who, from various causes, principally because

he was married and had a family—had been kept in the relation of a hired local preacher—now, after seven years' service in the hardest of the bush circuits, was also received into full connexion and ordained. He had proved himself strong and willing to labor, a good preacher, and very successful in winning souls. Each of these brethren spoke in considerable detail and with great feeling at their public reception.

178. There was a most formidable array of names presented as candidates for reception on trial for the ministry in connection with the Conference—no less than *nineteen* in all,—namely: *Richard Clarke, Joel Briggs, George McRitchie, David Sawyer, Alexander Campbell, Thomas Crews, James Preston, John S. Evans, D. G. Fletcher, William Sanderson, George McDougal, Aaron Miller, John Wesley German, Robert Brewster, David Robertson, Silas Huntington, Andrew McAllister, Henry McDowell,* and *Robert Hobbs.*

179. Six of these, namely: *Joel Briggs, John S. Evans, George McDougal, Aaron Miller, John W. German,* and *S. Huntington,* as having been employed by chairmen on circuits the preceding year, have already had their antecedents and character considered. And it is now recollected or ascertained that four others also rendered similar service during the same period, namely: *George McRitchie, David Sawyer, Alexander Campbell,* and *Thomas Crews.* The first three spent the whole of the past year on circuits, the last one the latter half of that year.

180. Indeed, *Alexander Campbell* had been called out so early as 1846, under which year we gave an account of his nationality, qualities, and early history. From some cause he retired during 1850-51. He is taken up again, and destined to complete his term of probation, and to be fully received into the body, and to perform several more years of

useful labor. His apparent health and great strength little augured that he would fall suddenly in middle life.

181. *David Sawyer*, an Indian preacher, had also been in charge of a mission among his native brethren, not the last only, but the last two years—called the first year by the name of "Owen Sound," the second by that of "Newark." Mr. Sawyer, himself a chief, was a son of old Chief Sawyer, of the Credit tribe, who was baptized in childhood, while living in a white family, by the Rev. Joseph Sawyer, one of the early presiding elders, who gave him his own name. Our present subject, at the time of his reception on trial, could not have been less than from forty-two to forty-five years of age; nor were the last two years' labors the first he had performed for the Church, as the writer remembers him to have been sent on distant missionary expeditions, by the ever-watchful Elder Case, so early as the summer of 1827. At that time he acted as interpreter, exhorter, and school teacher. In these capacities there are frequent letters from him in our foregoing history. He was a comely native, and sizable.

182. *Bro. Thomas Crews* had been taken from his manual labor in Goderich, during the winter of 1850-51, by Mr. Carroll, the Chairman of the London District, to meet the urgent solicitations of a neglected people in Kincardine, of whom Mr. Crews gave a good account at the next May district meeting. The calling out of Mr. Crews was somewhat of an adventure. He was, it is true, a trained, acceptable local preacher from Old England; but then he was at least twenty-six years of age, was married, and had not been liberally educated. The few months of his experimental labors had, however, wrought a great change in him; his short, compact, comely person had assumed clerical habiliments and appearance; his fair preaching talents had been encouragingly developed, and he had made a promising

offer to conquer the Conference course of study, which he ultimately mastered to the satisfaction of his examiners. The result was, the Conference received him and sent him back to the mission he had opened, where he remained another two years. *J. S. Evans'* case is well known.

183. As to *George McRitchie,* we simply adopt part of the sketch of him after he had risen to be a chairman of District and member of the General Conference in 1874 :—

" He was born in Dundee, Scotland, in 1827, which makes him at the present,* forty-seven. Just twenty years after his birth, here in Canada, he became a Methodist, under the ministrations of Rev. Wm. Young Two years after he was licensed as an exhorter. In another year he was a local preacher, and within a few weeks after, sent by the Rev. John Ryerson to the Georgetown Circuit.

" All the Scotch preachers we have had to portray are clever men ; as a preacher this gentleman is one of the best. He does not promise a great deal now, to look at him ; and he promised a great deal less when he commenced his career. But he has grown to be the thoughtful, original, and quickening preacher. He has not so much energy in delivery, but there is much in the thoroughness in which he " bolts his subjects to the brain," as the old divine would say, which reminds us of the late Henry Wilkinson. Nor is he unlike him in appearance ; he is perhaps a little taller, but his muscle is equally attenuated and hardened, and his complexion is equally as dark. We believe, also, he is equally as good a man, which is saying a great deal."

Brother McRitchie gave promise of what he afterwards became, before his trial year was ended on the Georgetown Circuit. Part of his probation was destined to enjoy the improving advantages of Victoria College.

184. So far as we have learned, *Richard Clarke, James*

---

* Twenty-three when called out.

Preston, D. G. Fletcher, Wm. Sanderson, Robert Brewster, Andrew McAllister, Henry McDowell, and *Robert Hobbs,** had not been employed on circuits. Clarke, Sanderson, McDowell, and Hobbs, were either born in Ireland, or were of Irish parents; Preston was English; Robertson a Canadian; and McAllister, we know not what as to nationality, most likely, either a Scotch, or North Irish-Canadian.

185. *Richard Clarke,* next to Mr. Preston, had more experience and ability as a preacher than any of the candidates. He was of the mature age or twenty-eight, but healthy and blooming to a degree. His compact, strong body, and clear, ringing voice, coming out of a deep chest, gave hope of long and vigorous labors. He had realized a diversified Methodist experience—converted among the Primitive Wesleyans in Ireland, with whom he remained until his emigration to Canada some years before. He allied himself to the Weslean Society in Canada East, and enjoyed the watchful care and familiar confidence of the sturdy Wesleyan ministers in such cities as Quebec, Three Rivers, and Montreal. In the prosecution of his business, as clerk and salesman, he found his way to Toronto, where he exercised as a local preacher in connection with the strong society of the Richmond Street Church, by whose Official Board he was recommended to the Conference. Brother Clarke, besides being educated better than most of the candidates, was particularly well-read in theology. The first part of this Conference year, he was the much approved colleague of the Rev. S. D. Rice, in Kingston, and after the opening of the McNabb Street Church in Hamilton, a second preacher being required, he was transferred to be my own assistant in that city.

*Since the above was written, a post-card from the veteran Shaler informs us that *Andrew McAllister* assisted him on the Osgoode Mission in 1850, and *Robert Hobbs* labored in the same capacity during the year 1851-52.

186. Of *James Preston,* we must also make his General Conference portraiture do duty:—Premising that he was then twenty-three years of age, and that he was twenty-three years younger than when his personal appearance was described as below, we adopt the sketch then made:—

"He is from a thoroughly Methodist English county, Lancashire, and the town of Lancaster itself. He is only forty-six years old,* thirty of which he has enjoyed the saving grace of God. Was cradled in Methodism, Sunday-school scholar, at nineteen a local preacher. In 1850 was recommended by the Lancaster Quarterly Meeting to the work of the ministry, passed his preliminary examinations before the Liverpool District Meeting, and was recommended by them to the British Conference, but decided to come and help us in Canada. At the ensuing meeting of the Canada Conference, in 1851, he was received on trial, and stationed in the town of Brantford.

"Mr. P. is a sound, scriptural preacher, who wears well, exemplary Christian, and diligent pastor. He has been District Secretary and Chairman. He is an impressive reader, especially of our liturgical services. No man enjoys the respect of his acquaintances more than does Mr. Preston. He is a stout, light-complexioned gentleman, comely enough; but, when speaking, has a slight twitching in the muscles of one of his cheeks. The excellence of his matter, however, soon withdraws the hearer's thoughts from this very small 'thorn in the flesh.'"

187. As *Drummond G. Fletcher* continued but a few years in the work, and as I know not his place of retirement, if alive (although I surmise he is alive, and a local preacher), I know not where to address him for information. From a slight acquaintance with him (subject to correction), I should pronounce him a personable man, above the medium

*In 1874.

stature, genteel in manners, well-educated, well-read, and possessed of good conversational powers, but either married or a widower when called out. I should call him of Scotch descent, but brought up near Bowmanville, and I suspect a good speaker.

188. *Wm. Sanderson* was the son of the Rev. John Sanderson, the first, not large in person, and very young. Also, not being very strong, he was destined, after a time, to have to lie-by to recuperate for two or three years before he resumed the work again. He was a pure, good lad, of earnest intentions, and of moderate, if not medium, abilities. He will come favorably to view hereafter.

189. *Robert Brewster*, after earning a worthy record, went to the United States; so that we have lost the means o readily learning his antecedents. He was certainly of Scotch parentage, and, if our recollections are not greatly at fault, brought up somewhere near Newboro'. He was a medium-sized, well-proportioned young man, fair of face, with dark hair, serious in deportment, very voluble in speaking, and full of zeal for God and souls. If he had been less voluble and rapid, his great impressiveness would have been still greater. He was destined to rank above the average in talents and for the circuits he commanded.

190. Alas, poor *Andrew McAllister*. He was, we surmise, either a Scotch or North-Irish-Canadian. He was destined to wear himself out on the large Clarendon and Onslow Mission in one year—to drag out the next year in ill-health—and to die within the third year thereafter. He had no further register in the Minutes, but we trust his record is on high.

191. *Robert Hobbs* was of an Irish Methodist family, brother of the devoted wife of the Rev. John Howes, brought up in Clarendon, Lower Canada. Not very large or strong, and only about twenty-one years of age when he went, the

year before, to the assistance of the Rev. Henry Shaler on the Osgoode Mission. The rest I leave his Conference obituary to say:—"He was born in Clarendon, Canada East, in 1830, and converted under the ministry of the Rev. Wm. Morton in 1843, from which time until his death he continued walking in the fear of God and the comfort of the Holy Ghost. He labored nearly two years in the capacity of a local preacher, prior to his being called into the more active work."

192. *David Robertson* was a very young man, but almost a giant for size and stature; yet, alas, his herculean strength was soon brought to succumb to the toils and exposures of the itinerancy. Not having much acquaintance with him personally, I simply copy a part of his short Conference obituary:— "D. R. was born near the Village of Kemptville, in the year 1829. At the age of seventeen he sought and obtained redemption in the blood of Christ. In 1850, he was employed by the Chairman of the Brockville District to labor on the Mississippi Circuit; at the ensuing Conference he was received on trial and appointed to the same circuit."

193. On page 473, of the fourth volume of this work, the author made the regretted blunder of using *Henry McDowell's* name instead of his brother *David C. McDowell's*, who was received on trial that year; that is, five years before our present date. *David*, therefore, one of our naturally gifted young preachers, one of the purest of men, and one who was destined to fill some of the most respectable stations in the Connexion, to exercise the office of Chairman for several years, and, what is even better, to be the instrument of bringing hundreds of souls to God, went unnoticed. The reader must recall what we said of the younger brother in the place referred to, and to remember that the senior brother had always somewhat the advantage in other respects

as well as years. They were both a great acquisition to the ministry.

194. While so very many were coming forward to recruit the ministerial hosts, some had "put off their harness" forever. Three were reported dead. One was a very aged man for years, another was old, but still older in complicated infirmities, induced by exhausting toils and exposures in the vast circuits of the early days—but one was but a boy for years, although like a middle-aged minister for the maturity of his mind and talents: we are referring to the venerable *James Wilson*, the laborious *George Ferguson*, and the gifted and saintly *Alexander Sturgeon Byrne*. Canada had owed them all to Ireland. But we need not recapitulate their history.

195. Of *Mr. Wilson* his obituary notice says: "The period of his superannuation was unusually protracted; but whatever strength remained was cheerfully devoted to the Redeemer and for the advantage of his beloved Church, to sustain the interests of which he made a generous centenary gift. For some" (many) "years he professed to enjoy the choice blessing of sanctification. Nearly" (quite) "all his children were members of the Wesleyan Church—God was his life, his hope, his all. 'In age and feebleness extreme' the doctrines he preached were vital to his heart. A few months before his death, at a quarterly meeting, he was assisted in ascending the pulpit, when he preached with apparent youthful liveliness; but it was his last effort. The final hour came, and when heaven opened, his words were, 'Jesus is precious; I want to go!'"

196. Of *George Ferguson*, his brethren's recorded testimony was as follows: "His career from the beginning was marked by singularly zealous efforts to promote the Redeemer's kingdom. Thus it was during the six trying years of his life that were spent in the army, and subse-

quently through the entire twenty-seven years of his effective ministry. He travelled many circuits from the Far West to the eastern boundary of Canada West, and his labors were signally crowned with the Divine blessing in the conversion of hundreds of sinners and the edification of believers. To our Church he firmly adhered through all her trials. He was a burning and a shining light, and will long live in the affectionate remembrance of thousands throughout the Province. After a long and painful illness, throughout which his piety shone with great lustre, he departed this life, in great peace, on the 1st of January, 1851, in the Township of Trafalgar, C.W., in the 65th year of his age."

197. As young *Mr. Byrne* was simply a prodigy of precociously matured talents in very boyhood, though reproducing some statements made before, I will give his Conference obituary entire, that all may have a complete, although transient view of his meteor-like appearance across our Canadian ecclesiastical horizon :—

"ALEXANDER STURGEON BYRNE was a grandson of the Rev. Alexander Sturgeon, for many years a distinguished member of the Irish Wesleyan Conference, after whom he was named, and the son of the Rev. Claudius Byrne, of this Conference. He was born in Dungannon, Ireland, June 20th, 1832; and was, consequently, at his death, (which happened in Brantford, in February last,) only aged *eighteen years* and scarcely *eight months*. He was a delightful and encouraging instance of the beneficial effects of the early consecration of children to God by their parents, and an early habituation of them to attend those social means of grace for which our Church is distinguished—he having been led to the class-room from the time he was able to walk. In advance of a blameless, amiable temper, and conduct, which he evinced from infancy, he was, after a livelong night of prayerful agony, brought into the glorious liberty of the sons of God. This important event took place about daybreak, on a Monday morning, in the month of February, 1845, and, consequently, about six years before his lamented removal. He was led, by a train of providential openings, almost immediately to exercise his gifts in public, which were of such an extraordinary character as to open his way, when not more than fifteen years of age, into many of the first pulpits of the Connexion in his native land, from which he had the privilege of proclaiming the unsearchable riches of Christ to large congregations, brought together by the fame of his precocious talents. In the winter of 1849, himself and father's family having emigrated to this country a few weeks before, he was called out by the Chairman of the Toronto District to labor on the Yonge Street Circuit, where he continued till the ensuing Conference; when, being received on trial in the itinerant ministry, he was appointed to the Town of London Circuit, where he was 'received,' to use the Apostle's language, 'as an angel of God,' and labored with much fidelity and success. At the next Conference he was appointed (then in an infirm state of health) to the East Toronto City Circuit. He labored with much acceptance, though in great pain and weakness, till increased indisposition forced him from his beloved employment, and obliged him to return to the parental home. Uniform patience characterized his lingering illness, and triumph his early death. His last words were, 'I know that my Redeemer liveth.' His *character* consisted of a rare and most harmonious combination of dignity and modesty, of fidelity and forbearance, of prudence and zeal, of gravity and cheerfulness. His *preaching* was distinguished for the ability to make the most practical and searching subjects attracting to all classes of hearers. Few have enjoyed, for the time, so much popularity; and still fewer have been so little affected by it. He ived and died one of the most faultless of religious characters. And the recollection which is entertained of him, is a pleasing illustration of that scripture, 'The memory of the just is blessed.'"

198. This Conference was noticeable among other things for a change of editor. *Mr. Sanderson* had, to the satisfaction of the majority of the electors and of the Connexion at large, occupied the office for five years, the longest term by two years that any incumbent had filled the editorial chair at any one time, albeit that the Rev. Egerton Ryerson had occupied that post seven years in all, but at three several times. Mr. Sanderson's removal turned entirely on the necessity of having variety and of a rotation in office. The *Rev. James Spencer*, who was elected in his place, had been brought forward by some admiring friends at two or three intervals before, but there had never been strength enough prior to this session to elect him. These two competitors were also great friends. They were born and had spent their days in Upper Canada, and they were fellow-students in the Upper Canada Academy, which afterwards expanded into Victoria College, and were among the very first who entered their names. They had some resemblances, with some dissimilarities. Spencer was the older, perhaps, by two yeas but Sanderson had entered the itinerant field one year the first: he travelled one year under a chairman; the other went into the Conference on trial the next year direct; that is, Sanderson in 1837—Spencer in 1838. Spencer had the wider scholarship; the other had the more taking accomplishments. Sanderson had the advantage in voice and appearance; Spencer's voice was sing-song, and his appearance by no means showy. Spencer's sermons might be the better written; the other certainly the better delivered. The retiring editor had excelled in selections, the new incumbent was destined to thrust his pen deeper into the questions ot the day. The first deprecated controversy, and labored for

the promotion of peace; the second was bound to have peace, if he fought for it. For several years previously it had been thought meritorious, on the part of many persons and papers, to keep up a carping sort of criticism of Wesleyan Methodist affairs, but Mr. Spencer soon conquered a peace. His ability in the use of the *argumentum ad hominem* and the *argumentum ad absurdum* soon taught the various comers to be afraid of some mischance, if they meddled with him. He took a very decided stand in favor of Temperance, and showed himself otherwise alert to the exigencies of the times through the whole of his long nine years' incumbency.

199. Any person who wishes to know where the several ministers were stationed during the ecclesiastical year 1851-52, and the consequent changes any of them underwent, has but to consult the printed Minutes for that year; but there are some vacancies in the stations themselves—vacancies part of which the painstaking Mr. Cornish himself has not been able to supplement in his valuable Hand-Book. The supplies for these vacancies I must now inquire after, and that the rather as they involve the commencement of some in the ministry whose origin and course of action I am desirous to trace out and record. The TORONTO DISTRICT has a few of these.

200. The Rev. Samuel Philp, sen., on the important *Humber Circuit*, seems to have gone to his field of labor incomplete in the matter of a colleague. Such a provision was made by the Rev. John Ryerson, co-Delegate, and Chairman of the District, in the person of a tall, strong young man, some twenty-five years of age, a native of Yorkshire, England, newly arrived in the country. He had come from the healthful labors of agriculture, and was said to have been an adept in that department of husbandry celebrated by Thompson in his *Seasons*, when he declares of noble Romans retiring from the defence of their country, " They seized the *plough*, and greatly independent lived." He had not had

5

great advantages of education, but he knew religion experimentally, had an aptness for making sermons, and was impressive in delivering them. He felt the usual awkwardness of one newly arrived in a new country, but ultimately mastered those difficulties, and made a preacher above mediocrity. We are contemplating our strapping, stalwart friend *William Richardson*. The *Nelson* Circuit, according to the Minutes, needed a third man. But the two that were actually there were more than ordinarily efficient and industrious—the Rev. Messrs. McCallum and Fish, and the former writes me that they "got on without any regular supply."

201. I am indebted to the *Rev. Lewis Warner*, now an invalid, but then an efficient chairman, for information relative to the supplies for the vacancies on the *Barrie District*. *Horace Dean*, whose *name*, as well as person, was this year in connection with the *Beausoliel and French Rivers*, was assisted by an Indian brother, *Solomon James* by name; but of his history and attributes we know nothing further. The indefatigable *George McDougall*, who had been sent to shepherd the Indians on the *North Shore of Lake Huron*, also supplied the lack of preaching to the neglected congregation at *Bruce Mines*. We have one more supply to introduce, who will require a little more particularizing.

202. *Nottawasaga* was often left "to be supplied." It was so the present year, and the supply, who was destined to spend six years in the regular work, must now be introduced: *James M. Clarke* was of Irish parents, but born in York (Toronto) in 1830. His father, Mr. William Clarke, was among the early Methodists of the city, and if his zeal had been as great as his gifts he would have been a preacher himself; but he never went beyond mere local efforts. The young man now under consideration was fair and florid in face and features, and stout and compact in frame and muscle, almost inclining to corpulency. He kept a journal

and says of himself: "Convinced of sin A.D. 1846, when nearly seventeen years of age; not satisfied as to justification by faith until eighteen months after. Believed for the blessing of 'perfect love' a few months subsequent to justification. Lost it in a few weeks; regained it at a camp meeting in 1851. Have retained it, though with a wavering faith, till the present time. Glory be to God!

203. "Deeply impressed, soon after conversion, with a call to preach the gospel. Received a call from the Church in 1851. Opened up my commission for the first time in October of the said year, on the Nottawasaga Mission, Barrie District, under the direction of the Rev. L. Warner, Chairman." Here we leave the brother for the present, reserving the right of drawing on his journal to show how the work was done in those days.

204. The Rev. John Carroll left the *London District* at the Conference of 1851, and was succeeded in the chair of the district by the Rev. Samuel Rose, who was, as we have seen, in charge of the Mount Elgin Indian Industrial School. There were four places not supplied by Conference men, but two of them I provided for during the Conference. I aided my successor in getting a young man for the district during the year, by which a young preacher was released to go to one of the vacancies, and a fourth was extemporized by the chairman. The details, I believe, were as follows :—

205. The first pair of supplies was from the Goderich Circuit. *Strathroy* was superintended by the Rev. James Armstrong, who was lacking a colleague appointed by the Conference. The young man engaged was *John Shaw*, the son of one of our Irish local preachers, born at Three Rivers, Lower Canada. The family removed to Goderich, where his father, though a farmer, sometimes taught a school, and for over thirty-five years was Township Clerk and Treasurer. At a special service, held by the Rev. John Williams and

the Rev. James Gray, young Shaw was converted, not from immorality, but Phariseeism, on the 12th of March, 1849. In three months he had been appointed assistant class-leader; and, three months later than that, he was sent to meet a class by himself where there were a great number of old members, which he found a sore trial. In the spring of 1851 after due examination under the pastorate of the Rev. Samuel Fear, he preached a trial sermon, and was fully installed in the office of a local preacher. He was therefore prepared to respond to my request from the Conference of 1851, and enter the opening left for him at Strathroy. Mr. Shaw, although a massive specimen of physical manhood, was very young, and diffident to a degree; but a tolerable elementary education, some practice in a mutual improvement and debating society, diligent private study, and one year at Victoria College, placed him in an advanced position at the end of his four years' probation, and laid the foundation for the eminence he has since attained.

206. A young man accompanied Shaw from the Goderich settlement to supply the vacancy at *Chatham*, under the superintendency of the Rev. William Price—*James Taylor* by name. Of him I have very slender information; but, partly from his early friend and partly from other sources, I came to the following conclusion about his history and character: He was less stout, but a little older than Shaw. Like him, he was of Irish parentage, and converted in the same revival. I would say he had less elementary training, but, perhaps, more reading, and certainly more cheek, than his junior friend. Shaw says he had "a great verbal memory." His first efforts attracted the most attention; but, if his life had been spared, he would scarcely have kept abreast with his more enduring companion. He was allowed to attend college during the last year of his probation, but he did not survive the year 1854, to which, when we come, we will give him a parting word.

207. *Wallaceburg* was left without any supply, and its necessities were so urgent that the chairman was fain to take from the Rev. John Bredin, at *St. Thomas*, his accomplished young colleague, Joseph Hugill, whose acquaintance the reader has already made, and send him to take charge of that isolated missionary circuit, who gave a good account of it for the balance of the year. [Since the text was written I have ascertained that Wallaceburg would have been totally destitute till late in the autumn, had it not been that the once robust *Thomas Harmon*, now in age and feebleness extreme, went there soon after Conference, and gave them half the amount of preaching which an efficient man would have given. The people showed their appreciation of his services by a testimonial.] The Chairman of the Hamilton District was applied to, if I remember right, both by Mr. Rose and Mr. Bredin, to learn if I knew of a supply. I had heard the fame of a young man whom I had once known somewhat when he was attending the Normal School in Toronto during its first session, who was, at the time of the application for a supply, teaching an advanced school in Dunnville, and rendering great aid on the circuit as a local preacher. Jonah-like, he had been fleeing from circuit to circuit to escape the responsibility of his call. Now, at length, however, he consented to go so soon as he could wind up his school, the ample emoluments of which he gave up for the scanty pittance, such as it was then, of a single preacher's salary. He came out with all possible despatch, spent a Sabbath with us at Hamilton, and preached with great acceptability in John Street Church, and took his way to his circuit the following week, where he succeeded to admiration. This was the ministerial beginning of *Edward Hartley Dewart*, born in Ireland of godly Methodist parents; converted in the wilds of Asphodel, near Norwood; encouraged in his first attempts to cultivate his mind by the

loan of books and words of cheer from the Rev. William Young, and, finally, trained at the Provincial Normal School, one of its earliest and best scholars. His powers of mind were quick and capacious, and he had devoured with voracity all the books which promised any information that had come in his way. His powers of private conversation and his gifts for public speaking were great, his voice loud and strong, and all other pre-requisites for a preacher good. By this time he has made himself so thoroughly, as well as favorably known—I might almost say to the Methodist world—as to need no further description.

208. The vacancy on the *Amherstburg* Circuit is the only remaining matter to be accounted for in relation to this district. As the St. Thomas Circuit furnished the supply for Wallaceburg out of its itinerant ranks, so it furnished the second preacher for Amherstburg out of its local ranks. A small and very young man, of a non-Methodist family, in very good circumstances, became converted under (I think) the powerful ministry of the Rev. William Pollard; and, after encountering some prejudice, if not some persecution, finally had the family look favorably on the Church of his choice and allow him to prepare himself for its ministry. His name was *William Williams*. He it was, if I mistake not, who went to the assistance of the sprightly *Richard Whiting* on the Amherstburg Circuit. He died at the early age of thirty-two, in 1861, which would make him but twenty-two when he went to the help of his brethren in the itinerant work.

209. The omissions on the *Brantford District* for this year are soon despatched. The *Ingersoll* and *Norwich* Circuits each lacked a second preacher; but the Rev. C. W. M. Gilbert, the Superintendent of the former, informs me that neither he nor his neighbor, the Rev. Francis Chapman, long since deceased, received an assistant, but had to struggle

on alone. The Rev. Matthew Whiting, in charge of *Walsingham*, I am informed by the venerable Matthias Holtby, then and now a supernumerary on that circuit, had a young preacher sent to his assistance from Brantford by the name of *Kirk;* but, as he soon went to the United States, nothing further is known of him.

210. There were three places to be supplied on the *Hamilton District*, all provided for by the retiring chairman, the Rev. Henry Wilkinson, as I know from my own recollection, having succeeded him in the charge of the district. And there was another case of exigency created by the failing health of the Rev. John Baxter, of the Nanticoke Circuit. Through his indisposition the circuit would have suffered very much, only that a young local preacher, who was teaching school in the circuit, went to the aid of his Superintendent by not only going far and near on Sabbaths, but by holding successful revival services on week nights besides. This young preacher was *William Tomlin*, who thus gave augury of the extreme diligence and success which were to characterize his after career in the itinerancy. More of him when fairly introduced to the work.

211. *Dunnville* was under the superintendency of the Rev. John Hunt, whose field was so extensive as to need an assistant. That assistant was a gentleman of middle age, who had been a member of the Irish " Primitive Wesleyan " Conference for several years, but, of course, not ordained, as that section of Methodism declined the right of dispensing the sacraments by its preachers. He was a fair preacher, willing to labor, companionable among the people, and much liked. We are writing of *George Washington* 1st, now a supernumerary minister of the Canada Methodist Church, residing at Oakville.

212. The *Rev. Solomon Waldron* was left without an assistant at *Elora*. I found and sent to his aid a young

man who had travelled a time on the Walsingham Circuit. He had some mind and many excellences, but such marked idiosyncracies (which after some years grew into spells of insanity) as to ultimately disqualify him for the work. This was *Edward Cooke*, a native of Cornwall, England, whence he had come in the standing of a local preacher.

213. A circuit still further north—the *Peel*—had no Conference supply at all, except that the ordinances were dispensed by the good and venerable Ezra Adams, who resided there as a superannuate. The work and management of the circuit were taken by Mr. Adams' son-in-law, who had lived within its bounds almost from the beginning of the settlement, and whose acceptability as a local preacher was so great that his brethren and neighbors gladly received him as their pastor. This was *Matthew Swann*, now a district chairman, the son of Governor Maitland's steward, born himself in York (Toronto); converted in old Adelaide Street Church; several years in the employ of the late Richard Woodsworth, and commissioned as a local preacher by the Rev. Henry Wilkinson. Mr. Swann, though married, was young and vigorous, compact and wiry, of average abilities, but uncommon zeal and laboriousness. Perhaps no preacher could have been got to do the same amount of service in that new country as himself.

214. There were three vacancies in the appointments of the Cobourg District for the year 1851-52, namely: Scugog Mission, an assistant for the Rev. William Case at Alderville, and the sole incumbent of the new missionary circuit, Metcalf, which seems to have been identical with Lindsay and its vicinity. Mr. Cornish's researches have led him to say that Scugog was supplied from adjacent circuits. All my inquiries have failed to reveal Mr. Case's assistant for the year.*
But we learn incidentally, from a communication in the

---

* Nay, we have just ascertained that the distinguished missionary

Guardian for that year, that the Rev. Thos. McMullen, who had travelled twelve consecutive years, and then retired into the local ranks from 1845 to 1849, and had supplied Cartwright and Manvers the preceding year, was now performing the same benefit to the *Metcalf* Mission, and not at " Aylmer, C. E.," as Mr. Cornish erroneously has it in the Hand-Book.

215. Under the date of November 3rd, 1851, Mr. McMullen writes as follows :—" We have the droppings of a shower falling on us already ; a number have been added to us since Conference ; we have union and love everywhere on the mission. The class in the Village of Lindsay is very much revived. Here our members and friends are commencing a new chapel ; they have subscribed very liberally, and they have got the heavy stuff on the spot, and expect to have it finished early in the spring. The building is forty feet by thirty feet. We are looking, and not in vain, for God to bless us on this mission this year.

> "Thy mercy make known, and sprinkle Thy blood,
> Display Thy salvation, and teach the new song
> To every kingdom, and nation, and people, and tongue."

216. The *Belleville District* had two of these vacancies to account for, namely : the second preacher's place on the old and valuable *Picton* Circuit, " who was to reside at Bloomfield." His then Superintendent, the Rev. Wm. McFadden, informs me that the brother of the chairman of the district, *Mr. Benjamin Jones*, whom we have seen enter the work in 1841 and retire into the local ranks in 1847, but serve as a chairman's supply of Owen Sound during the

the Rev. *Thomas Hurlbert*, who has spent the preceding six years assisting the Methodist Church in the United States, as Presiding Elder in their Indian Mission Conference, had returned to his native land, and was employed by the authorities to fill this vacancy.

preceding Conference year, is now brought down to assist Mr. McFadden in the district presided over by his relative, the Rev. Richard Jones. The second preacher for *Sidney* was *Henry Jones*, of whom more under the next year.

217. *Newboro'*, in the *Kingston District*, in charge of the laborious Michael Baxter, required the second preacher "to be sent," and was supplied by a young Irishman from the mother country. This was *John Mills*, a stout, compact person, with a semi-Scottish accent, newly from the North of Ireland, of good average abilities, fervent in spirit, and destined to do a great amount of work, and to realize a goodly measure of success on the very best class of our rural circuits.

218. *Hinchinbrooke* was to be supplied with a preacher, but who the supply was, we are unable to say, after applying to every likely source of information. As it was a new creation, it is barely possible that it was still supplied in connection with the circuit or circuits of which it had previously been a part.

219. The *Brockville* and *Bytown* Districts were each completely manned, and, therefore, require no remarks. *James G. Witted* was allowed a year's leave of absence to visit England.

220. This Conference year was one of unusual Connexional activity and labor. The ordinary routine of operations on the several charges seem to have been prosecuted with more than usual painstaking and success. Camp meetings and revival meetings were held in all parts of the Connexion, and attended with more than usual power, and followed by great results. The year was observable for the number of new churches erected, or completed and dedicated, or of old ones re-modelled and restored. Some newly-planted missions were so successful as to inspire special encouragement. The Missionary department seemed to have a warm place in the

Connexional heart. The anniversaries and missionary meetings were enthusiastically enjoyed and reported from almost every circuit in the work. These reports are so many and so full that even an abridged report of them would be impracticable. In a word, vitality and hope seemed to pulsate the entire body.

221. Camp-meetings were held in the following places, vigorously conducted, presently owned, and followed with more or less revival influence in the after years, as the glowing reports of them indicated. The places, and pretty much the order of them, were as follows—in the Townships of *Augusta, West Gwillimsburg, Whitchurch, Brock,* a union meeting for the *Bradford* and *Barrie* Circuits, *Waterloo West,* and two for the special benefit of the *Indians,* namely, one at *Muncey* and the other at *St. Clair.*

222. *New churches* came into existence during the year in a goodly number of places, of which we have certain account, and there may have been others not gazetted. It may be interesting to the several localities to know when their church was first erected, or specially enlarged and beautified. The localities were as follows, and pretty much the order in the year when they were completed: *Bradford* rejoiced in the opening of a church August 3rd, 1851; there was one completed in *Learn's* neighborhood, on the Chippewa Circuit; one in the Sixth Concession of *King;* one in *Jamestown,* on the Georgetown Circuit; *Kizer's* chapel, on the Humber Circuit; in *Burford,* on the Brantford Circuit; the *Stone Church,* in *McNabb Street,* Hamilton; the *Central Church,* in *Bytown;* the *Vandusen* chapel, Smith's Falls Circuit; *Port Hope,* enlarged and repaired; *Strathroy;* Village of *Northport,* on the Demorestville Circuit; *Waterdown; Prince Albert; Mercer Street,* Gosfield Circuit, and a parsonage at *Cookstown,* under the house-building L. O. Rice.

223. Good news came from a vast number of circuits,

containing various encouraging particulars. Some of these circuits will now be named, from many of which cheering ntelligence came several times over.

224. *George McDougall* sent thrilling intelligence from *Bruce Mines* and from *Garden River;* *Wellesley, Rawdon,* and *Nelson* sent good news; *Hamilton* city opened a new church, organized a second congregation, took on the second preacher, and advanced in all respects, despite the loss sustained by the removal through the year of Professor Van-Norman, who never returned to the country and the Conference, and the discontinuance of the Burlington Academy, the presence of which had in various ways strengthened Methodism in the city; good news came from *Madoc* and its new preacher, Rev. Robert Robinson, from the pen of the veteran Stephen Miles; *Proton,* a new mission, in the hands of the Rev. Joseph Hill, was uncommonly successful, numbering an increase of about one hundred members; the Rev. Thos. Bevitt, by no means a sanguine man, found the indications so good in the *Brockville* District that he predicted an increase of one-third in the total membership of the district; C. Byrne reported well of *St. Catharines* and neighboring circuits; twenty-five were added as the fruits of one revival service on the *Glanford* Circuit; there was a general revival on the *Markham* Circuit; cheery John Black sent good news from *Brighton;* *Owen Sound* and *Kincardine* both reported progress; *Chatham* netted a gain of *one hundred* members; *Waterloo* and *Kingston* sent good news by the *Rev. C. Taggart;* among the rest some pleasant news was sent from the *St. Thomas* circuit, with excuses for his temerity in writing at all, in a maiden communication from a chairman's supply, who is now, and has been for years, the editor of our Connexional organ, we need not name Edward Hartley Dewart; the *Alderville, Rice Lake,* and *St. Clair* Missions sent very cheering intelligence. The newly returned, Thomas Hurlbert,

was particularly happy and successful in his work at *Alnwick* ; the vivacious Dignam enjoyed a general revival on the *Mono* Mission,—ninety-eight were converted in a month ; *Port Hope* added thirty-five ; *Greenbush* and *Wardsville* had prosperity.

225. But the greatest amount of success in any one place was realized in the City of Toronto, which was the result of the presence and labors of that pre-eminently successful re vivalist, the Rev. James Caughey, seconded and followed up by the devoted stationed ministers in the two city circuits, the Revs. John Ryerson, E. B. Harper, H. Wilkinson, and John Douse. This was a revival of earnest religion in all its aspects, and resulted in a net gain in the two circuits of no less than seven hundred and thirty-one (731) in the year.

226. *Miscellaneous matters* were of a checkered character through the year. The *Financial District Meeting*, which the Conference had instituted at the Conference of 1851, was held in each district, consisting of a strict party of laymen and ministers, was found very satisfactory in regulating the matters relegated to it.

227. And had there been the same parity in the Legislative Conference then as now, there would not have been the Connexional disturbance there was attending an attempt on the part of the Conference to have the Connexional societies and institutions incorporated, such as the Missionary Contingent, Church Relief, and Annuitant Funds, including the Book-room and printing establishment. Some public journals, always showing more hostility than friendship to the body, at least its governing authorities, commenced an attack on the Bill when introduced to the Legislature. This awakened the fears of the members of the Church in some parts of the Connexion, who petitioned against the measure to the number of 300 signatures. But while Hamilton, and, perhaps, some other places, petitioned against it, the Toronto

Methodists petitioned in its favor. The Hon. Billa Flint introduced the measure and defended it by his pen as well. Although the objections to the Bill were founded on misapprehension and groundless suspicion, those who conducted it through the Legislature agreed to a compromise, and consented that the funds created by the ministers, and which they alone had a pecuniary interest, should be named in the Act and no others, and the others should be allowed to drop. It was a great loss and inconvenience to the interests of the Church for many years to lose those provisions. But with the introduction of laymen into the Legislature of the Church, a measure, all that could be desired, was secured. The history of this matter proves that ministers may be stupidly opposed to reasonable lay co-operation, and laymen may be unreasonably suspicious of their ministers. But the true way to disarm that suspicion is to give the laymen information of, and a voice in, all general interests of the Church.

228. A change of ministry from Conservatism to Liberalism took place during the lapse of this ecclesiastical year, which gave rise to some questions, such as the re-opening of the Clergy Reserve question and other matters, produced some under-currents which had a disturbing influence to a limited extent.

229. Some attempts were made to restore the machinery of the Sunday-school society in some quarters, and to form auxiliary Tract Societies in some others, but, upon the whole, such doings did not amount to much. A paper for the benefit of children, called the *Sunday School Guardian*, was started this year by the direction of the Conference.

230. Among the scores of excellent members of the Church who passed away to their rest and reward, we have specially noticed two, Charles Biggar, Esq., of Carrying Place, and Mr. John VanCamp, senior, long of Matilda; the

first was distinguished for his connection with the educational and other enterprises of the Church, and the other for his sanctity and long connection with the body.

231. Towards the close of this year the Rev. John Ryerson, co-Delegate, left the Province, *via* England, to visit St. Rupert's Land, preparatory to the measure which went into effect soon after, of supplying the Hudson's Bay and the Rocky Mountains with missionaries direct from the Canada Conference.

232. The total gain, in point of numbers in the membership, was not so great as might have been expected from the activity and revival character of the year. Still, it was the goodly number of *one thousand three hundred and seventy-two*.

233. The prospect is that we have a little more than the usually scarcity of materials for illustrating the labors of our brethren in CANADA EAST, with the result of their labors.

234. The Rev. John Borland communicated the following relative to the CANADA DISTRICT MEETING and District at large:—"Our District commenced its sittings on Wednesday, 21st of May (1851), nearly a week later than originally intended, to meet the convenience of the respected chairman, whom we are happy to receive once more, and especially in the honorable and responsible position of chairman of the district. After singing and reading of the Scriptures, prayer was offered by several of the brethren, and a gracious softening was devoutly realized by each person present. All felt it was good to be there.

235. "This season was followed by the usual business of the meeting; all of which was quickly and agreeably disposed of, save that of stationing the brethren for the ensuing year. This was found a more than ordinarily trying duty, owing to the peculiar circumstances of Montreal and

Quebec, and the openings in, and impressive appeals from many places in the townships. We earnestly and hopefully looked to your Conference for a continuation of that assistance so kindly and efficiently rendered us the last few years, and I very much regret to learn that you have been unable to accede to our wishes.

236. "The spiritual and financial condition of our work is generally encouraging; and when the very great number of removals, especially from our cities, is taken into consideration, it will be acknowledged that to be able to point to any ground of encouragement is to do much. We evidently want a French work in this district. The French population are swarming into our midst, while many of those speaking the English language are 'going westward.' It is, indeed, a serious question for our committee to consider, and not less, perhaps, for several members of the district, whether or not the Lord can view our proceedings favorably, and, therefore, bless us according to our wants and desires, while practically neglecting so large a portion of those among whom we sojourn. A prayerful attention to this subject is, I believe, becoming imperative.

237. "The spirit prevalent in the meeting was good and gracious. We had a blessed time reading the Liverpool Minutes and conversing together upon the best method of promoting the work of God amongst us. I feel persuaded that the brethren have but to follow the leadings of that Spirit, then richly enjoyed, in order to realize a large measure of prosperity in the year upon which we have entered. Oh! it is, as the sainted Fletcher has said, the unction of the Holy Spirit makes the preacher. A living, laboring, self-denying, believing ministry must be a successful one.

238. "The appointments for the year are as follows:—

MONTREAL :—
  St. James Street—John Jenkins.
  St. Gabriel Street—William Squire.
  Quebec Suburbs— ——— ———.*
QUEBEC—Charles De Wolfe, A.M.
THREE RIVERS—Thomas Campbell.
RAWDON—Henry Cox.
ST. JOHNS—G. H. Davis.
CHAMBLY—John Douglas.
ODELLTOWN—John C. Davidson (one wanted).
HUNTINGDON—James Brock.
RUSSELTOWN—H. Montgomery.
CLARENCEVILLE—Henry Lanton.
ST. ARMANDS—Edmund S. Ingalls.
DUNHAM—John Borland (one wanted).
SHEFFORD—Rufus A. Flanders (one wanted).
STANSTEAD—John Tomkins.
HATLEY AND COMPTON—Malcolm McDonald.
SHERBROOKE—Benjamin Slight, A.M.
EATON—John Armstrong.
MELBOURNE—Wm. Scott (one wanted).
LEEDS—Gifford Dorey."

239. Over the date of November 6th, 1851, the Rev. James Brock wrote from Huntingdon, Canada East, " Our beloved Zion is in a prosperous and healthy condition, and we are looking for a season of general revival." We have reason to believe that Mr. Brock's own labors while on that

---

* Only since the text was about to go to press have we learned that this vacancy was filled by a young preacher transferred from New Brunswick, who was received on trial that year, and who should receive some introduction to the reader. But it is now too late to get thoroughly authentic data. We are safe, however, in saying that Brother *G. N. F. T. Dickson* was a native of Ireland, well-bred, well-educated—report said educated for the ministry of another Church—thoroughly converted to God and Methodism, devout, circumspect,

circuit were remarkably owned in promoting a revival of unusual depth and extent.

240. The Rev. R. A. Flanders, over the date of December 5th, 1851, wrote a cheering account of a church-opening in the thriving and important Village of Granby, in connection with which he remarked as follows :—" The dedication of this new church was welcomed by our people as an important event in the history of our cause in the township. We were favored with the clear, powerful, and eminently practical ministry of our esteemed chairman, the Rev. Wm. Squire, who in the morning and evening preached to congregations which filled the house to its utmost capacity. During the fall the Holy Spirit has accompanied the ministry of the Word of life in His awakening power, and a few of the congregation has been led anxiously to inquire, ' Men and brethren, what must we do ?' These pleasing evidences of the Spirit's co-operation in the midst of our humiliatingly fruitless labors serve to inspire new zeal, and are hailed as pledges of increased spiritual prosperity."

241. Over the date of January 5th, 1852, the Rev. John Borland wrote from Dunham, Canada East, " We have no remarkable incidents to supply that would be either interesting or profitable to your readers. We have signs of prosperity of an encouraging character, and hope, ere long, to test their practical importance by a protracted meeting at one or two of the more central points of this extended circuit."

242. From the communication of a friendly Presbyterian, over the date of February 4th, 1852, it appears that a most enthusiastic " Wesleyan soiree " in behalf of missions was held on the 29th of January, at Leeds, Megantic, which enlisted the sympathy and co-operation of their fellow Protestants of the different denominations in a way to show how

possessed of the talents most available in the conversion of souls. His subsequent history has confirmed the above estimate.

high the Methodist cause stood in the public estimation in that region. And though they were disappointed of the presence of some celebrities from Quebec, the pastor, Rev. Mr. Dorey, a Rev. Mr. Wallace, several very clever laymen, and the returned missionary Hurlbert, so far succeeded in interesting the meeting as caused it to pass off with great animation and unusually good effect.

243. Having no other means of illustrating the progress of Wesleyan matters in the Canada Eastern District for 1851-52, we have nothing left to us but to inquire after the issue as it respected loss or gain in membership in the year; and find that, after all their assiduity and toil, they were fated to return a *decrease* of thirty. Their total membership stood at 3,739. This, added to the 27,585 members in the Canada West Connexion, made the total strength of Wesleyan Methodism in the two Provinces 31,324.

1852-53.

244. THE ecclesiastical year 1852-53 began with the usual session of the Canada Conference, which sat this year in Kingston, and commenced its sittings on June 2nd, 1852, and continued them until the 10th of the same month. At the request of the Canada Conference, and with the compliance of the British Conference, the Rev. Enoch Wood again took the chair. The Rev. John Ryerson had been, by the same means and authority, re-appointed co-Delegate; and the Rev. George Rivers Sanderson was, after fourteen years' itinerancy, appointed Secretary, a work which his ready penmanship and dignified manners well prepared him to perform. This was one of the most harmonious and truly religious Conferences known to Canada. There had been a great revival of inward holiness and earnest devotion, both among ministers and members throughout the Connexion the previous year, and the influence of it was felt, not only in the number, earnestness, and unctious character of the

religious services attending the Conference, including ser-sermons, prayer meetings, and Conference love-feast, which was pronounced the best ever remembered; but the result was seen in the increased kindliness and brotherliness of the discussions, and manifest religiousness of all the business transacted.

245. In following the order of routine proceedings, we have first to record the admission of no less than ten probationers into full connexion with the Conference. These were: *Charles Fish, Alexander Campbell, John G. Laird, John English, Thomas Peacock, John S. Evans, John B. Armstrong, Benjamin Jones, Edward White,* and *Francis Berry*. All but the last have been frequently before the reader, and their antecedents need not be recalled. There had been some interruptions in the continuity of the probationary relations to the Conference of three of them, namely: Messrs. *Campbell, Evans,* and *Jones;* but each had performed at least five years' labor, instead of four, which the rules only required.

246. But *Francis Berry's* case requires a more extended presentation. He was an Irish Canadian of Wesleyan parents, born in the vicinity of Toronto; trained religiously in the Adelaide Street Sunday-school, and educated in one of the best select schools in the city. His education and business learned had been commercial. His way into the ministry did not seem to open before marriage, and his union with the daughter of a highly-respectable and influential member of the Primitive Methodist body. At their solicitation Mr. Berry entered their ministry, in which he showed more than usual energy, and met with more than usual success. After several years' employment in that way, he thought well of retiring for a time into secular life, and entered on a commercial career in the Town of Brantford, in which, for the short time he was in it, he was very successful,

In that town he resumed his connection with his original friends, the Wesleyan Methodists; went upon their plan as a local preacher; was exceedingly acceptable and useful; was invited far into the neighborhood around on various occasions, and, finally, was pressed to close his secular business and to re-enter the ministry, and in the Church of his fathers. He was still young, was zealous, had lively preaching talents, and more than usual capacity for the business part of an itinerant's work. We need only add, in the words of the Editor for that year, the Rev. James Spencer, "Bro. Berry was furnished with satisfactory testimonials of his character and standing in the body with which he was formerly connected, and was received into the Wesleyan ministry in accordance with the provisions of regulations adopted by the Conference several years since" (in 1840), "for the admission of preachers from other bodies of Methodists."

247. The service for the reception of these brethren was conducted by the President of the Conference, the Rev. Mr. Green opening with prayer. The motion for their reception was moved by the venerable Mr. Case, seconded by the Rev. John Carroll, and supported by the Rev. Dr. Ryerson. The experiences of the young men, and every other part of the exercises, were very appropriate and impressive.

248. Among the nine names presented and accepted on trial for the ministry, there was only one with whom the reader has not been made acquainted already, not less than eight of them—namely, *William Richardson, James Clarke, John Shaw, James Taylor, Edward H. Dewart, James Harris, Matthew Swann,* and *John Mills*—having performed at least one years' circuit work already, and one of them indeed more than that.

249. *Henry Jones* is the only one who remains to be introduced; and we are sorry that we are so lacking in information of so worthy a man. He was a native of

England, but had been brought up in Canada, within the Shannonville Circuit, where he was converted and grew up into usefulness. He was very pious and blameless, and of bland and engaging manners. His abilities were medium and improveable. He was tall and commanding in person, but the strain of itinerant work demonstrated that his constitution was not very strong, which resulted in early retirement from labor, and death before middle life. He was re-appointed to Sidney, in which he had assisted the Rev. Michael Fawcett, then the chairman, the preceding year.

250. Two probationers retired for want of health, namely, *Alexander McAllister* and *James Preston*. The former died in the next year; the latter retired to the States and joined the Indiana Conference, where he graduated to elder's orders, and then returned, as we shall see. We might have said that Mr. Preston performed the pastoral work a good part of the ensuing year in Belleville, in place of the Rev. John Ryerson, who was absent in England.

251. On account of enfeebled health and other reasons, the *Rev. Charles Turver* took a supernumerary relation for the ensuing year, and visited England, I believe.

252. *Jonathan Loverin*, who once promised considerable, and enjoyed a large share of the affections of his brethren, was at this Conference "deposed from the ministry and expelled from the Church." He was not without sympathizing friends who thought him "sinned against, as well as sinning." But the lower depths into which he afterwards fell indicated that he was not possessed of the moral stamina necessary to a minister. His history should prove admonitory to preachers and people. Alas! poor Jonathan, that thou shouldst have so disappointed our hopes!

253. This Conference was visited by the *Rev. Jas. Brock*, as the representative of the Canada Eastern District, who

expressed the kindly salutations of his constituents, and bore back those of the Canada Conference to them. This was the beginning of courtesies henceforth recurring annually, and increasing in the number of visitors, until it ended (in 1854) in the incorporation of that district into the Canada Conference.

254. The Rev. John Ryerson being already in England, on his way to the Hudson Bay Territory, on a tour of inspection of the Wesleyan Missions in that region, was appointed representative to the then approaching British Conference. [It afterwards occurred that Mr. Ryerson returned to Canada direct, and went out the next season by way of the Red River.]

255. The usual Conference Missionary Meeting was of great interest. The addresses were of a superior kind. The speakers were the venerable William Case, the Revs. Jonathan Scott and Thomas Hurlbert, and Dr. J. W. Corson, of New-York. Two other speakers, who would have greatly interested the meeting, namely, Peter Jones and Lachlin Taylor, were excluded by the lateness of the hour.

256. At one stage of its proceedings there was a touching scene in the Conference, consequent upon its being addressed by the venerable Mr. Case, who wished to define his position, and to make a request concerning his relation to the work in future. He reviewed the way in which the Lord had led him since his first appointment to Canada in 1805. He had been now in the ministry forty-seven years, sixteen of which he had presided on districts; then there had been the care of all the churches for five years as President of the Conference or General Superintendent of the Connexional work. Since then he had experienced a great deal of care, as in charge of important missions and mission schools, and now, as he felt his memory failing, he wished to be relieved from further care, lest his mental powers, overbur-

dened, should give way. He did not wish to be understood as asking for a superannuated relation. He wanted an efficient relation, but a subordinate one. The Conference considered his appeal. The *Rev. James Musgrove,* a successful man in conducting the business matters pertaining to the itinerancy, was placed in charge of the Alderville Mission and Industrial School; and Mr. Case, whose name still stood in connection with the mission, had "permission to visit various parts of the work, as his health and circumstances might permit."

257. Another change of relation to the Conference deserves to be mentioned. The *Rev. Lachlin Taylor,* who had been the preceding year, as a supernumerary, gathering strength for the duties and labors of a wider sphere, "by permission of the Conference" accepted the agency of the Upper Canada Bible Society, and fixed his residence at Toronto for the present, and entered on his twelve long years of efficient service of that noble institution—serving, the while, the interests, to a great extent, of nearly every evangelical Church in Canada.

258. Without republishing the stations, which are to be found in the accredited Minutes, we must see how the work was provided for in the length and breadth thereof, premising, before we proceed, that the staff at the Connexional publishing-house was the same, Mr. Green being continued in the Book-Stewardship and Mr. Spencer in the Editorial chair, and Thomas Demorest was Agent for Connexional funds.

259. That important rural circuit in the *Toronto District,* the *Humber,* the second year in succession received for its junior preacher a chairman's supply. That supply was an ardent young Irishman, whose Superintendent familiarly "Likened to the spirited colt, which, though requiring careful training at the first, when once accustomed to the

bit, becomes the most serviceable and enduring horse; so, when the exuberance of youth in our friend had received its proper direction, he was sure to be one of the most energetic and efficient of men." Our subject was Irish by birth and parentage, and peculiarly so in mind and voice. We are writing of our aggressive and courageous friend, *William McDonough*. He was born in 1830, which made him twenty-two years of age at the time of his going into the field. Though young, he was not soft; but as his compact build, dark complexion, and black, curly, wiry hair indicated, had a constitution strong and enduring to a degree. The antecedents of this youthful laborer were as follows :— His birthplace was pre-eminently Protestant, namely, the County Fermanagh, near Enniskillin. His parents were Methodists. In conformity to the practice in that country, he was taken to all the meetings, class-meetings included, by them, and was converted in boyhood. He became a class-leader at the early age of seventeen. The family emigrated to Canada in 1847. About the time referred to, they had the misfortune to lose the husband and father in Montreal. The widowed mother and filial son came up the country to Brockville, where they resided for a time. All this while his young heart was agitated with the thought of public usefulness. A touching and significant occurrence happened about this time. When the people around the country turned out to attend the funeral of the much-loved Ezra Healey, the Rev. Joseph Wesley McCollum, in preaching the funeral sermon, made the following declaration and appeal : " The trumpet has fallen from the hands of one of Zion's watchmen. Who will take it ?—Who will take it up ? " A response broke involuntarily from the lips of a weeping, trembling stripling, " I will ! " and he immediately sank down upon the floor with extreme agitation and exhaustion. That stripling was young McDonough. About two months after he was placed on the local preachers' plan by the Brockville quarterly meeting. From Brockville he came to Toronto, and was a member of the Richmond Street Quarterly Board, whence he went into the work. We need not anticipate his reception on trial, or two years' training at Victoria College. He will often turn up in Methodist doings.

260. The extensive, or "six weeks" *Brampton* Circuit, required three preachers to do justice to its pastoral work. The Conference provided two—the fatherly *William Young* and the young but intellectual and studious *Blackstock*—and the chairman found a third. This was a young man whose good personal appearance, more than usual educational advantages, and whose relationship to several good men whose patronymic he bore, gave promise of more in his favor than was realized. There are some preachers—let them go where they may—who seem to have the misfortune to make a party, and that party is usually directed against their colleagues. They contrive to have some very warm admirers, but, in the end, to turn the reflecting and peaceable against them. This young man, as some experience of him as a hired supply in an after-emergency convinced me, was of this character. Such men may mean well; they certainly persuade themselves that they are very ill-appreciated and very unjustly treated; but those the most desirous to serve them find these their *protegees* utterly impracticable. As this brother never obtained a standing among us, and ultimately "left his country for his country's good," no one will be any considerable loser by not learning his name.

261. *Georgetown* is represented in the Minutes as entitled to another preacher, but the laborious Superintendent, the *Rev. Joseph Messmore*, assures me he worked it alone; and I know, from their own spontaneous testimony, that he himself won golden opinions among them.

262. *Nelson* was an extensive circuit in those days, and required a third laborer, but that one was " wanting " when the stations were published. The Superintendent, the *Rev. J. W. McCollum*, says they got on with what aid Father Prindle could render them; but Bro. George Washington (1st) claims to have been the supply. I am inclined to concede the palm of accuracy to him, having some recollection of the matter myself, as his family lived in Hamilton City, of which I had the charge. Where there are two such laborers as McCollum and John Hunt, no circuit will very much suffer if it have no more.

263. *Stouffville* was newly erected into a separate charge, and was promised a preacher, but none was found. The Brethren, Kerr and Sanderson, laboring on the Markham Circuit, supplied it trough this year. In the same manner *Snake Island, &c.*, was supplied by Brethren Willoughby and Longhead, from Newmarket Circuit.

264. The *Barrie*, as an interior and largely a missionary district, had, as usual, several vacancies. Fortunately, it had a chairman who had a facility in extemporizing provision in such emergencies—the *Rev. Lewis Warner*. His own circuit, the head of the district, was lacking a junior preacher, and he was fortunate in finding one valuable then, but also encouragingly improvable. About 1850 two pious young Wesleyans, who had known each other in England, came together to the United States. The one was *James Harris*, the other was *Andrew Edwards;* one was the son of a Wesleyan minister, the other of a peasant; one was classically educated, the other had but a plain English education, and, withal, an observable provincial *patois;* one was a druggist by profession, the other a farm laborer. Both had good minds, but Edwards' was quicker, though, mayhap, more superficial; but Harris', though slower, was stronger and perhaps more profound. The less educated

was the readier man, and, for the time being, the more passable preacher, and perhaps with some, always the more popular one ; but the other had a mind to wear bright, to improve ever on, and to satisfy the minds of the most thoughtful and the pious affections of the most devout. At the first start Edwards had most, in point of voice and elocution, in his favor as a speaker ; in the long run, the other, in voice and manner and everything else, became a most hearable and satisfying speaker. Edwards might be the more active in promoting revival meetings, but Harris led his hearers into all the heights and depths of holiness. Edwards overcame wondrously early illiteracy ; but Harris, by some of his later writings, showed a capacity for some of the higher types of literature. Harris, we have seen, rendered a great deal of help on the Dunnville and Nanticoke Circuits, without fee or reward, during the year 1850-51. During the year 1851-52 he had been a chairman's supply on the Elora Circuit, and now, at the Conference of 1852, was received on trial and sent to the Peel Circuit. His friend was still in the United States, where his old country peculiarities stood in the way of his becoming more than a local preacher. He wanted to enter the Wesleyan ministry, and we wanted him. Indeed, through his friend Harris, who informed me of him, I invited him to come to my district (the Hamilton), and left the junior preacher's place at Elora vacant for him, the vacancy his friend had filled the year before ; but, fortunately for Bro. Warner and the Barrie Circuit, when he arrived at Toronto he learned from the authorities about the destitution at the North, and, not knowing the country or the way to us, he went to them. His career has been good and his circumstances happy, and I believe they would have been so if he had gone into the Hamilton District ; but there has been, no doubt, a different tinge in the warp and woof of his fate from what they would have borne in the other case. Doubtless, Omniscient love directed it all for the best. These two good men have been enduring laborers. Mr. Edwards is not large, but wiry; Mr. Harris is stout and strong, but not unwieldy. After a quarter of a century, their natural force is none abated. Mr. Edwards' head corresponds with his dapper person, but Mr. Harris' cranium is disproportionately massive for even his large frame. The one was raised in refinement and a sedentary calling, is rather coarse in person than otherwise; the one whose boyhood was burdened with manual toil in the field, has the more delicate frame and features. Both have thoroughly qualified themselves for their work, and occupy about the same class of respectable circuits. Mr. Harris is a little the more prominent in Connexional matters.

265. There was "one wanted" to assist Alexander Campbell at *St. Vincent*, but no one obtained, and Mr. C. had to supply the circuit alone.* *Derby* was presented as a separate charge in the Minutes, with "one wanted" to supply, but it was supplied by the preacher on the Owen Sound Circuit, the late John Williams, very likely assisted by the venerable John Neelands, a supernumerary residing there.

266. The *London District* exhibited two such gaps. At *Sandwich* and *Windsor*, the Rev. Wm. Ames was in "want" of one to help him, but he writes me: "I had no colleague. I preached at Sandwich morning and evening on Sunday, and in the afternon at Windsor; besides which I had four or six week-day appointments, extending some twenty-six miles back from Sandwich. Each of these I took fortnightly in the evening." Some of the places must have been dreary enough, for he speaks of holding a sacramental service at one place where the mice actually disputed the sacramental

---

* So says the Chairman, but Mr. Cornish makes *S. E. Maudsley* the supply.

bread with him, and he had to fight them away while offering the prayer of consecration. That same neighborhood repaid exertions, and has for a long time rejoiced in a good brick church. The Conference sent no supply to *Mitchell,* and the then chairman has not informed me whether he succeeded in finding one.

267. *Hamilton* had two vacancies ; first, the second preacher's place at *Cayuga Heights;* and I, as the chairman, can remember soliciting a young local preacher in vain to go, but cannot remember who I found, if any, to go there, and alas, the Superintendent, Brother Thomas Jeffers, is not alive to refer to. *Elora* was in a similar plight, but the Brother *Edward Cooke,* mentioned under the preceding year, was still there assisting the Rev. Solomon Waldron.

268. Two Indian Missions in the *Cobourg* District were to be supplied, these were *Scugog* and *Mud Lake.* The former was probably supplied from some adjacent circuit, perhaps Cartwright, whose incumbent was the Rev. John Sanderson. The *Mud Lake,* with probably some adjacent white settlements attached, received a chairman's supply from the neighboring Township of Otonabee. He was of respectable American parentage, and may have been born in the States, but if so he was certainly brought up from early childhood in Canada. He was born in 1817, and born again in 1836, at the age of nineteen. His conversion was marked and decisive, and piety, even eminent attainments in piety, characterized his after-course. He had throughout a yearning compassion for perishing souls. He was only twenty-five years of age when called out, but had been five years laboring for the good of others as an exhorter and local preacher ; and had he not married young, would probably have been brought into the regular ministry some time before. But the fact that his wife was the daughter of godly parents and became an eminently pious, as she was a gifted

and accomplished woman, overcame the objection to him on account of matrimonial incumbrances. He had sought to qualify himself for the ministry by a period of study at Victoria College. His personal appearance and manners were very much in his favor. It is said of him in his Conference obituary : "He was a faithful minister of Jesus Christ ; his popularity as a preacher rested not so much on the brilliancy of his efforts, as on the plainness and unaffected simplicity with which he presented the vital truths of Christianity. He was particularly felicitous in introducing into his discourses illustrations from Nature's open book ; arresting the attention of his audience, and with the quickness of thought, sending the barbed arrow to the conscience and the heart." Thus constituted and equipped, the reader will be prepared to follow him with the expectation of a harvest of souls in all the fields of labors whither he went, an expectation destined to be realized.*

* By some means we have passed over the vacancies in the *Brantford District* for 1852-53, and in doing so, overlooked the provision for an important circuit and failed to introduce a valuable supply, who has occupied a peculiar place in the work in these Provinces. The second preacher's place in the *Simcoe* Circuit was vacant, and a supply was found for it in the person of a newly-arrived preacher from England. This was *Thomas Woolsey*, the nephew of the *Rev. Wm. Woolsey*, for many years a member of the "Legal Hundred" in the British Conference. T. W. was a native of Gainsborough, Lincolnshire, but had resided long in London, where he was ten years a member in the far-famed City Road Circuit. He had exercised his gifts as a local preacher no less than fifteen years on his coming to Canada, when he was a matured and experienced man of thirty-four years, strong and enduring, but still very active. The Simcoe Circuit, as then constituted, furnished no ill preparation for roaming the Saskatchewan for nearly a decade. Mr. W. says, "It then included what are now Port Dover and Windham, and I believe Waterford, but I am not certain." The delay of Brother Woolsey's letter to me has crowded him into a small space, and from the text into a note.

269. *Belleville*, although previously only a station for one man, had, in connection with the name of the Rev. John Ryerson, " one to be sent." There were two or three reasons for this : this town had a heavy membership, and a great amount of pastoral work. So much so, that if the superintendent were always there, he would be none the worse of a curate, but when in Canada, even, Mr. Ryerson, as co-Delegate, was often away from his station on official engagements, especially as the actual President, Mr. Wood, had the superintendency of missions specially in charge. But Mr. Ryerson had been away the latter part of the preceding Conference year, and expected to be away a large portion of this year. We have seen that Mr. Preston remained and supplied the station for several weeks after the Conference, but he was anxious to be away to the United States, whither he went on the second of October, so soon as a supply could be obtained. Such a supply God provided in due time. Towards the latter part of the summer a young gentleman arrived from England, coming, if I remember correctly, upon the recommendation of Mr. Ryerson himself, who was at the British Conference for that year. This young preacher came possessed of no ordinary qualifications. He was the son of an English Wesleyan minister, and classically educated at one of the Connexional Schools. He was further liberalized by acquiring what might be called a learned profession. Then, he had unusual advantages as a preacher; he excelled as a homilist, and in voice, volubility, or fluency, and tenderness and impressiveness in his delivery. Such was *Brother Thomas D. Pearson* when he first appeared among us. I have often wondered that, by this time, he had not won a higher Connexional position. Perhaps his known meek and retiring disposition is the cause. By the time his name comes before the Conference

as a candidate, I may be better furnished with the dates and salient points connected with his early history.

270. From the stations in the Belleville District it appears that Rev. J. G. Witted had returned from England, and was appointed as second preacher on the *Consecon* Circuit. From the same source we have learned, that the Rev. Cyrus R. Allison, had become superannuated, and resided in that circuit. He never felt himself equal to a circuit more.

271. *Hungerford* was left to be supplied. Such a supply was found in the person of a middle-aged local preacher, from either England or Ireland, who had lived in Kingston, and who moreover was single, being either a bachelor or a widower. Moreover, he was said to possess a prepossessing address and an impressive manner, with fair abilities as a preacher. He succeeded well on the circuit, reporting seven classes in a compact circuit, formed out of part of four adjacent townships, and returned a membership of 156. He never was received into the Conference, but regularly supplied circuits for six successive years thereafter, and report says, with great approval, when he retired under the plea of want of health, and gradually went into obscurity, and under a cloud, and finally passed away. This was *John D. Pugh*, who certainly had talents to be useful, if he had in all respects improved his opportunities.

272. The three remaining districts, the *Kingston*, *Brockville*, and *Bytown*, require brief annotation. The *Rev. M. Baxter* had no assistance on *Newborough ;* and I have not learned the supply for *Hinchinbrooke*. Richard Keegan, a hired local preacher, a mighty man of faith, was *Rev. S. Hurlbert's* assistant on the *Maitland* Circuit. *Edwin Peake* was second preacher at *Carleton Place*, of whom more anon. The *Rev. T. McMullen* had no helper at *Portage du Fort*, &c. ; and I cannot ascertain the supply for *Westmeath*.

273. This was a year of great activity and of great success. Every department of the Connexional work seemed to prosper. The editor met the many assailants of Wesleyan Methodism in a manner to give them an unpleasant recollection of the encounter. The *Guardian* was very popular and useful in the Connexion, and increased its circulation. The *Sunday School Advocate* also was making its way.

274. The *College* was performing great things considering the small money resources at its command. The attempt to create an endowment by the issue of scholarships, commenced in a previous year, was prosecuted with more vigor during this one. The *Rev. S. D. Rice*, though burdened with the duties of the important Kingston station and the charge of an important district, by the help of a curate, redeemed time to go extensively through the Connexion to a large extent and complete the endowment. He showed his usual business energy and directness, by eschewing a carriage and its luxurious accompaniments, but mounted a horse, and threaded his way into each hole and corner of the country, where, otherwise, he would not have found easy access. The scholarship scheme amounted to this : five hundred scholarships were sold at one hundred dollars each, which created a fund of $12,500 dollars, which was duly funded for the benefit of the College. The benefit, however, was rather to the holders of the scholarships than to the Institution. A holder was entitled to send one pupil for twenty-five years without tuition fees. It was also hoped the interest of the money, and the profits on board, would be a present indemnification to the College, and then there was the prospect, after a quarter of a century, of the whole $12,500 would constitute an unincumbered revenue, besides bringing the College into notice by increasing the number of students. Before the twenty-five years were expired, it is believed many, if not most, of

the holders of those scholarships surrendered them, as part of a measure for relieving and further endowing the College.

275. As an indirect means of helping the Institution, it was decided at the Conference of 1852, that as the Wesleyan Church edifice at Cobourg was neither corresponding in appearance to the character of a University Church, nor provided with accommodation for the increased number of worshippers furnished, in term time, by the students from all parts of the country, that wherever the Quarterly Official Meeting of a circuit would give permission, the superintendent of a circuit should take up a collection in each church and chapel within his charge to aid in the erection of a suitable University Church. The appeal was generously responded to from all parts of the Connexion, and a suitable church was erected and completed.

276. During both sessions of the collegiate year, the staff of professors and teachers was complete and the number of students was large:—One hundred and twenty in the autumn session. At that session, the vacancy created by Professor Wright's going into the ministry, was supplied by John Wilson, Esq., A.M., of Trinity College, Dublin, who has been a most efficient member of the College staff until this day.

277. This was to a very considerable extent a church and parsonage building year. I do not pretend to be able to furnish all that was done in that direction during that period. Suffice it to say, that a new brick church was erected and opened in the Village of *Grafton*, in the Cobourg Circuit, on the 27th of June, 1852. On the same Sabbath, a new Mission Church was opened at *New Credit*, furnished with a steeple with a tinned spire. The Superintendent of Missions, the Rev. Enoch Wood, performed this service, attended by Revs. David Wright and Peter Jones. The Indians upon this occasion, in accordance with a usual custom with them towards any one for whom they have regard, gave Mr. Wood the name *Ketche Metig*, the *Big Tree*.

278. On August, the 22nd, President Wood opened a church in *Essa*, on the then rising Cookstown Circuit, under the pushing superintendency of the Rev. L. O. Rice. A similar event took place in *Port Stanley*, under the superintendency of the Rev. Richard Whiting: the Rev. Messrs. Pollard and Taylor performed the opening services. The church at the head of the same circuit, St. Thomas, was during the year enlarged and improved.

279. The Methodist Indians at *Moraviantown*, at last, rejoiced in the possession of a suitable church. It was opened on the 22nd of September by the Chairman of the District, who was also Principal of the Industrial School at Mount Elgin—the Rev. Samuel Rose. The missionary in charge of the Wardsville Mission, in which Moraviantown was included, the Rev. Charles Silvester, reported at the same time the addition of twenty souls.

280. Mr. Wood also opened a new church in the township of *Reach*, four miles west of Prince Albert, in the Oshawa Circuit, under the superintendency of the Rev. John Law. This opening took place on the 24th of October, 1852.

281. Hewitt's Church, on the Mono Road, which had been burnt, was restored in a more substantial manner, and cleared of debt. This was due to the energy of S. C. Philp, the Superintendent of the Humber Circuit, within which the church was comprised. Fergus at last rejoiced in a substantial church, which was opened by the Rev. Messrs. Wood and Carroll, in the fall of 1852. The venerable Solomon Waldron was superintendent.

282. Another old itinerant, the Rev. Richard Phelp, put in charge of an extreme and neglected end of the former Chatham Circuit, *Morpeth*, now set apart as a separate charge, rejoiced in the completion and opening of the church in that place, which had long been in a state of suspense.

283. *Carlisle*, an outpost of the Dundas Circuit, at length

had its large society and congregation furnished with a suitable place of worship. The openings ervices and attendant festivities were of a profitable and pleasing character. *Thornhill* also got a new church. Devonshire was about to realize the comforts of a parsonage.

284. *Galt*, in the St. George Circuit, under the superintendency of the Rev. Ozias Barber, at length realised the long-desired accommodation of a convenient church. It was opened by the eminent brothers, the Revs. William and Egerton Ryerson. The seventh church in the well-provided *Malahide* Circuit was projected by the Rev. George Kennedy.

285. Camp-meetings, revivals growing out of them, protracted and special services, with conversions and addition of members under the ordinary preaching, were characteristic of the year.

286. Camp-meetings were held in the *Brampton* Circuit, Rev. William Young, promoter; *Chatham*, Rev. W. Price, Superintendent; *Strathroy*, Rev. Jas. Armstrong in charge, and *Mono*, in the Rev. Lewis Warner's district; and in the Township of *Woolwich*, in the Elora Circuit, under the Rev. S. Waldron. Great revivals in this and the adjacent Peel Circuit grew out of the Woolwich Camp-meeting. We repeatedly hear good news from these circuits, especially the Peel, during the year.

287. A similar result occurred on the *Strathroy* Circuit. *Toronto West*, under Wilkinson and Douse, was all in a blaze. *Norwich* had a great revival, under the Rev. M. Swann. *Jackson's School-house*, Oshawa Circuit, was the scene of a revival. *Garden River*, under George McDougall, was repeatedly heard from. *Bruce Mines*, with its pastor, E. Sallows, repaid attention.

288. There was a revival among the Tuscarora Indians, in charge of Abraham Sickles, the Oneida missionary. The

same was reported from *Middle Road,* Nelson Circuit. Indeed, this circuit, as was usual with circuits under the pastoral care of the laborious McCollum, reported favorably several times during the year. *Richmond* Circuit, under the energetic and indefatigable Greener, reported large accessions once and again. But no retired field of labor, all circumstances considered, enjoyed so long-continued a tide of prosperity and such a large influx of members as the *Proton Mission,* under the modest and retiring Joseph Hill.

289. But the greatest accessions were realized in two principal cities, *Kingston* and *Hamilton,* which enjoyed between them the evangelistic labors of the Rev. James Caughey, combined with the most untiring efforts of the ministers in those two cities—the Rev. Messrs. Rice and Lavell in Kingston, and Messrs. Carroll and Bredin in Hamilton. The clear increase of membership in the former city was one hundred and twelve, and in the latter one hundred and ninety-seven. The circuits adjacent to these two cities also largely partook of the benefits.

290. The only wonder is, that the general augmentation of numbers in the Province did not prove greater than what was counted up at the end of the year. The general gain was 2,739, making the total Connexional strength at the Conference of 1853 to be 30,325.

291. We turn briefly to CANADA EAST. A statement of the affairs of the Eastern District, under the hand of its temporary chairman, the Rev. Benjamin Slight, A.M., will obviate the necessity of constructing one myself. It was published in the *Guardian,* under the date of June 9th, 1852:—

292. "The ministers of the Eastern Canada District assembled together in the City of Montreal, Wednesday, 19th of May, 1852, to transact the usual business of the District.

293. "The entire sessions were eminently characterized by unanimity of feeling and brotherly love. Much of the

divine presence was experienced in the usual devotional exercises, and during one of the elucidations of the brethren on the several points of doctrine, discipline, and practice which designedly or incidentally came before the meeting; but more especially still when the question came up for consideration, 'What measures can be adopted to promote the work of God in this District?' The reading of the Liverpool Minutes of themselves produced a solemn effect, and furnished several suggestions of an important character, which appeared to be deeply impressive, on the minds of the assembly.

294. "It was matter of devout gratitude that, although sickness and death, in a more than ordinary degree, have been desolating the land, yet we met with undiminished numbers. A still greater cause of thankfulness was found to exist: all were alive in a much more important sense of the term—morally, spiritually so. The examinations of character elicited no defections and no cause of censure.

295. "The reports furnished of the spiritual state of the work have afforded matter of encouragement and gratitude. On every station there has been an ingathering of souls; and on some of them there have been witnessed remarkable displays of the power of God in the gospel. Yet, from the frequent removals and other causes, the increase of numbers is small.

296. "Three young brethren, who were probationers for our ministry, were examined on theological subjects and on other matters relative to our work, and passed in a highly creditable and satisfactory manner, and were recommended to be continued in their probationary career. From the peculiar nature and circumstances of the stations to which two of these brethren were appointed, they were designated to receive ordination, although the term of their probation had not expired. The ordination services were con-

ducted in Great St. James Street Church. A sermon was preached by the Rev. J. C. Davidson, and an impressive charge delivered to the young men by our respected chairman, the Rev. William Squire.

297. "The anniversary meeting of the District Branch Missionary Society was held in Great St. James Street Church on Tuesday evening, William Lunn, Esq., in the chair. Resolutions were ably moved and seconded by several clerical and lay brethren.

298. "Important business respecting the future position and relations of this District, as a portion of the great Wesleyan family, has occupied a considerable portion of our attention during the sittings of this assembly, and measures calculated to promote our future prosperity were adopted. We have every reason to believe that the members of our Church will efficiently co-operate with us.

299. "Our highly-esteemed brother, the Rev. Jas. Brock, has been unanimously appointed as a representative of this District, to present you our friendly and brotherly regards. As branches of the same common Methodism, residing in the same" (united) "Province of the British Empire, we feel anxious to take every opportunity of cementing the bonds of union and of strengthening each other's hands."

300. Two or three paragraphs of this partially-abridged letter give unmistakable indication that the idea of incorporation in the Upper Canada Conference, which took place two years later, had begun to take fast hold of the Wesleyan ministers and members in that part of the united Province.

301. Mr. Slight furnished the following list of stations for the year 1852-53 :—

Montreal Centre—John Jenkins.
Montreal West—William Squire.
Montreal East—G. N. A. F. T. Dickson.
Quebec—John Borland.

Three Rivers—Charles De Wolfe, A.M.
Rawdon and Wesleyville—John Douglas.
St. Johns and Chambly—John C. Davidson.
Huntingdon—George H. Davis.
Russeltown—Thomas Campbell.
Odelltown and Hemmingford—Jas. Brock, Geo. Douglas.
Clarenceville—Henry Lanton.
St. Armands—Edmund S. Ingalls.
Durham—Hugh Montgomery.
Shefford—Rufus A. Flanders.
Stanstead—John Tomkins.
Compton and Hatley—Malcolm McDonald.
Sherbrooke and Eaton—Benjamin Slight, A.M., John Armstrong.
Melbourne—William Scott.
Leeds—Gifford Dorey.

302. The first tidings we get from this district after their District Meeting is in a communication to the *Guardian*, from the Rev. John Borland, Quebec, under the date of July 22nd, 1852. It is as follows:—" We are moving on here in a quiet way, yet we think we hear the sound of a going in the tops of the mulberry trees. Three penitents were blessed with peace last Sabbath evening, and four others continue seekers. But what are these among so many! Scores! hundreds!! thousands!!! are hurrying to ruin, and but one now and then are drawn out of the fearful vortex. We have had some affecting providences here of late—one in the falling of a portion of the Cape, by which seven persons were killed, two of them members of our Church. The man (Robert Webb) was a worthy leader and local preacher. We lose much by his removal. Another case is a prominent inhabitant of this city. He spent the greater part of the Sabbath in fishing and in other flagrant forms of Sabbath-breaking, and by six o'clock on Monday

morning he was summoned into the presence of the Judge whose law he had so fearfully violated."

303. The next news was sorrowful, not unmixed with joy and hope, namely: the sudden but triumphant death of another of their ministers, the most influential in the district—the Rev. William Squire, of Montreal West. This occurred on Sabbath morning, the 17th of October, after a few hours' illness. He attended the funeral of a Mr. Samuel Young, a worthy Methodist from Canada West, who died at a hotel, of cholera, on Friday, the 15th. Mr. Squire attended the funeral of Mr. Young on Saturday evening, and shortly after returning home he was attacked with strong symptoms of the same disease. Medical advice was immediately obtained, but from the commencement of the attack he is reported to have had no hopes of recovery. All efforts to arrest the disease were in vain, and early on the Sabbath he ceased to breathe. He will come to view among the obituaries hereafter.

304. About this time a letter appeared in the *Guardian* from a spirited layman of Montreal, proposing to double the amount of missionary money raised in Canada, and to decline the receipt of any from England, as the Methodists of this country were better able to sustain their own missions in the Provinces than English societies were to spare them the balance between their receipts and their outlay. Something certainly true of all sorts of Methodists in those Provinces now, compared with those from whom missionary appropriations come in the British Isles. The Methodists of Montreal called a public meeting, and recommended a day of thanksgiving for the blessings of a bountiful harvest.

305. A layman had written to the *Guardian* rather despondingly about Lower Canada Methodist operations. The following was written as a corrective by "G. H. D." He says: "Blessed be the Lord our God we have peace in

all our borders, prosperity in many of our palaces, and never since the writer came to the country were the prospects brighter. Our cause in the cities, which during the last four or five years suffered somewhat from removals, consequent upon the commercial depression, fires, and other disasters that have taken place, is beginning to resume its former state, and both in Quebec and Montreal there are grateful signs of coming prosperity. Through the country circuits, with but one or two exceptions, a similar state of things exists. In some the work of God is being carried on blessedly. In this circuit" (Huntingdon) "the Lord is working mightily, and has been for months back. Sinners in scores are being converted. In every part of the circuit, through an extent of country measuring thirty miles in length and ten in breadth, the arm of the Lord has been made bare. No fewer than one hundred and twenty, and from that to one hundred and fifty, souls have during the last few months professed to obtain salvation, the forgiveness of sins, and the regenerating grace of God. Still the work goes on, and I solemnly believe it will go on till the whole of this extent of country is leavened with the heavenly influence of the love of God and the power of His Spirit." Then follows a detailed account of a fruitful missionary anniversary, tea-meeting, and bazaar for furnishing the circuit parsonage. Net proceeds over two hundred and eighty dollars.

306. As we have fairly illustrated the spirit and doings of the brethren, and our space is diminishing, we go in search of no materials, but inquire for the net numerical result of this year of labor. The numbers stood 3,740, an increase of *one* on the previous year. These 3,740, joined to the 30,324 in the ranks of Wesleyan Methodism in Canada West, made the total strength of the two sections of the noble army 34,064.

1853-54.

307. THE Conference at the beginning of this year was preceded with the tidings that the Eastern Canada District Meeting had voted unanimously for union with the Canada Conference; and was in due time visited by a deputation from that body, consisting of the Reverends John Jenkins, John Borland, and James Brock, who made their appearance by the third day of the Conference, and stated their business. But we must not anticipate the current of events.

308. As will be generally known, the Rev. Enoch Wood, in virtue of his appointment by the British Conference, took the chair of the Canada Conference on the morning of Wednesday, the first of June, 1853. The session took place in McNab Street Church, Hamilton, and lasted until the tenth of the month. A brother, distinguished by unusual ability and who had been seventeen long years in the ministry, but who had never been appointed to any very prominent office, who had, indeed, shrunk from notoriety, was this year elected by an almost " unanimous vote " to the highest position in the gift of the Canada brethren, the Secretaryship of the Conference. This was the first of a series of upward strides in Connexional confidence and favor of the Rev. Wellington Jeffers, now, and for many years, Doctor of Divinity. It is needless to say that he performed his duties efficiently. The Rev. Isaac Brock Howard was appointed Journal Secretary, and Rev. E. B. Harper and Rev. John Gemley were appointed Assistant Secretaries.

309. Four were received into full connexion with the Conference and ordained. Three of these had grown up under the eye of the Conference, and have been made known to the reader. They were thoroughly Canadian and Wesleyan in all respects. These were Isaac Barber, William Smith Griffin, and Andrew A. Smith.

310. But besides these, another brother came recommended from a smaller section of Canadian Methodism, and was received into full connexion, his orders being acknowledged. This was the *Rev. Ephraim L. Koyle*, a native of the Township of Kitley, who had received a respectable commercial education and had several years' experience of commercial matters. He had been converted in the central body, but became alienated from the society to which he belonged and had united himself to the Methodist Episcopal Church of Canada, re-constructed in 1834, and had been preferred by them to their ministry, in which he had occupied a respectable place for ten or twelve years. But becoming convinced in his own mind that the disruption which gave rise to the organization to which he belonged was not justifiable and that so many organizations were not needed, he sought to return to his former friends, and his advances were reciprocated. His reception was the result. He was a man of very considerable attainments adapted to the ministerial work, and otherwise well-informed. Furthermore, his urbanity and genteel deportment recommended him to favor. He was pious and laborious, but, from some cause or another, although often the secretary of his district, he has been scarcely appreciated according to his deserts.

311. The ranks of the probationers were recruited by no less than eleven candidates, who were received on trial for the ministry, namely : Richard John Forman, William McDonagh, Andrew Edwards, Samuel Edward Maudsley, Allen Salt, Thomas Woolsey, Orren H. Ellsworth, Edwin Peake, and Thomas Pearson. Messrs. McDonagh, Edwards, Ellsworth, and Pearson have passed in review before the reader, as having been known to labour on circuits under chairmen of districts the preceding year. The brethren, Maudsley, Woolsey, and Peake, might have been placed in the same category had I possessed the information while writing the

account of 1852-53 which I now possess at the beginning of 1853-54.

312. *Brother Samuel Edward Maudsley* was a native of England, and only came to this country a short time before being called out. He was a bachelor, but not so young a man as most are when they enter the field. He had evidently had considerable experience, both as a Christian and a lay preacher, when he came here, besides possessing powers of mind and gifts original and peculiar. He was a person of medium size, ordinary appearance, and of quiet, undemonstrative manner. This, added to the fact that I never labored in the same district with him, prevented me from obtaining much acquaintance with this excellent man, and his not being on the efficient list the present year, and without a known address, I am unable to go much beyond rumor and surmise. Furthermore, this brother having remained single, being equal to almost any kind of work, and having shown a disposition to obey the Connexional authorities implicitly, has been sent to such remote places, and has alternated between such wide extremes, that those in a central position have had a poor opportunity of cultivating his acquaintance. But of this I am sure, that the Conference, in the person of Brother Maudsley, received one of the best minds, unique preachers, and faithful laborers they ever numbered within their ranks, and from the few specimens he deigned to afford us, it is plain his writing was as elevated and original as his preaching. His was a sprightly and tasteful literary talent. According to the best information we can get, our subject labored during the foregoing year, namely, 1852-53, on the St. Vincent Circuit, as the colleague of Rev. Alexander Campbell.

313. *Thomas Woolsey* was a native of England, coming here from the City of London, where he had been an active local preacher for seven years. He was sizable, active,

voluble as a speaker, communicative among the people, and destined, as we shall see, to perform a work, distant and toilsome, for several years.

314. *Edwin Peake* was also English, from Devonshire, but not so old as either of the last two brethren, nor was he so large, being rather under, than over, the medium size. He had spent the preceding year along with the Rev. Wm. McGill, on the Carleton Place Circuit, which recommended him, at its close, to the Conference to be received on trial, and received him back the next year as their junior preacher for another twelve months. His talents were average at least, and while he remained in connection with Methodism he commanded medium circuits.

315. *Allen Salt* has come before the reader before in various relationships, and he had often fulfilled the duties of missionary before, although never till this year had he the honor, though an honor well deserved by him, of having his name in the Minutes of Conference. He was an Indian of the Belleville, Grape Island, or Alnwick band, naming them, if you like, according to their successive places of abode, but he was comely in boyhood, youth, and manhood. A thoroughly "red man," he was well-proportioned and symmetrical. He was a pretty little Indian boy, a lithe and sprightly stripling, and has become the majestic and well-developed man of middle age. Early brought under the power of converting grace, and among the most disposed to profit by one of the best mission schools in the work, he became one of the most advanced pupils and scholars, whether in childhood or youth. He was the pet and boast of the "Father of Indian Missions" throughout, who often exhibited him as a specimen of the success of mission teaching and the capacity of the Indian mind for improvement. Mr. Salt, at the time of his reception on trial, was married, and could not have been less than thirty-five years of age. The

matured, intelligent man was he, who had acquired experience in teaching and speaking in various ways and under various circumstances. His attainments and manners would have done no discredit to one of the civilized white race. Our subject has since proved himself a most reliable and valuable missionary among his own people.

316. *Richard John Forman*, though last, not least, was destined to prove one of the most quietly continuous laborers,—one of the wisest and best superintendents,—one of the best financiers,—and one of the soundest, wearing, feeding, satisfying preachers in the body. Our being able to say so much, at the outset, will awaken the inquiry as to his appearance, age, and antecedents up to the time when presented to the Conference as a candidate for the ministry of the Church. We are glad we have authentic data for satisfying these reasonable inquiries. Bro. Forman was then a young man of twenty-four years of age, medium-sized, rather tall than short, spare but muscular, dark-complexioned and enduring. Just the sort of man to work long and efficiently without breaking up. He was of English parentage, but born in Radnorshire, Wales, November 19th, 1830. His parents were religious, and he himself was converted to God in Dudley, under the ministrations of the Rev. Samuel Hulme, New Connexion minister, which people he joined at the early age of eleven years. The family came to Canada in 1845, when he was a youth of fifteen years, and settled in Pickering, near Toronto. He joined the Wesleyans at Duffin's Creek, and became a leader and Sabbath-school superintendent, and soon commenced preaching in a local sphere. The Markham Quarterly Meeting proposed him to the District Meeting as a candidate for the ministry, where he was examined and accepted, along with several others who have been mentioned, at Toronto, in 1853.

317. There was no change made in the staff officers at the

Book-room and Printing Establishment; the Rev. Anson, now Doctor, Green, recently honored with a degree from one of the most distinguished universities in the United States, was continued as Book-steward; and the Rev. James Spencer was re-appointed Editor. The Rev. Thomas Demorest was continued agent of Connexional funds, and was indefatigable and successful in his work.

318. Pre-supposing that the reader has access to the Stations of Conference through the published Minutes, I proceed to elucidate the points which the Minutes left unexplained, and that because the work I have assigned myself is to deal with the *personnel* of the laborers, and the starting point and early history of each is important.

319. Two of the most important circuits in the Toronto District had each a third preacher to be supplied by the chairman. The first was the noble *Brampton* Circuit, furnished with such matured ministers as Nankevill and Tupper, but it needed a third to aid in supplying the Sabbath appointments, at least. The circuit itself furnished the needed supply. A young man, born, I suspect, in the Town of York, whose very pious parents were residing in the "Harrison neighborhood;" who had been converted in boyhood, and showed himself grave and steady beyond his years, had pursued an elementary classical course, and was now attending term on week-days at the University of Toronto, where he afterwards graduated, was an eloquent preacher, and being strong and active, went out on Saturdays and took a-third of the Sabbath work on the Sundays, and thus helped to infuse considerable vigor into the circuit. He was then, perhaps, in the neighborhood of twenty, slightly more or less, sandy-complexioned, medium-sized, but compact and heavy. We are writing of *Brother Joseph E. Sanderson*, A.M., now Governor of the Ladies' College at Whitby. He needs no further introduction.

7

320. The strong *Nelson* Circuit, as it often happened, was in want of a third man. He was a worthy associate of the Prestons, Pearsons, Woolseys, and Maudsleys, with whom the Connexion were favored about that time. This brother was a bachelor, but, perhaps, nearer thirty than twenty. He was the son of an eminent English Wesleyan minister, classically educated, a skilful physician by profession. One of the most conscientious and upright of men was he, and an experienced and able local preacher. Never very smooth in his elocution, but destined to be one of the best preachers and ablest Conference debaters in the body. I need nothing further than to pronounce his name, *Robert Fowler, M.D.*

321. The *Hamilton District* had its share of vacancies to be filled. The venerable Solomon Waldron, at Nanticoke, required an assistant. The first part of the year he was aided by a young Canadian of good education, the son of a loyal local preacher, and brother of an itinerant preacher's wife prospectively. This was *Ira B. Kilborn*, who, for some cause which I cannot recall, although I was the chairman, removed before the year was out to the Guelph District. He ultimately became a minister in the United States. His place was supplied for the balance of the year by a very dissimilar man. The first supply was a Canadian, this one was thoroughly Irish. The former had come from the employment of school teaching, this one was dragged from the roughest of bush-farming. That one had more education, this one proved to have most mind, when once developed. And when the itinerancy and the College had ground off the native roughness, there were few preachers of more volubility and power than Brother *John V. Wilson*, who came to the rescue of the work in an emergency, and who did good service to the cause in positions which were not sinecures. He was destined to spend another year under the chairman, but on the same circuit, and when received on trial he was sent

there again. Surely, with the disadvantages under which he began, a brother who could sustain himself, almost in sight of his original home, three consecutive years must have had stamina and resources.

322. *Dunnville's* second man was a supply provided by myself, of whom we have had some glimpses in this work already. He had stood by his partially disabled superintendent in the Nanticoke Circuit, within the bounds of which he taught a school during the two preceding years. This was our beloved *William Tomblin*, a native of England, but spiritually born in Canada, An attempt to conduct a Sunday-school in a destitute neighborhood, convinced him of the need of religion, and led him to seek and find it. He soon began to preach as a local preacher. He came to our help with the reputation of having been a virtuous boy, a filial son, a punctual and laborious local preacher, and the amiable and prepossessing young gentleman. He was acute, studious, and well informed on all subjects ; but, though one of the most diligent pastors and best superintendents, the great demand for vocal power, commanding person, and brilliancy has prevented his being as prominently stationed as others in no wise his superiors. Happily he has been principally concerned to commend himself to his Master as "a workman who needeth not to be ashamed, rightly dividing the word of truth."

323. We must supplement such omissions of the *Brantford District* as we have required data for, leaving the other points. perhaps, to be elucidated before we go to press. The district was in charge of the old itinerant, the *Rev. William Ryerson*, whose own immediate appointment was the Indian mission on the Grand River. He was to have "one sent" him, but suspect his only, and certainly a very efficient, assistant was the *Rev. Peter Jones*, who resided on his own estate near Brantford, and who was placed under the " direction of

the Superintendent of Missions." But as his distant work was not onerous, I suspect the two Indian missions on the Indian Reservation enjoyed a large part of his ministrations. This had practically been his position since 1849, and continued so until his lamented death in 1856. The *Rev. Ozias Barber* needed an assistant at *Ingersoll*, but was fain to get on with an aged and unwieldy superannuate, Father Prindle, whose original thought made up for the lack of activity. The Rev. Matthew Swann, on the *Norwich* Circuit, had no less than two such helpers during the year. The first was a young man by the name of *Ditch*, who failed after three months, and the rest of the year was supplied by a local preacher. The quiet but laborious and faithful *Joseph Sheply* stood for *Paris* both this year and the next, with " one wanted" appended to his name. But we have authentic information that neither year was the " want" supplied, but the uncomplaining brother went on with his work in the best manner he could. It will be fulfilling one of the purposes of this book, which is to give a portraiture of all the labors, to say, that by some mischance the usual description of this excellent man, now twelve years in the work, has never been given. He was a native Canadian, from the neighborhood of Chatham. A Methodist of the Methodists, converted young, decently educated, a correct speaker, a good penman, a correct writer, a sound preacher, and one of the most upright men who ever lived. Nothing but want of "cheek" prevented his taking a much more prominent position than he did. He was loyal to the Church to the very core, and accomplished much in a quiet way. Rev. George Kennedy's assistant at *Aylmer* was a chairman's supply, *D. M. Hill*, of whom more anon.

324. The *London District* had but one vacancy. *Sandwich* and *Windsor*, in charge of the strong and energetic Edward White, "wanted" a second preacher; the chairman, the

Rev. Samuel Rose, supplied that want with a small-sized young man of respectable connections, who himself had received some preparatory training at Victoria College, from St. Thomas. He had been converted under the powerful ministry of the Rev. Wm. Pollard, at first met with some discouragement from his friends, but at length his prudence and piety won their sympathies to Methodism. His abilities were probably average, and we shall see that after his *early* death, his brethren bore a strong testimony to his character.

325. The newly-created *Guelph District*, presided over by the pioneering *Lewis Warner*, found itself with three vacancies at the beginning of 1853-54. Two of these we are sure the chairman, usually fortunate in such matters, succeeded in supplying. These two vacancies were first, the second preacher's place in the *Elora* Circuit, and the entire charge of the new and important *Mitchell* Mission. The two supplies were young men above the average in excellence, the one destined soon to seize his crown in the skies, the other to fill a number of important positions in the Canada Church for nearly a quarter of a century, and then to be the bearer of the gospel idings to the people of a "strange speech" and a stranger civilization in the Southern hemisphere. Some will surmise that we write of our modest and lovable *George Cochran.* Mr. Cochran was born of Protestant parents, in the County of Cavan, Ireland, January 14th, 1834. He came to Canada with his parents in 1837, a child of three years. They spent some time in Tecumseh. Next they removed to Sullivan and settled on a new bush farm. George was converted on the 10th of March, 1852, at the early age of eighteen, and a little more than a year thereafter, that is to say, in August, 1853, at the age of nineteen years and five months, he obeyed Mr. Warner's call, and went to be the colleague of the *Rev. James Armstrong,* on the *Elora* Circuit. Nothing could be more remarkable than this person's previous and subsequent course.

How wonderful that a young man, not twenty years of age, without the advantages of College or Academy, nay, of ordinarily good schools, all of whose experiences of the world had been gained in back townships amid land-clearers, and nearly all of whose time had been spent in chopping, logging, harrowing, reaping, threshing, and the like, should have been fit to occupy the pulpit at all! But all that knew him at the time of his setting out say that (despite a naturally plain exterior and a boyish uncouthness, the result of having seen nothing of polished life, and his coarse farmer's garb) he was the impressive and gifted preacher at the first blush, and how great has been his improvement since! Only to think that his rough hand should have learned to handle the pen of the elegant and "ready writer," and that his untrained mind, without an hour at college, or a day's exemption from circuit work, should have become the accurate accountant and correct Financial Secretary, the thorough grammarian, the elegant speaker, the eloquent city preacher, the able expositor, and the very considerable Latinist, Grecian, and Hebraist! And still more wonderful, that in his conversation he should have become tasteful, free from vulgarisms, and that he should have learned to deport himself with ease and politeness in genteel society. The whole speaks volumes for his native talent, sound good sense, tact, and untiring industry. Mr. Cochran's height, was five feet ten inches, and his weight about 139 pounds. His face was not uncomely, but his figure was better than his face. Now, at the age of forty-three, the head of the most successful mission in the Empire of Japan, it is impossible to say what he may not achieve before he reaches three-score years and ten, with the blessing of that God who has so remarkably favored him.

326. *Mitchell*, which was left without a supply, and which received none until February, 1854, was singularly fortunate in the supply it did receive when at length he came. Re-

peated communications to the *Guardian* during this and the following year declare the man and the success which crowned his labors. His Conference obituary, which we give entire, will exhibit the whole of his short career :—

"Brother Lucius Adams was a son of Rufus Adams, Esq., of Acton, C. W. He was born in Esquesing, in the year 1830, and converted to God in childhood. He was distinguished by his assiduity in study and his proficiency in learning while a student at Victoria College, and at Albion Institute, in the State of Michigan. In February, 1854, he was sent to the Village of Mitchell, in the County of Perth. Here he labored with great acceptability and usefulness until the following Conference, when he was regularly received on trial as a candidate for our ministry, and re-appointed to the same field of labor, in compliance with the earnest request of the Mitchell Quarterly Meeting.

"Brother Adams was a young man of great promise, both in piety and talent. In Mitchell a cheering revival took place under his ministry, and many members of our Church who had been "scattered abroad," were gathered into classes. But in the midst of usefulness, his life and labors were suddenly brought to a close. He fell a victim to fever, on the 29th of August, 1855, in the twenty-fifth year of his age.

"His closing hours were marked by no other anxieties than he felt for the prosperity and advancement of the work of God on this mission. His end was peaceful and happy."

It will, perhaps, interest the reader to know that this young man was the nephew of two excellent ministers who have often come to view in the pages of this work, from the very first volume downwards, namely : the Rev. Messrs. Ezra and Zenas Adams. He was also the brother of several ladies known as educationists, and one as a minister's wife.

326. Of the second preacher for *Mono*, along with the godly and devout *Wm. Steer*, we have no certain information to this date. Rev. L. Warner thinks it was *Edmund Cooke*. But Cornish's Hand Book informs us that *Wellesley* had a strong laborer, and gifted preacher, in the person of a newly-arrived local from Ireland, whom, we have been told, did service for God through his favorite Methodism in that land. He was married on his entering the work; and this was the reason, perhaps, why his reception on trial had failed at the late Conference, although he had done good service in the *Erin* Mission the year before. He was fairly educated, lively in his ministrations, and successful. But, for two reasons, l cannot be very minute: I never had the pleasure of being his neighbor, and the data upon which I had relied for information has eluded my search too late to seek its replacement. But Brother *John L. Kerr* is not unknown to the Connexion in Canada.

327. As to the *Owen Sound District*, the printed stations leave *Proton* as to be served by a chairman's supply, whereas all our information goes to say that *S. E. Maudsley* labored on that mission through the year 1853-54, and the Minutes of Conference inform us that he was "received on trial" at the Conference which began the year. *St. Vincent* was to have had a second preacher "sent," but the then chairman, Rev. C. Vandusen, is of opinion that "A. Campbell had no colleague." *Derby* had a strong, stout brother, English, but thoroughly Canadianized, sent to take care of it, whose antecedents I may know better when I record his reception on trial. This was David Hunt. The *North Shore of Lake Superior* and that region was supplied, in two separate missions, by two Indian brethren, namely, *George Blaker* and *James Esquob*. The chairman went along in person and placed them on their missions. Mr. Blaker was a man of some education: of Esquob I know nothing.

328. We have had no response from the then *Barrie* chairman, and the only omission is scarcely worth looking up.

329. *Cobourg District* had three vacancies. The second preacher's place, along with the Rev. Thomas Hanna, was supplied by a young Canadian, overtopping his superintendent greatly in point of size. He was the son of excellent Methodist parents, who lived in the extreme end of the peninsula of Prince Edward's, who had enjoyed the advantages of Victoria College in addition to good school opportunities in his own locality. His cranial developments indicated mental power, and he was said to be gifted and powerful, but I can lay claim to no data by which to speak with more accuracy of our almost gigantic friend, *Brother Garrett J. Dingman.*

330. A young man by the name of *John Fawcett*, who labored on some other circuits both before and after this year, but who never passed through a regular probation and entered the Connexion, was the assistant of the indefatigable *J. C. Slater*, on the *Norwood* Mission.

331. The *Belleville District* had only one vacancy, *Hungerford*, and that vacancy had a rather unusual supply. A native of the United States, who had served in the American army during the war of 1812-15, then a mere boy, came into the Province after the war, married young, and settled in business in the Town of Brockville. Soon after his marriage he became converted and joined the Church, and was one of the first class-leaders of that town, if not the very first. His house was a stopping-place for all the ministers who came and went, for many years. He was a liberal contributor to all the funds of the Church, both local and Connexional, trustee, and often steward as well as leader. He had stood by the cause through all the most painful crises through which it had passed. He had acquired substance, and his not very large family, all strongly attached to Methodism,

7*

settled in the world, and he now partially retired from business, and wished to spend the evening of his days in usefulness. No one had thought of Brother *Luther Houghton* as a preacher. He was an instructive leader, powerful in prayer, and a good Sabbath-school superintendent, but he did not seem to have the readiness of speech that marks out the preacher. Nevertheless, when a distinguished local elder, Rev. Samuel Heck, passed away, and his loss was much felt, Brother Houghton thought he should try to supply his lack of service, and began to preach as a local preacher. In this work he had been employed some three or four years, when the thought occurred to him, though in the neighborhood of fifty, to offer himself for a circuit, and he was accepted to supply this vacancy. Ultimately he was received on trial, and in the end ordained. It was the most unusual case which had occurred in later times, but his piety, long experience, loyalty to the cause, and respectable character throughout carried him through. This I afterwards found as his chairman: that he would cheerfuly go to bush missions to which it was hard to find a single young man in the district willing to go.

332. The *Kingston District* had three preachers' places to be supplied. *Hinchinbrooke* and *Storrington* I give up in despair, as all my applications for information have failed. Of the second preacher at *Bath*, who was sent as the assistant of the Rev. George Beynon, I believe I have authentic information. The supply was *Wm. Bryers*, a short, stout, compact young Irishman, within four years from the Old Country, with a face, making allowance for the difference of years, very much like that of the Rev. Dr. Burns, late of Toronto, and with a thoroughly North of Ireland accent. He had heroism, dash, and courage, joined with a fund of patient good-humor. His native talents were good, and he had information which, with a year at Victoria College,

raised him above mediocrity in the hard work he was destined to perform. The following salient points in his history are from himself, and therefore authentic. He says of himself, " I was born near the Village of Moy, County Tyrone, October 16th, 1826. I came to New York State in 1849. After years of deep religious anxiety I was enabled to claim Christ as my Saviour in 1851. I immediately joined the M. E. Church in that state. About six months after my conversion I came to Canada, and gave my certificate to the Rev. John Black, then on the Napanee Circuit. In a few months he gave me license as an exhorter. In May, 1853, Rev. D. B. Madden had me authorized to preach as a local preacher and in July of the same year I was placed in the Bath Circuit."

333. The *Brockville District* exhibited one vacancy. The *Rev. Vincent B. Howard*, on the *Cornwall* Circuit, had to look to the chairman's arrangement to provide him a colleague. He was, however, disappointed of any assistance throughout the year. This was a not very agreeable change from his first two years in that circuit, during which he had the efficient assistance of the acceptable and laborious William Burns.

334. The *Bytown District* had two apparent vacancies. *Lochaber* was left with a provisional supply. But it is now known that *Brother Richard Wilson*, whom we introduced as being received on trial in 1848, and who supplied the abovementioned mission during the preceding year, also remained this succeeding one.

335. There was a veritable chairman's supply of the second preacher's place, along with the Rev. Thomas McMullen, on the *Clarendon* and *Portage du Fort* Mission. This supply that section of country, so fortunate in the number of candidates for the ministry, produced. He was a young Irish-Canadian (if not born in Ireland), the third preacher from the one

family, *Andrew Armstrong* by name, and brother of James and Noble Armstrong. He was a dark-complexioned young man, of even greater physical proportions than his sizable brothers, and of average, improvable abilities, and though by no means favored with easy circuits, destined to labor through the intermediate twenty-four years between then and now with undiminished vigor.

336. The cases of two members of Conference and one probationer require to be stated. *Aaron D. Miller*, a member on trial, through indisposition, was required to take a year's respite from circuit work. The Rev. *William Andrews* was lent to the Canada Eastern District for a year, and stationed at *Compton*. And the Rev. *Erastus Hurlburt* was more than lent, for he was destined to be found in that district the next year and comprehended in the scheme of amalgamation, which went into effect after the Conference of 1854. Mr. Hurlburt's Lower Canada circuit was *Rawdon*, where he was respected and useful.

337. It will be in the reader's recollection that at the Conference of 1852 the Rev. Mr. Case, our principal subject, was released from all local charge, and suffered to visit any part of the Connexion where he thought he might subserve in any way the interests of the cause. One object he evidently had in view was to visit his early friends throughout the Province, with whom his many engagements, for the latter half of his life, had prevented him from having much intercourse. One of the scenes of his most successful early labors was in what was usually called "The Thames country." There, during the Conference year 1809-10, he had succeeded in organizing an extensive circuit, and was the instrument in promoting an extensive and saving revival. His heart had yearned after the Western people for many years, and this autumn, it would appear, those yearnings were to be gratified. Gosfield was the centre of the original "Thames

Circuit." To that township, which now gave name to a circuit, the active and enterprising William Dignam was appointed at the Conference of 1853. He, like Mr. Case, has long since gone to his reward. Many of his papers have come into my hands, and among them I found an autograph letter from the Rev. William Case, carefully labelled and kept. It would seem that Mr. Case had passed through the country by the main road to the Province line (indeed, the letter was written from *Detroit*), and he was purposing to return eastward along the Lake Erie shore. But the letter, which I give entire, will speak for itself; and it will be furnishing one of the few remaining glimpses to be had of one whose public life gives name and character to these collections :—

338. "DETROIT, Sept. 20th, 1853.

"DEAR BROTHER,—Being on a tour through the societies in the Western portion of our Church, I take this means of saying that I design to spend the ensuing Sabbath in Gosfield, and that you are at liberty, if you judge it expedient, to give me two appointments, if in two different settlements. I am to be at Amherstburg on Friday night, and, if time allow, please drop me a line (informing me) of the place and of the services, as also of the friends on whom I am to call.

"I have my own conveyance, and Mrs. Case is with me.

"Please do me the favor to have the appointments as general" (generally given out) "as may be, as I shall wish to see as many of my old friends and their children as convenient.

"I go on down the Lake Road and cross to Chatham Monday and Tuesday, and am to be at the district meeting on Wednesday next.

"With kind regards to all, farewell !

"WILLIAM CASE."

We may have something more of this kind to chronicle before this year is ended.

339. The ministerial strength of the body—now approaching two hundred, between pastors and Connexional officebearers, besides the hosts of local preachers and circuit

officials in the stations, circuits, and missions in Canada West, and the outlying missions—were in the most intense state of activity during this ecclesiastical year (1853-54), as will appear from the following details.

340. As spiritual vitality and the influx of members truly converted constitute the only real foundation for safe and abiding success in the more exterior doings of the Church, I will first endeavor to furnish something like a summary digest of the multitudinous and diversified communications that came to the Connexional organ, besides information from other sources.

341. We have referred to the revival that occurred in Hamilton City Circuit during the latter part of the preceding year. The result was published in the *Guardian*, under the hand of the Superintendent, Mr. Carroll, at the opening of the year we are now considering. It is embraced in the following excerpt:—"A careful record was kept of the revival, a synopsis of which I now give, as furnished me by the assiduous Secretary, Mr. R. D. Wadsworth:—During these special services, which commenced March the 24th and closed July 5th, 1853, eighty youths, boys and girls, professed conversion, aged from nine to seventeen years; three aged men were converted, whose ages severally were fifty-six, sixty-seven, and seventy-four; four Roman Catholics professed conversion—one man and three women; and one Indian—teacher of Mount Elgin Industrial School. The whole number entered in the register as having received some special blessing was 1,028. Of this number 705 were justified, of whom 183 afterwards professed to be sanctified. There were 142 backsliders restored; purified, in all 458. Of the conversions, 630 were *from the world*, 103 were from other Churches, and 324 were from the country around. Besides the above, the books present fifty-four as 'quickened or revived.' These, perhaps, should not have come into the

account; but we are persuaded that there were a much larger number of *conversions* of which no record was made, so that we may let the original aggregate stand as it was. Of the persons converted, 492 have been appointed to class, full 400 of whom are meeting. But as quite half of these have been brought in since the last renewal of tickets, they do not appear in our Conference return. This revival has been free from extravagances, while it has been characterized by the most extraordinary power. And we are glad to say that, though the special services are 'closed,' the revival has not ceased. Some have been saved at nearly every prayer-meeting since the departure of God's faithful servant," the Rev. James Caughey.

342. The first impulse to the revival work of the year was given by camp-meetings. This year they were numerous, spiritually conducted, and divinely owned. The key-note was struck so early as the 10th of June, 1852, by the enterprising preachers and people on the *Peel* Circuit. Next came the great "Union Camp Meeting" for the *Yonge Street, Humber,* and *Newmarket* Circuits, held in the Township of *Vaughan*, July the 17th, under the supervision of an old adept in such matters, the Rev. Richard Jones. Almost coincidently with this campaign—for it opened the next day, the 18th—a similar one was in progress for the benefit of the Cookstown and Barrie Circuits; and a little later in the season, on the 30th of the same month, and a little farther north, perhaps, the Rev. Thomas Hanna and neighboring ministerial brethren began a field of operations in the township of *Mariposa,* for the quickening of that region.

343. I have not preserved the dates, but the camp-meeting spirit and camp-meeting operations extended from Cookstown north-westward to *St. Vincent,* thence on to *Garden River,* where a wondrous Indian camp meeting, patronized by

Methodist missionaries and their embronzed flocks from the shores of the United States. Finally, the brethren on our south-western frontier felt the reflux of the camp-meeting wave, and one was held in the *Dunnville* Circuit, which was followed by wider and more permanent results. Also in the *St. George* Circuit another. The brethren concerned furnished minute and encouraging accounts of all these onslaughts on irreligion and carelessness. Finally, the old *Augusta* Circuit took up the battle-cry, and held a similar meeting in the township of *Elizabethtown*.

344. The reader will not be surprised to hear that the Province resounded with the notes of revival from east to west, from north to south, and from the circumference to the centre. News of revival came (in some cases two or three times over), embracing accounts of tens, fifties, and hundreds added to the Church, with scores of believers quickened or sanctified, from *Lachute, St. Andrews, L'Orignal, Westmeath, Matilda, Crosby*, and the *Brockville* District, while an echo of the same came back from *Bruce Mines, Garden River, Goderich, Windsor, Wardsville, St. Thomas, Blenheim*, and *Dunnville*. The north glowed with the holy flame: *Normanby, Bradford*, and *Wellesley* sent in their quota of cheering news. The centre and the south felt the pulsations of this spiritual life, and sent it throbbing back to the extremities; *Napanee, Port Hope Circuit, Newcastle, St. George*, and *Lundy's Lane* sent tidings of victory and triumph.

345. Wesley is reported as having said, in reference to the boast of Archimedes, "Give us ground whereon to stand, and we will move the world." The early laborers in this country were not so profoundly convinced of the value of church edifices to the extension and permanency of the work of God as they ought to have been. But this mistake had begun to be corrected, for a few years before the time of

which we write. The year 1852-53 was a great church-building year, but the one now under consideration was even more so. Churches large and small, cheap and costly, churches in the city and the country, were projected, built, or repaired and modified, and dedicated every month in the year. A few of these enterprises may now be mentioned, taking the order in which they were reported.

346. August the 8th, 1853, the Rev. G. R. Sanderson gratefully chronicled the opening of the much-needed new church in Cobourg, furnishing accommodation at once for students at the College and the congregation from the town and country around. The collection at the dedication—for the place, in that day, was unusually large, namely, two hundred dollars. That was the beginning of an upward course for Wesleyan Methodism in that town and neighborhood.

347. A revival at *La Chute*, that old appointment in the St. Andrews Circuit, originating in a visit from the Rev. Henry Cox, a year or so earlier, so strengthened the society that they resolved to "arise and build," and a long, much-needed church in that village was the result. The church at *Peterboro'* was enlarged and re-opened.

348. In November, 1853, a new church, which received the name of "*Bethel*," was opened in the *Norwood* Circuit. A similar event took place on Christmas day, for the accommodation of the Christianized Indians at *Garden River*. And a church was also finished and opened at a place called *Percy Mills*, in the Percy Circuit.

349. A new one at a place called *Tosotoronto*, in the Mono Mission, was reported. This field of labor, under Brethren Steer and Cooke, was wondrously favoured this year in all respects.

350. The Brighton Circuit, under the devoted John Black and his active young colleague, J. W. German, had a "deep-

spreading, blessed work," and a new church at the beautiful new Village of *Frankford*, where Cold Creek comes tumbling down into the Trent, was the result.

351. Bro. William McCullouch's circuits usually progressed, and this year was no exception. A revival and a class at " Perrytown " on the *Port Hope* Circuit issued in a church.

352. *London* built " the largest and most commodious church in that town." And the Methodist miners at the far-off Bruce Mines rejoiced in the completion and glad opening of a tabernacle suitable to them, thirty-five by twenty-five, under the always successful labors of the Rev. Joseph Hill.

353. And to crown all, the growing town of *Woodstock* welcomed the completion of a large and convenient church about the close of the Conference year—the 14th and 21st of May—the opening celebrated by some of the great lights of the Connexion for two consecutive Sabbaths.

354. The miscellaneous occurrences and interests of the year may be glanced at before we end the account of Connexional matters in Canada West. Among the first of these was the commencement, on the recommendation of the Conference, of what has grown to be a measure of great importance, namely, the taking up of a collection in the several circuits, to assist in defraying the expenses of indigent Conference students, and thereby benefitting the College itself.

355. The Clergy Reserve question was re-opened during the course of this year; but the Conference and its organ, referring to its former recorded declarations, chose not to take any very overt part in the current discussion, on which account they were liberally censured by some whose liberalism was newly-born. This was, perhaps, the cause of some obstruction to the usefulness of Wesleyan ministers in the

minds of a good many; but the Editor, Mr. Spencer, ever on the alert, continued to make his trenchant replies so difficult to digest, that no one long continued the discussion with him. This is a fitting place to say that the *Guardian* and its conductor were steadily growing in Connexional favor, and also in the respect of the country at large. It did good service to the interests of temperance, and favored strenuously the Prohibitory law endeavors which were then before the country.

356. The University of Victoria College, considering the disadvantages under which it labored, was prosecuted with vigor. The Rev. S. D. Rice, during this year as well as the last, besides his responsibilities at Kingston, travelled largely to promote its interests, and advocated them and cheered its friends in his frequent communications to the organ of the Connexion.

357. About the close of the civil year the venerable *Heman Hurlburt*, the father of no less than five members of the Conference, passed away, and his life and character, combined with many touching reminiscences of the past, were portrayed in a lengthened article by the venerable *Case*, a most fitting biographer for such a man.

358. The missionary meeting efforts of this year were too many and too extendedly reported to be conveniently abridged. The deputations were able and generally faithful, and some of them, such as Thomas Hurlburt and William Herkimer, who had large experience in the aboriginal field, lent their aid most efficiently to the anniversaries. The missionary income for the year advanced from $22,691 87 to $30,159 86, an increase of $7,467 99 on the year, and making the advance from the time of the reunion (or, rather, 1848) till the Conference of 1854 no less than $10,899 85.

359. The chronicles of the year, both domestic and missionary, home and foreign, may well be made to close with

a short reference to an interesting valedictory service held in Toronto, May the 24th, 1854, at which an affecting farewell was taken of the Revs. Thomas Hurlburt, Robert Brooking, and Allen Salt, who were designated to the far-off Hudson Bay Territory, consequent upon the British Conference missions of that region being transferred to the care of the Wesleyan Methodist Church in Canada, which had been a subject of negotiation during the preceding year or more. The deferred visit of exploration on the part of the co-Delegate, the Rev. John Ryerson, was now to coincide with the exodus of these outward-bound missionaries.

360. The numerical gains of this year of activity were not so great as might have been expected, but still they were very considerable. The total returns at the Conference of 1853 were 30,321. The total at the Conference of 1854 was 32,364, making the gains of the Conference year 1853-54, *two thousand and forty.*

361. We have now arrived at the last year of the existence of the Canada East District separate from the Upper Canada Conference, and happily we have a little more materials than usual for illustrating its history and doings.

362. The Annual District Meeting for this section of the work sat earlier than usual, although the precise date of its session cannot now be determined. It was one of peculiar interest and solemnity. It was presided over by the Rev. Enoch Wood, who had been appointed its chairman by the British Conference, third President of the Canada Conference, on account of the important question pending, affecting the District in its past relation to the British Conference and its prospective relation to the Canada Conference. Mr. Wood's visit was greatly valued, as appears from a resolution passed by the brethren at the close, and their presentation to him of Bagster's Bible, elegantly bound, embossed, and illustrated.

363. That having been a Missionary District, had never allowed the participation of laymen in any part of its deliberations, unlike the practice in England. But now, as a prudential measure—and, in my opinion, a very wise and just piece of policy—the Circuit Stewards and other official friends were invited by circular to attend from all the circuits. Many of them did attend, and on the subject being laid before them, they were invited freely to express their opinions.

364. The meeting was most harmonious and interesting throughout, and the question of amalgamation with the Canada Conference secured a unanimous vote.

365. Unhappily two of the brethren had become so enfeebled by affliction as to have to sue for a supernumerary relation. These were Brethren Ingalls and John Douglass. The former returned to the work after some years' rest; but the latter, although useful to the Church in every place where he afterward resided, never returned to the itinerant field—at least in Canada.

366. The deputation already mentioned, consisting of the Rev. Messrs. Jenkins, Borland, and Brock, was appointed to convey the decision and wishes of the District Meeting to the Canada Conference.

367. The stations, supplemented as they were with the loan of two brethren from the Canada Conference, were as follows:—

Montreal Centre—John Jenkins; John Douglas, supernumerary.
Montreal West—William Scott.
Montreal East—George Douglas.
Quebec—John Borland.
Point Levi—One wanted.
Three Rivers—Charles De Wolfe, A.M.
Rawdon and Wesleyville—(Erastus Hurlburt).

St. John and Chambly - John C. Davidson.

Odelltown and Hemmingford—James Brock, one to be sent.

Huntingdon—George H. Davis.

Russeltown—Thomas Campbell.

Clarenceville—Henry Lanton.

St. Armand—Gifford Dorey.

Durham—Hugh Montgomery, one to be sent; E. S. Ingalls, supernumerary.

Brome, Sutton, &c.—One to be sent.

Shefford and Granby—Rufus A. Flanders, one to be sent.

Stanstead.—John Tompkins.

Compton—(William Andrews.)

Bornston—One wanted.

Sherbrooke and Eaton—Benjamin Slight, one to be sent.

Dudswell—One wanted.

Melbourne—Malcolm McDonald.

Danville.—One wanted.

Leeds—John Armstrong.

Gaspe—One wanted.

368. The above stations require some annotations. First, the brethren whose names are within in a parenthesis were members of the Canada Conference. Secondly, the Rev. G. N. F. T. Dickson's name was in the first published draft of stations set down for *Rawdon*, but ultimately he was exchanged for the Rev. E. Hurlburt, while he himself was sent as junior preacher to Kingston. Falling into the Canada Conference by the arrangement of the next year, this excellent minister of Christ has never removed from the Upper Province from that day to this. Third, we have reason to believe that the "one to be sent" to the aid of Mr. Brock at Odell Town was a younger brother of Mr. Dickson, who never formally entered the itinerancy, but who ultimately became a physician. Fourth, the assistant of Mr. Slight at

Eaton was the Brother *Robert Graham,* whose peculiar case has been described, and who was ultimately incorporated in the Canada Conference. Fifth, who assisted Mr. Montgomery at *Durham;* and who supplied *Brome* and *Sutton, Dudswell, Danville,* and *Gaspe,* if any, it is impossible to say.

369. We must now endeavor to catch some glimpses of their labors and success, and, it may be, their joys and sorrows, through the year 1853-54.

370. The next glimpse of Canada Eastern interests is found in an editorial of the *Guardian* for October 19th, 1853, headed " *Canada East Methodism to be one with Canada West,*" containing the following passage from the Annual Address of the British Conference to its Canadian *confrere,* to be read at the ensuing session of the Canada ecclesiasitical assembly. It is as follows :—" We have heard with great satisfaction of the desire which exists on the part of the ministers and members of the churches in the Eastern Canada District to be incorporated with the Western Canada Conference. We believe that the consummation of this purpose will greatly increase the stability and usefulness of Wesleyan Methodism in your country. We cordially approve of the steps you have already taken with reference to the matter ; and we have great pleasure in assuring you that all suitable means will be employed by us to complete this most desirable arrangement as speedily as possible."

371. In Quebec, in the early part of the winter of 1853-54, revival services were conducted for the space of fourteen weeks, sustained by that eminent revivalist, Rev. James Caughey. They were remarkably owned to the conviction and conversion of sinners both in and out of the church ; two hundred and twenty-two were added from the world. The number reported pardoned was three hundred and

eleven, fifty-four of these, with seventy-one old members of the church—one hundred and twenty-five in all,—professed to receive the blessing of entire sanctification. The cases of special good were in all no less than three hundred and sixty-four. The new converts were solemnly confirmed, and the series of meetings closed with a serious, loving, social tea-meeting. The above particulars were furnished to the *Guardian* by an excellent lay friend, Thomas Vaux, Esq., whose acquaintance the reader has already made.

372. There was evidently a greatly-renewed current of life-blood coursing through the district during this last year of its first ecclesiastical relationship. We do not arrive in the usual way at a conclusion relative to the numbers in Canada East for the year 1853-54, because the numbers on the several circuits are not given, nor even the totals, in the British Minutes for 1854, as had been usual, as the Parent Conference regarded them as already transferred to Canada West, but we find, from other sources of information, that their increase for the year 1853-54 was the very considerable gain of two hundred and nineteen. This placed the membership of the two sections of Wesleyan Methodism in the two Canadian Provinces, on the eve of their consolidation at the Conference of 1854, at about 36,333.

BOOK THIRTEENTH.

CASE AND HIS COTEMPORARIES AMALGAMATED INTO ONE HOMOGENEOUS WHOLE.

1854-55.

1. WE are entering now on a new and final epoch in our biographical history. Although short, it is important, and requires to stand out by itself, as the beginning of long years of harmony and prosperity.

2. The epochal Conference of 1854 sat in the strongly Methodist Town of Belleville, on the 7th of June, and continued its sessions until the fifteenth. There was an unusually large attendance of no less than 133 ministers of the Conference, besides juniors who had no legal seat or voice in the assembly. The brethren, John Borland, James Brock, and Malcolm McDonald, came as a deputation from the Eastern Province, and were accompanied by the Rev. Thomas Campbell.

3. The Rev. Enoch Wood was announced as the appointee of the British Conference for President; and although not present, the Rev. John Ryerson as his co-Delegate. The urbane and amiable *Isaac Brock Howard*, after fourteen years of faithful ministrations, and many years' experience as Journal Secretary, was honored by the consecration of his elegant penmanship to the office of principal Secretary. He chose Brethren Tupper and Gemley as his assistants.

4. The other Connexional offices were filled by nearly the same persons as the year before. The Rev. James Spencer was continued in the editorial office; but the Rev. Anson Green, D.D., after nine years' incumbency, during which the institution greatly advanced, was relieved of the responsibilities of the Book-stewardship, and the Rev. G. R. Sanderson, was once more brought back to the " Book and Printing Establishment" by being elected in the Doctor's place. The Rev. Lachlin Taylor's name stood still in connection with Toronto First Circuit, as the permitted Agent of the Upper Canada Bible Society; and the Rev. Thomas Demorest continued the Agent for Connexional funds.

5. The absence of one distinguished name from this central position (as it happily turned out, however, for *one* year), as it was connected with an important question of Church polity, cannot be ignored; and may afford occasion for presenting some of those lessons which history teaches.

6. The leading minister referred to, who had privately mooted the question some years before, in view of the many excellent persons who sit in the Methodist churches and partake of the sacred symbols at our communion rails, but who are not recognised and utilized as members, because they shrink from meeting in class; and in view of the fact of another large class of persons, nominal members, apparently religiously habited in other respects, whose attendance at class is reluctant, and maintained very fitfully, barely to retain their membership, believing that it would be wise and proper to abolish the class-meeting condition of membership, gave notice of, and moved a resolution to that effect. His principal argument was that the test was only adapted to the mere *society* stage of Methodistic organization, but that, as it had now developed itself into a *Church*, it was wrong to make church-membership dependent on the use of a prudential means of religious edification. There were a few sympathizers

with the measure proposed who approved of the arguments by which it was sought to be carried, but it is not uncharitable to say, that they were such brethren as, however excellent, are averse to the strict details of disciplinary administration. But the great majority of the ministers were strongly, and some of them vehemently opposed to the innovation. This will especially apply to Brethren R. Jones, Wilkinson, Carroll, and W. Jeffers, who took a prominent part in the debate, with some others whose names elude our recollection. These brethren maintained, that though the name of the institution, like many other essentials of our Church organization, does not appear in the New Testament, the substance of its doings are strongly enjoined therein; that it is essential to the maintenance of the vital integrity of Methodism; that the enforcement of the class-meeting rule did no one any injustice, inasmuch as our Church organization was perfectly voluntary, and everyone had the means of knowing that his membership could not be begun or continued without an attendance at class; and that as to fastidious ones, they had, by the provisions and usages of the body, the privilege of access to the Lord's table and that of having their children dedicated to God in holy baptism. These considerations prevailed, and the overture was rejected by a vast majority, and there has been no formal attempt to unsettle the Church on that point to this day. The author of the overture felt so strongly on the subject, that he tendered his ministerial standing, and it was accepted. It is, however, but just to him to say, that he was not opposed to class-meeting itself, but to the use of it as a test of adherence to the Church. For one year he dropped quietly into the local ranks,—preached as occasion required, and united with a class and met regularly therein. And the present writer feels great pleasure in the recollection that he had the honor of proposing at the next annual session of the Conference an-invitation to the brother concerned to resume his connection with the Conference, which carried, and the recalcitrant member returned.

7. But it may, perhaps, be averred by some, that what was sought to be accomplished by direct enactment has come about by the slow process of events, and that in many circuits the class-meeting condition is a practical nullity, and it must be confessed that through the habitual disposition of some members to oppose and resist what they are bound to uphold, and the still more deplorable tendency of some ministers to ignore and neglect the details of a Discipline they are pledged to enforce, that there is too much truth in the above averment, but it is none the less a pity and a shame that it is so for all that. And this is a good opportunity for saying, that a little tact and painstaking on the part of leaders and preachers would correct this neglect, and render the class-meeting at once popular and an untold blessing to the Church. Let the minister make much of the class-meeting, after announcing and commending it, and after throwing himself into them and giving the leaders an example of strictness, variety, and life in their management; and, at least, always doing this *once a quarter*, examining the class-book and giving the ticket into each member's hand, instead of merely handing them to the leader. So also, if the leader would forecast his work, seek a preparation of mind and heart for its edifying and lively performance, eschewing stiffness and hackneyed ways, and striving to show some genius and generalship, as well as piety, in the management of the meetings from time to time, and particularly, always producing and marking his class-book in the presence of his class, to show that the attendance of members was a matter expected, and that its neglect was recorded; I say if these things were done, and the members co-operated, more would be accomplished twice over in securing permanent

members, and in upbuilding the Church in order and holiness, than by those spasmodic efforts by which is sought to stave off and remedy the deterioration occasioned by our ordinary and ruinous neglect.

8. The proposals of the Canada East brethren for amalgamation with the Canada Conference, backed as it was by the hearty concurrence of the British Conference, was unanimously accepted ; and skilful financial minds were set to work to devise the terms on which the incoming brethren might be invested with equal financial claims on the funds of the Conference with the original members, which terms, when agreed on, the Parent Connexion enabled them to fulfil. The details of this measure must be sought for elsewhere.

9. The effort to endow the College by the sale of scholarships during the course of the previous year had been to a considerable extent successful. Four hundred scholarships had been sold, and it was thought that the number might be increased to seven hundred, which, at $100 each, would yield an endowment of $70,000, the interest on which was a much-needed supplement to the other moderate resources of the institution. To complete the canvass, seven ministers, in as many different parts of the Connexion, were appointed to issue scholarships to applicants.

10. No less than sixteen brethren were received into full connexion with the Conference, and all but two, who had been previously ordained for special purposes, were solemnly set apart by imposition of hands. Their " public reception," at which six, selected from among the number, gave an account of their conversion and call to the ministry as a sample of what was required in the Wesleyan ministry, and three of the ablest ministers of the body, namely : the venerable Mr. Case, Dr. Green, and Rev. John Borland, of the delegation, addressed the assembly in an efficient manner.

11. The brethren received were *Nelson Brown, Wm. Burns, Joel Briggs, Wm. Creighton, Thomas Culbert, John Wesley German, Robert Graham, John Hutchinson, Richard M. Hammond, Silas Huntingdon, Joseph Hugil, George McRitchie, George McDougall, Thomas Stobbs, Matthew Swann,* and *Richard Wilson.* They had all graduated with the Canada Conference in the usual way, excepting Messrs. *Hutchinson* and *Graham*, who had come from lesser Methodist bodies through the Eastern Canada District.

12. The number beginning their probation for the ministry was still greater. These were: *John S. Clarke, Robert Fowler, John Wakefield, William Williams, John L. Kerr, Luther Houghton, David Hunt, George Blaker, Ashton Fletcher, John Fawcett, William Bryers, William Scales, Joseph E. Sanderson, William Tomblin, Peter German, George Cochran, Lucius Adams, S. G. Phillips, George Jaques, George L. Richardson, Garrett J. Dingman, Jay S. Youmans, William Briden,* and *Andrew Armstrong.*

13. Eight of these brethren are marked in the Minutes as having travelled *one* year under the direction of a chairman, some of whom we have mentioned, though there were one or two of whose labors and place of labor we were not informed. But several who assuredly labored under a chairman, and whom we have so presented, have no credit given them in the Minutes. Among these are *William Williams, John L. Kerr, David Hunt, William Bryers, Lucius Adams, Garrett J. Dingman, Andrew Armstrong, George Cochran,* and *George Blaker;* and we are morally certain that one or two others ought to be placed in the same category.

14. We must now give a presentation to the reader of such of these new laborers in the field as we have not already noticed; albeit, for lack of authentic information, in some instances we fear that we cannot go much beyond probable conjectures.

15. *Ashton Fletcher* appears in the list. There were two of this name—father and son. The son, I believe, is here intended. The father will come to view after the lapse of a year. The son was a very young man—not, probably, above nineteen or twenty, if up to that; nevertheless, if I am not greatly mistaken, he had labored the whole or a part of the preceding year on a circuit under a chairman—perhaps the circuit to which he was about to be appointed for 1854-55, the Nelson. He was the son of a good local preacher, who was destined to offer the evening of his days for usefulness; like his father, he was a native of England, and by all who witnessed his juvenile efforts, pronounced exceedingly gifted and promising as a speaker. But he was destined to labor only during this year on a circuit. The next two years, being still very young, he attended Victoria College as a Conference student, at which institution, I believe, he graduated. But while passing through College, his views became altered about his vocation for life, giving up the study of theology for the study of law, in which profession he is reported very successful, while still connected with the Church of his childhood and his choice. Seeing " he went not with us to the work," we can afford him no larger niche in the temple of fame.

16. *Jay S. Youmans*, a brother beloved, appears for the first time as a preacher in this list. Although he now sojourns in another land, to which we cannot say we cheerfully transferred him, yet he left the writer data for furnishing the reader an account of his early physical and spiritual life. He was of a good and godly stock, born in Prince Edward County in 1832; converted clearly in 1843, when only eleven years of age. The Rev. R. Jones and the Rev. Mr. La Dow were the instruments. Soon after, receiving the blessing of perfect love, he lived a beautifully devoted life from boyhood upwards. He had fair opportunities for

liberal training, although not a graduate. He had also a capable, active mind, and made good improvement of his opportunities. But the principal thing in his favor was the possession of the qualities that give a man success in the ministry, namely, ardent piety, an emotional nature, sympathy and fervor of spirit, great ease and volubility in speaking, a manageable, musical voice, and an easy, popular, though not exactly colloquial style. His personal appearance, also, was in his favor—sizable as to stature and dimensions, a thorough blonde as to hair and transparency of skin. His character was indicated by a prominent nose, and vocal capacity by a wide mouth. He early began to exhort and preach, and was only about twenty-one when proposed for the ministry. No wonder that a laborer constituted like the one I have described should have proved gloriously successful in winning souls. He has won a good position of usefulness in the Erie Conference, whither he has gone, and also a Doctor's degree.

17. *John S. Clarke* has not yet furnished me with specific data. I must therefore present him, as best I can, in a general way, leaving a space for the particulars, to be used if they arrive before I go to press. He was Irish we know, and stayed long enough in Ireland to give his accent a good broad sound. His voice was loud and rolling; his person good and commanding, and his temper generous, and his manners genial. Like Richard Clarke, William McDonagh, George H. Cornish, and Alexander Drennan, he came out of that prolific hive, the Richmond Street Society, Toronto. Bro. Clarke's youth gave promise to the ministry of the ability, activity, and success by which his public life has been characterized.

18. *John Wakefield* is one of those whom I surmised to have labored the preceding year under a chairman, and now I see from his General Conference sketch that he went out

in 1852; and Cornish's Hand-Book informs us the year was spent between the Blenheim and Stratford Circuits. Had we not overlooked this, he would have been noticed before. The next year, 1853-54, he was at Cobourg as a Conference student. This year he comes, Minerva-like, fully armed for the itinerant battle. He was born in Warwickshire, Old England, in 1830, so that on this occasion of his introduction to us he was the stout, compact young man of twenty-four years of age. He had a good physique, good resonant voice, great readiness of utterance, and immense hortatory power. He was converted at his starting-place in the ministry, Blenheim, and favored with advantages of education better than many others.

19. *William Scales* was a native of John Wesley's town and county, Epworth, in Lincolnshire, England. He had been a very laborious local preacher in his own country, where he had conducted a business. But coming to Montreal a matured man, he was called out for a time, I am almost certain, under a chairman, and recommended to this Conference for the ministry. He was well stored with Scriptural and theological furniture as a thoroughly instructive and impressive preacher. Mr. Scales was somewhat tall and slender, but wiry.

20. *Peter German* was a married man, had been very comfortable and respectable in private life, and invested with a commission of the peace. His residence had been within the St. George Circuit, where he had very acceptably exercised his talents as a local preacher for several years. Indeed, his marked usefulness as a lay preacher in the country around suggested the idea of urging him out into the itinerant field, in which he had labored the preceding year, under a chairman, on the Dumfries or St. George Circuit. We are glad, since the above was written, to have the following more precise particulars come to hand:—He

8*

was born at the "Fifty," in 1818; converted at a campmeeting in 1833; received license to exhort in 1835, and became a local preacher in 1839.

21. *William Braden* (who must not be confounded with *William Briden*—the latter was English) was an Irish-Canadian, if not born in Ireland, the son of thoroughly Irish Wesleyan parents, as thoroughly Canadianized. He was well-sized and proportioned, well-educated, and a most amiable young man, but seems to have had an aversion to public ministrations, and was destined to remain only a few years in the ministry, while his whole life was to be given to the Church. He came out from Pembroke, and settled at Carleton Place.

22. *Samuel G. Phillips* was a native of England also, not very large of stature, active-minded, and, we suspect, largely self-educated—an education which has been going on ever since. He came from the Lower Canada section of the work, where he had labored at least one year as a supply. When a Wesleyan standard-bearer went over to another section of the militant Church—the year preceding, at St. Johns—Bro. Phillips had been called to supply the vacancy, and did it courageously. This young man was destined to get up his Conference studies well, to advance his circuits, to preach good sermons, and to write and publish saleable and useful books.

23. *George L. Richardson* was also English; but, unlike the last, he was large in person and was married. We have never had the pleasure of hearing him, but imagine he was a fair average preacher and an agreeable pastor.

24. *George Jaques* was English also, but young, and possessed of physical qualities destined to be called into requisition in the hard back circuits he was fated to labor on and work up. The brother had always a bright, intelligent look, and appeared well-informed in conversation, but the distance

we have been apart has prevented me from forming a proper appreciation of his preaching abilities. To all appearance, he has proved himself an uncomplaining, enduring laborer.

25. These young brethren were needed to fill some vacancies created by withdrawals and by deaths. Two had withdrawn in Canada East during the preceding year. These were the *Revs. John C. Davidson* and *Hugh Montgomery*. They were both Irishmen by birth and education. Both were educated above the average of their day; both had taught school; both had been brought up into the ministry under the auspices of the Canada Conference, and both had retired from that Conference in favor of the British Conference during the early part of the seven years' rivalry in Canada West. They differed somewhat in age, size, and ability. Mr. Davidson was the senior, and had the advantage in the other two particulars. But in several things they were alike: they were both rather more than usually urbane and courteous, but both had that sort of parsonic, perfunctory manner and taste which, I think, always gave them a predilection for liturgical, not to say ritualistic, services. These things, with the possible expectation that their circumstances would be less comfortable under a Canadian Conference *regime* (in which, however, they were greatly mistaken), induced them to go over to the Episcopalian or Anglican Church.

26. It is more pleasing to turn to those who had "finished their course with joy, and the ministry which they had received of the Lord." Of these there were two.

27. The first was simple-minded, honest-hearted, affectionate *George Poole*. Although his life and labors for near thirty years have been before the reader, yet we will honor him by reproducing his short Conference obituary:—
"GEORGE POOLE was born in Gory, County of Wexford, Ireland. He died in Brantford, September 11th, 1853, in

the fifty-fourth year of his age. Bro. Poole was converted to God and became a member of the Wesleyan Methodist Church at eighteen years of age. In 1827 he was admitted a candidate for the holy ministry. Full of faith and zeal, he declined no labor and recoiled from no self-denial by which he might promote the cause of God and fulfil the mission assigned him in the Church of God. He deemed it his highest happiness to be in 'labors more abundant,' insomuch that when the Providence of God, by most painful affliction, laid him aside from the effective ministry, he was often heard to exclaim, 'That word *superannuated* presses like a leaden weight upon my heart; I cannot endure to think of it.' During the last seven years before his death his life was a scene of extreme and almost uninterrupted suffering. But amidst all he was eminently supported by the power of grace. His latest hours were especially characterized by calm respose and holy joy in the God of his salvation. In life men beheld in him a true and constant friend, an earnest and deeply-fervent Christian, and a faithful and useful minister. In death they saw him borne up as by the vision of God, in expectation of the 'crown of life' and a home in heaven."

28. The *Rev. James Booth* was the other. He also has been so long before the reader, that all that will be required will be to reproduce the very short obituary of him which appeared in the British Minutes for the year of which we write, he having always held relations to the English Conference:—" JAMES BOOTH, who entered upon the mission work in the year 1816, and prosecuted it diligently and faithfully, until growing infirmities compelled him to retire from active service. In a letter to the Missionary Committee, written a short time before his decease, he expresses himself thus : 'I now only live a day at once ; and I am striving, with all my powers, to be ready when the Lord

shall call me. Thank the Lord, my soul is happy in a sense of my acceptance with God, and a lively hope of a safe arrival at my heavenly home. Bless the Lord, O my soul, for all His mercies to me! Truly the Lord is my God, and I will praise Him.' He died at Kingston, Canada, January 22nd, 1854, in the seventy-third year of his age."

29. The Clergy Reserve question came before the Conference, but it was disposed of, in a quiet way, by the passage of a resolution setting forth the reasons for which the Conference declined taking any further action on that subject.

30. By the list of stations—which we shall transcribe by districts, seeing it is the beginning of an epoch—it will be discovered that no less than two hundred and thirty-eight preachers were stationed. Yet, by the same means, it will be discovered that between thirty and forty were needed. How this need was supplied, it will be also our duty to try and ascertain.

31. In pursuance of the plan of which I have given intimation, and for which I have assigned the reasons, of giving the "stations" for this epochal year by districts, with any annotations which they may require, I herewith furnish the first instalment, relating, as it does, to the main central district of the Connexion—the Toronto District :—

ENOCH WOOD, President of Conference and General Superintendent of Missions.

Toronto East—John Gemley, John Bredin; Anson Green, D.D., who is our Representative to the English Conference ; Geo. R. Sanderson, Book-Steward ; James Spencer, Editor ; Lachlin Taylor, Agent of the Upper Canada Bible Society, by permission of the Conference ; Thos. Demorest, Agent for Connexional Funds, under the direction of the Book Committee.

Toronto West—John Borland, Ephraim B. Harper, Chas. Lavell.

Yonge Street—Richard Jones, William S. Blackstock.

Humber—Robert Lochead, Benjamin Jones.

Brampton—Samuel C. Philp, Reuben E. Tupper, Joseph E. Sanderson.

    N. B.—Bro. Philp's address is Streetsville.

Cooksville—Benjamin Nankevill; Jonathan Scott, superannuated.

Oshawa—David B. Madden, Robert Fowler; Peter Ker, superannuated.

Markham—John Law, Henry Jones; David Youmans superannuated.

Nelson—Thomas Campbell, Ashton Fletcher; David Wright, superannuated.

    N. B.—Bro. Campbell's address is Trafalgar.

Milton—John Hunt.

Georgetown—William Andrews.

Stouffville—Cornelius Flummerfelt.

                      RICHARD JONES,
                       Chairman of the District.

There are no vacancies in the above stations. Remarks, therefore, are not required.

32. The next in order was the Hamilton District:—

Hamilton—James Elliott, William Haw, George N. A. F. T. Dickson; Samuel Belton, superannuated.

Dundas—Isaac B. Howard, James Harris.

Waterdown—Joseph Messmore.

Glanford and Seneca—Thomas Williams, James Clark; Andrew Prindel, superannuated.

Nanticoke—John Goodfellow (to be supplied).

Dunnville—Luther O. Rice (one to be sent).

Grimsby—Simon Huntingdon, William Richardson.

Stony Creek—John English.

St. Catharines—George Goodson.

Thorold—Thomas Bevitt, E. H. Dewart, who is to reside at St. Johns.

Drummondville—Alexander T. Green.

Niagara—Claudius Byrne.

>N. B.—The preachers on the Drummondville and Niagara Circuits shall change regularly.

Welland—Thomas Jeffers (to be supplied); John Baxter, superannuated.

>N. B.—Bro. Jeffers' address is Crowland.

Cainsville—Robert Corson (one wanted).

THOMAS BEVITT,
Chairman.

33. From the above list it will be seen that *Nanticoke, Dunnville, Welland,* and *Cainsville* each lacked a ministerial laborer. Beginning, for sufficient reasons, with the last *(Cainsville)*, which went the year before by the name of " Cayuga Heights," when it was in the same state of destitution, the now very aged incumbent, the Rev. Robert Corson, tells me with his trembling pen : " I was disappointed " (of a supply). " Peter German and the Rev. R. Heyland, superannuated, gave me one Sabbath in two weeks the first year. The second year a local preacher from Burford gave us the same amount of labor. We paid them for their time." He who wrote the above says : " I am in my eighty-fifth year." Peace to the dear old soldier of the cross ! The supply for *Nanticoke* was the same as the year before—our energetic Irish friend, *John V. Wilson,* whose promising characteristics have already been described. The supply for *Welland,* at this writing, we cannot determine, the then Conference appointee, the Rev. Thomas Jeffers, having been called to rest from his labors.

34. The next in order according to the Minutes was the Brantford District :—

Brantford—Noble F. English ; Hamilton Biggar, Rowley Heyland, superannuated.
Mount Pleasant.—Wm. S. Griffin (one wanted).
Paris—Joseph Shepley (one wanted).
Woodstock—Wm. McCullough, James Dixon.*
St. George—Thomas Fawcett.
Galt—George Kennedy.
Ingersoll—Ozias Barber, John Wakefield.
Norwich— Peter German (to be supplied).
Simcoe—Edwin Clement.
Dover—Wm. Chapman ; E. M. Ryerson, superannuated.
Walsingham—Matthew Swann (one to be sent); Matthias Holtby, supernumerary.
Aylmer—Francis Berry, William Williams.
Vienna—O. H. Ellsworth.
New Credit—Matthew Whiting (one wanted).
Grand River—Wm. Ryerson ; Peter Jones, who is under the direction of the Superintendent of Missions.

WILLIAM RYERSON, *Chairman.*

* *Woodstock* unhappily requires a note. Its faithful superintendent, *Rev. S. C. Philp, sen.*, was afflicted by an indiscretion of his junior colleague, who had to be dismissed. We find, from the Minutes of the Conference of 1855, there was a Brother *James Morgan* received on trial and credited with having "labored a year under a chairman." Turning to our invaluable referee, Mr. Cornish, we find a brother of this name was the junior preacher at *Woodstock*. Turning, yet again, to the Hand-Book for that name, we find that he died in 1858, in the Minutes of which year we look up his obituary, from which we get all the information of this brother that I am able to furnish, and which I give *in extenso* :—

" Bro. Morgan died in Dundas, on the 4th of February, 1858, in the twenty-eighth year of his age, and in the third of his ministry, after an illness of nearly two months.

He was a native of England, and the son of Mr. John Morgan, of

35. The "one wanted" for *Mount Pleasant* and *Paris* in each case, continued to be wanted to the end of the year. The reader has heard in advance from the Rev. Mr. Shepley, that Paris had no supply but himself for the present year as well as the last. As to *Mount Pleasant*, the preacher in charge for that and the following year writes as follows :— " In those years, namely, '54-55 and '55-56, I had no colleague. I believe the Minutes say 'one to be sent ;' but none was sent. I worked the circuit alone, and had glorious success. —W. S. GRIFFIN." We have heard from the *Rev. Peter German*, who says in reply, " I had no colleague in 1854, at Norwich. A young man by the name of *Stone* was appointed, but never came. I worked the circuit with the aid of the local preachers." We leave, for want of present information, *Walsingham* and New Credit supplies unaccounted for.

Franch Road, near Kidderminster. To the fifteenth year of his age he manifested no concern for his soul, and was, therefore, in great danger of being led astray by a wicked associate. He was not without friendly warnings and the strivings of the Holy Spirit. He began to reflect. At the same time he was pressingly invited to attend a class and engaged to do so ; and, though he afterwards regretted having made the promise, yet he went. On that very night, however, the arrows of truth pierced his soul. He was in deep distress during the following week, till the next class night. At that time he was enabled to believe in Christ, when he received a full assurance of God's pardoning mercy. From that hour he went on his way rejoicing in God.

Mr. Morgan's first circuit was Woodstock ; his second, Aylmer ; his third, Ingersoll ; and his last one Dundas. To increase in love to to God seemed to be his ardent desire for months previous to his last illness.

In his last illness he showed that he possessed a genuine piety and a clear experience of personal salvation. His life had been character- ized by simplicity of purpose · and as a gospel minister, by an ardent and well-tempered zeal for God and the prosperity of His Church,"

36. The next in order was the London District:—

London—Henry Wilkinson, Thomas Stobbs.*

London Circuit—Thomas Cleghorn, Thomas Crews; Edmund Stoney, Thomas Harmon, superannuated.

Mount Elgin and Muncey—Samuel Rose, whose attention shall be principally directed to the Industrial School; John Sunday, Abraham Sickles.

* There were peculiarities which affected the *London* Circuit for the Conference year 1854-55 which occasioned an exchange between two brethren and led to the calling out of one of the most precious young men who ever exercised his ministry in the Canada Connexion. These matters, as my mind was recalled to them after the text was written, I present in a note. At the beginning of the year, the *Rev. K. Creighton* was appointed to *Bytown*, with the chairmanship of the district. Towards autumn, a sad affliction took place in the family of Mrs. C——, near London, which required her husband to remove thither for the rest of the year. His circumstances would allow him to render some help on Sabbaths to the city circuit; those services were accepted, and the junior minister appointed for London, *Rev. Thos. Stobbs*, was despatched to Bytown to take charge of that important place until the ensuing Conference, while a senior brother was placed in charge of that district by the Conference Special Committee. The removal of the young preacher out of the Town of London occasioned a deficiency of pastoral attention. But one of the best pastors, as I can attest by having him afterwards for my own colleague, was found to replace him. This was the beloved *Joseph L. Sanders*, whose history may be learned from his Conference obituary, which I give entire :—

"Brother Sanders was born in Co''wall, England, in the year 1832. His father and mother were both me   bers of the Wesleyan Methodist Church, thus giving him the advant   s of a pious home. In addition to parental instruction and example '   had the sound Scriptural teaching of the 'ministers of the Parent (nnexion in England; therefore his views of Christianity were in perfect harmony with the standards of our Church. He was never troubled with misgivings or doubts respecting the importance and necessity of experimental religion. At the age of sixteen he gave his   t to God, finding peace and accept-

St. Thomas—William Price, Samuel E. Maudsley.
Port Sarnia—John G. Laird (one wanted).
Strathroy—John K. Williston.
Warwick—To be supplied.
Port Stanley—Francis Chapman.
St. Clair—Solomon Waldron.
Devonshire—John Webster.
Belmont—Richard Phelps.

SAMUEL ROSE,
Chairman of the District.

ance with Him, while listening to the preaching of a local preacher. He soon began to exhort others to seek like precious faith, and was in due time put upon the plan as a local preacher in his native town. While the Superintendent of the Devonport Circuit, England, was negotiating with him to enter the itinerancy there, he received a letter from a friend in Canada, informing him that men were needed here. Regarding this as a providential call, he at once decided to leave all and come to Canada. He arrived here in the fall of 1854, and was at once appointed to assist the late Rev. Henry Wilkinson in the City of London, C.W., where he labored with great acceptability until the Conference of 1855, when he was received on trial and appointed to the Yonge Street Circuit, in the Toronto District. The work, however, proved to be too much for his strength. His health failed ; and at the district meeting of 1856, he requested to be allowed to retire, fully intending to return to his native land ; but after a few months' rest among his attached friends on the Yonge Street Circuit, his health was measurably restored, which led him to change his purpose of leaving Canada, so he went to Belleville, to assist the Rev. John Carroll. From this time he continued to labor with more or less usefulness on the Three Rivers, Bradford, Lloydtown, Weston, Brampton, Whitby, and Oshawa Circuits. On the last-named his health failed again, and a change to an Indian mission, as being less laborious, was deemed desirable. At the end of two years his health was so far restored as to encourage him to ask for an appointment in the regular circuit work. In 1871 he received an appointment to the Baltimore Circuit, in the Cobourg District. During the greater part of the time he was able to do his work with some degree of comfort, and the usual success attended his faithful labors. In the latter part of the year the disease which at last brought him down to the grave began to

37. The assistant preacher at *Sarnia* along with the *Rev. John G. Laird*, according to Cornish's Hand-Book, was *Wm. Hawke*, a chairman's supply, a brother who afterwards placed his name prominently on the roll of the Church's pastorate. Though married, he was young—of average size—a native of Cornwall or Devonshire, England, who had come out to Toronto some time before, and was useful as a local preacher, being one of the efficient laborers who have gone forth from Richmond Street Church.

38. *Warwick* had in some respects a similar, but a very excellent supply—this was *John Wesley Savage*. Like Brother Hawke, he was English; like him, had "given pledge for his good behavior," according to the doctrine of Dr. Franklin, by having a wife and family; and like him, had gone out from Toronto. He was the son of an English Wesleyan minister, brother of the Rev. Wm. Savage, said to be a most soul-saving laborer; and he had been thoroughly educated in the "schools for the preachers' children." His education was not only classical, but commercial: he was an excellent accountant, and had for some time been a bookkeeper in our Connexional Book-room. He had been a lively local preacher, and business and accounts could not extinguish his love to souls or his ardor to join the itinerant battle

appear. His days were numbered,—the messenger had come to take him from his labors to the promised reward. The Master was calling for him, and he *must* go. He, however, had to be made perfect through suffering. In his case, patience had its perfect work. His sufferings were severe, yet not a murmur ever fell from his lips. At times, such was his consciousness of the Divine presence, as to raise him above his bodily sufferings; and, as his end approached, his confidence grew stronger. "There was not a cloud to darken his sky." He could say, "*I am ready* to depart and be with Christ, which is far better." "*Christ is all.*" Thus lived and died Joseph L. Sanders, a brother beloved; in the forty-first year of his age, and eighteenth of his ministry.

against the hosts of sin and darkness. His powerful voice, both for singing and speaking, and his glowing manner, preeminently qualified him to take part in revival services. His personal appearance and manners were excellent; cordiality gave him access to the people's hearts.*

39. The next list we have to present is that of the Chatham District :—

Chatham—Edmund Shepherd, Thomas D. Pearson.
Wardsville—William Ames.
Wallaceburgh—(Joseph Forsythe).
Morpeth—Joseph Hugill (one wanted).
Gosfield—William Dignam.
Sandwich and Windsor—Edward White, Thomas Peacock.
Amherstburg—E. L. Koyle.

EDMUND SHEPHERD,
Chairman of the District.

40. Who shall tell us of the supply to the vacancies in the above list? Brother Hugill, who "wanted" a colleague at

---

* We have referred to a senior brother of the laborer just mentioned, and this is the best time and method to introduce him. *Belmont* had the Rev. Richard Phelps appointed to its charge; but we suspect his health failed, for the next year he was returned as "superannuated." In his place a very vigorous supply was found. This was *William Savage*, a married man, but with a not very large family, and having a most Christian lady for a wife. He was, as will be inferred from what we said of his brother, the son of an English Wesleyan minister, said to be a great revivalist, from whom his sons imbibed their zeal and push. William had quite as good opportunities for education as his brother, and had been brought up to the liberal profession of medicine. He was a long-practised local preacher, and he threw himself into the work with the efficiency of an experienced itinerant. New appointments, new classes, conversions and revivals, and church-building were the order of the day in that circuit, as they have been in every subsequent circuit: joined to these, he espoused and promoted the temperance cause in all its aspects. The next year he was received on trial.

Morpeth, is no longer on earth to answer inquiries; and the chairman himself has long since gone to his account. Alas, that he should have "fainted" before he fell! Early in the year a charge of immorality was brought home to him, and the judiciary of the Church, jealous for its honor, expelled him. The *Rev. John Hutchinson*, whom we have seen admitted into the acknowledged ministry of the body at the preceding Conference, and who had been designated to *Newcastle*, was countermanded and sent to the town at the head of this district.

41. Our next is the Guelph District:—

Guelph—Lewis Warner, Richard Clarke.
Elora—James Armstrong (one wanted).
Berlin and Blenheim—John Williams, Andrew Smith.
Peel—Henry Reid (one wanted); Ezra Adams, superannuated.
Stratford—George Case.
St. Marys—C. W. M. Gilbert.
Clinton—Alexander Campbell.
Goderich—Charles Sylvester, George Cochran.
Mitchell—Lucius Adams.
Kincardine—Wm. Creighton.
Arthur—One to be sent.
Mono—John L. Kerr; William Steer, superannuated.
Erin—To be supplied.
Wellesley—To be supplied.
Grey—John Armstrong, 1st.
Morris—To be supplied.

LEWIS WARNER, *Chairman.*

42. I believe I have found the clue, after some sort, to the solution of the unexplained matters in this district for the year 1854-55. *Elora's* supply, at the beginning of the year, we have reason to believe, was *James E. Dyer*. Though then but a chairman's provision, he was destined to make, so

far as labor, integrity, and success are concerned, one of the "strongest men" in the body. I am sorry that, at this late hour, I discovered that he was appointed to a circuit that year, I have not time to secure precise data for the salient points in his previous life; but I know the man, and gathered some scattered hints from his conversation. I s ll not be far wrong if I say he was of English parents, and possibly, born in England himself, but had lived in early life in one or more of the larger cities of Lower Canada. His energetic organization had exposed him, while in an unregenerated state, to habits which placed him on the verge of ruin. But in one of those powerful revivals, for which Toronto was famous a good many years, he became the partaker of transforming grace, and speedily threw his constitutional energies into efforts for the advancement of the cause of Christ. He had a strong, clear, quick mind, and his rapid speaking was very forceful. His early opportunities may not have been very great, but after conversion, he assiduously improved his mind. Brother Richard Clarke had been appointed to Guelph, but, for some reason, an exchange was made after the year was half gone, and he went to *Elora*, while Brother Dyer was brought to *Guelph*. Dyer's dark hair and skin, with his compact frame, gave augury of the large amount of labor and toil he was to undergo.

43. The vacancy at *Peel* was destined to be filled by a young man not large in stature, and whose appearance was rather indicative of frailty, but who was to perform long years of service in the itinerant field with vigor and spirit. This was *Alexander R. Campbell*, born at Mount Pleasant, September 12th, 1827, but left fatherless at the early age of two years. The cruelties of a drinking stepfather led him to seek his fortune abroad at the age of fourteen. The Township of Blenheim became his residence until he commenced preaching. The heavy occupations of bush farming

were his first employment. Next, by incredible assiduity, he qualified himself for school teaching, which he followed for some years. The hardships of his youth were cheered and ameliorated by converting grace, received in a revival, conducted principally by two excellent local peeachers, Messrs. Jared Kilborn and Dennis Thompson, at the age of eighteen. This brother, who says he "obtained the little knowledge he possessed under great difficulties," had the good fortune, after some years, to marry a lady of education and talent, whose conversation and suggestions, it is not likely, were of any dis-service to him.

44. Mr. Cornish assigns the supply of *Erin* to *James Berry*, a brother of the Rev. Francis Berry, who, like his brother Francis, had labored in some smaller Methodist body —the Episcopal, I surmise. He gave so much satisfaction during this year, that he was received on trial at the next Conference, and received ordination at the one after that; but, as he then left and went to the States, I follow him no further.

45. *Morris* scarcely yet assumed the status of a circuit, but was supplied by the ministration of the *Clinton* preacher, the *Rev. Alexander Campbell*. He was a man of great strength, and could easily perform extra work.* The

---

* Since the above was written, a letter from the brother concerned, which I have recovered from among my papers, gives the true solution. About three years before this time, there fell under my pastoral care in Hamilton, a young man, the son of one of our leading friends in Guelph, who possessed a good mind and unmistakable talents for usefulness, whose reluctance to public efforts I endeavored, with no very great success, to overcome. I was, therefore, glad when I heard, a few years after, that he had entered the work. Here is his own account of the matter:—"On the 4th of July, 1854, Brother Warner met me at a camp-meeting at Bond Head, and he and many others insisted on my going immediately into the work. I had just consecrated myself anew to God; and after spending the night in prayer, with

brother labored on from that time, but he was so hesitating about his call, that he did not allow his name to appear in the Minutes, as received on trial, till 1857. *Arthur* I cannot account for like Morris, it may have been supplied still from the circuit with which it had previously stood attached, for it was a new creation. It may have been supplied, as a chairman's employee, by him who served it the next year (Mr. Lawson), of whom more anon.

46. We proceed to another section of the work, the Owen Sound District:—

Newash and Colpoy's Bay—Conrad Vandusen.
Owen Sound—Samuel Fear; J. Neelands, supernumerary.
St. Vincent—Te be supplied.
Saugeen—Peter Jacobs.
Southampton—George Jacques.
Derby—David Hunt.
Durham—To be supplied.
Walker's Mills—One wanted.
Proton—Thomas Culbert.
Osprey—To be supplied.
Bruce Mines—Joseph Hill.
Garden River—George W. McDougall.
Lake Superior, North Shore—George Blaker.

CONRAD VANDUSEN, *Chairman.*

47. It will be seen that four supplies were required for the district, and I believe they were found; but, even after consulting the chairman for that year, I am not positively certain about them all, or how they were arranged. There were about that time, embracing several years, three or four

some friends, I consented to go. I was at once sent, under Brother A. Campbell's (1st) superintendency, to Clinton. My destination was Morris Mission, then just forming." This letter is signed JOHN HOUGH.

brethren adapted to present usefulness, whom, for various reasons, differing in each case, it was thought well not to bring forward for admission into the Conference, employed in that region as temporary supplies. If "history is philosophy teaching by examples," then the teaching of Canadian Methodist history relative to the employment of supplies, whom it is never intended to introduce into the permanent ministry of the Church, may be very necessary at some times to prevent the work from suffering, yet it is an experiment not unattended with future inconvenience and injury. My own humble opinion is, that if the brother is not likely to answer in all respects for the ministry let him go back as soon as possible to his secular calling; otherwise you may be doing him a great dis-service by taking the active years of his life and then turn him off without any provision for old age; and if he go away discontented, he may throw himself into the arms of some little rival community, of whom there are quite enough, who will avail themselves of his knowledge of our denomination and his influence in it to introduce devisive measures among societies which would be otherwise peaceful. Therefore, if fairly useful, and we need them, they should receive ordination with some prospect of provision for their declining years, or else sent home. The cases of Richard Williams, Wm. Gundy, and George Cooke, to mention no more, may be produced as examples.

48. I do not intend to apply the above remarks to all, if any, of those I am about to mention; but I have to say, that the following brethren seem to have been available to man the breaches in the ranks on the Owen Sound District during the year 1854-55, namely: *Edward Cooke*, who has come into view several times before, a little Englishman, with a pious, honest heart, some unique qualities of mind, which, among other things, fitted him for effective writing on some topics in a proverbial sort of style, but whose manners

were so peculiar and whose idiosyncracies of mind, amounting to such marked eccentricities as to render it unwise to "lay hands" upon. Indeed, he ultimately became subject to seasons of derangement, which in the end removed him from all connection with the work, and I opine that he went to the United States. It is but just to say that this brother never acted the part of a traitor, or betrayed any trust.

49. Next there was a *"Father Atkey,"* a good, instructive, and exemplary local preacher, from England, who was ever ready to advance the cause of Christ in any way he could, and who was sometimes, if not often, a very useful supply on a circuit. He adhered to Wesleyan Methodism till his death, which was a fragrant one, and his name in that region now is as "ointment poured forth," and he has left descendants who sympathize with the cause their father loved.

50. Then, for that year, there was a superior young man, a native of Ireland, tall and sightly enough, but so modest that he was scarcely prepossessing, yet with a good mind and a respectable education, and was also a good preacher, who that year supplied a vacancy under the chairman, and did good service. He was received on trial at the next Conference, and has risen to a very respectable position in our ministry. We are writing of our much-esteemed and loved brother, the *Rev. William Shannon*, to whom we applied for specific data, which has not yet arrived. Subsequent information enables me to say, that he was born at Lough Point, in the Sligo Circuit; knew scores of Irish Wesleyan ministers, who preached and lodged in his father's house; joined class at fourteen, converted at eighteen, and made a leader at once; ten years a Hibernian school teacher; came to Canada with his friends in 1850; settled in the woods of Artemesia in March, 1853; eighteen months after, went into the work.

51. There is yet another to mention. There are in many

of our circuits gifted local preachers, who, had they abstained from marriage, and offered themselves for the full ministry of the Word in youth, and assiduously cultivated their minds while ductile and susceptible, would have risen to eminence as local preachers, but who have let the golden opportunity pass by. They love preaching, and render themselves very useful in their several circuits ; and while the geniality and unsuspiciousness of youth continue, they are willing and amiable auxiliaries of the circuit preachers. But after a time they begin to value their own labors very highly, and think that they are not properly appreciated. They grow into the habit of criticising and depreciating the regular pastors, and generally stand opposed to their receiving sufficient support, citing their own gratuitous labors. In such a case as this they must receive more occupation, or "Satan" will "find some mischief still for their idle hands to do." The brother I am about to introduce was of this kind. He was a Bay Quinte man, a Palatine, the son-in-law of one of the early pillars of the Church ; he was a gifted, gracious young man when an exhorter and in the early days of his local preaching, but gradually he fell into the spirit and habits I have described. His family grew up and were settled in life; he thought he might be useful in a wider sphere, and others thought so too. He was consequently put in charge of a circuit, and employed for some years—usefully, I believe—and could he have received ordination he would probably have been content ; and I am one of those who think it a pity he could not have received it, and been utilized to the Church. But the majority voted against his reception into the Conference. He was disgusted, and other arms were open to receive him; he united with a section of Colonial Methodism, which, unhappily, cherishes and magnifies an old feud against the great central body, which has embittered their own spirits and often placed us in a disparaging light. The reader will not be surprised to learn, that wherever he afterwards went he showed anything but a friendly spirit towards " the mother that bore him." I am writing of *Peter Empey*, who was one of the supplies indicated for the year.

52. There was yet another, whom I ought, perhaps, to have mentioned before. He was a married man, with one child, but young, who was called out as a chairman's supply, with the expectation that he would become an acceptable and permanent laborer in the ministry, which he did become. He had a very commanding, handsome person, a pleasant elocution, and all the elements of a preacher above mediocrity, which he became. I am writing of *Bro. W. R. Dyre*, who gave me his antecedents, but, now they are wanted, I cannot fully recall them. That he was a Canadian and trained in the Wesleyan Church I am sure, but further, till more inquiry, I cannot go.

53. I have mentioned five disposable men, and but four vacancies. It is likely that Mr. Atkey was not employed this year. How, then, shall we distribute the other four? The chairman says that *Mr. Empy* supplied *St. Vincent*, which is most likely correct; but while he says E. Cooke supplied *Osprey*, Mr. Cornish gives it to *Mr. Shannon*. And to the correctness of this last I incline, because Mr. C. obtained his information from DANSE'S REGISTER, or the brethren themselves. The chairman gives *Walker's Mills* to *Mr. Dyre*. These conclusions would throw *Edward Cooke* on to *Durham*. Thus, between Conference preachers and hired locals, was the district supplied.

54. The next was the Barrie District :—

Barrie—John Douse, John S. Clarke.
Bradford—William Young, Richard J. Foreman.
Cookstown—Joel Briggs.
Newmarket—William Willoughby, William McDonagh.

Holland Landing—Andrew Edwards.
Snake Island—To be supplied.
Brock—George T. Richardson.
Rama—Horace Dean.
Orillia—To be supplied.
Penetanguishene—Stephen Brownell.
Beausoliel and French River—To be supplied.
Collingwood Harbor—Edward Sallows.

JOHN DOUSE, *Chairman.*

55. There were only three vacancies in this small district, and two of them such as were usually provided for by temporary expedients. *Beausoliel, &c.*, were likely provided for by some gifted Indian brother, of whom there were several, in various relationships, in the employ of the missionary department of the Church. Good *Bro. Edwards*, at *Holland Landing*, most likely gave the Snake Island Indians all the regular pastoral oversight they had from the ministry; the rest would be afforded by the devoted teacher, Mr. Law, and the gifted Indian officials. As to *Orillia*, it was supplied by one of the useful young men who had swarmed out of Richmond Street Church, Toronto. This was the stout and enduring, but very pious and devout-spirited *Jabez Bunting Keough*, brother of the now *Rev. Thomas Keough*. His having received the name of the great Methodist sage and administrator, Jabez Bunting, was not merely because of his parents' pious admiration of that great man, but because they were lineally descended, on the maternal side, from the family of that good man. The settlement of the family in a bush neighborhood while the boy was of a tender age was the means of depriving young Jabez of some educational advantages which others of the family had enjoyed. I have reason to believe that Leeds, Canada East, had proved his spiritual birthplace, and that the advantages of Toronto had

been the means of quickening him into a higher state of religious enjoyment. The natural slowness of his mind, and deliberateness in speaking, did not at first promise much for him, considered merely as a pulpit man; but his deep experience of the things of God, and the unction that rested on him, compensated for this lack, and diligent and patient study, and no less than three years at Victoria College as a Conference student, went far to supply the lack itself. For prudence, piety, and pastoral care, he was to prove entirely unexceptionable.

56. Our next stage will comprise the stations of the Cobourg District :—

Cobourg—George H. Davis, Samuel S. Nelles, A.M., Principal of Victoria College; Samuel D. Rice, Governor; James Taylor, John Shaw, students; John Beatty, superannuated.

Port Hope—Joseph W. McCollum, William Tomlin.

Bowmanville—Thomas Cosford, John Mills.

Newcastle—John Hutchinson.

Cartwright and Scugog—Thomas Hanna (one to be sent).

Millbrook—James Hughes (one to be sent); Moses Blackstock, supernumerary.

Peterborough—William H. Poole.

Mud Lake*—John Sanderson.

Rice Lake—William Herkimer.

Alderville—James Musgrove, whose attention shall be principally directed to the Industrial School; William Case, with permission to visit different parts of the work, as his health and circumstances may permit.

Colborne—James G. Witted.

* Mr. Cornish's Hand-Book says that *James A. Iveson* labored on that mission during the year 1854-55, but whether in *Mr. Sanderson's* place or as his assistant we have not now time to learn.

Lindsay—John C. Osborne, who will exchange with the minister at Metcalfe once in six weeks; Garrett J. Dingman.

Metcalfe—To be supplied.

Norwood—George Carr, John Fawcett.

JAMES MUSGROVE, *Chairman*.

57. The first deficiency in the number of preachers required was in Lindsay, whose Superintendent was the *Rev. Thomas Hanna*. An exceedingly well-informed and active member of the district at that time, the Rev. James Hughes, informs us by letter: "T. Hanna was alone in Lindsay both in 1853-54 and 1854-55." This settles the matter for this year, and confirms my supposition for the year before.

58. *Millbrooke* was the next place where there was a vacancy. The then Superintendent, Mr. Hughes, tells me that *Samuel Down* was his assistant. For this I was not prepared, supposing that Mr. Down was not employed till a year later. I have therefore learned this too late to acquire a knowledge of the facts of Bro. D.'s previous history definitely. But I know enough of this good brother to be safe in saying: He was a native of England, of either Devonshire or Cornwall. In that hotbed of Methodism he was warmed into spiritual and official life. He possessed a mind with a strong proclivity for theological studies, in which he afterwards became both profound and accurate. His mind and manners were sober and Christian-like. He was calm, self-possessed, and correct in speaking, and if his address had been as impassioned as it was solemn and impressive, his ministry would have been as attracting as it was respectable. He was destined to be a quiet, faithful laborer in circuits where his ability was not always appreciated. Mr. Down was in person tall, intellectual-looking, with light curly hair,

59. *Metcalfe* was provided for by a chairman's supply, a married man, but without children, and his wife was a capable, worthy person. He was a man of superior personal beauty; alas! perhaps too much so. A man who, in his slap-dash way, acquired the fame of working up his circuits, but who, in the end, grossly wronged his wife and disgraced the cause; and I shall abstain from polluting my pages with his name.

60. These were all the vacancies; and all I have further to remark is, that for some reason—unless, perhaps, because he was the better preacher, and more qualified for the place —*Mr. Dingman* was changed through the year from *Lindsay* to *Norwood*, and Mr. Slater's colleague at the latter place, who had been there the preceding year, sent to *Lindsay.*

61. We take another step eastward, in the Provincial Connexion, and come to the Belleville District :—

Belleville—George Young.
Consecon—Michael Fawcett, Charles Taggart; C. R. Allison, superannuated.
Picton –J. C. Slater, William Bryers; Gilbert Miller, Daniel McMullen, supernumeraries.
Sidney—John Lever (one to be sent).
Brighton—William McFadden, Thomas Woolsey.
Demorestville—Vincent B. Howard.
Shannonville—Peter German.
Hungerford—Nelson Brown.
Madoc—Michael Baxter; Stephen Miles, superannuated.
Rawdon—John Black.
Percy and Seymour—W. H. Williams, Jay Youmans.

WILLIAM McFADDEN,
Chairman.

62. There was but one vacancy in the district, and that was satisfactorily supplied. The vacancy was the second

preacher's place on the old *Sidney* Circuit. It was supplied by a young Irish Canadian, born near Perth, and brought into the Methodist faith. He was not converted, however, till the family moved westward from their first Canadian home. This event took place about the age of eighteen. He showed a vehement zeal for God from the time he first tasted of His love, and proved to have talents as well as zeal. He was gifted, voluble, and fervent in spirit, hortatory and awakening. These gifts were apparently enhanced by physical strength and energy, and constitutional vehemence. He was furnished with all that was comprised in an English education: he held a first-class certificate, and had been a popular and successful school-teacher. He was medium in height, but his weight was greatly beyond his apparent size; and when we say he was a blonde, with curly hair and beard, there are many who will know that I am describing *David A. Johnston.* He succeeded well on his circuit, and staid there a second year. He was the means of promoting many revivals.

63. Our next stride eastward brings us to the Kingston District :—

Kingston—John Ryerson, Geo. Douglas, Geo. McRitchie; Henry Byers, supernumerary.
Napanee—George F. Playter (to be supplied).
Wilton—John A. Williams, Abraham Dayman.
Bath and Amherst Isle—George Beynon, Aaron Miller.
Waterloo—William Philp.
Gananoque—Charles Turver.
Newborough—Robert Robinson (one to be sent).
Farmersville—David Clappison, J. W. Germain.
Newburg—Charles Fish; I. B. Aylsworth, supernumerary.
Sheffield—To be supplied.

Hinchinbrook—John D. Pugh.
Storrington—To be supplied.

JOHN RYERSON, Co-Delegate,
Chairman.

N. B.—Rev. S. D. Rice will take charge of this district until the co-Delegate returns from Hudson Bay.

64. There were four laborers required to fill the blanks in the printed list of stations for this district. I am morally certain they were all supplied; but by whom two of the places were supplied at this writing I cannot say. *Sheffield* was supplied by a *Bro. William Briden*, a married man, and a thorough Englishman. He had been a laborer on a circuit as a hired local preacher in England itself, and I am quite sure he so labored in Canada, before being received on trial. Though married, he was young and blooming. A compact, strong, healthy man was he, well adapted to the toils of the Canadian itinerancy. He possessed an active, fair mind, which, whatever he may have lacked, had been carefully cultivated, with a view to usefulness in his ministerial work. An amiable man, a considerate pastor, and a plain, sound preacher was William Briden.

65. Of the supply for *Storrington*, we are certain this time. Just remember that "Battersea" is a village in the Township of *Storrington*, and that the mission at first took its name from the Township, and afterwards from the village, and all that is said in the obituary, which I am about to quote, will be intelligible. And I may attest, that as far as I know, that the brother referred to was all that was said by those entrusted to draw up the following statements :—

"*James Thompson* was born at Switzerville, on the Newburg Circuit, on the 24th of September, 1829, and converted to God on the 16th of November, 1840.

"From the time of his conversion, till his entrance into

the ministry, and—as his brethren know—until his death, his life was blameless. His voice was always heard in prayer-meeting. He never missed his class but once when at home and able to be present. Very soon after his conversion, feeling the importance of mental culture, in order to the ministry of the Word in connection with our Church, he applied himself faithfully to study, and in August, 1834, was sent to the Battersea mission. His next Circuit was Bradford. He was then sent to College for two years, after which he labored on the following Circuits in this order: Napanee, Brewer's Mills, Oil Springs, Milford, and Rednerville, where he finally broke down in health from overwork, and was obliged to superannuate. From Rednerville he removed to Napanee, and there, so far as God gave him strength, he labored with great zeal and fidelity until his death; but, though early called from labor to reward, it was only after he had done a work of deep and abiding value to the Church of God.

"That life is long which answers life's great end."

"On all his Circuits he was favored with extensive revivals, or he prepared the ground for them. The reasons of his success were as follows: he had great singleness of purpose, he was firm in his adherence to what he bel'eved to be right, and faithful in his denunciation of all he believed to be wrong. His love for his Master and his work was absorbing. He was converted to God, and knew it. He had a profound conviction that he was called of God to preach the Gospel, and to fight with every form of evil about him. He believed himself guided of God habitually. He served the Lord Christ, and counting himself the servant of the Church, for Jesus' sake gladly gave to the promotion of its interest all his energies, and all his time, and when laid aside, he was not content with past achievements, but because he loved his Master and the souls of men, he was "instant in season and out of season," perpetually planning new works. And seeing what obstructions intemperance and ignorance offered to the spread of religion, he labored for the overthrow of the license system, and for the introduction of Methodist literature into the homes of the people."

66. We pass to the next division of the work, the Brockville District.

Brockville—Richard Whiting.
Prescott—James Gray.
Maitland—Asahel Hurlburt, Edwin Peake.
Perth—David C. M'Dowell.
Kemptville—James Greener. To be supplied. Henry Shaler, superannuated.
Matilda—Francis Coleman. One to be sent.
Smith's Falls—Sylvester Hurlburt; Wm. Brown, Supernumerary.
Carleton-Place—Joseph Reynolds, William Braden.
Packenham—John Armstrong 2nd.
Merrickville—David Jennings.
Cornwall—John Howes, Robert Hobbs.
Winchester—Robert Brewster.
Sherbrooke—David Hardie; Alvah Adams, Superannuated.

ASAHEL HURLBURT,
Chairman of the District.

67. For reasons, hereafter to be assigned, I reserve annotations on this district till a future page, and present the stations of the Bytown District :—

Bytown—Kennedy Creighton.
Aylmer—William McGill.
Richmond—William Coleman, Henry M'Dowell.
St. Andrew's—Thomas W. Constable, William Scales.
L'Orignal—William Morton, Andrew Armstrong.

Cavignall—One to be sent.
Lochaber—William Burns.
Osgood—Wm. M. Pattyson. One to be sent.
Gatineau—Silas Huntingdon.
Clarendon and Portage-du-Forte—Luther Houghton. One to be sent.
Westmeath—Richard Hammond.
Huntley—Thomas McMullen.
Grenville—To be supplied.

KENNEDY CREIGHTON,
Chairman of the District.

68. In the above are four supplies required. Three of them, at least, we can account for, and the other may turn up as we pass on. *Cavignall* was supplied by a brother *Wm. T. Hewitt*, a middle-aged, if not elderly man, a native of Yorkshire, England, who had been a zealous and useful local preacher, at first in his own country, and afterwards in Bytown and vicinity. His zeal and usefulness suggested his being employed. If I am not much mistaken this is not the first vacancy he supplied. He was not a star of the first magnitude, but the star made up in heat what it wanted in brilliancy.

69. The Rev. Wm. M. Pattyson's colleague at *Osgoode* was an Irishman like himself, large, strong, and well-proportioned, with dark hair. If converted in his native country, he had been quickened into usefulness in one of the Canada East Circuits—Huntingdon, I think—whence he had been brought up to supply this vacancy. In those days his zeal and activity compensated for the experience and mental furniture which he had not yet had time to acquire. He was destined to make a diligent student and a painstaking laborer. This was the commencement of our stalwart friend *John A. Dowler*. He was a student at the Durham Academy.

70. Of the second preacher at *Clarendon*, if any, sent to

the aid of Brother Luther Houghton, we are not informed; but, fortunately, we can speak more deffinitely of *Grenville*. Many a first-class minister has been raised up in the pious, though, some would say, aristocratic, St. James Street society. Some time before our present date, a young man of Scotch-Presbyterian parents, Calvinistically trained, and educated in the first stages of classical learning, had been converted, if not wrongly informed, in one of Mr. Caughey's series of revival services, and despite the necessary sacrifice of early religious associations, he cast in his lot with the Methodists, whose social meetings soon develop his speaking talents, which were naturally good; and being full of zeal and unction from on high, he began to preach with a good degree of power. This led to his employment on a circuit in this tentative way, which proved no vain experiment. All who knew him, and he is extensively known, will believe this when I say, I am writing of the *Rev. James Roy, A.M.*, who has since been city preacher, college professor, &c. These two last-named brethren were amongst the first benefits accruing to the Canada West section of Methodism, from its union with that of Canada East.

71. There were twenty-eight vacancies in the Upper Province, and I have accounted for nineteen of them. To supply the remaining nine I have only three, believed to have travelled that year somewhere in that section of the work. These were: 1st, *David Costello*, of whom I know nothing; 2nd, *W. M. C. Luke*, whose early promise was followed by a mournful termination; and 3rd, excellent *James Masson*, whom it is strange I cannot locate, for I saw him at the Book-room that year on his downward way to his field of labor somewhere in the lower part of the Province—early labors which he and I so often talked over; and hurry does not now enable me to consult him. He was a Scotch-Presbyterian by birth and early training, but lived till he was twenty-four or twenty-

five years of age before he knew God experimentally. He lived on the north of Dundas Street, and was induced to attend revival services in one of the churches on the Nelson Circuit, where he and many other young men were converted to God. He had not been very remarkably favored with education before he began to study for the ministry, but he was, like all of his nationality, observing, and a considerable reader. His natural adaptations for the ministry were such, that had he not been unambitious, would have made him a more advanced man, forward as he is, than he has become. His quick perceptions, ready appropriation of passing ideas, good voice, easy utterance, rich doric accent, skill in analysis and sermonizing, calmness and self-possession in the pulpit, and ready elocution, made him the acceptable preacher from the first, and in a few years placed him among the very best. His affability and communicativeness with the people made him truly acceptable as a pastor; whether he taxed himself as slavishly as some is not for me to say. At the time of his starting, he must have been almost twenty-six years of age, and, though plain in his appearance, he was agreeable and prepossessing in intercourse with others. He was a blonde, long-vissaged, and above the medium size. But whither did he go the first year? I surmise to fill either the vacancy on the *Matilda* Circuit or that on the *Kemptville*, where he labored the following two years.

72. Another brother ought to be mentioned in this category before we close. A year or so before this time, a good sound local preacher from England, *via* Prince Edward's Island, made himself known to me in Hamilton, inquiring for some place to commence his business of blacksmithing. He fell somewhere within Brother Warner's jurisdiction, and dear John Williams falling at his post during this year, this brother was applied to to supply his place on the *Berlin* and *Blenheim* Circuit, and went. He was so satisfactory as

to be received on trial the next year, and to be continued in the work as a faithful laborer ever since. This was the way our *Brother Richard Punch* came to be a travelling preacher.

73. The urgent demand for "copy" on the part of my printer, obliged me to close the account relative to some brethren before I had received the answer to my inquiries concerning them. The needed information having arrived, I am induced to put the additional facts in a paragraph by themselves, arranged in alphabetical order :—

(1) The data furnished by the *Rev. Wm. Hawke*, summarized, amounts to these items. He was born in Lostwithiel, Cornwall, England, August 21st, 1832, and converted in the same place, in his eighteenth year, under the ministry of the Rev. Richard Whiting, then a local preacher, with whom and the now deceased Francis Chapman, Mr. Hawke met in class. Being slow to consent, he had only been a local preacher three years before his coming to Canada. The rest has been stated.

(2) The furnished items concerning the *Rev. George Jacques* are these: He was born in the parish of Frodingham, Lincolnshire, England; was brought up in the Church of England, but remained without a radical conversion until his twenty-first year, which occurred in the ordinary services of the Wesleyan Chapel in the Village of Sculthorpe, in the Brigg Circuit. He began to exhort in his own country, and saw a great revival. In 1851 he came to Canada and settled in Artemesia, where he soon became both an exhorter and afterwards a local preacher, and in February, 1854, was sent by the Rev. Conrad Vandusen, then Chairman of the Owen Sound District, as a supply to Durham, till the Conference of that year, when he was received on trial.

(3) The *Rev. L. O. Rice* says of his two two years at *Dunville*, namely, 1854-55 and '55-56, "I had no colleague

the first year. The Chairman sent me one the second year, 55-56, *George B. Johnstone.* He staid six months and left. Brother *Jacob Kennedy,* of Smithville, supplied for the remainder of the year. During 1856-57, I had no supply."

(4) *Rev. George L. Richardson,* in addition to what I have given, enables me more precisely to state that he was born in Oakhampton, Devonshire, removed with his parents to St. Austle, Cornwall, when four years of age; was converted when thirteen years old, January 1836, under the ministry of Rev. H. W. Williams (now Dr. Williams), Secretary of the British Conference. Was put on the Local Preachers' Plan when eighteen years of age, came to Canada in the summer of 1853, to enter the ministry, and was sent to *Orillia* by Dr. Wood and Rev. J. Douse, in February, 1854, till the ensuing Conference; when he was received on trial.

(5) *John Wesley Savage* informs me that his father was connected with the Wesleyan Ministry forty six years, and was a member of the legal hundred. J. W. himself began to labor on the plan as an exhorter in 1848-49, and was a local preacher in two several circuits after that. He came to Canada in 1854, and was sent to *Warwick.* Says he has had camp-meetings and revivals on all his circuits. Is in the midst of a revival now.

(6) *Wm. Scales* was indeed born in " *Lincolnshire,*" not in " Epworth," but at Westwoodside, in the Isle of Axholme, February 13th, 1818. "Born again," in 1832. Began to preach at the age of nineteen, and was a local preacher sixteen years and three months.

74. The stations for Canada East were put all together, as for one great district, but no chairman or financial secretary was appointed. Things were puposely left in that state till after the ensuing British Conference should have affirmed the whole proceeding. I do not give them *in*

extenso now, but leave them till after the work in that section was subdivided into the then several districts. I may remark, however, at this stage, that it was quite observable, that a large infusion of Canada Conference men was injected into Canada East. Thus, to particularize, *Montreal Centre* received *Rev. Wellington Jeffers; Quebec, Rev. Wm. Pollard; St. Johns, Rev. John Carroll;* second preacher for *Odelltown* and *Hemmingford, Rev. John S. Evans; Huntingdon, Isaac Barber;* and *Russeltown, Richard Wilson.*

75. In the *Guardian* of the 13th of September, 1854, the following manifesto was put forth under the sanction of the Conference authorities, which speaks for itself:—

CANADA EAST.

"The English Conference having finally ratified the Union of the Eastern Canadian Wesleyan Missions with the Canada West Conference, in May last the brethren assembled at their Annual District Meeting recommended the division of the Eastern Canada work into three separate districts. A copy of this, signed by the Rev. J. Borland, Secretary, having received the sanction of our Committee at the late Belleville Conference, it is thought advisable, for the welfare of the Church of God in that part of the Province, that this arrangement should go into immediate operation. From this date the following will be the ecclesiastical relationship of each minister, circuit, and mission in Lower Canada for the

MONTREAL CIRCUIT.

Montreal Centre—Wellington Jeffers.
   Do.   *East*—William Scott.
   Do.   *West*—James H. Bishop.
Rawdon—Erastus Hurlburt.
St. John's—John Carroll.
Chambly—John Douglass, Supernumerary.
Odell Town—James Brock.

Hemmingford—John S. Evans.

Odelltown and *Hemmingford* Circuits are worked together for the present year.

Russelltown—Richard Wilson.

Huntngdon—Isaac Barber.

JOHN CARROLL, *Chairman*.

QUEBEC DISTRICT.

Quebec—William Pollard.
Point Levi—To be supplied.
Three Rivers—Charles De Wolfe, A.M.
Leeds—John Armstrong.
Chaudiere—To be supplied.
Melbourne—Malcolm McDonald.
Danville—To be supplied.
Sherbrooke—Benjamin Slight, A.M.
Eaton—Robert Graham.
Dudswell—To be supplied.

BENJAMIN SLIGHT, A.M., *Chairman*.

STANSTEAD DISTRICT.

Stanstead—John Tomkins.
Hatley and Compton—John B. Selley.
Coaticoke—John Pugh.
Shefford—Gifford Dorey.
Granby—Barnabas Hitchcock.

These two circuits are worked together for the present year.

Dunham—Rufus A. Flanders, Samuel E. Philips; E. S. Ingall, Supernumerary.
Sutton—To be supplied.
St. Armand—James Norris.
Clarenceville—Henry Tomkins.

JOHN TOMKINS, *Chairman*."

76. It will be seen, by casting the eye over this list of stations, that there were four vacancies in the three dis-

tricts, or rather in two, for there were none in the Montreal District—three of which were in one of them, and only one in the other. The Quebec District, in which the three vacancies existed, obtained a supply for one of them; and the other three in those two districts, so far as I could learn, went unsupplied. Some portions of the ground they embraced no doubt continued to receive some attention from the minister of the circuit to which they had severally belonged previously.

77. The place supplied in the *Quebec* District was *Point Levi*. How, when, and by whom will appear from the following letter addressed to me some years ago. The writer of this epistle was dapper in person, with dark hair, but not dark-skinned. He is now known to many, from the east to the extreme west. The letter was signed *Edward Cragg* :—

"TYRCONNEL, April 7th, 1873.

"DEAR SIR AND BROTHER,—As you have no acquaintance with me, it would perhaps be well to give you an item or two of information. I was born in the town of Kendal, England, 1829; converted to God in 1843; commenced to call sinners to repentance in 1851; a candidate for the regular work of the ministry in 1853, but was recommended by the Rev. J. Rigg, Chairman of the Macclesfield District, to join the Canada Conference. *The agitation was then in full blast in England.* Accordingly I came out in October, 1854; travelled the remainder of the year under the chairman, as assistant to the Rev. W. Pollard, in Quebec. At the Conference of 1855, was sent to the Chaudiere, in 1856 to Dudswell, but in June of that year was requested by Dr. Wood to take the place of a young man who had suddenly deserted his post at Millbrook. Accordingly, in the depth of winter, I drove four hundred miles in a jumper specially made for the occasion. In 1857, was requested for Newcastle."

78. One of the first matters that will devolve upon us will be, to follow the " ambassadors sent unto the heathen," and to see how they were distributed. The stations for that

north-western section of the work (the Hudson Bay and Rocky Mountains District) were as follows :—

Norway House, Lake Winnipeg—Thomas Hurlburt.
Oxford House—Robert Brooking.
Lac La Pluie—Allen Salt.
Edmonton and Rocky Mountains—Henry Steinhaur.

THOMAS HURLBURT,
Chairman of the District.

79. The missionary party consisted of four gentlemen, namely, the *Revs. John Ryerson, Thomas Hurlburt, Robert Brooking*, and *Allen Salt*. Four more considerable men are seldom combined in one enterprise. Mr. Ryerson—who of course was only going for a time as their guide, as the explorer of the country, and as the diplomatist (if any were needed) with the officers and agents of the Hudson Bay Company—though still a vigorous man, had been no less than thirty-four years in the itinerant work in Canada, the most of the time embracing a period when it was no trifle to be an itinerant preacher, about ten years of which time he had been a travelling chairman, or presiding elder, whose rounds of travel were the most extensive; had been a regnant mind in the infant Conference during at least three-fourths of this time; and up till that date not the least breath of suspicion had been breathed against his moral habits or character.

80. The next member of the missionary party was almost as remarkable a man—at least, in his own particular way. This was *Mr. Hurlburt*. He, like his brother Ryerson, was one of an old Canadian family, and one of as large a band of preaching brothers as the other. He, too, had been a long time in the work—since his outset, not less than a quarter of a century—and besides that, his work had been peculiar and trying: almost wholly among the Indians, varying from school-teaching, at Grape Island and Muncey-

town, to pioneering along the rocky northern shores of the great lakes; to traversing a presiding elder's district across mighty stretches of prairie embraced within the vast boundaries of the "Indian Annual Conference." He had mastered the Chippewa with its dialects, and learned to hold verbal intercourse with the Cherokees, Chickasaws, and I know not what other tribes, as he was destined to do among the Crees and other wild tribes of the far north-west. He was going out as the Superintendent of the isolated missions of that region.

81. *Mr. Brooking* also was scarcely less remarkable in his own way. He was from Old England, but he had been a missionary all his public life, beginning with the coast and interior of Western Africa, among savages of the most loathsome and bloodthirsty character, where he had remained six years. His next remove was to Canada, to be a missionary among the Ojibways at Rice Lake and of St. Clair. Whatever his facility in acquiring their language, he knew the habits and prejudices of untutored men to an extent which must have furnished him with great facilities in dealing with the savage mind.

82. If two of these gentlemen knew the aboriginal mind, the third was one to whom that mind was indigenous, only that it was expanded, elevated, and improved by Christianity and Christian civilization. Perhaps *Mr. Salt* was not the least respectable and important man among them—a gentleman in whom all the qualities of a commanding manhood united—that is, everything that relates to physical advantages, qualities of mind, and special adaptation to his appointed vocation. But we will not repeat our sketch of him on a former page.

83. The missionary party, embracing the four gentlemen mentioned, and Mesdames Hurlburt, Brooking, and Salt, with some children, availed themselves of steamboat navi-

gation to Fort William, after which they took to smaller craft, and finally to the inevitable canoe, threading many streams, running rapids, crossing portages, and tossing on the boisterous inland lakes. On the way they met with Sir George Simpson, the Governor of St. Rupert's Land, on the Savan River, on his downward way to Montreal, accompanied by Mr. Hopkins, his private secretary. His Excellency informed them that a house had been provided for Mr. Salt and his family at Lac La Pluie (or "Rainy Lake"), and that the Honorable Hudson Bay Company had granted £50 ($200) per annum to each of the Wesleyan Missions in the Territory.

84. Mr. Salt was the first one of the missionaries who arrived at his post. According to Sir George's promise, things were found in readiness, so far as temporal comforts were concerned; but the prospects of success among the Indians themselves, at the opening of his efforts, did not seem to be great. It was a lonely thing for him and family to be set down there, in a place isolated and uninviting. Messrs. Hurlburt and Brooking, with their wives, remained there twenty-four hours, to attend to some necessary matters, but Mr. Ryerson went on. His parting with his brother Salt was very tender. He says of him : " As a good man and Christian minister, I very much esteem Mr. Salt. He grew daily in my affections and confidence during the month of our journeying together."

85. The voyageurs passed on, sojourning some time in the Red River country, which struck the observant eye of the leader of the party even then as necessary to be occupied by the denomination, in order to an effectual prosecution of our missions in the country.

86. Thence they trended away north-westward, through the great Winnipeg Lake, into and through Play Green Lake; thence up the Lach River, twenty-four miles, to the old

establishment of Norway House, where they were kindly received by Mr. Barnston, the Hudson Bay Company's factor. Two miles from the fort was situated the Rossville Wesleyan Mission, planted by the indefatigable Jas. Evans, who had been removed to his account. Amid the general destitution that had prevailed among the Wesleyan missions of that region, occasioned by the mishaps and removal of the devoted Barnley, the temporary removal to England and death, while there, of Mr. Evans, and the return of Peter Jacobs to Canada, this mission had been occupied by the last surviving, or remaining, European missionary, *Mr. Mason*, and, therefore, was kept in repair. Now this one also had seceded from the enterprise, and had sought ordination from the Anglican Bishop of St. Rupert's Land, so that the missionary party came just in time to save the Wesleyan missions from extinction. *Mr. Hurlburt*, the chairman of this missionary district, was placed at this central mission. Of his situation Mr. Ryerson says:—" The local situation of the place is remarkably pleasant, and the land very rich and productive. The garden looks beautiful; it is large and full of the most useful vegetables, all of which are in fine order and growing most luxuriantly. There is also a field of potatoes that looks remarkably well, so that Mr. Hurlburt, instead of finding himself in a waste, howling wilderness, living on pemmican or buffalo tallow, and surrounded with savages and eaten up by musquitoes, finds himself in a most comfortable and well-furnished parsonage, surrounded with not only the necessaries, but even the luxuries of life, and with a Christian society, far advanced in knowledge and practical piety. Indeed, there is no Indian mission in Canada which, for pleasantness of situation and means of domestic comfort, will compare with Rossville Mission."

87. Messrs. Ryerson, Brooking (with his wife and child), and Mr. Henry Steinhaur, a native missionary whom they

met by the way, leaving Rossville and pursuing their voyage northward, perhaps bearing east, two hundred and fifty miles further, they (by August the 20th, 1854) arrived at *Oxford House*, which was Mr. Brooking's station, displacing Mr. Steinhaur, who was to remove to *Edmonton*, under the Rocky Mountains.

88. Mr. Brooking, however, needing supplies, and Mr. Steinhaur coming out to civilization for a time to obtain ordination and to assist in missionary anniversaries, the whole party accompanied Mr. Ryerson to York Factory, on the shores of the Hudson Bay, where he and a number from the colony were to sail by the annual ship for England once more.

89. After a short sojourn in England, Messrs. Ryerson and Steinhaur re-crossed the Atlantic to Canada, the former to resume his duties as pastor at Kingston, Chairman of the Kingston District, and to attend to the many Connexional engagements which devolved upon him as the President's representative in a great many cases. Mr. Steinhaur spent the intermediate time between his return and the ensuing Conference of 1855 (where he received ordination) in visiting his native brethren in this Province and attending various missionary anniversaries.

90. It is fitting that a short notice of this brother should here be given. He was a thorough Indian, of the Credit band, and one of the first little boys in the Mission School at that place. On condition of assuming his name, Henry Steinhaur, a gentleman in the United States, had defrayed the expenses of his education for a number of years. The liberal part of it had begun, if I mistake not, at either Cazenovia, or Lima, New York, and after the opening of the Upper Canada Academy, it had been carried on in that institution till 1840, at which time the Rev. James Evans went to the North-west, and Steinhaur, along with Peter

Jacobs, was induced to accompany him. In that country he married and remained, and performed at least *quasi* missionary services at various posts for the long-intervening fourteen years. He received ordination at the London Conference in 1855, and accompanied the Rev. Thomas Woolsey to take charge of the work vacated by the Rev. William Rundle in the *Saskatchewan* and *Rocky Mountain* department of it. Mr. S. was rather shorter in stature than most of his nation, and stouter. He had proved himself enduring physically, and reliable in all respects.

91. We must now see what report we can make of the labors and experiences of this important climacteric year.

92. The summer was improved by holding not less than a dozen camp-meetings, ranging from one end of the Upper Province to the other, and from south to north: the *Bradford, Owen Sound, Toronto District, Guelph District, Peel, Glanford, Dunnville, Brampton,* and *Napanee Circuits* gave name to these meetings. *Meetings* followed each other in rapid succession, if they were not in full blast at the same time, covering the summer months from early in June till late in September; and, if we may judge from the glowing accounts of them from their promoters and lookers on, from ministers and lay brethren, they were seasons of power and delight while in progress, and of lasting influence for good after they were over.

93. Revivals in the several circuits, whether arising from the camp-meetings, promoted by special services arising in the ordinary ministrations of the word, or brought about by some extraordinary intervention of Providence, were of repeated and widespread occurrence, and of varied character and effect, whether calm or boisterous, adding tens or adding scores to the Church.

94. We are almost afraid to try to particularize all the places from which good news came; suffice to say there were

sixty converts in *Osgoode,* and yet we hear from it a second time ; a powerful revival in *Guelph,* twice heard from ; twenty conversions and more in *Milton; Clarendon* and *Portage du Fort* were twice heard from, from which revival correspondence we learn that *Bro. Houghton* had a helper the last two-thirds of the year, in the person of the young *Bro. William Bradin; Peel* partakes largely; *Waterloo, Cookstown, Quebec, Kemptville, Sherbrooke, Storrington,* and *Belleville,* under the successful *George Young,* are revived and blessed ; the London Township Circuit receives forty at a time; fifty or sixty at *Russeltown,* and revivals in *Lochaber, St. George, Consecon,* and *Walsingham* Circuits. And yet we have not enumerated them all, much less particularized their blessed details.

95. Missionary meeting or anniversary news, which was full and glowing, mingled the revival of the work at home with the prospect of extending it abroad, and these came from the far east and the far west, from north and south, from the centre and the circumference of the work.

96. We have not recorded or noted all the churches and chapels projected, finished, enlarged, or opened in their order, and with minuteness ; but we know such things were rejoiced over in *Aurora, Yorkville, Ingersoll, Dunnville, Mars Couche, Barrie, London, Plainville, King, Temperance Mills,* &c., &c..

97. There were matters miscellaneous not without interest : The Rev. Dr. Green returned from England and the British Conference September, the 16th, and gave a pleasing account of his visit in a series of letters in the *Guardian.* A *Christian Union Convention,* embracing a meeting of converted Indians from various Protestant missions, which met at Onondagua, near Syracuse, New York, was attended

by Rev. Peter Jones, who gave a cheering report of it through the Connexional organ.

98. Some things were sober or trying, and some were sad. The Haldimand and Four Corners Methodists lost their beautiful church by fire—soon, however, to be restored again. There were several deaths of ancient Canadian Methodists long identified with the cause, among whom might be mentioned *James O'Loan, Esq.*, one of the first and long a Professor in our institution at Cobourg.

99. An important assemblage of an unusual character took place during the course of this Conference year, which led to material modifications of the Church's temporal economy. For several years there had been very strongly expressed convictions on the part of some of the most enlightened and worthy laymen of the Church that the disciplinary allowances to the ministers and their families were entirely too small. But the Constitution of the Legislative Conference ever since the organization of the Church in 1828, embodied the following " restriction," that " No new rule, or regulation, or alteration of any rule or regulation now in force respecting our temporal economy: such as the building of meeting-houses, the order to be observed therein; the allowance to the ministers and preachers, their widows and children, the raising of annual supplies for the propagation of the gospel (the missions excepted); for the making up the allowances of the preachers, &c., shall be considered as of any force or authority, until such rule, regulation, or alteration shall have been laid before the several quarterly Conferences throughout the whole Connexion, and shall have received the consent and advice of a majority of the members (who may be present at the time of laying such rule, regulation, or alteration before them) of *two-thirds* of the said Conferences. '

100. The utmost deference had been paid to this requirement in any and all the modifications that had been made affecting the people's contributions and the preachers' pay; but as there were a number of details to be arranged which would require deliberation and concert, it was proposed to apply the principle in a way somewhat new, that is, by a method resembling in some measure "a joint committee" between two branches of a national legislature. It was decided to ask each quarterly meeting in the two Provinces to elect a layman to meet the Conference Special Committee at some time and place to be fixed by the President, to take all these matters into consideration. In pursuance of this decision, the following call was made at the date indicated in the notification :—

"MEETING OF REPRESENTATIVES.

"The representatives of Circuits in Western and Eastern Canada, and the Conference Special Committee, will meet in Kingston (D. V.), in the Vestry of the new Church, at 10 o'clock in the morning of October eighteenth, 1854, according to resolution and direction of Conference.

"ENOCH WOOD,
"Toronto, September 19th, 1854. "PRESIDENT."

101. As the time drew near, the prospect of a meeting so unusual in Wesleyan Methodism, and partaking so much of the nature of lay-delegation, awakened the solicitudes of those who had always been affected, more or less, with *layphobia*, if we may coin a new word, became uneasy and apprehensive; nor were those apprehensions allayed, but increased, by the proceedings of a few of a revolutionary tendency, before the meeting had properly settled to business, but the conduct of the great majority very soon evinced the unfounded character of such apprehensions. And this meeting confirmed our experience of every new extension of privilege to the lay members of the Church, whether in quarterly

meeting, district meeting, committee, or otherwise, that the great majority of the Wesleyan laity were law-abiding, quiet, and the very best aids to the executive in conserving order and rule, by keeping the fractious in their places.

102. *One hundred and two* quarterly meetings appointed delegates, *fifty-two* of whom were present at the opening of the meeting, and many came after. The President assumed the chair, the Reverends Wm. Case and Dr. Green led in prayer, and a lay-Secretary was appointed in the person of John Matthewson, Esq., of Montreal, along with the Rev. I. B. Howard, Secretary of the Conference. Every part of the proceedings were of the most orderly and business-like character, showing that the experience of secular men may raise the character of deliberative proceedings in ecclesiastical assemblies.

103. We have not room for the Minutes of these deliberations, but the gist of their recommendations from the modifications of our Connexional economy embodied in the registered enactments of the ensuing Conference, after submission to the quarterly meetings, which I append in this place in the form of a foot-note.*

---

* *Resolved,*—That the following scale of allowances recommended by the Kingston Delegate Meeting, and submitted to the Quarterly Meetings, and passed by them by a much larger majority than required by the Discipline, be now adopted by the Conference, viz.:—

I. That Art. 1st of second Section of Discipline be altered so that £25 shall be read £35, and that Art. 2nd as at present, viz., £25.

II. That a preacher's salary, after he is received into full connexion and ordained, shall be £45 per annum while he remains single.

III. That each child shall be allowed £7 10s. per annum until the age of 18—unless otherwise provided for.

IV. That in case of the death of a preacher's wife, instead of the provision for payment of board for children, &c.,—that no difference

104. The missionary anniversary of the Canada Conference Missionary Society was held in connection with this meeting, and the financial statement for the Conference year 1853-54 was made. The brief report of the meeting is as follows :—

MISSIONARY REPORT FOR 1853–54.

" From the report which has just been published we learn that the amount contributed to the Wesleyan Missionary

shall be made in the salary—provided that such preacher has a family to provide for.

V. That a fund be established for equalizing the support of preachers' children upon the principle adopted by the English Conference.

VI. SUPERANNUATED PREACHERS' FUND.—*Scale of Allowances :—*

CLAIMANTS.	ALLOWANCES.
Of 15 years	£32
16 "	34
17 "	36
18 "	38
19 "	40
20 "	42
21 "	44
22 "	46
23 "	48
24 "	50
25 "	52
26 "	54
27 "	56
28 "	58
29 "	60
30 "	62
11 to 15 years	32 } for 4
8 to 11 "	20 } years
Widows of 15 and upwards to receive two-thirds of husband's allowance.	
Widows, 10 to 15 years	16
Under 10 years	12 10
Rev. E. Stoney	36
" David Yeomans	25
" John Harmon	25

VII. That when the claims upon the Superannuated Preacher's Fund for any year shall be more than the income of such year, each

Society, by the various circuits and stations in Canada West, during the past year, is £7,539 14s. 4d., an advance of £1,866 14s. 10½d. on the contributions of the preceding year. The expenditure of the year in carrying on the extensive operations of the Society were, £6,559 13s. 7d.; leaving a balance in the hands of the Treasurer, last June, with which to commence the present year. The extent and state and prospects of the work under the superintendence

claimant shall receive a percentage in proportion to his claim, to the full amount of the current income.

The following resolutions were adopted by the Conference :—

Resolved,—That as a principle, it is just and expedient that all our Connexional Funds, raised wholly or principally by the exertions of ministers and others, and the contributions of our people at large, should be managed by mixed committees, composed of equal numbers of ministers and laymen, conjointly ; so that they, who by personal services or pecuniary benevolence have contributed to their accumulation, may have a fair and equitable share in their management and distribution.

The Conference, in accordance with this principle, places the Contingent Fund, Chapel Relief Fund, and the Fund for the Education of the Candidates for our Ministry, under the direction of Mixed Committees.

Resolved,—That, instead of the election of one delegate from each District, who, with the Chairman and lay members, now constitute the Contingent Fund Committee, the Contingent Fund Committee shall be constituted as follows :—

The Conference shall elect fifteen of its number on the first day of its session in each year, who, with fifteen laymen, chosen as directed in the following resolution, shall hereafter be the "Contingent Fund Committee."

Resolved,—That half of the Contingent Fund Committee which is to be composed of laymen, shall be annually chosen from the districts most contiguous to the place where the Conference shall be. The selection of such laymen to be made by the Recording Stewards and Representatives of each district, at the ordinary district meeting in May (at the close of the financial business to be transacted at that meeting), from and out of the members nominated by the respective

10*

of the Wesleyan Missionary Society in Canada, are exhibited in the following extract from the interesting report of the Committee:

"The Committee have great pleasure in stating that the Auxiliary Society in Canada last year supported fifteen Indian missions, sixty-two domestic missions, twenty-one missionaries to Indians, seventy-nine ministers on the domestic missions, sixteen day-school teachers, six interpreters, fifteen

quarterly boards of such districts at their fourth Quarterly Meeting for the year.

Resolved,—That any Circuit which in the past year has received assistance from the Contingent Fund may or may not obtain aid the next year, as the Financial District Meeting may see fit, even though the said Circuit may or may not have been considered in the Contingent Fund Committee assembled at the Conference.

Resolved,—That no deficiencies brought from any Circuit be allowed at the final meeting of the Contingent Fund Committee, unless the circuit has raised during each quarter the average sum of two shillings and sixpence currency per member, as required by the long-established rule, of each member paying one penny sterling a week, and a shilling per quarter.

Resolved,—That no application for grants to Circuits or special claims be entertained by the Contingent Fund Committee or the Financial District Meeting, unless they have passed the Quarterly Meeting, and have been signed by the Circuit or Recording Steward.

Resolved,—That it is very desirable and expedient that as many lay members from each circuit—one of whom shall be Recording Steward—be authorized to attend the May District Meetings, and take part therein during the transaction of financial business—as there may be preachers travelling on the same circuit.

DIVISION OF CIRCUITS.

Resolved,—That no circuits supporting their own preachers shall be divided till such divisions have been approved of by their respective Quarterly Meetings, and their approval signified in writing by the Recording Steward, or otherwise by a two-thirds vote of the May District Meeting at the time when the lay representatives are present.

Resolved,—That we are of opinion that provision should be made for the education, at Victoria College, free of expense for board and tuition, of young men intended for the ministry who may be recommended

day-schools, two of which are largely industrial ; and that there are on the different missions 10,624 members of the Church, 1,142 of that number Indians; and that the increase during the year is 1,330 members. Such are the results, under the blessing of the divine Spirit, of the application of the truths the Society's agents inculcate, and of the uniformity on all the missions of their instructions. An unlettered Namacqua forcibly said on a Wesleyan Missionary occasion in Africa, "All our teachers preach the same

by the Quarterly and District Meetings—and that a fund for this purpose be created and sustained by annual collections and donations.

Resolved,—That in view of the important and widely extended educational interests with which the Wesleyan Methodist Church in Canada is identified, a Committee of lay members of the Church from different parts of the Province should annually be named by the President and Executive Committee of the Conference—such Committee when appointed to co-operate with the Board of Victoria College, and in all other suitable ways to further the interests of education in connection with the College and other educational institutions of the Church.

Resolved,—That this Conference appoint a Select Committee to revise the present Book of Discipline, so as to provide for the renting of pews in our churches, and otherwise to adapt it to the wants and requirements of Canadian Methodism.

Resolved,—That this Conference alter the first clause of answer first of the 5th section of the Discipline, and that every Circuit be required to furnish the house or houses of their married preachers : and that, in order to enable circuits to do this, an appropriation shall be made out of the amount reserved of the Contingent Fund for extraordinaries, of such sum as the Contingent Fund Committee may think expedient.

Resolved,—That the Committee of Estimates appointed by a Quarterly Meeting, shall report to the Quarterly Meeting so appointing.

Resolved,—That the resolutions of the Kingston Delegate Meeting, relative to the Constitution of the Missionary Society, be referred to the Book Committee for careful revision, and for the purpose of adopting, as far as its relation to the Parent Missionary Society will allow, the principle on which the Committees of other funds of this Conference are constituted.

gospel; yes, though there are many teachers, the word is the same, the school is the same.'"

105. The newly incorporated work in Canada East was prosecuted much in the same manner as in other parts of the Connexion, and with no observable friction in any place, or department, excepting at the head of this humble historian's own district, the *City of Montreal*. It is a matter that cannot be ignored, besides its teaching its own historic lessons, but as it resulted in my first and only Connexional censure and humiliation, I must treat it with all the candor of one bound to sink self in Connexional interests, and the man in the historian. Withal our space obliges us to be concise.

106. The two suburban Wesleyan Churches in Montreal had been built by the Central Board of Trustees, and their ministrations had been sustained by general circuit funds common to the city circuit. Furthermore, although they had stood in the Minutes for several years in the form of separate charges, (and perhaps were, so far as *pastoral attention* was concerned), by the names of *Montreal Centre, Montreal West,* and *Montreal East,* yet there had always been a regular and systematic exchange of pulpits among the ministers. At the last District Meeting under the old *regime*—the one in May, 1854—there had been an attempt made, indeed it was decided, that this separation of circuits should be *real* as well as apparent, and their provisional stations were made with that view. To this, all the members in both the East and West Circuits were opposed, and a number of official members who worshipped in the Central church as well, and they objected to its going into effect, and their objections were based on the following grounds: the District Meeting, like all Missionary Districts, was a purely clerical body, and the request for the dismemberment had not received the consent of the City Quarterly Meeting, which they claimed was necessary to make it constitutional. But the sole Board of

Trustees, whose funds were ample, were determined to end the dependence, and do away with the presence of the extremities in their circuit meetings. They were willing to vote them a donation from time to time, they would see that their church edifices should be kept in repair and kept afloat, but they would have no intermingling of funds or of ecclesiastical business.

107. After the new antonomy for the Montreal District was fairly launched, both parties made their appeal to the President of the Conference of the Wesleyan Methodist Church in Canada. Early in the winter of 1854-55, the President and Secretary of the Conference and a large representation of the Conference Special Committee, including several respectable brethren long connected with Canada Eastern affairs, met all the office-bearers, of all grades and kinds, belonging to all the charges in the city, together with all the ministers stationed in the city, in a vestry of Great St. James Street Church, and the whole matter was gone over in a conversational way. The first business was to see how the matter had arisen; under which head the several parties did not agree as to all the antecedents of the matter. Next, the preferences and wishes of every brother was inquired into. These inquiries elicited two inevitable conclusions: first, that the whole affair was extraordinary, according to Canada Conference usages, and must be disposed of by a somewhat extra-judicial process; secondly, if it went by the number of votes, a considerable majority of the official members of the city were opposed to the dismemberment of the original circuit, but if weight was to be attached to the amount likely to be contributed in carrying on the work, then dismemberment had the preponderating influence. There was much sympathy felt for those who clung to their old united relation, and I must confess to feeling at the time disposed to do something to meet their wishes; upon the whole, how-

ever, it was decided by the Conference Committee, that the decision of the district meeting which had been acted on by the Stationing Committee, and lastly, by the President in his final act in dividing the work into three districts and appointing chairmen, *should remain undisturbed—that there should be three circuits.*

108. Soon after my return to my station at St. John's, I received official information from the pastor of *Montreal West*, the Rev. Wm. Scott (now President of the Montreal Annual Conference), that all the official members in the two suburban circuits had resigned their offices, and that unless something could be done to induce them to reconsider their resignation, the circuits would be so crippled that it would be hard to sustain the cause; furthermore suggesting a plan, involving a sort of compromise, which would save the pride and, in some measure, meet the feelings of the malcontents, and preserve them to the Church, till some final arrangement could be made by Connexional authority at the next district meeting and Conference. I consented to go and meet them. All concerned were assembled in a vestry of the Griffintown Church. The two ministers of the east and west were present of course, and the Rev. James Brock, one of the oldest and most influential ministers connected with that section of the work, gave us his presence and counsel, upon request. The minister of the Central Church, the Rev. W. Jeffers, perhaps wisely, was not present. It would be idle to detail all that was said by angry men, or all that was advanced to pacify them. Suffice to give the agreement that was come to, which was this: that the two suburban churches should be worked as one circuit for the balance of the year. The Rev. J. H. Bishop, in charge of the east, voluntarily surrendered his superintendency to Mr. Scott, who was to be in charge of the whole; there should be a common plan, a rotation in the pulpits, and, I think, " a share

and share alike" in the funds, which it was thought would be improved by the people being pleased by interchange and combined action. Upon this arrangement being agreed to, all the leaders took up their class-books, and every other office-bearer resumed his portfolio; and the thought was now that they would never ask to go back to the Centre, as they had found the true solution of city matters, at least for the near future.

109. This was no doubt a bold measure on my part, and it was only resorted to for the following reasons : (1) The forcible dismemberment of a people who refused to be separated seemed a measure somewhat hard; (2) The carrying of it through was effected by means of extra-judicial, the Conference Special Committee having no definite powers, indeed, was not then known in the *letter* of discipline; (3) Our arrangement was no infraction of the arrangement made by the committee, but a provisional one to meet an emergency which had arisen subsequently; and (4) Such provisional arrangements I had known chairmen or presiding elders to make years before, a notable one of which I had in my recollection as having taken place in the winter of 1832-33, relating to the Bytown and Hull Circuits.

110. Lest what I had done should appear as in contempt of authority, I wrote a full account of the emergency and the arrangement to the President, and hoped I might "receive a bill of indemnity," in view of the evil I had staved off. With his usual caution, he made no explicit avowal of opinion, although he thought it "a grave matter." Sometime after I received a set of resolutions passed by such of the Special Committee as were at hand, if not censuring me, repudiating my action. Still, I believe my arrangement would not have been disturbed till the end of the year, had not certain leading lay influences in the Centre written to the Connexional authorities on the subject. This I thought they might have

omitted, as they were now in no wise interfered with or troubled by the brethren of the extremities. Yet they saw proper to invoke Connexional authority to disturb an arrangement in which they were not immediately concerned. Perhaps, as they were directly appealed to, the authorities thought they were bound by the first arrangement to see it carried out. The co-Delegate came down, summoned me to Montreal, and required me to undo what I had done. This I declined, on the ground of the extraordinary circumstances which I thought justified the measure, and because I would not stultify myself. Bearing the President's authority, he proceeds to do it himself. My arrangement was disallowed, and the two ministers were to keep the circuits to which they had been originally appointed.

111. The results were, as I had feared, the recalcitrant officials withdrew from the Church altogether, and with them about seventy members out of the two charges (which had but a small membership at best), and these among the most gifted and active ones. The consequences were that these two places had to be sustained several years by an amount of Connexional aid which, in the other case, might have been saved. Wise and weighty ministers who succeeded, voluntarily expressed their sorrow that my arrangement had to be broken up, as it was just the expedient for the emergency, and the opposite course resulted in the calling in of another body, and the establishment of a cause inevitably rival to ours. Happily, the great comprehension of 1874 has come and remedied all that.

112. There are many things to be learned by occurrences of the above kind; such as that none of us should be too hot and positive, and we should be careful of being too exacting to our erring brethren, especially, as in this case, when there is no express law or precedent to guide us. The brethren of the extremities, perhaps, made too much of their grievances;

the central brethren may have let them alone, when once they were dismembered from them, although their dismemberment did not take the shape they had expected; and perhaps I expressed my indignation too warmly for having been censured for a measure which I had no chance of verbally explaining to those who registered the censure.

113. As it was I was punished sufficiently, being, by the counsel of the Advisory Committee, left out of the office they supposed I had mismanaged, and a junior placed over me; albeit, as a matter of favor, I was allowed at the last meeting of the Stationing Committee to exchange into another district, where my humiliation was not so much felt. After a year my former status was regained, and after several years I, perhaps, received some measure of the confidence again, accorded to me before. My falling so directly into the current of inevitable events must plead my excuse of nearly the only bit of egotism I have perpetrated in the five volumes I have issued.

114. At the Legislature which sat during the year 1854, a Reform Government being then in power, a Bill was brought in for the secularization of the Clergy Reserves. The lay Wesleyans attending the Convention at Kingston availed themselves of the opportunity to hold a meeting by themselves on the subject, and passed a series of resolutions approving of their alienation from all religious purposes, and recommended the ministry of the Church to decline the reception of any part of their avails for any denominational purpose, and pledging the laity of the Church to indemnify the funds of the Church for any loss which might result from such a declinature; and all the lay brethren who were still at the meeting, subscribed to the declaration, and the resolutions and names were published in the *Guardian*. I had at first thought to give them *in extenso*, but, from economy of

space, conclude to dispose of the subject with this briefer allusion.

115. We are in the midst of the last Conference year of the venerable Case, whose public life we have made the thread by which we have connected his fellow-itinerants in these Provinces, during his own times, together. We have already told how he spent this year, as well as the last, in public Connexional engagements, and we are glad that we have the means of giving his occupations, views, and feelings in a letter to one of his coevals and fellow-laborers of an early day. It will speak for itself:—

116.   "ALNWICK, March 16, 1855.

"DR. BANGS: REV. AND DEAR BROTHER,—What scenes and changes have passed in review since we commenced our ministry! Most of our early associates in the ministry in this country have passed triumphantly to their great reward; yet the Church is supplied abundantly and ably. The membership, too, have increased from scores to hundreds and thousands.

117. "Once we addressed the few in private dwellings; larger assemblies were congregated in barns, for churches were 'few and far between.' We now preach to thousands; churches have arisen, large and numerous, in our cities, towns, and circuits! Brother, after more than half a century of toil, you, perhaps, are scarcely able to visit the scenes of your former labors. Would it not be delightful to do so? Your appearance among the descendants of your early Christian friends would fill them with delight; and could you not do more for God and the Church by travelling at large than by treading a thousand times the streets of a city? Your experience in the things of God, your counsel in the interests of the Church, would have its influence favorably in the *closing scene* of so lengthened a ministerial course. Could you not again visit Canada, the land of your youth, of your conversion to God, your early ministry, and of the mission field you have aided to cultivate? The railroad would bring you to Kingston, or to Hamilton, in a few hours. Once we toiled on horseback through wild forests from two-and-a-half to four miles an hour; now, forty miles is the speed we move! Brother, try it before leaving for the 'fairer climes.' Sickness prevented, last season, your meeting your

appointment in Toronto. Perhaps you may be with us at our Conference in London, the first Wednesday in June. The two or three hundreds of Canada preachers would be happy to meet you there.

118. "During the winter just passing I have enjoyed the unspeakable pleasure of visiting the scenes of our early labors (yours and mine). I passed through Hallowell, Belleville, Kingston, Elizabethtown, Brockville, Augusta, Matilda, and thence to Bytown (Ottawa City); thence to Perth and Wolford, on the Rideau; then home, through a portion of the northern new settlements. In this route I found some, though few, of our former religious friends now living. Arthur Youmans, Rufus Shorey, Mrs. McLean (formerly Widow Coate), and William Brown are yet living, at the ages of from eighty to ninety-one. Youmans, at the latter age, was one of the members of the first class formed in Hallowell, January, 1793, by Darius Dunham. A class paper of the same class was written by Elijah Woolsey in 1795. But the parents of the Johnsons, Congers, Vandusens, Roblins, Germans, Huffs, Emburys, Detlors, Clarkes, Parrots, Maddens, Keelers, Colemans, Hecks, Coons, Brouses, Aults, Dulmages, Lawrences are all gone; yet they live in the example, of piety, integrity, hospitality, and Christian benevolence. These virtues are prominent to a great extent in their numerous descendants. The progeny bears a striking impress of their worthy patriarchal fathers.

119. "You will remember the names of Samuel and Jacob Heck, of Augusta, and the Emburys, of Bay of Quinte—the former the sons of Paul Heck and his worthy companion, the parents of Methodism in the City of New York and in America. The parents are gone, and the sons have followed them in the way of holiness to glory; but a numerous train of grandchildren are pursuing the Christian course 'their fathers trod'—intelligent, pious, and wealthy. 'Blessed are the meek, for they shall inherit the earth.' A few years since I visited John Embury and his worthy companion. He was then ninety-eight years old. The scenes of early Methodism in New York were revived in his recollections, and he referred to them as readily as if they had recently occurred. He said : 'My uncle, Philip Embury, was a great man—a powerful preacher—a very powerful preacher. I had heard many ministers before, but nothing reached my heart till I heard my Uncle Philip preach. I was then about sixteen. The Lord has since been my trust and portion. I am now ninety-eight.—Yes, my Uncle Philip was a great preacher.' After this interview he lived about a year, and died suddenly, as he arose from prayer in his family, at the

age of ninety-nine. The Emburys, Detlors, Millers, Maddens, Switzers, of Bay of Quinte, are numerous and pious, and some of them ministers of the gospel—all firmly grounded in Methodism. Their Palatine origin is prominent in their health, integrity, and industry, and their steadfast piety by Irish training on Mr. Wesley's knee. Old Mrs. Detlor forty years ago told me, 'When a child in Ireland, Mr. Wesley took me on his knee, when I sang for him :—

> " 'Children of the Heavenly King,
> As we journey let us sing.'

120. "You will remember the Rev. William Brown, of Wolford, River Rideau. He was once, as you know, one of our most efficient and talented travelling ministers. He is now eighty-six. A few weeks since I spent a Sabbath at his house. He is yet vigorous in mind, his voice pretty clear and full. He took part in the exercises of the quarterly meeting, opened the love-feast, and addressed the congregation at the close of the sermon. He spoke of the early ministers and the piety of our steadfast saints who had gone to glory, and seemed animated with the prospect of soon joining them in the song of redemption. I should not close without referring to the extent and success of our Indian missions, in which you took an early and deeply-interested part, but have at present only to say that they are still in progress, and have extended a thousand miles north into the Hudson Bay Territory. You will, perhaps, remember two of the Indian boys with us in New York, viz., Henry Steinhaur and Allen Salt. The former has lately returned, after an absence in that country (the Hudson Bay) of fourteen years. While in that country he has labored as a school-teacher, minister of the gospel, translator, and printer. He has translated the New Testament into the Cree language, a dialect of the Ojibway, and printed the Gospel of John, as also a hymn-book, in that country. He has brought with him portions of his printed translations. His addresses at our numerous missionary meetings created a great and lively sensation. Allen is now, also, laboring in that country, being ordained to the ministry. How little we thought, when those little boys were delighting the congregations with their musical voices—lately converted in the woods of Canada—that they would extend the mission of Christianity to their pagan people thousands of miles into the wilderness. Henry continues with us till about the last of May, when he will leave again for that country, and begin

a new mission one thousand miles west of his former station, near the Rocky Mountains.

"With Christian respects to Sister Bangs and your family,
"Yours, W. CASE."

121. Before we conduct the reader to the last Conference Mr. Case attended, and the one at which he, at the request of his brethren, preached his notable jubilee sermon, it will be well for us to inquire what had been the results of that year of activity and what were the state of the members in society in 1855. From the incorporation of so many different elements, it was hard to say what had been the gains of 1854-55; but the membership at the Conference of 1855 stood at the goodly aggregation of 39,015 (of which 1,068 were Indians), which was larger by 6,651 than the total set down to the Canada Conference one year before.

1855.

THE BALANCE OF THE YEAR, AND THE DEATH OF CASE.

122. THE Conference of 1855 was a time of deep depression to this humble chronicler, and one the remembrance of which awakens thoughts disagreeable to the mind. Yet it was a glorious one in itself, and the occasion of jubilation to his brethren; and he intends endeavoring to write of it in the spirit which becomes the theme.

123. It was convoked in one of the most pleasant, growing cities in the richest part (agriculturally) of our best grain-producing colony—that is to say, in *London*, Canada West, a place strong in Methodism, as in every other branch of Protestantism, and where the assembled itinerants from Gaspe to the upper lakes—yea, we might add (for Woolsey and Steinhaur were there), to the Rocky Mountains—were there, or their representatives, and were treated to a princely hospitality.

124. It met in the most genial month of the year, its sessions extending from the 6th to the 14th of June, and the weather was fine for the time of year.

125. Its managing authorities were representative of the many interests involved. The *Rev. Enoch Wood* (afterwards D.D.), an Englishman, a member of the British Conference constructively, who embodied twenty-nine years of foreign labor, President; the *Rev. John Ryerson*, who might be taken as the representative of the old Canadian graft-stalk, co-Delegate, or Vice-President, was there in memory, though absent in the North; and *Samuel Dwight Rice*, also a prospective D.D., a sort of representative of every possible interest, element, and nationality in the body, was chosen Secretary. Then, also, the Conference was favored with the presence of the *Rev. James Beecham*, one of the General Missionary Secretaries. The *Rev. Dr. Richey* also was there as a visitor from a branch of Wesleyan Methodism in the Eastern Provinces. Besides whom, no less than seven ministerial brethren from the Methodist Episcopal Church in the United States—unofficially, but in a friendly manner—visited the Conference, mingled with its members, and received a most cordial reception from each individual and from the Conference collectively. These were the Rev. Messrs. Collins, Pervine, Hickey (Detroit), and Jacobs, of the Michigan Annual Conference, and the Rev. Messrs. Fuller, De Puy, and Robie (editor of the Buffalo *Christian Advocate*), of the old Genesee Conference, with which the Canada work once stood connected. But last, not least, the apostolic Case himself, without title or office, stood there as the hero of a thousand battles and the toil-worn laborer of half a century.

126. Just fifty years before he had crossed the St. Lawrence to Kingston in a ferry, his horse and saddle-bags, with

their contents, his sole possession. How truly might he not have sung :—

> "With my pastoral crook
> I went over this brook,
> And, lo! I am spread into bands."

Then there were eight circuits in the two Canadas—now there were 210 under the direction of the Canada Conference; then there were nine laborers employed—now there were no less than 305; then there were 1,787 members in society—now there were 37,895; then there could not have been above half a dozen humble houses of worship—now they might have near a thousand. All this in the central body, irrespective of the numerical and other strength of no less than two or four offshoots either from the parent stocks of Europe or Canada.

127. According to the previous unanimous request of the Conference, made one year before, and in pursuance of consequent arrangements for that purpose and announcement, on the first evening after the Conference—that is to say, on the 6th of June, 1855—the man of seventy-five years and of fifty in the toilsome Canadian itinerancy, tall, unbent, and with even elastic step, but with ample locks of snowy whiteness, ascended the commanding pulpit of the spacious North Street Wesleyan church, and surveyed a vast concourse of persons brought together by the extraordinary character of the services, to deliver his expected JUBILEE SERMON.

128. His text and sermon were both in the very best taste—not adapted to recall his own exploits, or to celebrate his own achievements, but to celebrate the loving-kindness of the Creator and Provider to his human creatures at large, and to His covenant people in particular. He announced as the subject of meditation the words of the royal

poetic prophet, as recorded in the 103rd Psalm and 17th verse: "But the mercy of the Lord is from everlasting to everlasting upon them that fear Him, and His righteousness unto children's children." After a brief exposition of the theological aspects and teachings of the text, the venerable preacher, with booming, undulating voice, launched forth into a pæan of triumph in the displays of God's mercy and faithfulness to himself and the people of Canada, especially its religious people, during the fifty years of their connection with each other. The straits, and toils, and sufferings of the early settlers, and the exhausting journeys and the destitution of the early preachers came into review, followed by a presentation of the deliverances that had been wrought, the improvements that had taken place, and the wondrous extension of the work of religion. The discourse occupied an hour and a-quarter in delivery, but it did not weary.

129. So healthy and hale was this active, though aged man, that he and his friends little recked at that time that he was substantially chaunting his own requiem. That session of the Conference had to register the deaths and record the excellences of four of their brethren, fallen since their last assembling—the promising lads *James Taylor* and *Lucius Adams* had fallen before their period of trial had expired. Of the latter, especially, it might have been sung:—

> "The stranger's eye wept, that in life's brightest bloom
> One gifted so rarely should sink to the tomb;
> For in ardor he led in the van of the host,
> And he fell like a soldier—he died at his post!"

John Williams, the graceful pulpit man and the soul-winning revivalist, also was cut off in the midst of his days—in his prime,—and left a comparatively young widow to mourn his loss. But *Prindle—Andrew Prindle,*—the coeval in years and the compeer in ministerial labors of Case, the man of massive proportions—of body and mind,—the acute, original theologian and mighty preacher, had just crossed the flood before his early friend, having been barely permitted to enter the climacteric year of his ministry, in the seventy-fifth year of his age (for he died January 15th, 1855), all of which might have been interpreted as premonitory of his own sudden removal.

130. But while the Head of the Church was "burying His workmen," He was making provision for "carrying on His work." Mr. Case, in his jubilee sermon, had said that, if required, he could give the names of two hundred men, whites and Indians, in our own and other Christian Churches, whom he knew to have been converted and raised up into the ministry in Canada. And this, his last Conference, was particularly prolific in recruits to the ministerial ranks.

131. We cannot indulge ourselves in the minuteness which has characterized our details hitherto. All I can presume to give will be an outline of character here and there. The ministry seemed likely to be kept full. Besides the fifteen who had graduated to full connexion in our own ranks, with whom the reader has become acquainted, two matured men, from lesser sections of Methodism, were taken into the full ministry at this Conference. These were *Thomas Robson* and *Thomas Lawson.* Both were Englishmen, and destined to be exceedingly successful laborers; but both have, years since, gone to their rest. The former came to us from the "M. E. Church of Canada;" the latter had labored among the Primitive brethren. They were both average preachers, and very faithful to their work. They both died suddenly: the first "died at his post, having scarcely time to lay down his weapons." "Bro. Lawson was in the act of crossing the Grand River in a scow, when suddenly the chain snapped asunder, and he was precipitated

into the rolling flood, and soon was numbered with the dead."

132. The real augmentation of the ranks of itinerant laborers on circuits for the year 1855-56 was to the number of *thirty-one*. That was the number of those formally received on trial, and printed in the Minutes as such. But that is not the reason why we say that augmentation was produced, for all but five or six of these brethren whose names are given labored on circuits under a chairman during the preceding year (1854-55), and nearly all of these, in some form or another, were presented to the reader. Still, there was an augmentation of the actual laborers this year over the last, to the number of thirty or thirty-one, but this was because, as we find from inquiry, some twenty-three or twenty-five, were discovered and placed in the many vacancies that had to be left in the vast list of appointments. Taking, therefore, say, the seven actual candidates not before described, and the twenty-five supplies, the new recruits did not amount to less than thirty or thirty-one; and if you add thirty-one to the printed list of laborers in the Minutes, which was 305, the whole number of those doing battle for God in the two Canadas and the Hudson Bay Territory was not less than 335. Three in this list I pass over in sorrow, because, although they were personable men to look at, and in their respective ways gifted and capable; and although, from their activity and apparent zeal, they gave augury of more than usual enterprise and success, were destined, after a few years, to "vilely cast their shields away," and to disgrace themselves and to dishonor the Captain of their salvation. We cover their names with the mantle of oblivion, hoping that every one "who putteth on the harness" may take warning at their fate. I am shut up, therefore, to the consideration of twenty-seven or twenty-eight good men and true to be presented to the reader.

133. And of these themselves I will not promise the minute details furnished in most cases concerning those of whom we have written, but simply present their characteristic features by a few bold lines, that the animus of the men, who were soon to grasp the fallen standard and trumpet of him who ere long was to put off his harness.

134. There were seven worthy men among those in the list of candidates of whom the reader has not been informed. Their names were the following: *W. R. Morden, James Latimer, Ashton Fletcher, Sen., Samuel Tucker, Amos E. Russ, William H. Laird*, and *Isaac Crane*, the last of whom, there can be no doubt, labored on a circuit the preceding year. A word or two concerning each of the above.

135. Three of these, namely, *Morden, Latimer*, and *Fletcher*, were destined not to labor " affectively " very many years :— *Morden*, I suspect, was a young Canadian, I surmise from Flamboro' Country, took tolerably fair circuits, spent one year at Victoria College as a Conference student, and filled up his four years' probation, and was then " dropped," but whether voluntarily on his part, or involuntarily, I cannot say. He must be by no means confounded with *T. E. Morden*, who entered the work in 1875, an English-speaking Canadian, who has, out of love to the Teutons in our midst, mastered the German language as to be thoroughly bi-linguil, being qualified to write, and think, and speak in German, and to render a great amount of service to our evangelistic efforts as one of our most useful and trusted German missionaries. A fellow-laborer in that department pronounces him to be one of the purest-minded, unselfish, and upright ministers he ever knew, and one pre-eminently qualified for his work.

136. *James F. Latimer*, I think, a Bay of Quinte man, of a good stock, tall, straight, and commanding, though rather silent than otherwise, was destined to spend one year at

Victoria, and ten full years on circuits, and then to succumb to chronic infirmity, and to become a supernumerary, but to keep as near under the shadow of the Conference as possible.

137. We have already made some references to Mr. Fletcher. He was a local preacher of fair gifts, long experience, and ample means for his support, who, like many another old Methodist, wished to spend the balance of his days given up to the work of God. He was an English gentleman, but has become thoroughly Canadianized. He was soon ordained, labored three years on circuits, and then was placed in the ranks of supernumeraries, thus giving him a ministerial status until now.

138. *Crane* and *Tucker*, both Englishmen, the first married, the other single, the one profound, the other more taking, but both exceedingly laborious and reliable, and destined to elevate all the circuits on which they have labored to this day. Crane was trained in the Normal School, one of the first students, along with Dewart and some other men of mark. Tucker, however, or wherever educated, was a man of varied attainments, one of which attainments is a considerable amount of medical knowledge.

139. *Laird* and *Russ* are Canadians; one of Irish pedigree, the other of German; one short, stout, and plump, the other tall, big-boned, muscular, strong, and springy as a steel trap. They both received some advantage from Victoria. The larger had more vigor, the less, perhaps, more polish. Ladies would admire the preaching of the lesser man, sinners would have to stand from under when the larger was fulminating his thunders. Brother Laird was to pass through town and city pulpits to the chair of a district; Russ's enterprise, after turning his circuits upside down in Canada, was to send him to listen to the surf battling on the Pacific shore, and to be the " Great Heart "-guide of miners and pioneer pilgrims.

140. Some of the supplies employed to fill long lists of vacancies, which made unsightly gaps in this year's list of stations were decidedly valuable, and destined to purchase to themselves a good degree.

141. I propose to take them as they turn up without reference to alphabetical order, age, or nationality :—

(1) *Edward Ward*, the self-consuming home missionary from the cities of Yorkshire, transferred to Canadian fields of labor, has proved one of the mightily successful laborers in this land. He served the *Humber* Circuit during 1853-54 and 54-55.

(2) *Thomas Cobb*, the neat, compact, studious, little Englishman, unique, original, and peculiarly emphatic and impressive in preaching, has demeaned himself like a gentleman, and quietly worked up the good circuits (scarcely equal to his abilities) to which he has been appointed. He labored his first year under the chairman on the old *Grimsby* Circuit, with the gentle *Simon Huntingdon*.

(3) Here comes *William Hansford*, English too, good in physique, strong in mind, industrious in research, clever in conversation, and able in the pulpit. He is the ready Financial Secretary and accountant, and he, too, has been a chairman. His first circuit, *Quebec*, was enough to try his metal, and the metal proved to have no flaw.

(4) Here comes an Irish-Canadian, *Thomas S. Howard*, who though married and in a successful business, sold out his stock and his stand, and obeyed the call, through Rev. Henry Wilkinson, and went out on the *Strathroy* Circuit, worked it up, and has been in a revival ever since.

(5) *John Nelson Lake*, a native of the Bay of Quinte, descended from an excellent Methodist stock, and called after the Yorkshire Methodist hero, himself not much his inferior in size, symmetry, stature, and strength, being a healthy looking blonde, five feet and nine inches in height, and one

hundred and sixty pounds in weight, had been converted at the age of nineteen, licensed to preach at twenty-one; although embarked in a successful business, for which he is well adapted, left all at the call of the Church and went, October 1st, 1855, out as the third minister on the then extensive *Picton* Circuit, including, as it did, what are now the Picton, Frankford, Bloomfield, and Cherry Valley Circuits, embracing twenty-two appointments, as the colleague of Brethren Slater and Tomblin, where he remained the balance of that year and the next year also, entering on the circuit October the 1st, 1855. In twenty months no less than three hundred new members were added to the Church. It is but just that this dear brother should be allowed to assign the reason why he is not now performing the work of a circuit:—

"The cause of my retiring from the work was a nervous affection of the eyes, which prevented me studying, and hindered my reading with any satisfaction, and I am afraid I will never recover fully. I would be so glad if I could again enter the work, my heart longs for it, and, like Payson, 'I would rather a man would eat my dinner than preach for me.' But this Sherbourne Street Church has been a very great 'safety valve' for me. The Sabbath-school, of which I am superintendent, has kept me in sympathy with the work I love, and then I have contributed towards the church $1,700 in all, which keeps me from the love of money. I may add that I married a grand-daughter of the Rev. Thos. Whitehead, on 9th June, 1859."

(6) *Wm. Norton*, an Irishman, but rather quiet for that nationality, married, supplied the frontier *Bayfield* Circuit, and was destined so to commend himself to his brethren as to be received on trial at the next Conference, and to be allowed to labor on these succeeding twenty-two years. I am so little acquainted with this dear brother as not to know how to describe him. From what I do know, I should

be inclined to say he was average in ability, quiet in operation, and medium in success.

(7) Now comes a specimen of what Lower Canada townships can do in the supply for the vacancy at Dudswell. A warm-hearted Methodist family on the St. Francis River, of American origin, by the name of Fowler, were identified with the cause when it was under American, or Methodist Episcopal, supervision, and would talk with rapture of Ayre, and Virgen, and Streeter, and Hibbard, and Luckey, but who also cheerfully adopted the British missionaries when the arrangement of 1820 took place, had a pair of twin sons, both of whom were destined to be ministers, though in different sections of the Church—Horace had yet to try the work; *Hiram (Fowler)* was the supply for Dudswell. He ultimately became an able preacher, and is now chairman of a District; but before his mind was matured and stored, I know of no one who, by a sympathizing spirit, a persuasive voice, and voluble utterance, could make a moderate capital go further. He was fairly up to man's estate, medium-sized and comely looking.

(8) Of *Henry H. Perdue*, who, it appears, supplied one of the vacancies, I know very little; and our painstaking investigator, Cornish, has overlooked him altogether. Of this I am sure, he was of a good Irish Methodist family, who lived a number of years in the Township of Chinguacousy. We find he took very good circuits for several years, mostly in the lower districts. Looking for his name in the alphabetical list of ministers names for 1860, I found opposite *Henry H. Perdue*, "out of health." This I suspect was the harbinger of an early grave, found by so many young preachers in this country.

(9) Here comes a brother of whom, though I have been furnished with no data, I have the happiness to know more. He was tall and prepossessing in appearance, an Englishman

by birth, who, I suspect, came from that country a local preacher. He found an opening in the noble *Brampton* Circuit under the chairman for the year 1855-56, and was adopted by the Conference. He is not fussy or demonstrative, but amiable and pleasing in his manners. He does not obtrude his well-doings in the papers, but his name never comes up for evil-doing. He has had the good fortune to secure a wife, who, for piety and gifts, has proved herself a helpmeet for him. Some will surmise that I am writing of Brother William Short.

(10) A fatherless boy, brought up with a Methodist family, on the Yonge Street Circuit, where he was converted and became a local preacher, *William L. Scott* by name, is invested with the responsibility at once of managing the *Wellesley Mission*, and succeeded so well as to be recommended and received the next year. He was quite young, but his light hair and fair complexion made him seem younger than he was. His being sent a little later to the neighborhood of Peterboro', was the means of an alliance with one of the best Methodist families in the land, by marrying their only child. The mention of Mr. and Mrs. Thomas McBerney is enough. Indeed, Mr. McB. preached so much and so ably as to deserve a place with these worthies himself.

(11) *James Berry* has been mentioned, and *Joseph Jones* had not better be further mentioned. If everything had been equal to his gifts, all would have been well.

(12) *Charles Stringfellow*, a local preacher from England, came out in time to release Bro. Hansford from *Point Levi*, who was taken into the City of Quebec, and Brother S. gave a fair specimen of the honorable and useful career which has succeeded, including ten or a dozen years at *Oxford* and *Norway Houses*, in the far North-West, in all of which positions he has proved himself capable and reliable. Not large, but active was he.

(13) Two married men were admitted as supplies, who did well; one was a local preacher from England, *John Davies*, who was sent— a needed supply—to *Hatley*. He has maintained himself in that Province ever since.

Alas! we have buried poor, worthy *Atkinson*, and must let his obituary tell the story of him :—

" Bro. Atkinson died in Maitland, on the 29th day of December, 1874, as he had just attained to fifty years of age. He was born in Ireland, and came with his parents to this country when he was very young. Through the instrumentality of a godly mother he was early led to give his heart to God, and united with the Wesleyan Methodist Church, in the Village of Newburgh. He became a most zealous and active Christian worker, constantly bearing his cross at every opportunity. He then felt that God had called him to preach the gospel. Removing to another part of the country, he became connected with the Methodist Episcopal Church. Here he soon gave evidence that he was a suitable person to be employed in preaching the gospel, and was accordingly licensed a local preacher, and soon after entered the ranks of the travelling ministry. For four years he labored usefully in this relation, but his preferences and early associations led him to seek connection with the Wesleyan Methodist Church, and in the year 1855 he was received into its ministry, and stationed on the Rochester Mission. He entered upon his work with great zeal and activity, and continued in it with unabated earnestness until the Master summoned him home to rest. The greater portion of his ministerial life was spent west of the City of London, where his name will long be held in affectionate remembrance by many who were led to Christ through his labors.

" Bro. Atkinson was a man of deep and fervent piety, with a glowing zeal for the salvation of men. In his preaching, all his energies were bent on its accomplishment. On his circuit he was a most diligent and zealous worker, and the blessing of God attended his labors, so that he was the means of gathering many souls into the fold of the Chief Shepherd. With one exception, he held a camp-meeting on every circuit he travelled. The promotion of the work of God engrossed all his time and energies. Indeed, there can be little doubt that he often labored beyond his strength ; but he loved the work, and was happy only when actively engaged in it. On account of failing health, he once sought rest, and was left without a circuit for one year ; but he was not satisfied in this position, and at the end of three months, a vacancy occurring, he resumed his labors. He was not suffered, however, to continue many years longer. Disease began to prey upon him and render his work difficult. His last year was one of much suffering, in which he struggled hard to perform his duties, encouraged by the great kindness of his people and by the prosperity of the work. In his last sickness he proved the genuineness of his faith and the sufficiency of God's grace. There were no fears, but holy joy and glorious hope. The messenger came as the old year was closing, and found him ready. A faithful minister of Jesus Christ triumphed over death, and went home to receive his reward."

(14) *Edmund E. Sweet* and *Benjamin Cole* came out into the work from places in Lower Canada, and were appointed to supply circuits in that Province. Sweet was sent to *Huntingdon* and Cole to *Melbourne*. Cole has ended his labors, and we will let his obituary give his brethren's matured estimate of him.

" Bro. Cole was born in the ancient City of Quebec, in 1825, where he spent the days of his youth in follies and amusements too common to that period of life. Having become converted to God under the ministrations of the Wesleyan Methodists in 1849, he gave himself up at once without reserve in entire consecration to his Redeemer. Of a sanguine temperament, impulsive in his disposition, and thoroughly Protestant in his views and feelings, at the time of the unhappy Gavazzi riots in Quebec and Montreal, he was one of the volunteers who rallied around that champion of Protestantism, and very narrowly escaped with his life. After laboring for some time as a Sabbath-school teacher, superintendent of the school, and organist of our church in Quebec, he became convinced that it was his duty to devote himself to the work of the Christian ministry, and he hesitated not; but though filling a lucrative situation, with every prospect of speedy advancement, he cheerfully abandoned all and entered upon the self-denying and laborious life of a Wesleyan minister. This was in 1855. His circuits were large and laborious, but Bro. Cole never spared himself nor shrank from duty. He was generous, cheerful, social; a good and enthusiastic musician, a true friend, and, better than all, deeply pious. These qualities made him a welcome inmate at the dwellings of our people, who were always ready to greet him with a smile. But he was popular in the best sense of the word : he was useful in saving souls and building up the Church of the Redeemer. At the Conference of 1870 he was compelled, by total physical prostration, to accept a superannuated relation. For the last twelve months previous to his decease his sufferings had been great, but he sustained them with Christian patience. Although himself suffering from intense pain, he had always a cheerful smile and loving word for those who visited him. The young looked up to him as a father—the aged blessed the day they first saw him. As he drew near the last struggle, his consolations were abundant. '*Precious Jesus! Nearer home; every pin loosened so gently; ready to go!*' When asked if he wished to live, he said : 'I would like to labor a little longer in the vineyard, but I am ready to go.' He particularly desired that while he was passing away those around him should sing his soul into bliss. His favorite hymn was 'My God, I am thine,' etc. This beautiful hymn was sung and another was begun; but, rousing all his energies, he cried, 'Rock of Ages;' and as these words passed the lips of the singers, his happy spirit winged its flight to everlasting bliss. Thus triumphantly passed away our dear friend and brother, at the residence of his endeared friend, Robertson Lincoln, Esq., in Abbotsford, in the forty-sixth year of his age and the fifteenth of his ministry, on the 2nd of August, 1870. 'They that be wise shall shine as the brightness of the firmament; and they that turn many to righteousness as the stars for ever and ever.'"

Mr. Sweet was not very young, but single, a well-furnished Bible student, an able, searching, very impressive preacher, enterprising and industrious in his circuits. If any one wishes to have his person described and to contemplate his attributes as a preacher, he must read the sketch of him among the " Conference Crayons " in the pages of *Past and Present*. He was a native of Devonshire, but made himself thoroughly a Canadian.

(15) This year's list of extemporaneous supplies yielded three very considerable men, who are yet to be mentioned. The first of these was a married man, but of such inherent energy as to make him a prize to the Connexion. This was *Alfred Andrews*, born in Suffolk, England, 1833, and therefore now about twenty-two years of age. He was the eldest child of Wesleyan parents, who had come to Canada and settled in Toronto twenty years before, where Alfred was religiously trained in the old Adelaide Street Sunday-school, for which institution he imbibed a great regard, and was destined to be placed at the head of the Sunday-school operations of his denomination. He was convinced of sin under the address of a Sunday-school superintendent in Toronto. When the family removed to Aurora, for some

reasons, they united with the New Connexion, among whom he seems to have begun to preach. But returning to the old body again, the Rev. Lewis Warner induced him to supply the *Mount Forest* Circuit, in the Guelph District, in which work he was destined to hold on. He had many things in his favor—a good constitution, an active mind, a thorough schooling under good teachers, serious piety and enterprise.

(16) *Stephen Bond*, a young Canadian, born in the Township of Dumfries, but of English parents, who was called out this year by a chairman on the *St. Mary's* Circuit, was destined to be no mean man. He possessed a quick, self-reliant mind, the training of which had been by no means neglected. Rather under than over the medium size, he was the sort of man for activity and endurance. Over the average for preaching ability and business capacity, he has worked up his circuits well, and performed any Connexional trust assigned him in a complete and respectable manner.

(17) Next comes a brother larger and heavier than Brother Bond, young and single, but not a boy ; not indigenous to the country, for he came from old England to help us. His life had not been sedentary nor professional, but comprised the skill and activities of a builder, yet his strong, sound mind, along with an average school training, had been directed to every branch of study that relates to the function of preaching; and he sat at the feet and enjoyed the friendship of many of the great lights of the British Wesleyan Conference. He had been long on the plan, and was a capable city preacher when sent to the aid of the ministers of the *Hamilton Circuit.* He was destined often to have a town or city station, and upon occasion, to fill the chair of a district. Such was *Jonathan E. Betts.* The above has been learned merely by former conversations with our friend.

142. And now I have yet another, whom I have reserved to the last, that I might afford him a section to himself.

True, he was a boy just "out of his time" at a printing office; and he says of himself, "When I entered the work I had no books, no money, and very slender educational acquirements." The "educational acquirements," I am inclined to think, with his present enlarged views and attainments, he underrated. No person capable of the elegant calligraphy, and evincing the accurate orthography and ready accountantship of this man, could otherwise than have had a good elementary English education. Then, put a boy of such attainments and of a quick, observing mind into a printing office for seven years, and he will come out with no ill education. And then, there was an education of heart and of the moral nature which had been going on in the Sabbath-school and Bible-class, and, since his conversion, under the fervent, emotional, and paternal Goodson, in 1852, three years before; the training I say, he received in the class and prayer and fellowship meeting, and on the exhorters' and local preachers' plan. These meetings and the temperance platform would soon make a person so easy in utterance, so graceful in elocution, so facile in expression, and so naturally eloquent as *Alexander Sutherland*, no mean orator at once. Such a man with such alert and vigorous powers of mind, would be sure to make his mark. And make it he did. It was soon rumored in Wesleyan circles that Brother Warner had taken a young Scotch lad (he was of Scottish parents) out of Guelph, who was distancing his compeers by a long way. And when, in a year or two, he was allowed to go to Victoria as a Conference student, and to measure himself in the recitation room, in the debating society, and on the rostrum with others, he was pronounced by President Nelles to have a mind of the first class. Pity the exigencies of the work would allow him to remain in college halls so short a time. Everything this brother undertook was done well—not so much because of the plodding slavery of his application, as it was because it came easy to him, and he could hardly help doing as he did. Now then, here in this extemporized supply, we have the forcible city preacher, the trenchant writer, and the ready administrator that was to be. Little did the "Father of Canadian Missions" think before he lay down to his long last rest, that a lad on a bush circuit was, within the next twenty years, to come up and be one of the helmsmen of the great Methodist Missionary Society which supervises its missions from New Credit to Whitefish Lake, and from the Bermudas to Japan. The *Rev. Alexander Sutherland* has physical advantages; well-proportioned, he stands five feet ten in height, and weighs one hundred and seventy-four pounds. Need we say, his complexion is sandy, and his hair, which was once abundant, curly. While he is what he is now, we need not want a secretary, a chairman, an editor, or a *President of Conference*. He has been already twice Secretary of the original Conference, besides a Chairman of District.

143. This Conference was addressed at great length, and in a very instructive and encouraging manner, by the Rev. Dr. Beacham, the representative from England, expressing the warm attachment of the British Connexion for this affiliated Conference and for the Church and work under its care; and the sentiments he uttered were cordially reciprocated by the Conference in appropriate resolutions, and the same sentiments were embodied in the address to the British Conference.

144. The Conference closed in the usual form, on Thursday, the 14th of June, and the brethren parted with a renewed determination to prosecute the great work in which they were embarked with all possible diligence and fidelity. They might be seen in twos and threes, and in half dozens, or more, or singly, and solitarily—in rail-cars and steamboats, in stages and buggies, for days after, wending their way to

their several fields of labor, whether in city or country, in the cultivated or wilder parts of the Provinces they occupied.

145. There were instances reported then as well as now, of ministers receiving some token of affection, in the shape of a much-needed purse, to help them on towards moving and getting settled in their new circuits.

146. Every report made in the early part of that Conference year from any and every interest of the Church, was of an encouraging kind. Glowing accounts appeared in the *Guardian* from the camp-meetings, held east, west, north, and south, for single circuits, or several, or for districts; from the many, the whites, and the fewer, but not less interesting, the Indians.

147. The Rev. Samuel D. Rice, as moral Governor and Chaplain of the College, was making his business energy to bear on the material and financial interests of the institution; and an agent was set apart to extend and consummate the scholarship system. The annual commencement or convocation was characterized by interesting exercises, and by the graduation of some who afterward became distinguished in the Connexion and in the community at large. Among these was *Edward B. Ryckman*, who had been converted while an undergraduate, and about the time of which we write began to preach. He remained, however, that year as a tutor in the College, and the next year was received on trial and appointed to the Yonge Street Circuit the following year. This worthy descendant of a worthy German-Canadian Methodist family near Dundas, was destined to become one of the most able conscience-stirring preachers, efficient administrators in circuit and district, college professors and governors, and city pastors of the body. *Mr. Albert Carman*, now the Bishop of the Episcopal Methodist denomination in this country, graduated at the same time, and was fated to

pursue an almost similar course to Mr. Ryckman's in his own body. *B. M. Britton, Esq.*, now an eminent lawyer, and *Dr. Moses Aikens*, also distinguished as a physician, took their degrees in arts at that time, preparatory to their entrance on their professional studies. An undergraduate also, who was mentioned with approval for some prelection which constituted a part of the exercises, *Wm. R. Parker*, then a devout student and local preacher, was preparing for a course of activity and usefulness nearly parallel to that of Ryckman. Less conspicuous in educational matters, but more conspicuous in pastoral ones.

148. The autumn session of the college began under very encouraging auspices. The following is a brief statement of its prospects copied from the pages of the Connexional organ, the *Christian Guardian* :—

"We are glad to learn that the fall session of Victoria College has commenced with about one hundred and fifty students, a larger number, we believe, than have been present at the commencement of any previous fall and winter session. An addition to this number is still expected. The winter session of the Medical Department of Victoria College will commence in Toronto, on Monday next, Oct. 1st."

149. One of the most pleasing pieces of intelligence during the summer of 1855, was an account of the revival which broke out among the children of the Richmond Street Sabbath-school, Toronto, which issued in the conversion and incorporation of an encouraging number of the children in the society classes, something very necessary to the stability of youthful converts.

150. There were notes of triumph from as far East as Eaton, and from points in other directions as extreme from the centre. Thus early was there an augury of between one and two thousand net increase, that was to crown the year; and yet this was but a small earnest of the annual gains

which were to swell the augmentation of the next thirty years.

151. Mr. Case stood in the same relation to the work this year as last, and he and Mrs. Case were cheered by a beautiful letter from their protege, *Henry Steinhaur*, on his way back to his life-long scene of labor in the far, far west, dated "June the 26th, 1855," and written from the "Upper Mississippi." They shared the pleasure of its perusal with their friends, by publishing it in the *Guardian*.

152. Father Case was an exceedingly happy old man. There was with him "The remembrance of a life well spent," and unlike many old men, he was by no means querulous, or inclined to say, that "the former times were better than these." Nay, he exceedingly rejoiced in the material, commercial, and educational improvements that had taken place and were going on. Instead of envying the younger generation the comforts and refinements which an advancing Christian civilization had brought them, or grudging them those advantages, he was glad and thankful that they had not to undergo the inconveniences their fathers had to endure. This will appear from a letter to his friend, Rev. Dr. Green, written near this time, and which the Doctor considerately gave to the public. It is as follows:—

"Rev. and Dear Bro.—Our voyage down the Lake, on Saturday, was windy, but off shore, so that we were quite comfortable, and arrived safely about eight o'clock. A good boat is the '*Maple Leaf*.' Kind officers and attentive waiters. How little we once thought of such accommodations in travelling, when we rode in mud, knee deep, in three or four days, from 'York' to Hamilton Township! Then no Cobourg nor villages on the way. Now ten or twelve flourishing villages, with churches on the route; and how little we thought of a Cobourg, with its College, Grammar School, three Ladies' Schools, and eight Common Schools!

"Yesterday was a pleasant and devout season in the new church—well filled—amon wh were about one hundred and fifty students of Victoria College,—mostly devoted Christians—a scene of thrilling interest!

"In the College are youth from all parts of the Province—to return to their friends, when their education shall be completed, to bless the country in morals, science, religion, and various useful professions! My feelings were intense while addressing this interesting assemblage. God grant we may be increased fourfold." We look for it. With the Divine blessing it may be accomplished.

"As ever, affectionately,

"WM. CASE."

153. But the time drew near when the younger prophets were to have "their Master taken from their head." Although Mr. Case had passed his seventy-fifth year, he was still active; he could harness his horses, if need required, and drive them also. He, like all the early preachers, was a lifelong equestrian. He often took short journeys on horseback. Early in the month of October, or late in September, 1855 (for I have found it impossible to determine the precise day), he had mounted his horse, at his own door, for one of these short excursions, when an accident occurred of which we have the particulars in a letter from the Mission School teacher to the *Guardian*, which I give entire :—

"REV. SIR,—As it appears there are some wrong impressions abroad relative to the accident that recently befel the Rev. Mr. Case, some supposing that it was caused by his horse having run away, &c., he has requested me to state a few of the particulars, which you will have the kindness to give an insertion in the *Guardian*, for the satisfaction of his numerous friends who have manifested so much solicitude and sympathy in his behalf.

"The accident occurred in the yard, in front of his own door, as he was in the act of mounting his horse. Reaching over to adjust the stirrup on the opposite side he lost his balance, and falling over, fractured the neck of the thigh bone just below the hip-joint, leaving the joint itself uninjured.

"The fracture was reduced by Dr. Gilchrist, who was in attendance the same evening. By suitable application inflammation has been kept down, so that he has suffered but little pain from the wounded limb, which is now rapidly healing, and bids fair for timely recovering its strength.

"As may be supposed, however, the sudden change from very active habits to such close confinement has had the effect of greatly reducing his strength, and at times producing considerable fever, though for the last few days, I am happy to state, he has been improving in this respect; and through the unwearied attention and skilful treatment of Mrs. Case, we trust he will in time be fully restored.

"I am, Sir, yours, &c.,
"JOHN CATHAY.

"Alnwick, 15th Oct., 1855."

154. In the *Guardian* of the 3rd of October, intimation had been given that Mr. Case had fallen from his horse and broken his leg. In that of the 17th, the letter of Mr. Cathay, above given, was published, holding out hopes that he might recover. But the same paper contains the following short but sadder editorial notice :—

"After our paper had gone to press, we heard with unaffected sorrow of the death of our venerable Brother Case, at Alnwick. The accident referred to a few weeks since was the immediate occasion of his removal, just after he had passed his 75th year. More hereafter."

155. And in the *Guardian* of the 31st, in a long editorial with a deep margin of black, we have the particulars of his funeral, of which we give a paragraph below :—

"Shortly after the *Guardian* was put to press last week the mournful intelligence was received that our venerable and beloved "Father Case" had gone to his eternal reward. A brief notice of this event was inserted in the numbers of the paper printed after the intelligence of his death was received. We had been led to hope, from the favorable account given in the *Guardian* of the week before last, that his recovery was probable, and that he would be spared a little longer to his friends and the church; but it appears that he began rapidly to sink very soon after the letter was written by Mr. Cathay. The exhaustion was occasioned by bed sores, which brought on hectic fever, and hastened his death. We understand that while his consciousness continued he still entertained the hope that he would recover. During the last twenty-four hours he was scarcely conscious of his state, except at times for a few moments, when his mind appeared quite clear; but even to the last he could be roused by Mrs. Case. He died on Friday, the 19th inst., about one o'clock in the afternoon. His mortal remains were consigned to their last resting-place on the following Sabbath, at eleven o'clock, after a sermon suitable to the occasion, by the Rev. J. Carroll, of Belleville. The Revs. C. Vandusen, S. D. Rice, J. Beatty, S. S. Nelles, and Jas. Musgrove were also present at the funeral."

156. The way in which so many ministers chanced to be present, in a place so much out of the way and upon such short notice, was as follows:—The Missionary and Special Conference Committees had been sitting in Toronto, and their session covered the time of Mr. Case's death. There was then no railway down the margin of the lake. The brethren whose stations were in the country between Cobourg and Belleville, came from Toronto to the former place by steamer, and expected to take the stage at Cobourg for their homes; but a head-wind kept them back, and when they arrived at the wharf, they found the Brighton and Belleville stage had left. They were, therefore, detained over Sunday, upon which day they heard their venerated friend was to be buried. A number of them accepted the kind invitation of the Governor of the College and drove the intervening twelve or fifteen miles in his double-horse waggon to the funeral at Alderville. Just as they arrived, the Rev. James Musgrove, Missionary and Chairman of the District, was about to preach, when he insisted on men who were his seniors in the work, and who had known the deceased longer,

should address the people on the occasion. It was finally arranged that Mr. Carroll should preach, and the Rev. John Beatty follow with an address, and Mr. Musgrove read the burial service at the grave. There was a large concourse of whites and Indians who assembled to pay their last tribute of affection and respect to their friend and father; and there was the stricken widow of the departed. The text on which the sermon was based embraced the triumphant language of the great Apostle of the Gentiles, "I have fought a good fight; I have finished my course; I have kept the faith; henceforth there is laid up for me a crown of righteousness, which the Lord, the righteous Judge, shall give me at that day, and not to me only, but unto all them also that love His appearing." 2nd Timothy, fourth chapter, seventh and eighth verses. THE FAITHFUL MINISTER AT DEATH, HIS RETROSPECT AND PROSPECT, was the theme of the discourse.

157. From the many aspects, and scenes, and circumstances in which our central figure has been presented during the fifty years comprised in this biographical history, any extended account of his character will not be required. One short paragraph from his official obituary will be sufficient:—

"His body was never robust, and his habits were always temperate. His presence was dignified and prepossessing. His mind though never trained scholastically, was vigorous, searching, and tenacious, and by much reading, observation, and experience it became enriched with knowledge as practical as it was adapted for all the purposes which his diversified positions in the Methodist Church required. His acquaintance with Wesleyan doctrines, discipline, and usages was correct and comprehensive; his publication of those doctrines judicious, experimental, persuasive --often pathetic; his enforcement of that discipline in its integrity, while there was no lack of fidelity to our incomparable system, was invariably marked with moderation and caution; his pastoral assiduities for adults and youth, parents and children, were spiritual, fatherly, and unremitting. He was a warm well-wisher of our ministry and Connexional institutions; and in his entire intercourse with the ministers he loved, especially at the sessions of Conference, there was a good sense, a prudence, and a heartiness which made all revere and love him."

158. His admiring friends in Belleville, almost immediately, placed a tablet to his memory in the old Pinnacle Street Church, in which he had often ministered; which tablet has been transferred to the Great Bridge Street Church, since its erection. Although tardily performed, a monument to his memory was erected by his ministerial brethren, at Alderville, where he labored so long and where he died, the inscription on which is the following:—

[Since writing the above, it has been ascertained the matter has been delayed, and the inscription we sent for, and expected to give, has not been executed, and therefore, cannot be given.]

INDEX.

A.

Abbott, Rev. Jacob, reference to, i. 160.

Adams, Rev. Alvah, introduced, iii. 206; R. on T., 210. Perth, 273; Bonshire, 301; Bytown, 346, 389; Augusta, 415; located, 444.

Adams, Rev. Ezra, his account of Enoch Burdick, i. 267; ditto of Densmore, 269; of H. Ryan, 285; his own history, 286; R. on T., ii. 1; Bay Quinte, 11; Ottawa, 184; ord. 217; Hallowell, 331; Success on Thames, 355; Niagara, 416; located, iii. 3; readm., 277; Y. St., 296; P. Elder's letter, 334; Muncey, 365; death of Mrs. A., 385; fully occupied, 417; discouragements, iv. 125; superannuated, 151.

Adams, Mr. Joshua, short account of, ii. 179.

Adams, Rev. Lucius, a supply, v. 149; obit., 151.

Adams, Rev. Zenas, short notice of, ii. 189; his b. and conv., 190; death, 194; old Toronto Circuit, iii. 414.

Addoms, Rev. John T., short notice of, i. 276; located, 280.

Address to the Gov. of Can., ii. 271; ans., 273; to Can. Meth. from Am. G. Conf., 284; to Sir F. B. Head, iv. 120; dissatisfaction on account of, 125; to Brit. Wes. Conf., 200; of Rev. Wm. Case before Am. Genl. Conf., iv. 69.

Adelaide Academy, v. 40.

Adelaide Mission, v. 17.

Adherents of Royalty, i. 3.

Adventism, Dr. Cooney's account of, iv. 380; in Can. East, 408.

12

Adventures of Peter Van Nest, i. 76; of itinerants, 91; of Alex. Rose, 129; of Rev. Wm. Case, ii. 43; of John Dempster, 58; of Geo Ferguson, 69; midst rocks and mud, 469; of R. Phelps, iii. 291; of Benham and Indian boy, 368; of Tomkins and Knight, 437.

Aikens, Mr. James, short account of, ii. 363; his sons, 363; James C., one of the first merit students of Vic. Coll., iv. 374.

Aikins, Rev. James, notice of, i. 15; obit., 62; correction, 329.

Aikins, Moses, a graduate, v. 257.

Aikman, John and Hannah, i. 161.

Albion Circuit, its first supply, iii. 268; Huston, 332; S. Rose, 381; G. Miller, 414.

Alder, Rev. Robert, portraiture of, iii. 88; Montreal, 140 208; Exeter Hall Miss'y Meeting, 305; again in Can., 351; his views on the union, 392; at the Conf., 440; his third mission to Canada, iv. 237; his letter to Lord John Russell, 303; at Toronto Conf., v. 1; President, 2.

Alderville Indian Mission, why so named, iv. 128; manual labor school, 209; Case there in secession, 375; number of members, 467; an assistant, v. 73; Case and Hurlburt, 105.

Allegorical preaching, i. 131.

Allison, Rev. Cyrus R., portraiture of, iii. 135; R. on T., 143; his first Circuit, 203; Ottawa, 247, 272; among the Indians, 296; Rideau, 347; agent, 418; letter from, iv. 48; stewardship, 117; success, 155; sup'd, 129.

America and American Methodism, Dr. Jobson's quoted, ii. 84.

American Gen'l Conf., resolutions on Can. Meth., ii. 284-287; Delegates to, iii. 169; iv. 6; Cincinnatti Conf. and Can. Episcopals, Mr. Lord's letter, 100; comments on, 134; decisions, 399.

American Republic, i. 3; Loyalists leave, 3; independence of, 5; war declared with, 246; continuance of, 257.

American Meth. Mag., publication of, ii. 131.

Ames, Rev. William, short account of, iv. 363; his work at S. and W., v. 125.

Amherstburg Circuit formed, iii. 129; E. Stoney, 150, 245; Messmore, 266; Whiting, 337; Harmon, 385; interesting news, 470.

A night in the woods, i. 43, 106; ii. 18.

Ancaster Circuit and Wm. Case, i. 159; extent of, and leading laymen, 163; further notice of, ii. 10; labors of Youmans and Culp, 40; of Isaac B. Smith, 130; large decrease, 416; Smith and Culp, 453; Atwood, iii. 11; Gatchell, 56; its boundaries, 125; success, 126; Madden and G., 148; death of Slater, 243; W. and S., 265; increase, 292; revivals, 329; a small circuit, 380; Wilkinson, 413; Evans and Watson, 454.

Ancaster Conference of 1829, where held, &c., iii. 253; defections, 254; subjects considered at, 256.

Andrews, Rev. Alfred, portraiture of, v. 252.

Andrews, Rev. Wm., introduction of, iv. 407; a supply, 466; in Can. E., v. 156.

Anecdote of Wm. Losee, i. 7; of N. Bangs, 31; of Dunham, 37; of Dunham and the squire, 38; of Dunham and the Lutheran, 38; of the crying child, 39; of frontier life, 91; of a fiddler, 95; of H. Ryan, 286, 287; of Peter Bowslaugh, 161, 303; of John Platt and Wm. Losee, ii. 51; of a sceptic, 57; of a wicked father, 65; good sauce, 67; forgetting to pray for onions, 68; of Isaac Puffer, 137; of an Indian's gratitude, 142; of a bad road, 178; scarce timber, 250.

Anson, Rev. Wm., notice of, i. 15, 16; again, 64; his death, 66.

Appeal of C. Meth. Epis. Ch. to Genl. Conf., and its results, iv. 399.

Armstrong, Rev. Andrew, short account of, v. 156.

Armstrong, Rev. James, a supply, iv. 454.

Armstrong, Mr. James R., a guide, iii. 71; a director, 168.

Armstrong, Rev. John, a supply, iii. 58; Niagara, 149; Long Point, 244; on trial, 253; discontinued, 278;

Dumfries, 292, 311; L. Point, 336; Nelson, 381; Ancaster, 455.

Armstrong, Rev. John B., a supply, v. 37.

Armstrong, Rev. Noble, a glimpse of, v. 30.

Articles of Union between the Eng. and Can. Methodists, iii. 405; also, v. 3.

Arnold, Rev. John, short account of, ii. 14; sup'd, 37.

Asance, John, sad account of, iii. 180.

Asbury, Bishop, his com. to Garretson's band, i. 6; letter to, from Case, 180; his visit to Canada, 228; accident to, 232; his estimate of Canada, 233; preaches in Kingston, 234; letters to Rev. J. Benson, 256; to James Mitchell, 332, 333; his death, ii. 27; his burial, 29.

Ashgrove; where and by whom settled, i. 17; seat of N. Y. Conf., 17; District, 144.

Asphodel Mission, its first missionary, iv. 363; name changed and why, 447.

Atkinson, Rev. Thomas, his obituary, v. 249.

Atley, Father, a good supply, v. 195.

Atwood, Rev. John S., portraiture of, iii. 104; Whitby, 108; on trial, 143; a mighty revival, 191; not at home, 269; not in time, 292; removal, 337; a soul-saving assistant, 384; ill-health, 412; Canboro', 454; located, iv. 116.

Atwood, Rev. Joseph, on trial, ii. 393; his character, 466; removal, iii. 3.

Augusta District formed, iii. 98; account of, 132; divided, 269; its. P. Eld., 297, 344; stations for 1835, iv. 42; divided, 198; its P. E., 258, 364.

Augusta, Methodist settlers in, i. 6; Circuit formed, 158; its extent, ii. 12; Isaac Puffer, 134; successful year, 178; Goodwin and Smith, 329; opposition, 471; increase, iii. 35; Metcalf, 133; alteration of boundaries, 204; revival, 246; two popular men, 345; good tidings, 390; two young men, 415; united to Prescott, iv. 42; secession, 43; Manly taken away, 46; defection, 125; a supply, 364; revival, v. 77.

Ault, Mrs. Jacob, i. 172.

Austin, Mr. John, short notice of, ii. 363.
Axtle, Rev. Nathan C., a widow's son, iv. 473.
Aylesworth, Mr. Bowen, ii. 48.
Aylesworth, Rev. Isaac B., portraiture of, iv. 390.
Ayre, Rev. Philip, appointed to Stanstead, i. 140 ; located, 330.

B.

Badger, Major, some account of, ii. 147-151.
Bagot, Sir Charles, death of, iv. 372.
Bailey, Mr. John, short notice of, i. 42 ; his sister Chloe, 124 ; his home, 128.
Bailey, Rev. John, a supply, iii. 265 ; his history, 277 ; on trial, 278 ; his colleague, 293 ; another, 337 ; a new Circuit, 385 ; still on trial, 413 ; in opposition, 422.
Baltimore Methodism, i. 151.
Bamford, Robert, a supply, iii. 38 ; applies for orders, 76 ; Rice Lake, 107 ; his visit to the Indians, 112.
Bangs, Rev. Nathan. Conf. of 1802 sends him to Can., i. 16 ; Oswegotchie, 19 ; his early history, 27 ; his opinion of Seth Crowell, 61 ; his trust in Providence, 91 ; his frontier life, 93 ; conversion of a fiddler, 95 ; escape from wicked men, 96 ; at an Indian dance, 98 ; a drunkard pacified, 101 ; typhoid fever, 102 ; a night in the Long Woods, 106 ; his marriage, 125 ; his account of Wm. Snyder, 134 ; his work in Quebec, 136 ; providential supplies, 138 ; goes to Montreal, 138 ; to Niagara, 144 ; leaves Canada, 150 ; goes to the Gen'l. Conf., 151 ; Dr. Luckey's opin., 152 ; volunteers for Montreal, 271 , his loss to Canada, subsequent career and death, 272 ; on the origin of the Reformed Secession, ii. 48 ; Haldimand Camp-m., iii. 74 ; preaches at the Conf., 94 ; again visits Can. Conf., 142 ; his views on union, 393 ; visits the Conf. in Brockville, v. 66 ; his comments, 67.
Barber, Rev. Isaac, a supply, 53 ; a recruit, 62 ; his ord., v. 140 ; in Can. East, 212.
Barber, Rev. Ozias, a supply, iv. 344 ; his antecedents, 347 ; Dalhousie Mission, 367 ; at Ingersoll, v. 184.

Barlow, Rev. William, Ass't. Sec'y. at Elizabethtown Conf., ii. 90 ; on trial, 100 ; work in Montreal, 132 ; withdrawal and subsequent career, 353.

Barnes, Elijah, a faithful class-leader, iv. 474.

Barnes, Miss Eliza, short account of, iii. 169 ; Rice Lake Indians, 193 ; visit to N. Y., 222; Lake Simcoe, 302 ; Dorcas Society, 321.

Barnston Circuit, how supplied, iii. 50 ; united with Stanstead, 89.

Barton, Rev. King, from the Irish Conf., iii. 311 ; his death, iv. 2.

Barrie District, first named in 1850, v. 69 ; its supplies, 70, 98 ; a miss'y. Dist., 123 ; "one wanted," 153 ; its stations and men in 1854, 197.

Barrie Mission, its first missionary, iv. 281 ; T. McMullen, 320 ; two laborers, 339 ; Wm. Steer, 375 ; 49 members, iv. 466 ; Camp-meeting, v. 107 ; well manned, 197.

Barry, Rev. John, York, iii. 395 ; Montreal, 437.

Baxter, Rev. John, a supply, iii. 337 ; on trial, 364 ; Hallowell, 386 ; a helper, 413 ; Canboro', 454 ; ord., iv. 1 ; Gosfield, 16 ; Waterloo, 124 ; Albion, 320, 338 ; needing a colleague, 388 ; Nanticoke, v. 73 ; superannuated, 183.

Baxter, Rev. Michael, his portraiture, iv. 364 ; Madoc, v. 201.

Bay Quinte Circuit, first meetings, i. 7 ; in the list of stations, 19 ; D. Pickett in 1801, 26 ; its extent, 111 ; increase of members, 118 ; revival, ii. 11 ; Madden and R., 138 ; sad event, 245 ; Jeffers and Spore, 325 ; two Americans, 376 ; death of Peale, 421 ; a year of turmoil, 468 ; tokens for good, iii. 34 ; glorious revival, 69 ; twin spirits, 78 ; appointments on, 102 ; Kingston set off, 187 ; changes, 233 ; ably served, 267 ; G. Ferguson, 295, 342 ; Whiting and Poole, 386 ; W. and Musgrove, 415 ; interesting letter, 468 ; New church, iv. 32 ; well supplied, 123 ; success, 124.

Bay Quinte District, how formed, ii. 372 ; a prosperous

year, 418 ; its stations and men, 466 ; Case, P. E., iii.
5 ; particulars from, 25 ; more, 66-69 ; further reports,
150 ; W. Ryerson, P. E., 218, 266, 295, 338 ;
changes, 386 ; its station, and men, 456 ; state of the
work, 482 ; stations for 1835, iv. 30 ; the Di t. Meeting, 258 ; stations for 1841, 339 ; a gain of, 224, 390.

Beam, John, some account of, i. 289.

Beatty, Rev. John, short notice of, ii. 364 ; iii. 18 ; a supply,
108 ; on trial, 210 ; Newmarket, 238 ; Belleville, 267,
295 ; London. 413 ; Toronto, 455 ; Yonge St., iv. 23 ;
Steward U. C. Academy, 156.

Beckwith, Rev. James, his obit., iii. 308.

Beecham, Rev. John. his visit to Can. Conf., v. 238 ; reference to his address, 255.

Belton, Rev. Samuel. on trial, iii. 140 ; early life, 145 ; appearance, 151 ; York, 226 ; Westminster, 305 ; Hallowell, 374 ; his zenith, 419 ; increase, 466 ; Belleville,
iii. 33 ; Perth, 85 ; B. Quinte. 100 ; Del. to Gen'l.
Conf., 170 ; Earnestown, 187 ; Fort George, 241 ;
gracious revival, 264 ; Westminster, 293 ; Ancaster,
329 ; Nelson, 381 ; L. Simcoe, 417 ; Dumfries, iv. 26 ;
retired, 117 ; sup'd., v. 182.

Belleville, Circuit org., ii. 139 ; conv. of Asa Yeomans, 171 ;
a vacancy, 254 ; Thos. Madden. 324 ; Jeffers and W.,
374 ; George Poole, 467 ; no increase, iii. 33 ; Indian
members, 69 ; D B., 105 ; a glorious revival. 190 ; success and extension, 233 ; well manned, 295 ; 5 new
classes, 341 ; a station, 415 ; letter from H. W., 464 ;
encouraging, iv. 36 ; vicissitudes, 192 ; H. Lanton,
487 ; Gemley and revival, v. 17 ; Geo. Young, 201.

Belleville Conference of 1830, iii. 276 ; of 1836, iv. 115 ; of
1840, 287 ; of 1848, v. 24 ; of 1854, 169.

Belleville District, stations all full, v. 37 ; one vacancy, 53 ;
its needs, 74 ; how supplied, 105, 128 ; unusual supply,
153 ; its stations and men in 1854, 201.

Benham, Rev. John B., first mention of, ii. 406 ; a student
at Cazenovia, iii. 168 ; supplies Cobourg, 170 : at Rice
Lake, 174 ; Case's letter to, 178 ; Grape I., 189 ; a miss'y.
helper, 232 ; his piety, 260 ; L. Simcoe, 262 ; visit to

L. Huron, 281 ; his school at Sahkung, 288 ; visit to L. Simcoe, 302 ; letter from Case, 325 ; Saugeen, 366 ; Journal, 367 ; perilous voyage, 368 ; reasons for his removal, 377 ; Oneida Conf., his subseq. labors and death, 378.

Bennett, Rev. Leonard, Memoir of, i. 275.

Bennett and Black, Messrs., at Am. Gen'l. Conf., ii. 31.

Benson, Rev. J., letter to, i. 175 ; another, 203.

Bentonville and Russeltown Circuit formed, ii. 437 ; James Booth, 485 ; iii. 46.

Berney, Rev. Daniel, introduced, iii. 442 ; on trial, iv. 2 ; ord., 45 ; letter from, 56 ; unfaithful, 454.

Berry, Rev. Francis, his portraiture, v. 116.

Berry, Rev. James, short account of, v. 192.

Betts, Rev. Jonathan E., portraiture of, v. 253.

Bettis, David, short notice of, iv. 451.

Bevitt, Rev. Thomas, a good supply, iii. 257 ; on trial, 277 ; an able preacher, 296 ; his circuit described, 339 ; Cobourg, 415 ; letter from, iv. 9 ; Sec'y. of Conf., 357 ; Chairman, 358 ; Sec'y. again, 444 ; President, 472 ; cheering account from, v. 78 ; Thorold, 182.

Beynon, Rev. Geo. portraiture of, iv. 293.

Bidwell, Marshall S., Esq., at a miss'y. meeting, iii. 167 ; a leading Reformer, iv. 184.

Biggar, Rev. Hamilton, first glimpse of, iii. 152 ; at Rice Lake, 160, 193 ; on trial, 210 ; Hallowell, 267 ; in charge, 296 ; London, 337 ; Westminster, 384 ; L. Point, 413, 454 ; "four days'" meeting, iv. 38 ; Sec. of Conf., 472 ; sup'd., v. 184.

Binning, Rev. Wm., short notice of, ii. 108.

Bishop, Rev. Luther, a stranger, i. 16 ; Long Point, 19 ; slender memorials, 34 ; he returns to U. S., 155.

Bissel, Rev. Geo., on trial, iii. 1 ; Ottawa, 41 ; Camp-meeting, 45 ; woods and swamps, 75 ; a long move, 136 ; married, 207 ; revival, 247 ; Bay Quinte, 267 ; wearing well, 295 ; large increase, 332 ; Toronto Circuit, 366 ; he went not, 414 ; he located, 444.

Black, Rev. John, portraiture of, ii. 474; his journal, 477; took the new part, iii. 38; on trial, 53; no sombre shade, 73; extract from diary, 74; Black and Green, 122; in orders, 143; amusing examination, 144; two colleagues, 195; Perth, 249; Mississippi, 273; old starting place, 299; ever-loved, 345; Ottawa, 389; wants a colleague, 416; letter to *Guardian*, 432; happy results of union, iv. 38; two letters from, 39; Bay Quinte, 123; Murray, 339; Rawdon, v. 201.

Black River Conference, visitors from, iv. 187.

Blackstock, Rev. Moses, a local preacher, ii. 323; further notice of, iii. 75; withdrew, 237; again received, iv. 295; early life, 296; removal, 297.

Blackstock, Rev. Wm. S., portrayed, iv. 472; Yonge St., v. 182.

Blaker, Geo., a native helper, v. 152.

Bloomfield, its first Meth. class, ii. 420.

Boardman, Rev. Elijah, a new import, ii. 218; probabilities, 255; U. S., 352.

Boehm, Rev. Henry, his account of Joseph Samson, i. 173; of Bishop Asbury's visit to Canada, 228; preaching in Matilda, 232; his touching account of Asbury's funeral, ii. 29.

Boice, Mrs., incident related by, ii. 42.

Bonchire Mission, and Geo. Farr, iii. 249; A. Adams, 301; James Brock, 347; far off, 390.

Bond, Rev. Stephen, portraiture of, v. 253.

Book Concern, N. Y., claims on, iv. 5; complaints, 120.

Book Estab. Toronto, Report of, iii. 444; origin of Committee, iv. 152; its Steward, 152, 191.

Booth, Rev. James, notice of his arrival, ii. 74; short notice of, 79; in perils often, 120; Kingston, 338; Quebec, 390; indefatigable, 437; difficulties, 486; decrease, iii. 48; Quebec, 88, 140; Kingston, 209; Stanstead, 274; Barnston, 308; Shefford, 351; an old field, 396, 438; sup'd., iv. 190; withdrew, 334; again effective, 486; obit., v. 180.

Borland, Rev. John, quoted, ii. 75; again, 77; an ass't.

12*

miss'y., iv. 108 ; early life, 144 ; Melbourne, 234 ; quotations from, 236, 284, 329 ; Montreal, 355 ; trials and difficulties, 411 ; his account of Foster, 439 ; Melb., 470, 489 ; letter from, v. 111 ; another, 137 ; Delegate to Can. Conf., 165 ; at the Conf. of 1854, 169 ; Sec. of Dist., 211 ; Toronto, 182.

Botfield, Rev. James, on trial, ii. 329 ; early life, 334 ; plans thwarted, 351.

Botterell, Rev. E., introduced, iv. 107 ; W. Can., 464 ; London, v. 14 ; P. E. Isl., 38.

Bottome, Frank, a supply, v. 53.

Bowen, Rev. Elias, D.D., short notice of, ii. 185 ; further account, 229.

Bowman's Chapel, i. 159 ; names of first class, 160 ; Conference there, iii. 253.

Bowman, Peter, some account of, i. 159.

Bowmanville, effects of disunion, iv. 484 ; a new church, v. 79 ; its men in 1854, 199.

Bowslaugh, Peter, a zealous man, i. 161 ; anecdote of, 303 ; another glimpse, iv. 371.

Boyce, Mr. Jehoida, his home, iii. 75 ; his death, iv. 106.

Braden, Wm., short notice of, v. 178 ; a helper, 220.

Bradford, a new church opened, v. 107.

Brant, Chief John, his sympathy, iii. 333 ; his death and burial, 379.

Brant, Colonel, short notice of, i. 164.

Brantford, its first class, iii. 14 ; its first church, iv. 14 ; sep. from the mission, 122 ; a brick church built, 342 ; N. F. E. there, v. 184.

Brantford District, first org. in 1848, v. 35 ; account of, 53 ; one to be sent, 72 ; omissions, 102 ; Wm. Ryerson its chairman, 147 ; its stations and men, 184.

Breckenridge, David, junr., short account of, ii. 468 ; Smith's Creek, iii. 31 ; Cobourg, 73 ; unwilling to wait, 80 ; a coming storm, 105 ; defection, 106.

Breckenridge, David, senr., portraiture of, i. 128 ; a mar-

riage, 177 ; hospitality of, 232 ; ceases to preach, iii.
35 ; an exception, 80.

Breden, Rev. John, his portraiture, iv. 376 ; Goderich, 406 ;
letter from, 436 ; Peterboro', 486 ; St. Thomas, v. 101 ;
Toronto East, 181.

Brewster, Rev. Robert, short reference to, v. 91 ; Winchester,
205.

Briden, Rev. Wm., some account of, v. 203.

Briggs, Rev. Joel, his early life, v. 71 ; Cookstown, 197.

British Wes. Conf., letter of, to Am. Gen'l. Conf., ii. 31 ; Canada stations, 37 ; friendly relations desired, iii. 216 ;
union projected, 353 ; (see Meth. Union) organization
of a Dist. for C. W., iv. 325 ; stations, 325 ; C. W.
Dist., 341 ; dissolution, 349 ; the Dist. in 1842, 374 ;
Del. to Eng , v. 50.

Britton, Byron M., an eminent lawyer, v. 257.

Brock Circuit, how formed, iii. 415 ; D. Hardie, 456 ; one
wanted, iv. 28 ; a new supply, 252 ; G. S. useful, 363 ;
two hired l. p's., 389 ; G. T. R., v. 198.

Brock, Rev. James, introduced, iii. 300 ; on trial, 311 , a
single man, 347 ; Mississippi, 389 ; more labor, 416 ;
his address, iv. 315 ; visit to Can. Conf., v. 118 ; Rep.
to Conf., 136 ; Odelltown, 211.

Brockville, revival in, iii. 134 ; annexed, 204 ; a new creation, 246 ; Green and Williams, 299 ; a station, 345 ;
Wm. Smith, 415 ; a blessed shower, iv. 44 ; united with
Elizabethtown, 154 : Conv. of D. B. Madden, 259 ; revival, iv. 308 ; R. Whiting, v. 205.

Brockville Conference of 1844, iv. 417 ; of 1850, v. 61.

Brockville District, first named, v. 37 ; stations well manned,
75 ; complete, 106, 129 ; a vacancy, 155 ; its stations
and men, 205.

Bromley, Rev. Daniel, a local elder, ii. 16.

Brooking, Rev. Robert, early history, v. 10 ; H. B. T., 164 ;
remarks, 215.

Brouse, Peter, an early convert, i. 8 ; death, 207 ; his family,
209.

Brouse, "Uncle Joe," conv. of, i. 7.

Brown, Rev. Nelson, a native Canadian, iv. 274; Hungerford, v. 201.

Brown, Rev. Wm., i. 127; early life, 291; on trial, ii. 1; location, 88; Cornwall, 133; P. Elder, iii. 269; superannuated, 340; in old age, v. 236.

Brownell, Rev. John B., a glimpse of, iv. 286; another, 409.

Brownell, Rev. Stephen, a supply, iii. 416; Ottawa, iv. 42; made his way, 126; Owen Sound, 339; agent, 455; Penetanguishene, v. 198.

Bruce Mines, a new church, v. 162.

Bryers, Rev. Wm., his early life, v. 155.

Budge, Henry, a supply, v. 37.

Bundy, Richard, his class, i. 74.

Burch, Rev. Thomas, app't. to Quebec, i. 271; his birth, &c., 281; marriage, ii. 4; death, 5.

Burdick, Rev. Caleb, i. 267, 304; his ord., ii. 295; wife's death, iv. 371.

Burdick, Rev. Enoch, early life, i. 254; enters the min., ii. 4; located, 267.

Burge, Michael, i. 315.

Burgess, John, a supply, iii. 413.

Burkholder, Christopher, ii. 97.

Burlington Academy, v. 40; success, 76.

Burlington Bay, i. 164.

Burrett, Mr. Charles, his conv., iii. 261.

Burns, Rev. William, his early life, v. 62; Lochabar, 206.

Burt, Rev. William, ii. 78; his zeal, iii. 90; Odelltown, 140, 209; return to Eng., 251.

Burwash, Nathaniel, sen., his conv., iii. 136.

Butcher, Rev. George B., short account of, iv. 57; ill-health, 243; again called, 258; desisted, v. 14.

Byam, John Wesley, on trial, ii. 100; in opposition, iii. 425, 447.

Byers, Rev. Henry, a supply, iv. 159; withdrew Brantford, 405.

Byrne, Rev. Alex. S., early hist., v. 48 ; obit., 94.

Byrne, Rev. Claudius, notice of, v. 50.

Bytown District, its stations and men, iv. 340; vacancies and supplies, 345, 369, 392; two more, 429 ; well manned, 454, 484 ; its Chairman, v. 15 ; its needs, 37 ; one supply, 75 ; complete, 106, 129 ; two to be sent, 155 ; its stations and men, 205.

Bytown Mission, some account of, iii. 247 ; church burnt, 274 ; J. C. D., 300; another helper, 346 ; A. and W., 389 ; the work spreading, 391 ; J. C., 416 ; asks for two men, iv. 45 ; changes, 259 ; secession, 407.

C.

Cain, " Old George," i. 158.

Caldwell's Manor, a new Circuit, ii. 387; success, 437 ; change, 487, 489 ; Booth, iii. 48 ; one wanted, 98, 140, 208; Thomas Turner, 307.

Cambridge, N. Y., birthplace of Thomas Madden, i. 32.

Cameron, Hon. Malcolm, mention of, iii. 300.

Camp-meetings, first in Canada, i. 113 ; Dutchman's remarks, 147 ; near the Fifty, 222 ; near N. York, ii. 57 ; Indian, 410, 416; Ancaster, 454 ; Kitley, 481 ; Yonge St., iii. 9 ; Haldimand, 74 ; Ameliasburgh, 99; Cummer's Mills, 109 ; Waterdown, 149 ; Churchville, 266 ; Presque I. and Hay Bay, 267 ; Kingston, 270; three good ones, 298 ; Portland, 342; King, 385 ; Baltimore, iv. 193, 197 ; Vaughan, v. 55 ; Union, 76 ; Owen Sound, 78 ; in the year 1851, 107 ; in 1854, 218.

Campbell, Rev. Alex., notice of, iv. 483 ; extra work, v. 192.

Campbell, Rev. Alex. R., his early life, v. 191.

Campbell, Rev. Thomas, short account of, iv. 181.

Campbell, William, a supply, iv. 348.

Canada, none but natives and volunteers sent there, i. 18 ; Case, useful to, 18.

Canada, Annual Conference, first meeting of, ii. 492 ; second, iii. 52 ; third, 94 ; fourth, 142 ; Earnestown, 210 ; Bowman's church, 253 ; Kingston, 276; York, 309 ;

Hallowell, 355 ; York, 404 ; Kingston, 439 ; Hamilton, iv. 1 ; Belleville, 115 ; Toronto, 145 ; Kingston, 183 ; Hamilton, 239 ; Belleville, 287 ; Toronto, 309, 332 ; Picton, 356 ; Hamilton, 382 ; Brockville, 417 ; St. Catharines, 443 ; Kingston, 472 ; Toronto, v. 1 ; Belleville, 24 ; Hamilton, 46 ; Brockville, 61 ; Toronto, 84 ; Kingston, 115 ; Hamilton, 140 ; Belleville, 169 ; London, 237.

Canada Methodism, doings of Am. Gen'l. Conf., ii. 284 ; requests for separate Conf., 397 ; again, 440 ; Conf., 492 ; request granted, iii. 177 ; effected, 210 ; a successful year, 347 ; transition (see Meth. Union), iv. 332 ; report of delegates, v. 2 ; Union ratified, 2.

Canada Western District, Rev. Wm. Scott's account of, iv. 325 ; its stations and men, 374 ; corrected, 379 ; misleading, 435 ; scattered hints, 464 ; work, how provided for, 485 ; stations corrected, 488 ; union with Can. Conf. ratified, v. 2.

"Canadian Courant," pub. in Montreal, i. 152.

Canadian Wesleyan Methodist Church organized, iii. 250 ; changes, iv. 294 ; declension, 294 ; proposals for union with New Connex. Meth., 295 ; union made, 435.

Canboro' Circuit, its extent, iii. 291 ; Phelps and Griffin, 330 ; supplies, 381 ; Griffis, 413 ; Atwood, 454 ; name changed, iv. 122.

Canniff, Jonas, ii. 51.

Cannon, Rev. Ibri, short account of, ii. 336.

Canton Circuit, Hope Chapel, opened, iii. 387.

Carey, John, short account of, iii. 22 ; Muncey School, 54 ; prosperity, 63.

Carlisle, a new church, v. 132.

Carlton, Rev. Thomas, D.D., incidental allusions to, ii. 189.

Carman, Rev. Albert, v. 256.

Carman, Michael, his conv., i. 8.

Carpenter, Abraham, brief notice of, iv. 472.

Carpenter, Samuel, death of, iv. 457.

Carr, Rev. George, first glimpse of, iv. 364 ; his own account, 386.

Carroll, Rev. John, D.D., his first open air sermon, iii. 149 ; traded away, 167 ; return to Toronto, 177 ; first Camp-meeting exhortation, 179 ; meets and dines with Case, 186 ; appointed leader, 194 ; sent to Toronto Circuit, 199 ; Belleville, 233 ; on trial, 253 ; Cobourg, 267 ; his first charge, 300 ; Perth, 317 ; Ottawa, 389 ; a feast, 391 ; Bytown, 416 ; Brockville, iv. 2 ; hard times, 124 ; Cobourg, 157 ; results of excessive labor, 244 ; perilous journey, 259 ; Chairman, 340 ; losing patience, 345 ; Toronto, 484 ; London D., v. 33 ; enemies, 78 ; his record of Hamilton revival in the East, 211 ; friction, 228-233 ; preaches Case's funeral sermon, 261.

Carter, Robert, a supply, iv. 389.

Case, Rev. George, his early history, iv. 473 ; Stratford, v. 190.

Case, Rev. William, his antecedents, &c., i. 2 ; no journal, 9 ; exhorter, 17 ; on trial, 17 ; volunteers for Canada, 18 ; strength of Methodism when he entered, 19 ; Bay Quinte Circuit, 112 ; first Camp-meeting, 114 ; Oswegotchie, 126 ; ord. deacon, 141 ; returns to Canada, 159 ; account of the journey, 162 ; sympathy for Indians, 164 ; ord. elder, 168 ; Detroit, 180 ; his letter to B'p. Asbury, 180 ; worthy of imitation, 191 ; promoted, 202 ; Dr. Peck's remembrance of his person, 237 ; three years' labor in U. S., 313 ; his receipts, ii. 2 ; delegates to the Gen'l. Conf. of 1816, 2 ; his District in 1815, 7 ; at B'p. Asbury's funeral, 29 ; his return to Lower Can. Dist., 42 ; the Scotch woman, 43 ; his Dist. in 1817, 131 ; in 1818, 170 ; Conf. work, 216 ; his Dist., 228 ; Aurora Seagar, 239 ; Baltimore Gen'l. Conf., 284 ; Secretary of Niag. Conf., 292 ; P. E. Upper Can. Dist., 304 ; Dr. Fitch Reed's testimony, 354 ; sympathy for Indians, 360 ; his discernment, 362 ; Sec. of Conf., 390 ; other work, 391 ; glimpses, 398, 399 ; visits the Indians, 404 ; conversion of some, 443 ; more success, 461 ; org. of Miss'y. Society, 495 ; Canada for life, iii. 2 ; passing glimpses, 25-31 ; corner-stone, 39 ; contrasts, 41 ; missionary anniv., 42 ; visit to Red men,

45 ; Conf. of 1825, 53 ; visit Grand River, 61 ; letter to Paddock, 66 ; to Ezra Healey, 67 ; to R. Jones, 79 ; meets H. Pope at Ottawa, 92 ; Sec. of Conf., 94 ; further glimpses, 98 ; two letters to Healey, 99, 100 ; again Secretary of Conf., 142 ; abundant labors, 150 ; letter to Peter Jones, 151 ; to Z. Paddock, 154 ; to Healey, 156 ; to Peter Jones, 158 ; to E. Perry, 159 ; extracts from Healey's diary, 160 ; visit U. S., 168 ; return to Grape Island, 170 ; letter to Benham, 178 ; journey north, 179 ; 132 Indians baptized, 181 ; glimpses, 186 ; Pres. of Conf., 217 ; his home at Grape Island, 218 ; Peter Jones, 219 ; with Jones he visits U. S., 221-226 ; marriage, 227 ; letter to Z. Paddock, 228 ; more letters, 229-233 ; Pres. of Conf., 253 ; Indian Missions, &c., 257-263 ; birth of a daughter, 264 ; Sup't. of M. E. C., 279 ; journeys and labors, 279-289 ; Del. to Gen'l. Conf., 314 ; death of Mrs. Case, 315 ; letters, 316-326 ; the last of his General Superintendency, 365 ; interesting letters, 368-373 ; laborious voyage, 387 ; miss'y. to Indian tribes, 417 ; letter from, 472 ; Credit Mission labors, iv. 66 ; letter, 68 ; his address before the General Conf., 69 ; in partial retirement, 208 ; to visit the missions, 264 ; letters, 266 ; President of Special Conf., 308 ; his address, 315 ; Academy Board, 351 ; letter from, 377 ; his Indian work, 407 ; Alderville, 467 ; an incident, 487 ; gratitude, v. 3 ; Industrial School, 16 ; Chairman Cobourg Dist., 36 ; letter from, 39 ; addresses the Conf., 119 ; visiting the Thames country, 156 ; letter to Dr. Bangs, 234 ; at the London Conf., 238 ; his jubilee sermon, 239 ; letter to Dr. Green, 258 ; accident, 259 ; death and funeral, 260.

Castle, Rev. Joseph, short notice of, ii. 419 ; on trial, 441 ; removal, iii. 2.

Cataraqui, first appointment to, i. 12.

Catterick, Rev. Thomas, ii. 48 : history of, 107 ; Fort Wellington, 206 ; Johnstown, 279 ; Niagara, 282 ; more testimony, 340 ; breaking new ground, 389 ; success, 438 ; obit., 491.

Caughey, Rev. James, first glimpse of, iii. 491 ; another, iv. 183 ; Quebec, 330 ; Montreal, v. 81 ; Toronto, 109 ; Kingston and Hamilton, 134 ; results, 158 ; Quebec, 167.

Cavan Circuit, a substitute, iii. 193 ; sympathy with Ryan, 237 ; McMullen, 268 ; hard labor, 296 ; VanD. and Young, 339, 387 ; Law and Harmon, 415.

Cawthorne, John W., short notice of, iv. 421 ; a supply, v. 53.

Cazenovia Seminary, iii. 168, 189 ; a student from, 238 ; son of Reynolds, 260 ; Alex. McNabb, 331 ; another, 337.

Centenary of Methodism, iv. 246.

Chamberlayne, Rev. Israel, short account of, ii. 13 ; Lycoming Circuit, 38 ; Bay Quinte, 139 ; his visit to Hickcox, 301.

Chamberlayne, Rev. J. F., short account of, i. 273.

Chamberlayne, Wyatt, senr., ii. 13 ; his baptism, 54 ; marriage, 87.

Chamberlayne, Rev. Wyatt, junr., ii. 54 ; ord. deacon, 57 ; Augusta, 178 ; Canada again, 377 ; B. Quinte, 421 ; difficulties, 468 ; Augusta, iii. 34 ; delegate to Gen'l. Conf., 170 ; Hallowell, 190 ; sup'd. and subsequent history, 212 ; a telling address, iv. 357.

Chambly Village, some account of, ii. 22.

Chapman, Rev. Francis, contrasts, iv. 450 ; Port Stanley, v. 187.

Chase, Rev. Abner, i. 195 ; Ostego, ii. 146 ; brief notice of, 291 ; another glimpse, iii. 131.

Chase, Henry P., a native helper, v. 33.

Chatham District, its stations and men, v. 189.

Child, the crying, i. 39.

Chippewa, a new chapel, v. 79.

Chisholm, Wm., Esq., iv. 26.

"Christian Advocate," N. Y., begun, iii. 97.

"Christian Guardian," Toronto, pub. of, began, iii. 256 ; E. Ryerson, Editor, 412 ; a significant election, 444 ;

anxious discussion on, iv. 2 ; editorship made impersonal, 152 ; change of Editor, 185 ; files of, inaccessible, 282 ; rivalry, 342 ; editorial on consecration, 370 ; Editor's reports, 382 ; Editor's course, 396 ; Playter, 424 ; portraiture of Maffitt, 457 ; Sanderson, 475 ; re-elected, v. 15 ; gleanings, 17.

Church, Rev. Levins S., introduced, iii. 247 ; Ottawa, 272 ; on trial, 277 ; desisted, 299.

Churches, number of, in 1806, i. 140 ; in 1815, ii. 35.

Church Relief Fund approved, iv. 459.

Churchhill, Rev. Charles, account of, iv. 441 ; visit to Brockville Conference, v. 67.

Circuits, division of, resolutions on, v. 226.

Civil and religious privileges, committee on, iv. 247.

Clappison, Rev. D. C., introduced, iv. 464 ; Farmersville, 202.

Clarendon first named in stations, iv. 42 ; report from, 45 ; parsonage built, 56.

Clarke, Capt. Matthew, i. 305.

Clarke, Rev. James M., a supply, v. 70 ; his antecedents. 98 ; on trial, 117 ; Glanford and Seneca, 182.

Clarke, Rev. John S., on trial, 174 ; portraiture of, 176 ; his first Circuit, 197.

Clarke, Rev. Richard, his early life, v. 80 ; Guelph, 190.

Class-meetings as a test of membership, debate on, v. 170.

Cleghorn, Rev. Thomas, contrasts, iv. 449 ; his portraiture, v. 53 ; London, 186.

Clement, Rev. Edwin, his portraiture, v. 34 ; Simcoe, 184.

Clergy Reserve controversy, iii. 192 ; disposal of, 337 ; resolutions on, iv. 147 ; rescinded, 245 ; attempt to settle, v. 18 ; Bill to secularize, 133.

Cline, Henry, i. 103.

Cline, S., i. 161.

Clouse, Peter, his miss'y. speech, iv. 15.

Coate, Rev. Michael, i. 15 ; biography of, 51 ; death, 53.

Coate, Rev. S., i. 14 ; goes out of the country, 15 ; P. Elder,

16 ; early history, 19 ; controversy with McD., 21 ; visit to England, 145 ; P. Elder, 174 ; letter to Rev. J. Benson, 175 ; abundant labors, 176 ; locates, 196 ; further account of, 203 ; Playter's account, 210 ; correction, 327.

Cobb, Rev. Thomas, portraiture of, v. 245

Cobourg, first named as a Circuit, iii. 72 ; Slater and E. R., 191 ; societies decimated, 235 ; Wright and Carroll, 267 ; fair success, 339 ; Camp-meeting, 387 ; Bevitt and Jones, 415 ; good prospects, 464 ; letter, 469 ; four days' meeting, iv. 38 ; its extent in 1837, 157 ; a new church, v. 131 ; its dedication, 161.

Cobourg District, first named, iv. 363 ; vacancy, 452 ; two more, 483 ; its manual labor school, v. 37 ; Scugog Mission, 53 ; its needs, 104 ; Indian Missions, 126 ; its supplies, 153 ; its stations and men, 199.

Cochran, Rev. Geo., his early life, v. 149.

Cochrane, Rev. Samuel, short account of, i. 149 ; appointed to Quebec, 155 ; obit., 170.

Coke, Rev. Dr., sent to org. Am. Meth. Church, i. 5 ; his death, ii. 3.

Colborne, first society formed, ii. 418 ; first named as a Circuit, iv. 322 ; 70 added, v. 17.

Coldwater, Baxter sent, iii. 386 ; the settlement breaking up, iv. 162.

Cole, Rev. Benj., his obituary, v. 250.

Coleman, Rev. Francis, some account of, iv. 291 ; Albion, 338 ; exchanging, 451 ; Matilda, v. 205.

Coleman, Rev. James, i. 14 ; account of, 40 ; his piety, 43 ; his death, 44 ; reference to, 160 ; correction, 328.

Coleman, Rev. Seymour, funeral sermon for Samuel Howe, i. 71.

Coleman, Rev. William, brief notice of, iv. 151 ; Oxford, 337 ; Richmond, v. 205.

Collier, James, his conversion, iii. 383.

Committee on Union, iii. 356.

Conference of 1806, i. 118; of 1807, 141; of 1812-14, where held, 288; of 1815, ii. 1; of 1816, ii. 35; of 1817, 83.

Conference, General, first, in N. York, i. 282; second, in Baltimore, ii. 28.

Connexional troubles, iii. 428.

Connor, Matthew, some account of, iv. 292; Vic. Coll., 394; located, v. 32.

Consecon, revival in, iv. 41.

Constable, Rev. Thomas, first glimpse of, v. 14.

Constitutional Act promulgated, i. 9.

Contingent Fund, creation of, iv. 120; Committee, how constituted, v. 225; applic. for grants, &c., 226.

Cooke, Edward, a supply, v. 104; Elora, 126; Mono, 152; his portraiture, 194; Durham, 197.

Cooksville first named on Circuit plan, iii. 244.

Cooney, Rev. Dr., introduced, iv. 235; his autobiography, 380, 412; pleading for the truth, 415; in Toronto, 465.

Cooper, Rev. Edward, i. 198; some account of, 219; Bay Quinte, 256, 261, 305.

Copway, George, some account of, iv. 372.

Cornish, Rev. Geo. H., "Hand Book of Meth." refer'd. to, iii. 79; iv. 180, 182, 233, 234, 236, 248, 269, 285, 286, 287, 375, 388, 404, 405, 406, 410, 424, 436, 441, 465, 466, 467, 482; v. 47, 70, 97, 105, 125, 152, 177, 184, 188, 192, 197, 199.

Cornwall Circuit organized, i. 158; increase on, 178; prospects of, ii. 110; further notice, 114; Mr. Pope's labors, 121; extent of, 122; increase, 243; E. Boardman and D. W., 329; great revival, 474; Ezra Healey, iii. 38; Chamberlayne, 135; decrease, 247, Black, 299; Waldron, 389.

Corson, Rev. Robert, his estimate of Geo. Neal, i. 90; moves into Oxford Township, ii. 38; his opinion of Elijah Warren, 40; his good home, 399; on trial, 441; Dumfries, iii. 13; letter from, 14; ord., 53; Dumfries, 59; Westminster, 128; a good year, 149; Whitby,

236, 268 ; Toronto Circuit, 297, 331 ; Yonge St., 381, 414; Newmarket, 455 ; letter from, iv. 27 ; his 85th year, v. 18.

Cosford, Rev. Thomas, some account of, iv. 241 ; St. Catharines, 338 ; Bowmanville, v. 199.

Costello, David, a supply, v. 207.

Cotton, Wm., portraiture of, iv. 453.

Covell, Mrs., i. 142 ; ii. 194.

Covell, Rev. James, ii. 194 ; his obit., 195.

Covenhoven, Rev. Peter, i. 198 ; some account of, 218 ; located, 268 ; correction, 334.

Cow, Robert, a native helper, death of, iv. 62.

Cox, Henry, a glimpse of, v. 20 ; Sherbrooke, 44 ; his visit to La Chute, 161.

Cragg, Rev. Edward, his early life, 213.

Crandall, Rev. Phineas, brief notice of, ii. 336.

Crane, Rev. Isaac, introduced, v. 244.

Crane, John, incidents of travel, iii. 71 ; exhorting, 120.

Crane, Samuel, i. 24.

Crawford, Seth, short account of, ii. 409 ; Grand River Indians, 447-450 ; success, 462 ; a glimpse, iii. 21 ; good training, 66.

Credit Mission, Indians apply to locate, iii. 22 ; a kind offer, 63 ; settlement commenced, 68 ; James Richardson, 201 ; curious census, 240 ; Geo. Ryerson, 269 ; Youmans, 297 ; James Evans, 333 ; report, 451 ; Quarterly Meeting, iv. 63.

Creighton, Rev. Kennedy, some account of, iv. 297 ; Grand River, 338 ; Bytown, 205.

Creighton, Rev. William, his early life, v. 73 ; Kincardine, 190.

Crews, Rev. Thomas, a supply, v. 87 ; London Circuit, 186.

Crosby Circuit, how formed, iii. 204 ; included in Brockville, 246 ; secession, iv. 42.

Crosscomb, Rev. William, some account of, ii. 107 ; brief

notice of, 200; Montreal, iii. 437, 487; interesting letter, 488-493; Quebec, iv. 107; visit Belleville Con., 119; Dist. Meeting, 141.

Crowell, Rev. Seth, i. 15, 22; further account of, 60; his death, 62.

Culbert, Rev. Thomas, his ord., v. 174; Proton, 193.

Culham, Rev. John, account of, iv. 297.

Culp, Rev. David, his early life, i. 289; his ord., ii. 1; Bay Quinte, 11; Yonge St., 130; York, 165; sup'd., 228; Long Point, 400; located, iii. 52; opposed to union, 420, 427.

Cumberland Mission, its extent, iv. 263.

Cummings, Rev. Anson, his visit to Conf. iv. 420.

Cunningham, James, a supply, iii. 265.

Currie, Rev. James, appointed leader, iii. 194; short account of, 277; among the Indians, 296; Lake Simcoe, 334; Waterloo, 415; Richmond, iv. 50; Perth, 340; R. Lochead's conversion, 368; Andrew A. Smith's conv., v. 64.

Curry, Michael, a supply, iii. 351; Wesleyville, 399; still helping, iv. 125.

D.

Daily, Joseph, a Quaker convert, ii. 325.

Darlington, Rev. Robt., on trial, iv. 34; supernumerary, v. 32.

Davidson, Rev. John C., a supply, iii. 75; Cobourg, 107; on trial, 143, Hallowell, 190; success, 245; Bytown, 300; Belleville, 515; Kingston, 456; a thorough pastor, iv. 190; withdrawal, 356; Bytown, 467; again withdrew, v. 179.

Davies, Rev. John, a supply, v. 249.

Davis, Alpheus, ii. 143; his early life, 162; his first circuit, 163; his obituary, 164.

Davis, Chief, some account of, ii. 415.

Davis, Rev. Geo., H., portraiture of, iv. 469; Toronto, v 33; letter from, 138; Cobourg, 199.

Davis, Rev. Heman, a supply, iii. 384; Sidney, 415; marriage and its consequences, iv. 117; Cobourg, 124; a supply again, 350; Balsam Lake, 363; Brock, 389.

Davis, a Mohawk Chief, iii. 53.

Day, William, brief notice of, iv. 160.

Dayman, Rev. Abraham, short notice of, iv. 421; ord. v. 29; Wilton, 202.

Dean, Rev. Horace, first glimpse of, iii. 293; some account of, 311; Westminster, 336; Thames, 385; Gosfield, 413; letter from, 430; Gosfield, 454; in full connection, iv. 1; Newmarket, 21; report from, 24; his colleague, 252; Toronto Circuit, 338; a mistake, v. 70; Rama, 198.

Decrease, first reported, i. 15; after the war, ii. 8; after the missionary war, 337; after the disruptionion, iv. 133; second consecutive, 233; in Can. East, 469.

Delegates to Am. Gen'l. Conf. at Pittsburg, iii. 169; New York, 314; in 1836, iv. 5; Baltimore, 247; New York, 383, 399.

Demorest, Rev. Thomas, on trial, ii. 218; his early life, 245; Yonge St., 311; Thames, 355; marriage, 455; letter of 456; ord. Eld. iii. 3; Niagara, 7; Dumfries, 126; located, 145; re-admitted, iv. 357; trav. agent, v. 54, 181.

Demorestville, noted, iv. 56.

Dempster, Rev. John, D.D., history of, ii. 56-63; in good company, 83; his perseverance, 91.

Dennett, Rev. Joseph, brief notice of, i. 251; his return, 261.

Densmore, Rev. Geo. W. short account of, i. 253; further account of, 268; his return, 270; Dr. Peck's opinion of him. ii. 53.

DePutron, Rev. John, notice of, ii. 26; his letter to the Miss'y Com., 71; his early history, 77; illness, 119; Fort Wellington, 206; Melbourne, 338; death, iii. 47.

Detlor, Mr. Samuel, death of, iv. 456.

Detroit Circuit, first named, i. 170; further notice of, ii. 8;

the society in 1818, 128 ; great changes, 129 ; increase and church built, 219.

Deverill, William, a supply, iii. 455; letter from. iv. 38 ; Brock, 344.

Devonshire, a parsonage built, v. 133.

Dewart, Rev. E. H., his portraiture, v. 102 ; his maiden communication, 108 ; on trial, 117 ; Thorold, 183.

De Wolfe, Rev. Charles, v. 43.

Dickson, Rev. G. N. A. F. T., from N. B. V., 113 ; changes, 166 ; Hamilton, 182.

Dignam, Rev. William, first glimpse of, iv. 257 ; his portraiture, 289 ; St. Andrews, 340 ; Gosfield, v. 189.

Dingman, Rev. Garrett J., a supply, v. 153 ; Lindsay, 200.

Discipline, changes in, iv. 358.

District Meeting of Eng. Missionaries in Kingston, ii. 215 ; further account of, 270 ; Dr. Alder's visit, iii. 351.

Division of Circuits, resolution on, v. 226.

Dixon, Rev. James, D.D., President of Conf. v. 24 ; his early history, 25-28.

Dixon, Rev. Trueman, short notice of, ii. 218 ; Montreal, 334 ; Ottawa, 335.

Dixon, William, on trial, iv. 384 : his parentage, &c., 385.

Doel, Mr. John, his account of the York class, ii, 166 ; Dr. Fitch Reed's testimony, 367.

Dodson, Rev. Nathan B., i. 195.

Dorey, Rev. Gifford, his portraiture, v. 20.

Douglas, Rev. Geo., on trial, v. 42 ; Bermudas, 80.

Douglass, Rev. John, recommendation of, iv. 488 ; Sherbrooke, v. 21 ; supernumerary, 165.

Douse, Rev. John, on Grand River, iii. 458 ; labors, iv. 14 ; letter to Mr. Evans, 209 ; his address, 314 ; in Hamilton, 465 ; back again, v. 7 ; Barrie, 197.

Dow, Rev. Lorenzo, quotation from his journal, i. 49 ; return to Ireland 119 ; preaches at Camp-m., 235.

Dowler, Rev. John A., a supply, v. 206.

Down, Rev. Samuel, a supply, v. 200.

Doxtater, William, his conv., iii. 31 ; successful labors, 187 ; Genesee Conf., 229.

Draper, Rev. Samuel, i. 15 ; further account of, 59 ; his death, 60 ; account of a Quarterly Meeting held by him, 279.

Duchess County, the home of H. Ryan, i. 24.

Duffin's Creek, Circuit formed, ii. 130.

Duke of Richmond, death of, ii. 274.

Dulmage, Elias, i. 233.

Dulmage, Miss, the wife of S. Coate, i. 20; death of Mrs. D., 206.

Dumfries, pioneering, ii. 459 ; extent of Circuit, 460 ; R. Corson, iii. 13, 59 ; Demorest, 126 ; Geo. S., 149 ; Griffis, 265 ; P. and A., 292 ; Atwood, 337 ; a soul-saving time, 384 ; Van, 414, 455 ; letter, 461 ; Belton and N., iv. 26 ; Ferguson and Madden, 337 ; revival, 343.

Dunham, i. 139 ; how connected, 144 ; increase, 150, 191 ; further record, 276 ; Dr. F. Reed's statement, 277 ; history, 279 ; resumed, ii. 256-268 ; Ibri. Cannon, an incident, 336.

Dunham, Rev. Darius, one of Garretson's band, i. 6 ; Canada, 12 ; Lower Can. Circuit, 14 ; locates, 15 ; history of, 36 ; some characteristics, 37 ; Dunham and the Squire, 38 ; power in prayer, 39 ; another glimpse, ii. 423.

Dunning, Rev. Charles, his conversion, iii. 81.

Dutch Methodists of Matilda, iv. 47.

Dyer, Rev. James E., his portraiture, v. 190.

Dyre, Rev. William R., a supply, v. 197.

E.

" Early Methodism," Dr. Geo. Peck's, quoted from, i. 242, 314 ; ii. 13, 15, 41 ; on Hop Bottom Circuit, 55 ; on Dr. Dempster, 57 ; Gid. Lanning, 99 ; Dr. Paddock's letter, 143.

13

Earnestown Conf. of 1828, account of, iii. 210.
Easton, Joseph, a local helper, ii. 379.
Education, early movement for, ii. 217.
Educational collection, v. 162; Committee, how appointed, 227.
Edwards, Rev. Andrew, sketch of, v. 123; Holland, L., 198.
Elizabethtown Circuit, formation of, iii. 345; Madden and Wood, 388; good tidings, 390; C. Wood, 416; "a feast of fat things," iv. 43; " no bed of roses," 126; true state of the case, 348.
Elizabethtown Conference, account of, ii. 83, 86; local preachers, 471.
Elliott, Rev. John, short notice of, ii. 309.
Elliott, Rev. John Ferguson, a candidate, iv. 328; his death, 353.
Elliott, Rev. James, a supply, iv. 344; his diffidence, 345; Hamilton, v. 182.
Ellis, David and William, iii. 15.
Ellsworth, Rev. Orrin H., a supply for Mud Lake, v. 126; on trial, 141; Vienna, 184.
Embury, John, in old age, v. 235.
Embury, Philip, and his company, i. 5; reference to, ii. 74; his Bible, 262; his grandson's death, iii. 140; a powerful preacher, v. 235; death, 236.
Embury, Samuel, i. 8.
Emms, Joel, Cornwall Circuit, iii. 81; fruits, 247.
Emory, Rev. John, ii. 30; Del. to Brit. Conf., 288.
Empey, Peter, criticisms on, v. 196; St. Vincent, 197.
English, Rev. John, his parentage, v. 30; Stoney Creek, 182.
English, Rev. Nohle F., contrasts, iv. 449; a glimpse of, 484; Brantford, v. 184.
Enthusiasm of early Methodists, i. 10.
Episcopacy, resolutions to relinquish the, iii. 357.

Episcopal disruption of 1833, and Culp's sympathy with, iii. 53 ; a vortex, 338.

Escape, providential, i. 96.

Esquob, James, a native helper, v. 152.

European itinerants, dates of arrival, i. 5.

Evans, Rev. Ephraim, D.D., short account of, iii. 203 ; on trial, 210 ; Cobourg, 235 ; Kingston, 270 ; Niagara, 290; a good year, 329 ; Stamford, 380 ; agent for college, 418 ; editor, iv. 3 ; re-elected, 120, 152 ; London Dist., 190 ; author's comments, 217 ; his address on taking leave, 314 ; in other company, 341 ; John B. Selley's letter, 342 ; London, 375 ; a laborious colleague, 405 ; his whereabouts in 1844, 435 ; London fortunate, 465, 486; back again, v. 7 ; sent to Halifax, 33.

Evans, Rev. Henry, i. 139.

Evans, Rev. James, short account of, iii. 220 ; visit to Grape Island, 233 : Indian School, 268 ; on trial, 277 ; Rice Lake, 296, 301 ; Credit, 333 ; Ancaster, 381 ; St. Catharines, 413 ; St. Clair, 438 ; Ancaster, 454 ; letter from, 471 ; selections, iv. 75-85; always busy, 127 ; in England, 168 ; letter from, 169-175 ; letter to, 209 ; L. Superior, 214-233 ; Guelph, 250 ; private letters, 272 ; H. B. T., 277 ; death, 278 ; testimonials of character, v. 31.

Everts, Rev. Renaldo M., his birth and conv., ii. 183 ; Augusta, 244 ; his death, 302 ; his letter to Healey, 427 ; another glimpse, iii. 131.

F.

Facts passed over, iii. 348.

Fairbanks, Ira, i. 195 ; Dr. Peck's reminiscences of, 240.

Farr, Rev. Geo., his conversion, ii. 12 ; his first Circuit, 324, 329 ; vindication of character, 351 ; Augusta Circuit, 377 ; discontinued, 390 ; Rideau, iii. 84 ; again on trial, 96 ; great triumphs, 136 ; his marriage, &c., 206 ; Demas, 249 ; located, 254.

Father of Indian Missions, i. 1 ; his family scattered, 2. "See Case, Rev. William."

Faulkner, Rev. William, iii. 209.

Fawcett, John, a supply, v. 153.

Fawcett, Rev. Michael, some account of, iv. 359 ; he begins seven successful years in Bay Quinte, v. 74 ; Consecon, 220.

Fawcett, Rev. Thomas, a supply, iii. 384 ; Toronto Circuit, 414 ; Newmarket, 455 ; letters from, iv. 27 ; his address on separating, 314 ; Guelph, 375, 436 ; back again, v. 7 ; Sarnia, 33 ; St. George, 184.

Fear, Rev. Samuel, iii. 458 ; a supply, iv. 159 ; letter from, 213 ; Chinguacousy, 406, indefatigable, 467 ; ord., v. 29 ; Owen Sound, 193.

Fenton, Mr. John, short account of, ii. 339.

Ferguson, Rev. Geo., on Christian Warner's conversion, i. 89 ; his early life, 304 ; opinion of Montreal, 312 ; extract from his journal, ii. 18 ; on trial, 64 ; further history, 65-70 ; Niagara Circuit, 161 ; Ancaster, 225, 307 ; success, 355 ; Long Point, 400 ; Westminster, iii. 12 ; increase, 58 ; Amherstburgh, 129 ; Thames, 150 ; Hallowell, 234, 267 ; Bay Quinte, 295, 342 ; Waterloo, 386, 415 ; discouragement, iv. 125 ; sup'd., 294 ; again in the field, 321 ; travels and work done, 383 ; Credit, 394 ; his obituary, v. 93.

Fiddler, anecdote of a, i. 95.

Financial District Meeting created, v. 56 ; first held, 109.

Fingland, Thomas, his death, iv. 457.

Finley, Rev. John B., his first appt. as P. Elder, ii. 292.

Fish, Rev. Charles, early history of, v. 35.

Fisher, Daniel, Esq., ii. 74 ; obit., iii. 140.

Fisher, John, Esq., iii. 51.

Fisk, Rev. Wilbur, D.D., elected Bishop of Canada Meth. Church, iii. 215 ; in favor of union, 393.

Flanagan, John, iv. 1 ; four days' meeting, 38 ; located, 243.

Flanders, Rev. Rufus A., some notice of, iv. 353 ; Russeltown, 379 ; Rawdon, 410 ; Wesleyville, 458 ; v. 21 ; New Ireland, 44 ; Shefford, 57, 80, 113, 137 ; Dunham, 212.

Fletcher, Rev. Ashton, portraiture of, v. 175.

Fletcher, Rev. Ashton, Sen., brief notice of, v. 175; introduced, 244.

Fletcher, Drummond J., portraiture of, v. 90.

Flint, Billa, gives house rent free, iv. 46.

Flint, Calvin N., short account of, ii. 187; Augusta, 244; Rideau, 333; Bay, 337; revival, 419.

Flummerfelt, Cornelius, iii. 196-198; again in the field, iv. 345.

Forman, Rev. R. J., on trial, v. 141; portraiture, 144; Bradford, 197.

Fort George Circuit, its extent, iii., 241; revival, 264; name changed, 290.

Foster, William, a good supply, iv. 438; subsequent career, 439; examination satisfactory, 469; Rawdon, 470.

Four days' meetings introduced, iii. 290.

Four noted names, iii. 447.

Fowler, Rev. Hiram, his antecedents, v. 247.

Fowler, Rev. Robert, M.D., a supply, v. 146.

Frazer, Father, and his class, iv. 124.

Freeman, D. M., Esq., i. 248.

Freeman, Rev. Daniel, i. 198; history of, 220; Dr. Ryerson's testimony, 221; located, 247; death, 248; hospitality, ii. 158; a glimpse, iii. 22.

Frontier life, anecdote of, i. 93.

Froom, Mr. James, i. 157.

G.

Gabie, Robt. L., a glimpse of, iv. 475.

Gage, James, i. 42; Case's home, ii. 304.

Gananoque, first found in the list of stations, iv. 30; Steer there, 32; S. Miles, 330; C. Turver, 202.

Gardiner, Capt., introduced, iii. 330.

Gardiner, Mr. David, ii. 46.

Garlick, Rev. Heman, i. 215; further account of, 243; death, 244.

Garrett, Richard, a supply, iv. 181; on trial, 334; withdrew, 335.

Garretson and his band, i. 6; gives permission to visit Can., 7; Wm. Losee one of the number, 11.

Garry, Rev. Geo., i. 195.

Gatchell, Rev. Joseph, i. 223; marriage, 224; Smith's Creek, 256; located, 263; again in the field, iii. 56; Lyon's Creek, 149; Niagara, 243; Long Point, 265, 292; sup'd., 313; his subsequent career, 313; useful, 330; opposed to union, 404, 445; finale, iv. 4.

George, Rev. Enoch, elected Bishop, ii. 31; a reference to, 83; his portraiture, 84; visit to Canada, 196; Lundy's Lane Conference, 291; his piety, 318; visits Canada, 493; Hamilton Conf., iii. 94.

Gemley, Rev. John, some account of, iv. 348; Toronto East, v. 181.

Genesee Conference, formed, i. 193; first meeting of, 194; extracts from journal of, 196; of 1812 meets at Lyons instead of Niagara, 258; in 1817, at Elizabethtown, ii. 83; in 1818, at Lansing, N. Y., 140; in 1819, at Vienna, 216; in 1820, at Niagara, 288; in 1821, at Paris, 339; again, in 1822, 390; Canada affairs, 397; in 1823, at Westmoreland, 439; visitors from, v. 238.

German, Rev. John W., his antecedents, v. 75; Farmersville, 202.

German, Peter, a helper, iv. 371.

German, Rev. Peter, a supply, iv. 427; portraiture of, v. 177; a note from Norwich, 185.

Gilbert, Rev. C. W. M., introduced, iv. 420; his first Circuit, v. 15; St. Mary's, 190.

Giles, Rev. Charles, quotations from, i. 195; ord. Elder, 238; instrument of Dempster's conversion, ii. 57; his account of Bishop George's sermon, 85.

Gill, William, noticed, iii. 135.

Gillespie, George, a supply, v. 15.

Gladwin, Rev. Jonathan, Isle of Tanti, iii. 458; useful, iv. 86; death, 190.

Glass, William, a probationer, iv. 445 ; Mono, 451.

Glassford, Paul, Esq., i. 129, 232 ; headquarters, ii. 133 ; his generosity, 176.

Goderich, first named as a separate Circuit, iii. 413 ; Thos. Hurlburt, iv. 74 ; out of the Can. Conf., 321 ; J. Norris, 375 ; another name, 481.

Gooderham, James, his early history, v. 30.

Goodfellow, John, brief account of, iv. 385 ; ill-health, v 14.

Goodrich, Rev. Charles B., some account of, iv. 288 ; his address on leaving, 315.

Goodson, Rev. George, portraiture of, iv. 118 ; Matilda, 125; Crosby, 340 ; St. Catharines, v. 183.

Goodwin, Rev. Timothy, his early life, ii. 186 ; testimony, 244 ; Augusta, 329 ; death, 378.

Gosfield, Horace Dean there, iii. 413 ; Dean and Ker, 454 ; letter from P. Ker, 560 ; help needed, iv. 426 ; union working well, v. 17 ; W. M. Dignam there, 189.

Government House, visit of Dr. Alder to, iv. 248.

Government Money Grant, iii. 394 ; remarks on, 426 ; political aspect, 427 ; memorials on, and report, iv. 3 ; resolutions on, 47 ; rescinded, 245.

Grafton, new church opened, v. 131.

Graham, Rev. Robert, his introduction, iv. 410 ; his portraiture, 437 ; a supply, v. 167.

Graham, William, short notice of, iv. 482.

Grand River Mission, nature of the work, ii. 400 ; first convert, 406 ; successes, iii. 20 ; visit by Case, 62 ; visit by Loring Grant, 65 ; Alvin Torry, 130 ; Messmore, 150 ; visit by Jones, 241 ; Geo. Ryerson, 294 ; Phelps, 332, 365 ; report, 452 ; letter, 470 ; Quar. M., iv. 63 ; K. Creighton, 338 ; H. Byers in opposition, 405.

Grant, Rev. Loring, i. 238 ; visits Grand River Mission, iii. 65.

Grape Island, R. Phelps sent there, iii. 107 ; S. Waldron, 190, 201 ; Wm. Case, 365 ; report, 452 ; John Sunday in charge, iv. 86 ; removal, 128.

Gratiat, incident on board the, iv. 169.

Gray, Rev. James, short account of, iv. 481.

Green, Rev. Anson, D.D., short account of, ii. 420; active in labor, 467; new work, iii. 32; on trial, 53; recollections, 76; gratitude, 87; quotations from MSS., 125-126; in full connexion, 143; reminiscences of Ryan, 146; Ancaster Circuit, 148; Fort George, 241; sent to plead for missions, 242; a gracious revival, 264; first advent East, 299; his first station, 345; P. E., 380; letter of, 431; his report, iv. 42; Secretary of Conference, 333; President, 356; Del. to Eng., 478; D.D. conferred, v. 38; return home, 220.

Green, Rev. Alex. T., some account of, iv. 448.

Greener, Rev. James, account of, iv. 393.

Griffin, David, a local preacher, iii. 330; a supply, 381.

Griffin, Smith, Esq., account of, i. 302; his after life, ii. 141; ord., 295; his generosity, iii. 9; a glimpse of, iv. 371.

Griffin, Rev. Wm. Smith, short account of, iv. 49; ord., 140; note from, 185.

Griffis, Rev. William, a great favorite, ii. 417; on trial, 440; success, iii. 13; married, 56; fruit, 124; a good year, 149; Long Point, 244; Grand River, 265; Ancaster, 292; revivals, 329; Canboro', 381, 385, 413; letter of, 430; London, 454; letter from, iv. 19; located, 151.

Grimsby Circuit, how formed, iv. 122; glorious revivals, 363.

Grindrod, Rev. Edmund, President of the Conf., iii. 440; short account of, 445; his death, 447.

Guelph, how provided for, iv. 123; its first place of worship, 160; little society, 212-214; changes, 321; re-constructed, 335; Ezra Adams, 338.

Guelph District, its first Chairman, v. 149; its stations and men, 190.

Gundy, John, an assistant, iv. 405; Whitby, 467; excluded, v. 32.

Gundy, William, a local supply, v. 15 ; Brock Circuit, 33.

Guinness, William, short account of, ii. 335.

H.

Hallock, William, i. 27 ; further account of, ii. 87.

Hallowell, extent of Circuit, ii. 138 ; decrease, 249 : Wilson and Metcalf, 325 ; two marriages, 374 ; Smith and Wright, 467 ; decrease, iii. 33 ; twin spirits, 76 ; Waldron and Atwood, 104 ; another decrease, 190 ; Ryan's stronghold, 234 ; two masterly preachers, 296 ; two able incumbents, 340 ; a great staff, 386 ; Heyland, 415 ; letter, 466 ; a good report, iv. 34-35 ; Davidson and Haw, 124 ; Dis't. Meeting held there, 258 ; Campmeeting, 258 ; Warner and Philp, 322 ; Jones and W., 339 ; an M. D. supply, 390 ; a convert, 428 ; revival, v. 39.

Hallowell Conference of 1824, account of, ii. 492 ; of 1832, iii. 355.

Hamilton City, names of first class formed, i. 161 ; its first church, iii. 125 ; seeks to be a station, 148 ; revival, 333 ; made a station, iv. 190 ; John St. Church, 342 ; new church opened, v. 108.

Hamilton Conference of 1827, account of, iii. 142 ; of 1835, iv. 1 ; of 1839, 239 ; of 1843, 382 ; of 1849, v. 46 ; of 1853, 140.

Hamilton District, first organized, iv. 362 ; ranks all full, 427, 451 ; its Chairman, v. 15 ; its needs, 36 ; "one to be sent," 53 ; provided for, 103 ; two wanted, 126 ; its share, 146 ; its stations and men, 182.

Hamilton Township Conference of 1826, an account of, iii. 94.

Hamilton, Rev. John, his early history, ii. 39 ; facts, 92 ; located, 93.

Hammond, Richard M., his early life, v. 63.

"Handsome pair," the, i. 20.

Hanna, Thomas, a supply, iv. 430.

Hansford, William, portraiture of, v. 245.

Hardie, David, his first Circuit, iii. 415; Brock, 456; a supply, iv. 127; on trial, 151; ord., 288; an oversight, v. 54.

Harmon, Thomas, early history, i. 298: his loyalty, 300; his work in 1818, iii. 128-9; ord. deacon, 217; a stopgap, 452; war of 1812, iii. 18; a supply, 293; Waterloo, 342; Amherstburgh, 385; Cavan, 414; ord., 442; member of Conference, iv. 119; supplies Wallaceburg, v. 101.

Harnden, Ralph, a supply, iv. 391; failed, 429.

Harper, Ephraim B., a supply, iv. 344; his portraiture, 346.

Harris, Rev. Benoni, ii. 2.

Harris, Elijah, a supply, iv. 344; his large family, 345; removal, 362.

Harris, James, short sketch of, v. 123.

Harris, Rev. Reuben, i. 16; further account of, 71; death, 72; another glimpse, 139.

Hartman, John, death of, iii. 486.

Harvard, Rev. William M., D.D., Pres. of Conf., iv. 123; his early life, 130; notice of arrival, 144; Toronto Conf., 183; Lower Can. Dist., 199; complimentary, 200; L. C. D. M., 327; Selley's estimate, 329; Montreal D. M., 469; Can. West Dist. M., v. 1; visit to Toronto Conference, 2; England and his subsequent death, 7.

Haskell, Rev. Squire B., short account of, ii. 269.

Haw, Rev. William, a supply, iv. 40; Port Hope, 322; visit to England, v. 54; Glanford, 68.

Hawke, William, a supply, v. 188; his early life, 209.

Hay Bay catastrophe, ii. 246.

Hazzard, Rev. John, ii. 41.

Head, Sir F. B., his visit to the Credit Mission, iv. 129.

Healey, Rev. Ezra, first notice of, ii. 350; his early history, 425; letter from Everts, 427; on trial, 429; his journal, 430; extracts, 479; Cornwall, iii. 80; more extracts, 82; a profitable time, 94; home again, 97; quotations from his diary, 98-100; Kingston, 202; Brockville, 246 ; Augusta, 345, 388 ; Matilda, 415; good news, 431 ; Bytown, iv. 54 ; honors, 122 ; extracts, 193-197 ; details, 253 ; Camp-meeting, 258 ; his death, v. 66.

Heck, Jacob, i. 136.

Heck, Samuel, ii. 83 ; meets Rev. H. Pope, 143 ; his death, iv. 350 ; his antecedents, iv. 422.

Hecks, i. 5 ; they, Embury, and others, 6 ; at Big Creek, 8 ; at Ashgrove, 17 ; their descendants, 126 ; Barbara's funeral sermon, 128 ; their works follow, v. 235.

Hedding, Bishop, his opinion of Ryan, i. 25 ; he visits Canada, ii. 493 ; Conf. at the " Fifty," iii. 52 ; presides at the Conf. of 1827, 142 ; and 1828, 210 ; he visits the Conf. at Kingston, iii. 276 ; a letter from, 314.

Herkimer, William, to go to Sault Ste. Marie, iii. 373 ; some account of, iv. 281 ; another glimpse, 386.

Herron, James, i. 15 ; further account of, 67.

Hetherington, Rev. John P., his arrival in Canada, iii. 252 ; Kingston, 349 ; he visits Hallowell Conf., 363 ; Kingston, 396 ; in Toronto, 403 ; England, 465.

Hess, William, a native convert, iii. 187.

Hewitt, William T., a supply, v. 206.

Heyland, Edward, short notice of, ii. 455 ; Ancaster, iii. 57 ; death; 57 ; his grave, 127.

Heyland, Rev. Rowley, his first Circuit, ii. 456 ; new settlements, iii. 17 ; Long Point, 58, 126 ; Niagara, 147 ; Bay Quinte, 267 ; Hallowell, 296 ; success, 339 ; Hallowell, 386, 415 ; letter to " Guardian," 430 ; a gracious revival, iv. 32 ; Nelson, 338 ; superannuated, v. 184.

Hibbard, Rev. Robert, i. 142 : St. Francis, 213 ; incident, 214 ; Ottawa, 271 ; death, 273 ; further reference to, ii. 118.

Hick, Rev. John, his letter to Mr. Benson, ii. 74 ; short notice of, 77 ; another letter, 80 ; his labors in Quebec, 117 ; letter to Miss'y. Com., 200 ; Montreal, 338 ; Chairman, 387 ; record of success, 437 ; Europe, iii. 47 ; Stanstead, 307 ; Quebec, 437 ; death, 487.

Hickcox, Rev. Joseph, his early history, ii. 9 ; success, 39 ; Ancaster, 162 ; Thames, 219 ; located, 231.

Hierarchy overthrown, i. 5.

Higher education, early movement for, ii. 217 ; further efforts, iii. 256 ; an agent appointed, 315.

Hill, Darius M., a supply, v. 148.

Hill, Joseph, v. 108 ; great success, 134 ; Bruce Mines, 193.

Hilliard, Major, his testimony concerning Thomas Harmon, i. 299.

Hillier, Rev. Daniel, notice of, ii. 387, 439 ; drowned, 489-90.

Historic lessons, Montreal and its churches, v. 228-233.

Hitchcock, Barnabas, an exhorter, ii. 18 ; a supply, iv. 111 full account of, 182 ; desists, 328.

Hobbs, Robert, short sketch of, v. 91. ; Cornwall, 205.

Hodgins, Dr., his "History of Canada" quoted, iv. 176.

Holmes, Rev. Ninian, his nationality, &c., i. 146 ; further account of, 178; his usefulness and death, 264 ; his memoir, 265 ; his tomb, 266.

Holtby, Rev. Matthias, on trial, iii. 364 ; Toronto, 366 ; Guelph, iv. 321 ; secular things, 335 ; Oxford, 337 ; supernumerary, v. 184.

Hopkins, Caleb, Esq., iii. 149.

Hopkins, Silas, on trial, i. 255 ; located, 261.

Horning, Abraham and Isaac, i. 160.

Hough, James, glimpses of, iv. 160 ; letter from, 212.

Hough, John, a supply for Morris, v. 192.

Houghton, Luther, introduced, iv. 125 ; his liberality, 260; exhorting, 351 ; he enters the itinerancy, v. 154 ; Clarendon, 206.

Howard, Rev. Isaac B., introduced, iv. 321 ; on trial, 334 ; Vic. Coll., 394 ; Journal Secretary, v. 140; Sec. of Conf., 169 ; Dundas, 182.

Howard, Thomas S., obeys a call, v. 245.

Howard, Rev. Vincent B., a supply, iii. 415 ; Bytown and Hull, 457 ; Peterboro', iv. 339 ; Demorestville, v. 201.

Howe, Rev. Samuel, i. 16; further account of, 68; his obituary, 69.

Howes, John, first glimpse of, iv. 347; short notice of, 421; ord., v. 29; Cornwall, 205.

Hubbard, Miss, teaching at Grape Island, iii. 169; visits New York, 222; her marriage to Mr. Case, 227.

Hudson's Bay and Rocky Mountains District, its missions, beginning of, iv. 275; its first list of stations, v. 214.

Hughes, Rev. James, quoted, i. 161; teaching, iii. 344; a supply, iv. 261; his portraiture, 344; Millbrook, v. 199.

Hugill, Joseph, his early life, v. 65; a change, 101; Morpeth, 189.

Hulbert, Rev. Cephas, short account of, i. 148; success, 178; locates, 198.

Hull, Village of, ii. 17; circuit formed, iii. 136; boundaries changed, 207; McFadden there, 416; its extent, iv. 55; one sent back, 126; increase, v. 17.

Hunt, David, introduced, v. 152.

Hunt, John, a question asked, iv. 467; ord., v. 29.

Huntingdon, Simon, brief notice of, iii. 239; on trial, 253; Y. Street, 268; Westminster, 293; first charge, 346; Bonchire, 390; Augusta, 415; letter from, iv. 41; Grimsby, 182.

Huntington, Silas, his early life, v. 75; Gatineau, 206.

Hurd, Aaron, first notice of, iii. 236; Scugog, 241; ceased, 366.

Hurlburt, Asahel, short account of, iii. 205; on trial, 210; Brockville, 246; Westminster, 265; L. Point, 293; Thames, 337; Rideau, 389; power of God, 391; Elizabethtown, 416; three letters from, iv. 50; comments, 218; Chairman, 358; Secretary of Conf., v. 61; Maitland, 205.

Hurlburt, Erastus, some notice of, iv. 447; ord., v. 29; Can. East, 156.

Hurlburt, Heman, his death, v. 163.

Hurlburt, Jesse, on trial, 334; notice of, 336; Female Academy, 370.

Hurlburt, Sylvester, first mention of, iii. 262 ; Grape Island, 366, 417 ; short notice of, iv. 119 ; Lake Simcoe, 339 ; Smith's Falls, v. 205.

Hurlburt, Thomas, his early life, iii. 232 ; Muncey, 266, 366 ; Saugeen, 417 ; letter from, 471 ; on trial, iv. 2 ; light, 74 ; translating, 170 ; L. Superior, 214-232 ; church in the wilderness, 270 ; report of labors, 300 ; miss'y. travels, 373 ; a supply, v. 104 ; Hud. B. T., 164 ; exploring, 214.

Huston, John, first labors, iii. 19 ; St. Clair, 59 ; Westminster, 128 ; on trial, 143 ; London, 150 ; Thames, 245 ; a large gain, 274 ; Albion, 332 ; located, 412 ; in opposition, 450.

Hutchinson, James, portraiture of, iv. 252.

Hutchinson, John, New Ireland, iv. 471 ; Adelaide, v. 70 ; a change, 190.

Hutchinson, Richard, introduced, iv. 180 ; Adventism, 380 ; censure, 409.

Hyatt, Mr. and Mrs., i. 177 ; preaching in their barn, 214.

I.

Incidents : in Black River forest, i. 18 ; James Coleman and James Gage, 42 ; in journey of Peter Van Nest, 76 ; of clerical insolence, 122 ; characteristics of Case and Pearse, 130 ; of Case's journey from York to Hamilton, 163 ; of Bishop Asbury's crossing Lake Ontario, 236 ; of Van Nest, 269 ; of Ryan, 285; of the war, 317-321 ; romantic, ii. 18 ; of Wm. Case, 42 ; of an old Scotch woman, 43 ; at Father Waldron's, 67 ; horse trading, 153 ; a mother's sacrifice, 155 ; a rowdy arrested, 159 ; a wood bee, 189 ; journey on the St. Lawrence, 206 ; heroic daring, 215 ; thrilling events, 220 ; Metcalf's ministry, 254 ; Fitch Reed, 260 ; perils in a snowstorm, 264 ; conversion of a Roman Catholic, 265 ; a son of Belial, 313 ; a blacksmith, 313 ; State prison, 314 ; a child's experience, 331 ; an infidel's conversion, 332 ; preaching to Indians, 355 ; Infant baptism valid, 357 ; conversion of a R. C., 367 ; a prodigal son, 367 ; the providence of God, 370 ; perilous journey, 405 ; narrow escape, iii. 36 ; Indian converts, 95 ; wanted a wife, 129.

Increase of members, i. 15, 16 ; general, 118, 140 ; on Case's Dist., 242, 257 ; corrected, 334 ; in 1816-17, ii. 82 ; in Lower Province, 127 ; on Niagara Circuit, 130 ; in L. Canada, 201, 349 ; U. C., 384 ; for both Up. and L. C., 390. See end of each year in each vol. for report of incr. or decr.

Independence of U. S., when acknowledged, i. 5.

Indian affairs, first Committe on, ii. 349 ; applic. to Gov. for location at River Credit, iii. 22.

Indians, Six Nation, visit by Alvin Torry, ii. 358 ; Mission begun, 400 ; many conversions, 443-451 ; their first church, iii. 20 ; number of members, 24 ; a good visit, 45 ; conversions during Conference Sessions, 95 ; industry, 161 ; pagans converted, 179 ; extent of Indian work, 285 ; number of converts, 306 ; Manual Labor School, 361.

Indian Camp-meeting, full account of, iv. 78.

Indian names of lakes, i. 9 ; of Circuits, 12.

Indian tradition, i. 165.

Indians, Wyandots, their first missionary, ii. 360 ; further notice of, 463 ; number, iii. 54.

Ingalls, Rev. Edmund S., short account of, iv. 107 ; contrasts, 262 ; Sec'y. of Conf., v. 140 ; supernumerary, 165.

Intemperance, Indian resolution on, ii. 403 ; drowning whisky, iii. 113 ; craft in danger, 119.

Irvine, Rev. Alex., short account of, ii. 392 ; his history, iii. 309 ; B. Quinte, 342 ; York, 381 ; Stamford, 454 ; his removal and death, iv. 8.

Irvingite heresy, the, iii. 60 ; mischief of, 485.

Ivison, James A., a supply, v. 199.

J.

Jackson, Edward, his arrival in Canada, iii. 55 ; a glimpse of, iv. 153.

Jackson, James, on trial, ii. 96 ; early history, 98 ; Alvin Torry's estimate of him, 158 ; ord. deacon, 217 ; L. Point, 224, 306 ; success, 355 ; suspended, 391, 399 ; ord. Elder, iii. 3 ; Thames, 12 ; Westminster, 58 ; sup'd., 97 ; rival societies, 235 ; causing more division, 244-5 ; expelled, 254 ; another glimpse, iv. 294.

Jackson, John, his liberality, v. 36.

Jacobs, Peter, incidental meeting with, iii. 71 ; exhorting with power, 179 ; going to Hud. Bay Ter., iv. 278.

Jacques, George, his portraiture, v. 178 ; his early life, 209·

James, Solomon, a native helper, v. 98.

Jeffers, Robert, on trial, ii. 140 ; Augusta, 178 ; Bay Quinte, 325 ; his subsequent work and family, 375.

Jeffers, Rev. Thomas, first mention of, ii. 375 ; on trial, iv. 334 ; his antecedents, 336 ; Peterboro', 339 ; Welland, v. 183.

Jeffers, Rev. Wellington, D.D., first mention of, ii. 375 ; his conversion, iii. 344 ; portraiture of, iv. 128 ; on trial, 151 ; ord., 334 ; where born, 335 ; Belleville, 339 ; Montreal, v. 211.

Jenkins, Rev. John, his return from India, v. 41 ; visit to Hamilton Conf., 50.

Jennings, David, a probationer, iv. 445 ; Merrickville, v. 205.

Jewell, Rev. Joseph, i. 15 ; removes, 16 ; further account of, 57 ; location and death, 59 ; correction, 282, 326 ; additional, 329.

Jobson, Rev. Dr., his portraiture of Bishop George, ii. 84.

Johnson, Abbot, a local preacher, iv. 54 ; a helper, 125.

Johnson, James, Grape Island, iii. 366.

Johnson, William, his conversion, ii. 15.

Johnston, David A., introduced, v. 202.

Johnston, Rev. Edward, short history of, ii. 108 ; his non-arrival in Canada, 118 ; a Chairman, 203.

Johnston, George B., a six months' supply, v. 210.

Johnston, John, an assistant missionary, iv. 111.

Jones, Benjamin, some account of, iv. 388 ; a supply, v. 70 ; Picton, 105.

Jones, Henry, a supply, v. 106 ; further mention of, 117.

Jones, Joseph, a supply, v. 248.

Jones, Rev. Peter, 1st, his early history, ii. 52 ; marriage, 53 ; Ottawa, 132 ; superannuated, 352 ; located, iii. 444.

Jones, Rev. Peter, (Kakewahquonaby,) his early life, ii. 406-415 ; exhorting, 462 ; first Indian Church, iii. 20 ; fruits, 23 ; extracts from journal, 61 ; incidents of travel, 71-72 ; evangelizing, 111-121 ; on trial, 143 ; visit to Grape Island, 160 ; more extracts from journal, 161-167 ; journal again, 170-177, 179-185 ; with Case itinerating, 219-226 ; superintending, 240 ; extracts from journal, 257-8 ; passing notes, 269 ; still itinerating, 279-280 ; further labors, 301-303 ; voyage to England, 304-6 ; results of visit, 314 ; letters from Case, 316-326 ; vote of approval, 364 ; translating, &c., 366-67 ; ordination letters, 370 ; his journal again, 129 ; more quotations, 161-168 ; in England, 201-208 ; general miss'y. work, v. 54 ; encouraging letter, 77 ; in retirement, 147 ; visit to Syracuse, 221.

Jones, Rev. Richard, letter from, ii. 383 ; his conversion, 435 ; brief reference to, 482 ; setting out, iii. 78 ; Augusta, 133 ; on trial, 143 ; Perth, 206 ; death of his father, 207 ; open air preaching, 248 ; reminiscences, 272 ; Kingston, 299 ; Belleville, 341 ; three field meetings, 387 ; Cobourg, 415 ; good report, iv. 34 ; appointed Chairman, 153 ; effective labor, 198 ; President, 418 ; Yonge St., v. 182.

Jones, Rev. William, ii. 143 ; his antecedents, 152 ; Ancaster, 225 ; Rideau, 382.

Jones, Rev. Zenas, i. 195.

Jubilee sermon, William Case's extract from, i. 9 ; preached in London, v. 239 ; his text, 240.

K.

Karkaner, Father, i. 109.

Keagan, William, a supply, iv. 483; a mighty man of faith, v. 129.

Keefer, Geo., Esq., friendly to the last, ii. 341.

Keeler, Rev. Sylvanus, his first Canada Circuit, i. 14; further notice of, 15; his conversion, &c., 21; extent of his Circuit, 22.

Kelsey, Rev. James, a warm-hearted pioneer, i. 195.

Kendal, Rev. David, Lake Champlain, i. 11.

Kennedy, George, contrasts, iv. 359-60; Galt, v. 184.

Kennedy, Jacob, a supply, iii. 331; six months at Dunnville, v. 210.

Keough, Jabez B., first mention of, iv. 284; his portraiture, v. 198.

Keough, James, Esq., home of, iv. 284.

Keough, Thomas S., incidentally spoken of, iv. 284; fraternal relation, v. 198.

Ker, Rev. Peter, some account of, iii. 412; Westminster, 413; Gosfield, 454; super'd., v. 182.

Kerr, John L., short notice of, v. 152; Mono, 190.

Ketche, Metig, or Big Tree, v. 131.

Kilborn, Ira B., a supply, v. 146.

Kilborn, Jared, a local preacher, v. 192.

Kilbourn, Rev. David, i. 215; his life and death, 244-5; a correction, 327.

Kincardine Mission, by Mr. Muirhead, a local supply, v. 69; Wm. Creighton, 190.

Kingston, the first Canada Circuit, i. 9; its ancient name, 12; preaching in the market, 112; numb. of members, 22; request for help, 122; Dist. Meeting, 214; more pastoral work, 376; numbers, 385; glorious revival, iii. 69; how promoted, 71; Healey and Evans, 202-3; increase, 245; Evans and Bevitt, 270; faithfully served, 299; H., 307; a station, 343; Wm. Smith, 386; Wm. Ryerson, 415; Turner, 438; some account of, iv. 31; Sydenham St. Church, v. 77.

Kingston Conference of 1830, account of, iii. 276; of 1834, 439; of 1838, iv. 183; of 1846, 472; of 1852, v. 115.

Kingston District, John Carroll, its first Chairman, iv. 428; his supplies, 452; one vacancy, 483; its Chairman, v. 15; none wanted, 37, 43; well manned, 106, 129; three vacancies, 154; its stations and men, 202.

Kingston Meeting of Representatives, account of, v. 221.

Kirkland, John, iv. 160.

Knight, Rev. Richard, narrow escape of, iii. 437.

Knowlan, Rev. James, estimate of his character, ii. 386; Montreal, 436; Melbourne, iii. 50; Kingston, 88; Stanstead, 208.

Koyl, Ephraim L., his early life, v. 141.

L.

La Chute, i. 22; a society there, 109.

La Dow, Samuel, short account of, iv. 360; removal, 484.

Laird, John, G., his early history, v. 29.

Laird, William H., portraiture of, v. 244.

Lake, John Nelson, portraiture of, v. 244; his reasons for locating, 245.

Lake country, the, i. 9.

Lake Simcoe Mission, Miller and Currie, iii. 334-5; report, 451; its extent, iv. 281.

Lakes, Indian names of, i. 12.

Lambert, Rev. Chandly, some account of, i. 158; further notice, 178, 195; obit., 201.

Lang, Rev. Matthew, short account of, ii. 487; useful, 488; winning souls, 348; St. Armand's, 89, 140; Quebec, 307, 349; St. Armand's, 396, 438; his son's death, iv. 130; his address, 314; his death, v. 59.

Langlois, Peter, his early life, &c., i. 136; his journal, 145; joins the Church, 146; begins to study English, 156; app't. as a class leader, 211; begins to preach, 282; writes for a supply, 310; in England, ii. 27; new church, 76; Mr. Hick's labors, 117; the cholera, iii. 349.

Lanning, Gideon, his early history, ii. 99; his own version, 100; Detroit, 128.

Lanning, Ralph, at Quar. Meeting, i. 314; his character, 315; repeated, ii. 15.

Lanton, Rev. Henry, his portraiture, iv. 234; doubts, 285; probation, 328; recommended for ordination, 353; Hamilton, 405, 435; Belleville, 467; Canada East, v. 38; Clarenceville, 212.

Latimer, James F., his portraiture, v. 243.

Lavell, Charles, brief account of, iv. 385; Montreal, v. 54; Toronto, 182.

Law, John, introduction of, iii. 411; Cavan, 415; Dumfries, 455; letter from, iv. 17; Yonge Street, 250; Oshawa, v. 132.

Lawrence, George, i. 320.

Lawrence, John, his marriage to Embury's widow, i. 8.

Lawson, Thomas, short notice of, v. 241.

Lay celebrities, i. 128.

Lee, Daniel, some account of, iii. 397.

Lee, Jason, obituary of, iii. 397.

Lee, Rev. Jesse, his District, i. 9.

Lee, Rev. Luther, visits Canada Conf., iv. 187; incident of, 188.

Lever, John, a supply, iv. 28; letters from, 29; hard times, 253.

Lewis, James, Esq., and Niagara Circuit, ii. 40.

Lewis, John, short account of, ii. 19-20.

Lindsay, Father Purdy's shanty, iii. 344; class revived, v. 105.

Literary obligations of Canada to Methodist preachers, i. 153.

Liverpool Minutes, the, iv. 121.

Local preachers preparing the way, i. 6; Dunham's helpers, 14; pioneers and pastors, 326; their first District Conf., 327; its members, 328; covetous of orders, 345; their Conf. of April, 1821, 377; two helpers, 379; Seth Crawford and E. Stoney, 410; two old countrymen, 419; Rustan's revival, 437; demands, 465; Conf. of 1824, 471; extraordinary proceedings, 472; Conf. of

1825, iii. 9 ; praying Jimmy, 40 ; Conf. at Elizabethtown, 68 ; plan for Circuit first made in Canada, 270 ; three useful, 330; another, 331 ; two more, 346; four others, 383 ; oppose the Union, 420 ; meeting of dissatisfied, 420-422 ; letter, 434 ; conflict, 440.

Lochead, Robert, some account of, iv. 368 ; another glimpse, 390.

Lockwood, Rev. Joseph, introductory account of, i. 178 ; ord. deacon, 198 ; Yonge Street and the coon hunt, 224 ; located, 248.

London Circuit organized, ii. 452 ; E. Stoney, iii. 13, 59 ; a change, 127 ; M. Whiting, 244 ; Bailey, 293, 337 ; Griffis, 454 ; letter from Griffis, 460 ; union, v. 14 ; explanation, 186.

London, Conference of 1855, some account of, v. 237 ; prolific in recruits, 241.

London District, formation of, iii. 334 ; account of, 384 ; stations for 1835, iv. 16 ; reports, 16-21 ; David Wright in charge, 122 ; changes, 249 ; its stations and men in 1841, 337 ; changes, 362 ; its vacancies, 450 ; filled up, 481 ; its stations and men in 1854, v. 186.

Long, William, introduced, iii. 330 ; his visit to Yonge Street, 382.

Long Point Circuit, i. 19 ; extent of, 110, 289 ; Alvin Torry, ii. 154 ; success, 158 ; Camp-meeting, 159 ; large increase, 306 ; decrease, 356 ; Ferguson and Culp, 400 ; stationary, iii. 12 ; Heyland, 58, 126 ; increase, 149, 244 ; Gatchell and Patrick, 265 ; three men, 293 ; success, 336 ; W. and P., 384 ; notes of victory, 386 ; B. and W., 413 ; Biggar, 454; letter, 461 ; full details, iv. 10 ; name changed, 122.

Long Woods, a night in the, i. 106 ; Ryan there, ii. 484.

Lord, Rev. Wm., Pres. of Conf., iii. 475 ; labors, &c., 476-481 ; advice from, 496; apostolic labors, iv. 90-101 ; letter, 114 ; push and labor, 115 ; his return to England, 130 ; his last letter, 142.

Losee, Joshua, conversion of, i. 7.

Losee, Rev. William, his power in prayer, i. 7 ; Kingston, 9;

early history, 10; his age and appearance, 11; name and extent of his Circuits, 12; desists from the work, 13; in business, 14; visits Bay Quinte Circuit, ii. 50; his old age, 51.

Loverin, Jonathan, a supply, iv. 453.

Lovey's, Rev. John, wanted, iii. 260; his future, 261.

Lower Canada Camp-meeting, iv. 111.

Lower Canada and its missionaries, ii. 21; interesting details, 21-27; more missionaries, 37; their success, 71-82; their station list, 106; full reports, 107-127; labors and successes, 199-215; Kingston Dist. Meeting, 270; official documents, 271-275; stations for 1819, 276; letter from R. L. Lusher, 277; letter from T. Catterick, 279; interesting news, 280-283; the year 1820, 338-349; 1821 and its stations, 385; more facts of history, 386-390; meagre details, 436-439; a copy from the "Magazine," 485; letter from Mr. Booth, &c., 486-492; the year, 1824, iii. 46-52; the year 1825, 88-93; 1826, 139-142; 1827, 208-209; 1828, 250-253; Wm. Squire, Turner, and others, 274-276; change of several laborers, 306-309; a hurried glance, 348; hard to determine, 391; the celebrated Jason Lee, 396-398; two letters, 399-401; fragmentary references, 486-487; Mr. Lord's letter, 488; Mr. Crosscombe's letter, 489-492; revivals, 494-499; scattered inklings, iv. 107-110; camp-Meeting, 111; missionary meeting in Montreal, 112; Mr. Crosscombe's report, 141; letter from Mr. Lord, 142; from Mr. Harvard, 144; stations and men for 1837-8, 179; comments on, 180-183; gleanings, 233-239; stations for 1839, 283; no increase, 287; the "Wesleyan" published, 327; Dist. Meeting, 328; number of churches, &c., 329; manuscript minutes, extracts from, 352-356; Mr. Stinson called home, 375; changes in the stations, 379; numbers, 381; another laborious year, 408-417; Montreal Dist. Meeting, 437; comments, 438-443; more particulars, 469-472; a new name, 488; decrease, 489; a brief exhibit, v. 20-24; Quebec Dist. Meeting, stations, &c., 41-45; Rev. B. Slight's journal, 57-61; quota. from "Guardian," 79; stations for 1850, 80; Mr. Slight's record. 81-84; Rev. J. Borland's record, 111; appointments, 113; Rev. J. Brock's letter and labors, 113; Granby Church, 114; statement of affairs by Mr. S., 134-136; Mr. Borland's letter, 137; death of Rev. Wm. Squire, 138; efforts for union with the West, 140; last meeting of the District, 164; editorial on, 167; terms accepted, 173; union ratified, 211.

Loyalists, U. E., withdraw from the American Republic, i. 3.

Luckey, Rev. Samuel, his opinion of Bangs, i. 152; on Ottawa Circuit, 214; short account of, 250; letter to Dr. Bangs, 271; honors, 273; letter about Case, ii. 132; his visit to Can. Conf., iv. 382.

Luke, Wm. M. C., a supply, v. 207.

Lunn, William, Esq., his letter to the Home Com., iii. 399; another glimpse, v. 136.

Lusher, Rev. Robt. L., his arrival in Montreal, ii. 118; letter of, 125; another, 200; his work in Montreal, 177; Quebec, 338; Melbourne, 347; Halifax, 387; Chairman, iv. 180; editor of "Wesleyan," 327; again effective, 386; death, 440.

Lutheran ministers, i. 8, 325.

Lyon's Creek Circuit formed, ii. 309; why so named, 310; Alvin Torry, 357; decrease, iii. 100; Messmore, 57; increase, 124.

Lyons, an exhorter, holds meetings in Bay Quinte country, i. 7; his adherents, 11.

Lyscomb, Cyrus, introduced, iii. 246; marriage and removal, 272.

M.

Mack, Rev. Wilbur, brief notice of, ii. 194.

Madden, Rev. David B., his birth and baptism, i. 297; going to Cobourg, iv. 259; on trial, 334; Dumfries, 337; a year to rest, 361; Oshawa, v. 182.

Madden, Rev. Thos., first glimpse of, i. 16; Smith's Creek, 19; history of, 32; his appointment for 1807, 145; Montreal, 156; Ottawa, 177; removal to U. S., 246; returns to

Canada, 297 ; Conference Steward, ii. 1 ; Augusta, 12 ;
Bay Quinte, 48 ; Steward again, 90 ; Hallowell, 170 ;
Conference work, 217 ; on committee, 296 ; his talents,
373 ; Pres. Elder, iii. 5 ; Superintendent of Missions,
54 ; unabated zeal, 123 ; Rideau, 249 ; decay of energy,
270 ; Brockville, 299 ; Elizabethtown, 345 ; illness, 388 ;
sup'd., 412 ; death, 444.

Maffitt, Rev. John N., visits Toronto, iv. 457 ; portraiture of, 457-8.

Malott, Mr. Joseph, his obituary, i. 189.

Manly, Rev. John G., his conversion, iii. 300 ; Clarendon, 458 ; Augusta, iv. 42 ; Mr. Lord's curate, 46 ; his address on separation, 314 ; West Indies, 404.

Mansell, Mrs., out of candles, iii. 86.

Markham, a parsonage built in, v. 78.

Marmora and William Young, iii. 415.

Marriage, romantic, iii. 377.

Marsden, Rev. George, President of Conf., iii. 394 ; some account of, 409.

Marsden, Rev. John S., short account of, iv. 341 ; his death, 466.

Martin, Rev. Timothy, his first Circuit, iii. 12 ; on trial, 53 ; Long Point, 58 ; failing health, 126 ; death, iv. 350.

Marvin, Rev. Martin, conversion of, ii. 47.

Masson, James, portraiture of, v. 208.

Matthews, Abner, short account of, ii. 295 ; he preaches to Indians, 360 ; at Camp-meeting, 414 ; a precious time, iii. 23 ; letter from, 422 ; reference to, 473 ; glimpse of, iv. 371.

Matilda, Wm. Losee preaches there, i. 7, 11 ; Henry Boehm, 232 ; Henry Pope and Samuel Heck, ii. 133 ; a class formed, 206 ; missionary meeting, 280 ; W., H., and A. (see Cornwall), iii. 205 ; Waldron, 345; parsonage built, 390 ; Healey and Howard, 415 ; pruning, 469 ; no murmurs, iv. 43 ; both German, 47 ; both lively, 125 ; Nankeville serviceable there, 260 ; N. and Harmon, 340 ; a supply, 368 ; Francis Coleman there, v. 205.

Mattison, Rev. Seth, a shining star, i. 195.

Maudsley, Samuel E., a supply, v. 125 ; on trial, 141 ; portraiture of, 142.

Meetings of dissatisfied local preachers, iii. 420-422.

Melbourne, Circuit formed, ii. 106 ; R. Williams, 203 ; J. DePutron, 276 ; Sutcliffe, 338 ; Mr. Pope's letter, 388 ; vitality and hope, 438 ; Stinson, 488 ; Knowlan, iii. 50 ; Wm. Burt, 142 ; supplied, 209 ; Johnston, iv. 111 ; Selley and Borland, 236 ; Mr. Selley's letter, 284 ; Borland, 329 ; Raine, 410 ; death of Raine, 442 ; Borland again, 470 ; M. McDonald, v. 12.

Men who laid the foundation of Methodism in Canada, i. 129.

Merwin, Rev. Samuel, appointed to Canada, i. 83 ; his obituary, 84.

Messmore, Rev. Joseph, first notice of, ii. 454 ; Thames, iii. 13 ; Lyon's Creek, 57, 124 ; Grand River, 150, 245 ; Amherstburgh, 266 ; Stamford, 290 ; Niagara, 329 ; St. Catharines, 380 ; G. River, 418 ; letter from, iv. 10 ; again in the field, 388 ; Waterdown, v. 182.

Metcalf, Rev. Franklin, on trial, ii. 218 ; a beardless boy &c., 249-253 ; reason why, 391 ; recovery, 423 ; fruit 434 ; marriage, 483 ; letter from, 484 ; Hallowell, iii 33 ; sermon, 45 ; a model preacher, 76 ; Augusta, 133, 204 ; assist. editor, 256 ; his wife's death, 265 ; P. Elder, 298, Del. to Am. Gen'l. Conf., 314 ; Augusta Dist., 344 ; Niagara Dist., 380 ; sup'd., 444 ; St. Catharines, 455 ; located, iv. 3 ; Conf. of 1836, 116 ; letter from, 333 ; he visits the Conference, 419 ; his death, v. 66.

Methodism in Canada, its enthusiasm and activity, i. 10 ; doings of Am. Gen'l. Conf., ii. 284 ; separate Conf. requested, 397 ; again asked, 440 ; first meeting of Canada Conference, 492 ; Conf. at Saltfleet, iii. 52 ; at Hamilton, 142 ; pleasing news, 177 ; Earnestown Con. change of relations, 210 ; particulars, &c., 213-217 ; Conf. of 1829, 253 ; Belleville Conf., 276 ; first York Conf., 309 ; Hallowell Conf., a union projected, 353 ; editorial on, 354 ; delegation to England, 363 ; how viewed, 392-396; extract from Eng. Magazine, 400; union ratified, 404; opposition, 419; happy results, iv. 38; dividing wedge, 185; shadows, 237; seeds of discord, 248; antagonism, 270; spirit of the times, 279; disturbing elements, 298; delegatson to England, 300; events there, 302; the Canadian side, 307; a special Conf., 309-313; union dissolved, 317; comments, 318; choosing sides, 319; first step toward conciliation, 432; committee appointed 449; del. to Eng., 477; resolutions on, 478; action of Brit. Conf., 479; meeting of Canada Conference executive, 481; the Conf. of 1847, v. 1; articles of the reconstructed union, 3-6; consolidation, 7; consequent increase of laborers, 16; Conf. of 1848, 24; another epoch, 169; amalgamation of Canada Eastern District, 173.

Methodism, Provincial, what divided it, iv. 127; enmity to, 457.

Methodists, Episcopal, Jos. Gatchel meets a convocation of local preachers, iii. 313; David Culp's meeting, 420; another in Burford, 421; the Belleville sixteen, 422; John Bailey's case, 423; comments, 425-429; re-construction, 447-450; their del. to Am. Gen'l. Conf., iv. 6; false reports, 29; their episcopacy spurious, 101; political cry, 121; Bishop's statement, 134; "Guardian" editor, 134; Dr. Paddock, 135; judicial trials, 136-141; appeal to General Conference and its results, 399; making drafts, 437.

Methodists, Primitive, their first labors in Canada, 297; in Bowmanville, iv. 485.

Methodists, Reformed, secession of, ii. 48.

Methodists, union of (see Methodism in Canada).

Miles, Stephen, i. 153; short account of, iv. 118; superannuated, v. 201.

Miller, Aaron D., short notice of, v. 75; a year's rest, 156; Bath, v. 202.

Miller, "Father," i. 234; correction, 327.

Miller, Rev. Gilbert, a supply, iii. 267; on trial, 277; working hard, 296; Lake Simcoe, 334; Albion, 414; Rice and Mud Lake, iv. 71; Coldwater, 127; Peterboro', 253; Napanee, 339; supernum'y., v. 201.

Millerism, iv. 380, 396, 410.

Mills, John, introduced, v. 106; Bowmanville, 199.

Milner, James, introduced, iv. 241.

Minor, Timothy, glimpse of, i. 215.

Missionaries, British Wesleyan, instructions to, ii. 275; comments, 276; stations, 276; misled, 287; difficulties adjusted, 335-342; District Meeting of 1823, iii. 46, 88, 139, 208, 250, 274, 305; projected shadows, 348; more, 352; changes, &c., 396, 436, 486; v. 20, 41, 57, 80, 113, 136, 165; union, 211.

Missionary Society formed, ii. 492; report, 496; anniversary, iii. 53; first missionary meeting, 167; York seventh anniversary, 368; Conf. public missionary meeting, 410; report, 450; good increase, iv. 133; anniversaries, 395; Chinese Mission proposed, 461; out of debt, v. 77; report for 1853-4, 224.

Mississippi Mission, Ryerson and Belton, iii. 85; members, 86, 137; William H. Williams, 208; an increase, 249 John Black, 273; C. Wood, 300; Huntington, 346; Brock, 389; two chapels erected, iv. 49.

Mississxuoi Bay, a chapel proposed, ii. 126.

Mitchell, Rev. James, some account of, i. 212; removal, 260; his obituary, 331.

Mixed Committees to be appointed, v. 225.

Mockridge, James, brief account of, iv. 291; withdrew, 321.

Mohawk Christians, ii. 403.

Mohawk Mission Report, iii. 452.

Mohawk schools, iii. 54.

Money Grant Government, iii. 394; remarks on, 426; political aspect of, 427.

Mono, its first preacher, iv. 191; a good year, 250; ninety-eight conversions in one month, v. 109.

Montgomery, Rev. Hugh, a supply, iv. 48; in Canada East, iv. 378; illness, v. 20; withdrew, 179.

Montreal, Martin Ruter sent to, i. 86; visited by Joseph Sawyer, 121; clerical insolence, 122; first chapel, 177; state of society, 310; without a preacher, ii. 16; glimpses of, 18; letter of Mr. DePutron, 71; contributions to Quebec church, 76; District Meeting, 109; first Sunday-school, 120; Am. Meth. progress of, in, 132; further noticed, 185; number of classes and members, 277; church dedicated, 347; increase, iii. 48; R. Alder, 88, 140; prosperous, 208; John Hick, 274; Wm. Squire, 306, 349; Crosscombe and Barry, 437; additions, iv. 43; missionary meeting, 112; Dist. M., 112, 141; decrease, 234; revival, 330; a year's review, 355; two new churches, 413; friction, v. 228-233.

Montreal District, its stations and men, v. 211.

Moore, William Fitz., his conversion, ii. 46; his death, 47; a passing visit, iii. 71.

Moraviantown, Indian church opened, v. 132.

Morden, Thomas E., a useful man, v. 243.

Morden, William R., a candidate, v. 243,

Morgan, James, a supply, v. 184; his obituary, 184.

Morpeth, a separate charge, v. 132; Joseph Hugill there, 189.

Morris, Rev. Caleb, i. 15; obituary of, 66.

Morton, Lewis, a glimpse of, v. 30.

Morton, William, his antecedents, iv. 369.

Muirhead, a local supply, v. 69.

Mulkins, Hannibal, Long Point, iii. 454; Yonge Street, iv. 23; succeeding well, 192; subsequent career, 259.

Muncey Indians, Carey's school, iii. 54; prosperity, 63; a request, 68; confusion, 231; Thomas Hurlburt, 266; Ezra Adams, 365, 417; report, 452; Quar. Meeting, iv. 63; letters, 71; corner-stone of Indian school laid, v. 54.

Murray Circuit, how formed, iii. 415; letter, 466; Camp-Meeting, iv. 41.

Musician, the Devil's, burning his fiddle, i. 95.

Musgrove, Rev. James, introduced, iii. 341 ; on trial, 364 ; Whitby, 387 ; Bay Quinte, 415 ; his Conf. experience, 443 ; appointed Chairman, iv. 423 ; courage, 476 ; Secretary of Conf., v. 2 ; again elected, 85 ; Alderville Industrial School, 120, 199.

Mc.

McAllister, Andrew, on trial, v. 89; short notice of, 91 ; ill-health, 118.

McBerney, Mr. and Mrs. Thomas, worthy mention of, v. 248.

McCallum, Joseph W., first mention of, iv. 321 ; Waterloo, v. 75.

McCarty, a converted Irishman, i. 7 ; in the Bay country, 11.

McCarty's, Mr. John, Case's resting-place, iii. 151.

McConnell, Richard, a supply, iv. 369.

McCracken, George, some account of, i. 172 ; missed, 199 ; correction, 331.

McCullough, William, introduction of, iv. 292.

McCullough, Wm., 2nd, a glimpse of, iv. 475.

McDonagh, Wm., portraiture of, v. 120 ; on trial, 141.

McDonald, James, a local preacher, iii. 346.

McDonald, Malcolm, introduced, iv. 235 ; another glimpse, 378.

McDougall, George, his early history, v. 73 ; Bruce Mines, 98 ; sends good news, 108.

McDowell, Henry, short notice of, iv. 473 ; Richmond, v. 205.

McDowell, David C., an error noted, short sketch of, v. 92 ; Perth, 205.

McDowell, Robert, his controversy with Coate, i. 21 ; another glimpse of, iv. 256.

McEwen, Wm., received, iv. 360 ; U. S., 361.

McFadden, William, his conversion, iii. 247 ; his estimate of

Madden, 270; of R. Jones, 272; his first Circuit, 388, Hull, 416; letter from, iv. 49; Peterboro', 339; Brighton, v. 201.

Magee, Thomas, a converted native, begins to travel, iii. 301; journal of, 370; visits Credit Mission, iv. 68, 161.

McGee, Thomas, obit. of, ii. 101.

McGill, Wm., his early history, v. 12; ord., 85; Aylmer, 205.

McIlmoils, Squire, i. 157.

McIntyre, John, on trial, iv. 1; account of him omitted (see errata).

McKendree, Bishop, mention of, i. 196; travelling, 229; meets Asbury, 238; 2nd Gen'l. Conf., ii. 29; at Asbury's funeral, 30.

McLean, Hugh, i. 20.

McMullen, Rev. Daniel, conv. of, iii. 18; left his Circuit, 19; on trial, 53; success, 59; London and Long Point, 127; in full connexion, 144; located, 145; Yonge Street, 238; Cavan, 268; Cobourg and Belleville, 295; Hallowell, 340; Rice Lake, 365, 387, 417; super'd., iv. 151.

McMullen, Rev. Thomas, a supply, 381; Dumfries, 414; Whitby, 456; Metcalf, v. 104; extract from journal, 105.

McNabb, Rev. Alex., short notice of, iii. 330; a supply, 341; on trial, 364; Hallowell, 386; Prescott, 417; supernumerary, 443; letter from, iv. 8; Chairman and Book Steward, 358; Secretary of Conference, 382; D.D. conferred, v. 40; withdrew, 68.

N.

Nankeville, Benjamin, iii. 458; his work, iv. 213; usefulness, 260.

Napanee, Allison and Miller, its first pastors, iv. 332; a revival, v. 78.

Nasson, Peter, a faithful man, iii. 159.

Neal, Colonel, forms a class at Niagara, i. 7; his early life and old age, 88-90.

Necaunahby, happy death of, iv. 73.

Neelands, John, a supply, iv. 191.

Nellis, Samuel S., his early history, v. 13; President of Vic. Coll., 68.

Nelson Township, when named, i. 111 ; Circuit, how formed, iii. 381 ; J. S. Atwood, 414 ; Norris and Warner, 455 ; letter, 462 ; details, iv. 25 ; a good work, 250 ; well manned, v. 123.

Newbury, Arkle S., first glimpse of, iv. 159 ; on trial, 186 ; withdrew, 294.

New England schools, i. 19.

Newlove, Rev. George, Gananoque, iii. 352 ; his death, 353.

Newmarket Circuit, how formed, iii. 238 ; R. Corson and T. Fawcett, 455 ; letter from R. Corson, 462 ; Camp-meeting, iv. 24.

New Ireland, its first missionary, iv. 107 ; its second, 144.

New York Conference of 1805, i. 17.

Niagara, first class formed, i. 7 ; Circuit formed, 14 ; Gershom Pearce, 19 ; extent of, 110 ; increase of members, ii. 10; a new preacher, 40: increase, 42 ; Ferguson and Byam, 130 ; the Wolf, 162 ; again noticed, 211 ; increase small, 224 ; divided, 309 ; Isaac Puffer and Tackabury, 361 ; church opened, 416 ; Adams and Ryerson, 453 ; Demorest, iii. 7, 56 ; three men, 147 ; Circuit divided, 241; further changes, 290 ; Messmore and Wilson, 380.

Niagara District, stations for 1824, iii. 4 ; Thomas Madden, P. Elder, 54, 123 ; new P. Elder, 147 ; John Ryerson, 241, 264 ; large increase, 290 ; James Richardson, P. E., 326 ; F. Metcalf, P. E., 380 ; its stations, 454 ; its staff and Chairman, iv. 7 ; dismembered, 191.

Northrup, Rev. Charles, short notice of, ii. 188 ; success, 244.

Norris, Rev. James, his nativity, &c., iii. 143 ; a change, 189 ; Cobourg, 235 ; Yonge Street, 268, 296 ; Whitby, 338, 387 ; Sidney, 415 ; letter from, iv. 25 ; his address on leaving the Conf., 314.

Norris, Rev. Samuel, portraiture of, ii. 269.

Norton, William, portraiture of, v. 246.
Norway House, arrival of missionaries, v. 217.
Norwood Circuit. its change of name, and why, iv. 447.
Nova Scotia, Thomas Whitehead, missionary in, i, 132.

O.

Oakville, its first Methodist church, iv. 26.
Odelltown church built, ii. 486; William Burt there, iii. 90, 209; Knowlan, 308; Booth, 438; J. Hick, 487; probabilities, iv. 109.
Ogdensbnrg, reminiscences, i. 12.
O'Loane, James, Esq., death of, v. 221.
Onions, forgetting to pray for, ii. 168.
Oozhushkah and Mekagase, remarkable account of, iv. 75.
Organization of Can. Meth. Episcopal Church, iii. 213; its union with the British Wesleyans, 404; another M. E. Church constructed, and how, 447.
Orton, Henry, M. D., his liberality, iv. 160.
Osborne, John C., short notice of, iv. 472; his ord., v. 85.
Osgoode, beginnings, iii. 389; a revival, iv. 343; a supply, 346; sixty converted, v. 20.
Oswegotchie, first appointment to, i. 12; length of, 22; notice of, 42; extent of, 110; Wm. Case, 126; Baptismal register, 149, 156; divided, 158.
Ottawa Circuit formed, i. 19; in 1802, 22; D. Pickett, 26; extent of, 109; its scenery, ii. 14; a two weeks' Circuit, 17; the military preacher, 65; sifting, 132; humiliation, 379; a mistake rectified, 478; G. Bissell, iii. 41; Brit. Wes. send H. Pope, 92; increase, 206; C. R. Allison, 247, 272; Poole and L. S. Church, 299; Poole and Warner, 346; Black, 416; revival, iv. 44.
Ottawa District, how formed, iv. 198; R. Jones, Chairman, 248. See Bytown Dist.
Owen, Jesse, a supply, iii. 385.
Owen Sound District, C. Vandusen its first Chairman, v. 152; its stations and men, 193.

Oxford, a new Circuit, iii. 385 ; R. Phelps, 413, 454 ; Wm. Coleman, iv. 337.

Oxford House Mission, v. 218.

P.

Paddock, Rev. Dr., graphic account of his journey to his first Circuit, ii. 143.

Paine, Rev. Edward, a short account of, ii. 289, 290.

Palatines, the, i. 11.

Parent, Amand, a glimpse of, iv. 416.

Parker, John, short account of, ii. 398 ; subsequent career, 472 ; Genesee Conference, iii. 3.

Parker, Wm. R., a graduate, v. 257.

Pattie, Elias, some account of, i. 147 ; Cornwall, 178 ; Augusta, 224 ; further account of, 245 ; located, 246 ; effort to restore, ii. 96, 137.

Patrick, William, his conversion, ii. 166 ; short reference to, iii. 194 ; Yonge Street, 238 ; on trial, 253 ; L. Point, 265 ; Belleville, 295 ; Whitby, 338 ; Perth, 389, 416 ; located, iv. 48.

Pattyson, William M., introduction of, iv. 473.

Paul, John, begins to travel, iii. 301.

Peacock, Thomas, his early history, v. 51.

Peake, Edwin, a supply, v. 129 ; on trial, 141.

Peale, James G., a good soldier, ii. 66 ; his intended bride, 87 ; on trial, 140 ; Belleville, 171 ; sermon on baptism, 172 ; Cornwall, 243 ; Yonge Street, 311 ; his heroism, 383 ; his death, 421.

Pearce, Rev. Gershom, at Niagara, i. 19 ; history of, 133 ; success on Dunham Circuit, 150 ; obituary, 327.

Pearson, Thomas D., a supply, v. 128 ; on trial, 141.

Peck, Rev. Dr. Geo., his opinion about the Case family, i. 2 ; account of Deleware Circuit, 55 ; testimony concerning Jewell, 57 ; testimony concerning VanNest, 80 ; testimony concerning Chandly Lambert, 158 ; on organization of the Genesee Conference, 193 ; on doings of the General Conference, 196 ; his remembrances of Case,

228 ; quotations from " Early Methodism," 242, 314 ; on Israel Chamberlayne, ii. 13 ; on Jones and Densmore, 53 ; Wyatt Chamberlayne, 55 ; Gideon Lanning, 99 ; record of a sad event, 289 ; Susquehanna Dist., iii. 3.

Peck, Rev. Jesse T., visit to the Canada Conference, iv. 87.

Pembroke, twenty sheep gathered in, iv. 45 ; mission begun, 57.

Perdue, Henry H., a supply, v. 27.

Perth, introduction of Methodism into, ii. 382 ; Philander Smith and Metcalf, 433 ; Sol. Waldron, iii. 35 ; Ryerson and Belton, 85 ; W. H. Williams, 137 ; R. Jones, 207 ; Black, 249 ; A. Adams, 273 ; Carroll, 347 ; Patrick, 389, 416 ; expanded, iv. 48 ; Harmon and Tupper, 125 ; James Currie, 340 ; a supply from, 345, 346 ; David C. McDowell, v. 205.

Perry, Ebenezer, Hon., his family connections, i. 34.

Perry, Rev. Robert, on trial, i. 18 : Ottawa, 19 ; portraiture, &c., i. 34 ; Niagara, 131 ; his comments on a sermon of Wm. Snow, 157 ; Quar. M., 179 ; Long Point, 225 ; locates, 247 ; supplementary, 326 ; secession of, ii. 48 ; death, 50.

Peterboro' mentioned, iii. 344 ; preaching in a ball room, 432 ; first church built, iv. 362 ; Wm. H. Poole there, v. 199.

Peterson, Mr. Jacob, his narrative of Dunham's fidelity, 38-40.

Pettis, Charles, a supply, iii. 337.

Phelps, Rev. Richard, seeking God, iii. 81 ; Cobourg and Grape Island, 107 ; abundant in labor, 202 ; on trial, 210 ; Westminster, 244 ; Thames, 266 ; saddlebags experience, 291 ; conversion of Indians, 328 ; Grand River Mission, 330 ; graphic account from, 333 ; still there, 365 ; death of Brant, 379 ; Oxford, 413, 454 ; Grimsby, iv. 122 ; return from the States, 423 ; Belmont, v. 187.

Phillips, Samuel G., introduction of, v. 178.

Philip, Samuel C., his local influence, iv. 158; a supply, 192; Hamilton, 337; his energy, v. 132; Brampton, 182.

Philp William, a local helper, iv. 158; Sidney, 339; Waterloo, v. 202.

Philo, Geo. Washington, a supply, iv. 54; letter from, 55.

Pickett, Rev. Daniel, a new laborer for Canada, i. 15; Yonge St., 19; history of, 26; colleague of Bangs, 32; supplementary account of, 325; in opposition, iii. 447.

Picton, a great revival, iii. 31; Conference held in, 355; Conference of 1842 held there, iv. 356.

Pierce, Rev. Thomas C., his history, ii. 105.

Pinch, Richard, how he came to travel, v. 209.

Pioneers in Virginia, &c., i. 3; privations of, 4; local preachers and others among them, 6.

Plan for local preachers first made in Canada, iii. 270.

Playfair, Andrew W., a supply, iii. 137; his subsequent career and death, 138.

Playfair, Colonel, a funeral sarmon by, ii. 435.

Playter, Rev. Geo. F., his "Hist. of Methodism" referred to, i. 7; quoted from, 13; his account of Samuel Coate, 20; of Daniel Pickett, 26; Coate again, 210; Ryan's District, 226; Reeder's usefulness, ii. 15; about Wm. Losee, 50; his account of the Elizabethtown Conference, 86; the Hay Bay disaster, 246; the Gen'l. Conference of 1820, 284; statistics, iii. 209.

Playter, Rev. Geo. F., a supply, iii. 416; unappreciated, iv. 54; his thirty-five reasons, 397; appointed Editor, 424; at Napanee, v. 202.

Plumley, Daniel, short account of, ii. 70.

Pollard, William, some account of, 366-7; Quebec, v. 212.

Poole, Rev. George, Bay Quinte Circuit, iii. 101; on trial, 143; Richmond, 207; Bytown, 248, 274; Ottawa, 299, 346; Bay Quinte, 386; Murray, 415; letter from, 434; Hallowell, iv. 34; a baptism, 258; his death, v. 179.

Poole, Rev. Jacob, ii. 329; conjectures, 377; Yonge, St., 417; on trial, 440; finds a wife, 467; Hallowell, iii. 33; full membership, 53; Augusta, 78; Rideau, 137; Crosby, 204; Cornwall, 247; Albion, 296.

Pope, Rev. Henry, references to, ii. 74-77; further account of, 78; interviewed by Bishop George and Case, 84; letter to the author, 206; meets Elder Ryan, 211; his marriage, 214; Kingston Conference, 270; farewell sermons, 282; his person, 341; Montreal, iii. 48; Ottawa, 92; P. E. I. and Nova Scotia, 93; an octogenarian, 93.

Pope, Rev. Richard, safe arrival, ii. 74; place of labor, 75; promising, 77; his obituary, 79; letter to Miss'y. Com., 203; Fort Wellington, 338; success, iii. 48; Stanstead, 89; revival, 140; Shefford, 251; his death, 307; conversion of Jason Lee, 398.

Port Hope, first Methodist sermon in, iii. 32; first chapel dedicated, iv. 38; first resident Meth. minister, 249.

Port Stanley, church opening, v. 132.

Praying compact, the, i. 120.

Prescott, subtracted from Augusta, iii. 388; A. McNab, 417; rising, iv. 45.

Presiding Elders, changes of appointments by, i. 144.

Preston, James, portraiture of, v. 190; retires, 118.

Price, William, detained, iii. 459; a second glimpse of, iv. 129; his portraiture, 281; on trial, 288; St. Thomas, v. 187.

Primitive Methodists, their first labors in Canada, iii. 297.

Prindle, Rev. Andrew, his birth, education, and conversion, i. 133; Augusta, ii. 12; St. Lawrence, 138; labors in U. S., 189; Conference work, 216; Dumfries, 292; transferred, iii. 211; a vacancy filled, 243; superannuated, 311; his death, 313; the compeer of Case, v. 240.

Privileges, Committee of, appointed, iv. 153; another, 247.

Progress from 1790 to 1805, i. 16; at the close of 1823, ii. 494; numbers at the time of the union, iii. 396; on the eve of re-union in 1847, iv. 489; in 1855 Case's jubilee year v 239.

Proton Mission, successor, v. 108; a prosperous tide, 134.

Providential escape rom death, i. 40; providential deliverance, 78; from wicked men, 97; in a storm on the Atlantic, ii. 112.

Puffer, Rev. Isaac, some characteristics of, i. 195; ord. deacon, 238; Augusta, ii. 134; obituary, 134; his trust in God, 135; Bay Quinte, 172; Niagara, 309; second year, 361; visit to old fields, iv. 458.

Pugh, John D., a supply, v. 129; Hinchinbrook, 203.

Q.

Quakers, the, and Alvin Torry, ii. 220-224.

Quaaterly Meetings of the olden time, i. 226; in a smuggler's house, 279; at St. Davids, 307; Elizabethtown, ii. 137; revival and thunderstorm, 147; the first in new settlements on York Circuit, 366; Henry Ryan's 373; Perth, 435; Rideau, 484; York, iii. 6; Credit Indians, 170; Twenty Mile Creek, 326; Canboro', 328.

Quebec, first Meth. sermon in, in 1780, i. 6; attempt to introduce Methodism into, 83; Dr. Bangs appointed to, 135; Geo. McCracken, 172; how supplied during the war, 282; John B. Strong, 310; a lot bought on St. Ann Street, 312; first chapel, 313; Richard Williams' account of, ii. 23; dropped from the Aerican Minutes, 37; opening of new church, 76; letter of R. Williams, 76; increase, 205; further increase, iii. 52; no particulars, 88, 140; R. Rope, 208; Wm. Squire, 250, 275; Lang, 307; death of Mr. Pope, 307; three hundred conversionss, 349; Hick, 396; great fires, 411; Hick and Tomkins, 437; revival, 494.

Quebec District, its stations and men, v. 212.

R.

Raine, Rev. John, short account of, iv. 109; his death, 442;

Rattray, Rev. Thomas, a local helper, iii. 330; some traits of, iv. 448.

Rebellion in Canada, some account of, iv. 176.

Redner, Peter, conversion of, ii. 139.

Reed, Dr. Fitch, his account of Elijah Woolsey's death, i. 46; his account of Wm. Ross, i. 277; account of a Quar. Meeting, 279; of a battle, 306; his opinion of Case, ii. 132; Dunham Circuit, 356; reminiscences of Henry Ryan, 313; York, 315; letter to Meth. Mag., N. Y., 336; report, 365; report to U. S., 416; P. Elder, 440.

Reeder, Nathaniel, Dr. Peck's estimate of, i. 315; heavenly-minded, ii. 14; one hundred souls, 45; specimen of his sermons, 47; Cornwall, 179; his history, 180; death, 183.

Reid, Henry, a supply, v. 33; St. Vincent, 51; worked up, 70; his exceptional case, 85; Peel, 190.

Religious state of Canada in 1805, i. 10; value of religion to new settlers, 4.

Representatives, lay and clerical, meet at Kingston, v. 221; their doings, 222-228.

Reproof, a faithful, i. 236.

Republic, the American, its age in 1803, i. 3.

Revival Conference, the, ii. 86.

Reynolds, Rev. John, a native Canadian, i. 158; his first charge, 159; ord. deacon, 198; Smith's Creek, 225; Augusta, 256; located, 262; his after-course, 263; recom. to Annual Conf., ii. 324; defends the right, iii. 106; his opinion on Dist. Conferences, 408; his letter to the "Christian Guardian," 432; in opposition, 450.

Reynolds, Rev. Joseph, his conversion, iii. 415; called to work, iv. 257.

Rhodes, Rev. John, his early life, i. 252; ord. Elder, ii. 1; Bay Quinte, 48; going south, 93; his death, 94; his last visit to Canada, 416.

Rice Lake, a new Circuit, iii. 74; its extent, 75; R. Bamford, 107; Cavan substituted for, 193; James Evans,

296 ; McMullen, 365, 387 ; report, 451 ; letter from Gilbert Miller, iv. 62.

Rice, Luther O., introduced, iv. 321 ; on trial, 335 ; Cookstown, v. 132.

Rice, Samuel D., his early history, v. 10; Muncey, 54 ; Kingston, 68 ; College endowment, 130 ; Secretary of Conf., 238 ; Governor of Vic. Coll., 256.

Richardson, Geo. T., introduced, v. 178 ; his early life, 210.

Richardson, James, his conversion, ii. 419 ; York, iii. 17 ; on trial, 53 ; York, 60 ; Fort George and Queenston, 124 ; in full con., 143 ; Credit, 201 ; Secretary of Conf., 210; Niagara, 243 ; Sec. of Conf. again, 253 ; Kingston, 299 ; York Conference, 309 ; P. Elder, 326-328 ; Editor, 380 ; his views on the union, 393 ; valedictory, 418 ; Sec. of Conf., 439 ; elected Editor, 444 ; first to use the term Chairman, 459 ; letter from, 463 ; almost located, iv. 3 ; Toronto Dist., 21 ; his work, 27 ; U. S., 116 ; Meth. Epis. Church of Canada, 117.

Richardson, William, a supply, v. 97 ; on trial, 117.

Richey, Rev. Matthew, short account of, iv. 107 ; Principal U. C. Academy, 124 ; contrasts, 251 ; visit to Europe, 300 ; his defence of Powell, 397 ; acting President of Conference, v. 8 ; D.D. conferred, 28 ; Hamilton Conference, 46 ; Brockville Conference, 61.

Richmond Circuit, how formed, iii. 207 ; large increase, 274 ; C. Wood, 346 ; Wm. H. Williams, 389, 416 ; revival, 469 ; prospects poor, iv. 44 ; nothing remarkable, 50 ; a supply, 345 ; times of revival, v. 17 ; large accessions, 134.

Richmond St. Society, Toronto, a prolific hive, v. 176.

Rideau Circuit, how formed, ii. 333; its extent, 424 ; Healey's journal, 478 ; old landmarks, &c., 482 ; D. Wright, iii. 37 ; Farr, 84 ; Madden, 249 ; Sol. Waldron, 273 ; Healey, 299 ; Allison, 347 ; A. Hurlburt, 389 ; a great revival, 391 ; Shaler, 416.

Rideau District, formation of, iii. 269.

Roberts, Rev. Robert R., elected Bishop, ii. 31.

Robertson, David, portraiture of, v. 92.

Robinson, Rev. John, sent to Canada, i. 15 ; P. Elder, 16 ; his history, 54 ; his death, 56.

Robinson, Reuben, a supply, iv. 363.

Robinson, Robert, notice of, iv. 446 ; good news, v. 108.

Robson, Thomas, a successful laborer, v. 241.

Roise, Evan, a shouting Methodist, i. 231.

Rolph, Dr., a leading Reformer, i. 184.

Rose, Alexander, Esq., his adventures, i. 129.

Rose, Daniel, a local preacher, iii. 346 ; his subsequent career, 429.

Rose, Mr. John, a useful class-leader, i. 130.

Rose, Rev. Samuel, short account of, iii. 332 ; Albion, 381 ; Westminster, 413, 454 ; Muncey Indian Institute, v. 68 ; Chairman London Dist., 99, 187.

Ross, Thomas, a supply, v. 15.

Ross, William, his early life, i. 277 ; his death, 280 ; brief notice of, ii. 258 ; another call, 268.

Rossville Mission, some account of, v. 217.

Roy, James, M.A., his portraiture, v. 207.

Ryan, Rev. Henry, appointed to Bay Quinte, i. 19 ; his nationality and history, 23 ; Hedding's opinion of him, 25 ; incidents of his preaching, 113 ; E. Elder, 225 ; his extensive travels, 226 ; in charge of both Districts, 284 ; his labors and wit, 286 ; holds three Conferences, 288 ; faring well, ii. 2 ; a delegate to the Gen'l. Conf., 2 ; his impetuosity, 36 ; on U. C. Dist., 38 ; Gid. Lanning's testimony, 127 ; his zenith, 145 ; Conference work, 216 ; still successful, 218 ; his Dist. in 1821, 372 ; very effective, 373 ; ambitious, 465 ; jealousy, 468 ; superseded, iii. 5, 24 ; old Boanerges, 72 ; excitement produced, 80 ; sowing discord, 105 ; debate, &c., 145-7 ; Case's caution, 156 ; sowing seed, 190, 193 ; at the Conference of 1828, 213 ; Ryanites, 250 ; sends two letters to Conference, 253.

Ryerson, Colonel, his home at Long Point, ii. 306.

Ryerson, Rev. Egerton, his account of Daniel Freeman, i. 221 ; his memoir of Ninian Holmes, 264 ; his own conversion, 306 ; thrust out, iii. 7 ; sketch of, 9 ; on trial, 53 ; York, 60 ; champion of truth, 87 ; Credit Indians, 110 ; travelling north, 121 ; in full connexion, 143 ; the Clergy Reserve controversy, 192 ; editor, 256 ; representative to Eng. Conf., 362 ; sails for England, 393 ; editor, 412, 444 ; Toronto City, 455 ; U. C. Academy, iv. 31 ; his return from England, 146 ; Sec. of Conf., 184 ; editor, 185 ; to visit England, 247 ; again Sec. of Conf., 287 ; England again, 300 ; inaugural address, 351 ; his defence of Sir Charles Metcalf, 397 ; Conf. resolution on, 419 ; Sup't. of Education, 431 ; letter from Europe, 459 ; del. to Brit. Conf., v. 69 ; date of appointment as Chief Sup't. of Schools, 77.

Ryerson, Rev. George, on trial, iii. 210 ; short account of, 211 ; Credit Mission, 240, 269 ; Grand River, 294 ; visiting England, 294 ; his subsequent career, 294.

Ryerson, Rev. Edwy M., begins to be useful, iii. 265 ; a glimpse, 301 ; on trial, 364 ; Ancaster, 381 ; Stamford, 413 ; St. Catharines, 454 ; illness, iv. 192.

Ryerson, Rev. John, a supply, ii. 307 ; short account of, 350 ; Ancaster, 362 ; Niagara, 416 ; labor and love, iii. 34 ; Bay Quinte, 69 ; Perth, 83 ; a pleasant evening, 86 ; married, 124 ; P. Elder, 147 ; del. to Gen'l. Conference, 170 ; Niagara Dist., 241, 264 ; Metropolitan, 332 ; Bay Quinte, 380 ; letter from, 482 ; his Dist., iv. 30 ; Pres. of Conf., 382 ; extensive travels, 395 ; delegate to England, 478 ; to English Conference, v. 50 ; Co-Delegate, 67, 77 ; visit to the North West, iii ; exploring, 214 ; visit to England and return to Canada, 218.

Ryerson, Joseph E., a supply, iv. 425 ; desisted, v. 14.

Ryerson, Rev. William, short account of, ii. 440 ; laid aside, iii. 7 ; Stamford, 10 ; in full con., 53 ; a station, 55 ; York, 108 ; del. to Gen'l Conf., 170 ; return home—good news, 177 ; counselling Flummerfelt, 197 ; P. Elder, 218, 266 ; unusual activity, 295 ; del. to Gen'l. Conf., 314 ; letter from, 338 ; Brockville, 380, 388 ; Kingston, 415 ; letter from, iv. 7 ; his sarcasm, 242 ; contrasts, 251 ; deputation to England, 300 ; President, 332 ; again President, iv. 1.

Ryckman, Edward B., a College tutor, v. 256.

Rundle, William W., on trial, ii. 140 ; Yonge Street, 168 ; Long Point 224 ; St. Lawrence, 301.

Russ, Amos E., portraiture of, v. 244.

Ruter, Rev. Dr. Martin, a good man, i. 16 ; obituary of, 85 ; his domestic character, 88.

S.

Sabin, Benjamin, short account of, ii. 70 ; further account of, 393.

Sacket's Harbor, battle of, i. 316.

Salary of ministers, resolutions on, v. 223.

Sallows, Edward, first glimpse of, iv. 214 ; Sydenham, v. 33 ; Collingwood, 198.

Salt, Allan, on trial, v. 141 ; portraiture of, 143 ; H. B. T., 164 ; some remarks, 215, 236.

Saltfleet Conference of 1825, iii. 52 ; a boisterous time, 82.

Samson, Rev. Joseph, some account of, i. 173 ; P. Elder, 216 ; ord. by Asbury, 228.

Sanders, Rev. Joseph L., a supply, 186 ; his obituary, 187.

Sanderson, Rev. George R., a student, iv. 124 ; his first Circuit, 158 ; contrasts, 281 ; Editor of "Christian Guardian," 476 ; Secretary of Conf., v. 32 ; again Secretary, 115 ; Book Steward, 170.

Sanderson, Rev. John, received, iv. 295 ; some account of, 297.

Sanderson, Rev. Joseph E., his early piety, v. 145 ; Brampton, 182.

Sanderson, Rev. William, portraiture of, v. 91.

Sarnia, a sad state, iv. 209, John G. Laird there, v. 187.

Saugeen, John Benham there, iii. 366 ; his journal, 367 ; Thomas Hurlburt, 417 ; report, 453 ; David Sawyer's letter, iv. 73 ; a supply, 175 ; greatly quickened, v. 78.

Saul, Mr., a supply, iv. 450.

Savage, John Wesley, his portraiture, v. 188 ; his father, 210.

Savage, William, his antecedents, &c., v. 189.

INDEX. 331

Sawyer, Chief Joseph, embraces Christianity, iii. 21; exhorting, 303.

Sawyer, David, letter from, iii. 262; begins to labor and travel, 302; journal of, 370; his experience, iv. 63; letter from, 73; on trial, v. 87.

Sawyer, Rev. Joseph, a new man for Canada, i. 15, 16; P. Elder, 119; his early life, 119; portraiture of, 124; an accident, 125; locates, 198; a local helper, ii. 379; he visits the Conference, iv. 420.

Scales, William, short account of, v. 177; more, 210.

Scarritt, Josiah A., on trial, ii. 104.

Scotch woman, considerate conduct of a, ii. 43.

Scott, James, conversion of, v. 15.

Scott, Rev. Jonathan, from England, iii. 458; L. Simcoe, iv. 70; letter from, 86; editor of "Christian Guardian," 280; estimate of, 424; Secretary of Conference, 444; superannuated, v. 182.

Scott, Rev. William, from England, iv. 154; his address, 314; letter from, 325; St. Clair, 467; strong affinity, 487; Canada East, v. 38; Montreal, 211.

Scott, William L., a fatherless boy, v. 248.

Scugog Indians, their steadfastness, iii. 113; how supplied, 236.

Scull, Rev. Joseph, some account of, i. 174; return to U. States, 260.

Seagar, Rev. Aurora, a new name, ii. 218; his early life, &c., 230-242.

See, Mr. and Mrs. David, congenial spirits, i. 309.

Selley, Rev. John B., his arrival in Montreal, iv. 144; letter from, 284; another letter, 329; to the author, 342; in Toronto, 403.

Seminary, conference, efforts to establish, iii. 256; successful, 278; an agent appointed, 315.

Sermon on Ephes. v. 14, by Rev. John Sunday, iv. 87.

Shahwundais on trial, iv. 185. (See John Sunday.)

Shaler, Rev. Henry, introduced, iii. 70; Trafalgar, 244; on trial, 253; Albion, 268; Toronto Circuit, 297; a great revival, 342; Waterloo, 386; Rideau, 416; letter from, 430; revival, iv. 47; Richmond, 340; superannuated, v. 205.

Shannon, William, a supply, v. 195.

Shaw, John, his birth and early life, v. 99; on trial, 117; student, Cobourg, v. 199.

Strawbridge, Rev. Robert, plants Methodism in Maryland, i. 5.

Shefford, new ground, ii. 389; success, 438; M. Lang, 487; souls won, iii. 48; Wm. Squire, 90; advancement, 140, 209; R. Pope, 251; Shenstone, 396, 438; Tomkins, 487; iv. 180; an increase, 236; E. Botterell, 283; comments, 286; Tomkins, 328; E. S. Ingalls, 379; M. McDonald, 410; Montgomery, 441, 470; G. Dorey, v. 212.

Shenstone, Rev. William, his arrival in Canada, iii. 252; Shefford, 396, 438; Three Rivers, 487; ditto, iv. 110.

Shepherd, Edmund, his first appointment, iii. 296; on trial, 311; success, 339; Chairman, iv. 358; Bytown District, v. 38; expelled, 190.

Shepherdson, Daniel, new to Canada, ii. 143; his nativity, &c., 153; Niagara Circuit, 224; Lyon's Creek, 311; Ancaster, 362; Yonge Street, 417; Long Point, 452.

Sheply, Joseph, a supply, iv. 344; portraiture of, v. 148.

Sherbrooke, first mention of, iv. 326.

Short, William, portraiture of, v. 248.

Sickles, Abraham, short account of, iv. 384; Tuscarora Indian revival, v. 133; Muncey, 186.

Sidney Circuit, how formed, iii. 415; interesting letter, 467; laborers in demand, iv. 257; prosperity, v. 17.

Silvester, Charles, his first Circuit, iv. 471; success, v. 132; Goderich, 190.

Simcoe. (See Long Point).

Simmonds, George, an exhorter, iii. 295.

Simpson, John, a native supply, iv. 175 ; courtship, 176 ; comforts, 268.

Six Nation Indians, some account of the, ii. 402.

Slater, James C., his early life, iv. 485 ; Picton, 201.

Slater, Rev. William, short account of, ii. 339 ; a supply, 341 ; on trial, 392 ; Thames, 398 ; ord. deacon, iii. 3 ; labor and love, 34; glorious revivals, 69; never happier, 83 ; Cobourg, 106 ; Del. to Gen'l. Conf., 170 ; his death, 243.

Slight, Rev. Benjamin, Amherstburg, iii. 458 ; letter from, 470 ; extracts from journal, iv. 278 ; his address, 314 ; journal, 414 ; return to Three Rivers, 442 ; more from his journal, v. 22 ; degree of M. A. conferred, 45 ; more extracts from journal, 57-59 ; the year 1851, 81 ; report from, 134 ; Sherbrooke, 212.

Smith, Andrew A., his early life, v. 64 ; ord., 140 ; Berlin, 190.

Smith, Bela, some notice of, i. 216; obituary, 218; a glimpse, 229 ; his death, 236.

Smith, Benson, a supply, iii. 457.

Smith, Edmund, and wife, members of the first class in Ancaster, i. 160.

Smith, George, a local supply, iv. 363 ; Brock, 389 ; letter from, 427 ; Mono, 451 ; St. Vincent, v. 33; Owen Sound, 36 ; Nottawasaga, 70.

Smith, Isaac B., some account of, i. 147 ; removal, 170 ; located, 262 ; Ancaster, ii. 130 ; Niagara, 161, 224 ; Westminster, 305 ; Long Point, 356 ; Lyon's Creek, iii. 10 ; superannuated, 53 ; his subsequent course and happy death, 255.

Smith, Jacob, member of first class at Bowman's Church, i. 160.

Smith, Kenneth McK., conversion of, ii. 12 ; portraiture of, 297 ; Augusta, 329 ; his zeal, 365 ; ord. Elder, iii. 3 ; Lyon's Creek, 4 ; superannuated, 53 ; located, 96.

Smith, Mrs. Ann, the first Meth. member in Bowman's class, i. 160.

Smith, Philander, his conversion, ii. 88 ; further notice of, 300 ; a watch-night service, 323 ; success, 379 ; Kingston, 423 ; Hallowell, 467 ; ord. Elder, iii. 3 ; Augusta, 34 ; P. Elder, 182, 202, 245 ; health fails, 269 ; superannuated, 278 ; Prescott, 388 ; his subsequent career, iv. 155.

Smith, Thomas, B. and J. W., New York Conference, i. 236.

Smith, William, short account of, iii. 188 ; Cavan, 190 ; on trial, 210 ; Grape Island, 233 ; Ancaster, 265 ; Assistant Editor, 269 ; York, 297 ; Kingston, 343, 386 ; Brockville, 415 ; last visit, 371.

Smith's Creek in the first list of stations, i. 19 ; extent of, 110 ; how supplied in 1815, ii. 11 ; divided, 139 ; reconstructed, 255 ; its extent, 322 ; increase, 374 ; leading men converted, 418 ; now Cobourg, iii. 72.

Smithville, the first day's meeting in Canada held there, iii. 290.

Snake, Henry, letter from, iii. 263.

Snider, Solomon, short account of, iii. 455 ; dissatisfied, iv. 253 ; again in harness, 426 ; left, v. 32.

Snow, William, account of, i. 156 ; St. Lawrence, 178 ; subsequent career, 200 ; del. to Gen'l. Conf., 238 ; located, ii. 140 ; a Presiding Elder, 426.

Snyder, William, his conversion, &c., i. 134 ; Rev. Dr. Bangs' account of him, 135 ; a perilous journey, 144 ; Ottawa, 145 ; located, 172.

Sorel, Village of, ii. 81 ; visited by Rev. H. Pope, 113.

Sornborger, Stephen, short account of, i. 251.

Southwind, John, two letters from, iv. 273.

Sovereign, George, brief reference to, ii. 452 ; Toronto Circuit, iii. 60, 121 ; conversational powers, 149 ; Westminster, 244 ; located, 253 ; a supply, 265 ; Malahide, iv. 321 ; writes the obituary of S. Heck, 350.

Spears, Duncan, a member of Father Bowman's first class, i. 160.

Spencer, James, first glimpse of, iv. 158 ; a further account, 186 ; elected editor, v. 96.

Spicer, Rev. Tobias, his account of Henry Ryan, i. 24.

Spore, David, brief account of, ii. 296. Bay Quinte, 325; sent adrift, 381.

Springer, Oliver, first graduate of Vic. Coll., iv. 456.

Springer, Richard, some account of, i. 161.

Squire, Rev. William, some account of, iii. 51; Shefford, 90; success, 140, 209; Quebec, 250, 275; Montreal, 306, 349, 396; his letter to the Home Com., 400; Stanstead, 438, 488; his zeal, iv. 109; testimony, 180; return to Montreal, 330; review of work, 355; Quebec, 411; Chairman, Kingston District, v. 38; his death, 138.

Stamford Circuit, formation of, iii. 229; a good year, 329; Stoney and Evans, 380; Wright and Ryerson, 413, 454.

Stanstead Circuit and P. Ayer, i. 140; how connected, 144; increase on, 191; further increase, ii. 19; Benj. Sabin's labors, 70; details, iii. 48; a new man, 89; gracious revival, 140; gloom, 431; revival, 495.

Stanstead District, its stations and men, v. 212.

Steer, William, Kingston, iii. 456; his piety, iv. 32.

Steinhaur, Henry, at school, iii. 24; a native helper, iv. 278; visit to England, v. 218; portraiture of, 218; his labors, 236.

Stevens, Rev. Dr., his history quoted, i. 26, 27; his account of Wooster, 47; his estimate of Woolsey, 45; his account of Dr. Bangs, 104; account of the first Canada Camp-meeting, 113; account of Thomas Burch, ii. 5-7; of Wm. Losee, 51.

Stevenson, William, useful, iv. 214; short account of, 341; Whitby, 406.

Stewards, election of, to be annual, iv. 3.

Stewart, John, a missionary to the Wyandot Indians, ii. 360.

Stewart, Schuyler, a supply, iii. 456; letter from, iv. 25; his marriage and its consequences, 26.

Stinson, Rev. Joseph, his arrival from England, ii. t87; Kingston, iii. 47; Three Rivers, 89, 140; returns 4o

England, 251 ; Canada again, 394; letter from, 431 ; Kingston, 456 ; visiting missions, 474 ; letter from, iv. 31 ; daily employed, 58-67 ; mode of travel, 131 ; appointed President, 200 ; Hamilton Conference, 239 ; letters, 274 ; Belleville Conference, 287 ; deputation to England, 300 ; work in England, 375.

Stobbs, Thomas, short account of, v. 52 ; Amherstburg, 72 ; London, 186.

Stoddan, Rev. Goodwin, a staunch advocate, i. 195.

Stoney, Rev. Edmund, taken into society, ii. 212 ; a local preacher, 410 ; pioneering, 459 ; London, iii. 13, 59 ; Thames, 129 ; Amherstburg, 150, 245 ; Niagara, 290 ; Stamford, 329, 380 ; Yonge Street, 414, 455.

Stoney Creek, the battle of, i. 306 ; Ferguson at, ii. 30 ; notice of James Gage, Esq., 42 ; a visit to the battleground, 97 ; a convention, held there, 493 ; one hundred and seven conversions, iii. 328 ; revival, 330.

Stouffville, a new charge, v. 123.

Strachan, Rev. Dr., his address to the military, i. 299 ; his attack on Methodism, 386.

Stratton, Rev. John B., his election to the Bishopric, iii. 314.

Strawbridge, Robert, plants Methodism in Maryland, i. 5.

Street, John, Esq., of St. John's, never lost his piety, ii. 341.

Streeter, Rev. Squire, a successful worker, i. 191.

Streetsville, early settlers, ii. 364.

Stringfellow, Charles, a timely supply, v. 128.

Strong, Rev. John B., account of, i. 310 ; Montreal, 313.

Sunday, John, begins to travel, iii. 301 ; on trial, 364 ; missionary, 367 ; success, 370 ; ord., 443 ; speech of, iv. 62 ; first charge, 86 ; sermon of, 87 ; visit Engl., 132 ; in full connexion, 185 ; North West, 209 ; first pastorate, 268 ; Camp-meeting, 330 ; letter from, 468.

Sunday-school, the first, in Montreal, ii. 120 ; its prosperity, 126.

" Sunday-school Guardian," the, pub. in Toronto, v. 110.

Superannuated Ministers' Fund, scale of allowance, v. 224.

Sutcliffe, Rev. Ingham, at Three Rivers, iii. 396.

Sutcliffe, Rev. William, first notice of, ii. 338; org. a new Circuit, 387.

Sutherland, Alexander, portraiture of, v. 254.

Sutton, William, a supply, iv. 427.

Swann, Matthew, his antecedents, v. 104; on trial, 117; Walsingham, 184.

Swanston, John, letter from, iv. 272.

Swansea, Case's birth place, i. 1.

Swaze, Caleb, notice of, ii. 93; on trial, 96; Westminster, 130; located, 169.

Sweet, Edmund E., a supply, v. 250; portraiture, 252.

Sydenham, Lord, death of, iv. 352.

Sykes, Rev. Oliver, obituary of, v. 66.

St.

St. Armand, Circuit formed, ii. 203; R. Williams, 277; members, 349; increase, 387; Booth, 437; no increase, iii. 48; M. Lang, 89; Turner, 209, 307, 349; M. Lang, 396, 348.

St. Catharines, formerly Niagara Circuit, iii. 330; interesting facts, 383; Evans and Baxter, 413; good news, 429; R. and Metcalf, 455; a good state, 460.

St. Catharines, Conference of 1845, iv. 443.

St. Clair, its extent, iii. 13; increase, 59; merged into other Circuits, 130; James Evans, 438; letter from, 471; prosperity, iv. 75.

St. Francis Circuit, its location, i. 213.

St. John's, Que., some account of, ii. 22; further notice, 80.

St. Lawrence Circuit, i. 125; ii. 12; new men, 53; A. Prindle, 138; in 1818, 186; Black River District, 301.

St. Regis, i. 7; a crossing place, 11; a large Indian Village, 230.

St. Thomas first named as a Circuit, iv. 122.

T.

Tackabury, Rev. John, short account of, ii. 361 ; history of, 394 ; his death, 396.

Taggart, Charles, brief account of, iv. 392.

Taunchey, John, a native helper, iii. 374-5 ; the Credit Camp-meeting, iv. 430.

Tavern-keeper, conversion of a, i. 79.

Taylor, Rev. Andrew, his arrival in Toronto, iii. 456 ; Brockville, iv. 46 ; death, 320.

Taylor, Rev. James, introduced, v. 100 ; on trial, 117 ; death, 240.

Taylor, Rev. Lachlin, conversion of, iv. 54 ; contrasts, 262 ; lent to Canada East, v. 38 ; supernumerary, 76 ; Agent U. C. B. S., 120.

Temperance societies organized, iii. 265 ; in Perth, 344.

Templeton, the first class formed, iv. 55.

Thames Circuit, Nathan Bangs appointed to, i. 29 ; revival on, 186 ; an increase, ii. 129 ; Wm. Jones the preacher, 152 ; increase, 355 ; two vigorous men, 398 ; Jackson and Griffis, 451 ; another increase, iii. 12 ; divided, 129 ; Ferguson, 150 ; Huston, 245 ; Phelps, 266 ; Hurlburt, 377 ; H. Dean, 385 ; Burgess, 413 ; letter, iv. 19.

Things passed over, iii. 348.

Thomas, John, begins to travel, iii. 301.

Thompson, Dennis, a local preacher, v. 192.

Thompson, James, obituary of, v. 203.

Thornhill, a new church built, v. 133.

Three Rivers, Circuit formed, i. 169 ; R. Pope, ii. 385 ; difficulties, 438 ; chapel opening, 489 ; Knowlan, iii. 46 ; Stinson, 89, 140 ; Faulkner, 209 ; Beckwith, 308 ; Sutcliffe, 396.

Throckmorten, John, the death of, iv. 106.

Tomblin, William, a glimpse of, v. 103 ; a supply, 147.

Tomkins, John, a short account of, iii. 437.

INDEX.   339

Tomkins, Nehemiah U., in Canada, i. 16 ; Oswegotchie, 22 ; further account of, 82.

Toronto Circuit, first mention of, iii. 59 ; Sovereign and Black, 121 ; its extent, 122 ; John Black in charge, 195 ; preaching places, 199, 200 ; division, 238 ; called Trafalgar, 243 ; not efficient, 268 ; a net gain of sixty, 297 ; Corson, 331 ; Bissell and Holtby, 366 ; Thos. Fawcett, 414 ; John Beatty, 455 ; letter, 462 ; prosperity, iv. 24.

Toronto City, Turner and Ryerson, iii. 455 ; Lang and Davidson, iv. 22 ; three brothers, 191 ; excitement, 197 ; Mr. Cooney's letter, 465. (See York.)

Toronto Conference of 1837, iv. 145 ; of 1840, special, 309 ; of 1841, 332 ; of 1847, v. 1 ; of 1851, 84.

Toronto District, its stations and men, iii. 455 ; report from, 462 ; its stations for 1835, iv. 21 ; enlarged, 191 ; change of men, 250 ; its stations and men in 1841, 338 ; vacancies, 427 ; supplies, 451 ; a transfer, v. 32 ; vacancies in 1851, 97 ; the work, how provided for, 120 ; two supplies, 145 ; stations and men in 1854, 181 ; comments, 183.

Torry, Rev. Alvin, sent to Long Point, ii. 143 ; his early life, &c., 154 ; his appointment to Canada, 156 ; a great revival, 159 ; Bishop Asbury's travelling companion, 196 ; Westminster, 219 ; Ancaster, 307 ; extract from his autobiography, 347 ; Grand River Mission, 400 ; success, 446 ; Clarke's Commentary, 450 ; success, iii. 20 ; a Conference scene, 95 ; failing health, 130 ; return to U. States, 131 ; Genesee Conference, 150.

Townley, Adam, short account of, iv. 2 ; his subsequent course, 242.

Townley, Rev. Dr., a letter from, iii. 315.

Trafalgar Township, when named, i. 111 ; Circuit formed, iii. 243.

Trickey, Henry, on trial, v. 12.

Tucker, Samuel, introduced, v. 244.

Tuffy, ———, a local preacher in 1780, i. 6 ; again mentioned, 135.

Tuke, John, his early life, ii. 171 ; notice of, 217 ; indiscretion, 253 ; dropped, 300 ; license restored, 421 ; a supply, iv. 254.

Tupper, Mr. Horace, conversion of, ii. 136.

Tupper, Rev. Reuben E., a supply, iv. 125 ; again called, 258 ; Mississippi, 323.

Turner, Rev. Thomas, short account of, iii. 89 ; a great revival, 140 ; St. Armand's, 209 ; Kingston, 275 ; St. Armand's, 349 ; St. Clair, 352 ; Kingston, 438 ; York, 444 ; Toronto City, 455.

Turver, Charles, a supply, iv. 466 ; ord., v. 29 ; visiting England, 118.

U.

Unconditional perseverance, preaching against, i. 278.

Union Convention, a Christian, v. 220.

Union of the Canada Methodists with the British Wesleyans, projected, iii. 353 ; editorial on, 354 ; the Conf. of 1832, resolutions on, 356-364 ; how regarded, 392-396 ; extract from Magazine, 400 ; union ratified, 404 ; opposition to, 419. (See Methodism in Canada.)

University Bill, Hon. Mr. Draper's, iv. 433.

Upper Canada Academy, charter for, iv. 31 ; opened, 124 ; forty students converted, 158 ; a new Principal, 249 ; incorporated as Victoria College, 351 ; its first graduate, 456.

Upper Canada District, its extent, i. 108, 123 ; its stations and men, 143, 154 ; for 1809, 169 ; for 1810, 199 ; for 1811, 239 ; for 1812, 259 ; for 1815, ii. 3 ; for 1816, 36 ; for 1817, 90 ; for 1818, 142 ; for 1819, 218 ; for 1820, 304 ; for 1821, 353 ; for 1822, 397 ; for 1823, 442. (See Niagara District.)

V.

Valedictory service, a, v. 164.

Van Camp, John, senr., an early convert, i. 8 ; marriage of, 209 ; a class-leader, ii. 133 ; his death, v. 110.

Vanderlip, Rev. Elias, kind and fatherly, i. 141.

Vandusen, Rev. Conrad, conversion of, iii. 99; his first Circuit, 268; on trial, 277; Whitby, 296; a broken leg, 339; Cavan, 387; Dumfries, 414, 455; Secretary of Conference, v. 29; Treasurer and Agent of Vic. Coll., 68.

Van Nest, Rev. Peter, Canada in 1802, i. 16; Oswegotchie, 34; facts of his early life, 73; enters the ministry, 74-75; his death, 82; supplementary, 326, 330.

VanNorman, Rev. Daniel C., his antecedents, iv. 289; Female Academy, 370; Burlington Academy, Hamilton, v. 40; its vigor and success, 76; he removes to the U. S., 108.

VanNorman, Isaac, his remembrances of William Anson, i. 65; his account of Niagara Circuit, 163; his hospitality, ii. 226; his joy, iii. 148; his son, iv. 289.

Vaux, Thomas, Esq., some reference to, iii. 8; an incident, 7; teaching, 19; Toronto, 145; Sec. of Miss'y. Society, 368; his letter to the "Guardian," v. 84; account of revival in Quebec, 167.

Victoria College, incorporation of, iv. 351; opening of, 369; its first examination, 373; its scholarship scheme, v. 130; further advanced, 173; some distinguished graduates, 256; autumn prospects, 257. (See U. C. Academy.)

Virgin, Rev. Charles, obituary of, i. 167.

W.

Wakefield, John, a brief account of, v. 176.

Wakeley's Heroes of Methodism quoted from, ii. 291.

Waldron, Rev. Solomon, some account of, ii. 423; on trial, 440; his narrative, 469; Perth, 484; letter from, iii. 35; incidents, 36; melted, 45; in full connexion, 53; Hallowell, 103; Grape Island, 190, 201; Bay Quinte, 233; Rideau, 273; full of life and fire, 299, 389; Whitby, 414, 456; letters, iv. 71; explanation, 280.

Walker, Levi, a short account of, i. 149.

Walker, Moses, a Mohawk Chief, iii. 412 ; ord., 443.

Walpole, a new mission, iv. 212.

Walpole Island, an Indian mission, iv. 170.

War, declaration of, i. 246 ; its three years' continuance, 258.

Ward, Edward, a home missionary, v. 245.

Ward, James, a supply, iii. 455.

Warner, Christian, his conversion, i. 89.

Warner, Lewis, his first year, iii. 346 ; on trial, 364 ; Bytown, 389 ; Rideau, 416 ; Nelson, 455 ; fervent in spirit, iv. 33 ; a card from, 257.

Washington, George, a glimpse of, v. 73 ; a supply, 103 ; Nelson, 123.

Warren, Elijah, early history of, ii. 40 ; Thames, 129 ; his location and subsequent course, 140.

Waterloo Circuit separate from Kingston, iii. 342.; James Currie, 415 ; letter, 464 ; its extent, iv. 194.

Watson, John, a witness of perfect love, iii. 411 ; Long Point, 413 ; Ancaster, 454.

Webster, John, his ordination, v. 85.

Webster, Mr., a local preacher, i. 283.

Webster, Thomas, D.D., his history quoted, iii. 422-424, 447-450.

Wesley, Rev. John, his death noticed, i. 8.

" Wesleyan," the, pub. in Montreal, iv. 327 ; Toronto, 342$\frac{1}{4}$; discontinued, 433.

Westminster Circuit, formation of, ii. 38 ; members, 40 ; success, 130 ; large increase, 153 ; Smith and Belton, 305 ; increase, 399 ; decrease, 452 ; increase again, iii. 12 ; Jackson, 58 ; Corson, 128 ; M. Whiting, 150 ; its extent and losses, 244 ; Hurlburt, 265 ; Belton, 293 ; a revival, 336 ; Biggar and Davis, 384 ; Rose and Ker, 413, 454 ; letter from S. Rose, 461.

Whatcoat, Bishop, a reference to his death, i. 141.

Whitby Circuit, Meth. first organized, ii. 46 ; Circuit formed, iii. 108 ; R. Corson, forty preaching places, 236 ; Vandusen, 268 ; useful labors, 296 ; Norris and Patrick,

338; Norris and Musgrove, 387; divided, 414; Waldron and McMullen, 456; prosperity, iv. 27; hard times, 253.

White, Ebenezer, some account of, i. 315.

White, Edward, a supply, v. 34.

Whitehead, Rev. Thomas, his birth, &c., i. 131; appointed to Canada, 132; his portraiture, 133; a reference to, 313; on Committee, ii. 1; Ancaster, 10; Sup'd., 89; letter to Mr. Pope, 212; visiting the Indians, 360; his journal, 102-106; his death, 475.

Whiting, Rev. Lansford, i. 191; his obituary, 330.

Whiting, Rev. Matthew, a short account of, iii. 127; on trial, 143; Westminster, 150; London, 244, 265; Amherstburg, 337; Bay Quinte, 415; letter of, iv. 33 at Woodstock, v. 72.

Whiting, Richard, contrasts, iv. 450.

Wigle, Joseph, obituary of, i. 188.

Wilkinson, Rev. Henry, his conversion, ii. 453; preaching talent, 291; L. Point, 293; on trial, 311; some account of, 312; in labors abundant, 336; L. Point, 384; his modesty, 411; Ancaster, 413; Conference experience, 443; interesting letters, iv. 36; a Camp-meeting, 41; his first District, 154; efficient labors, 198; another move, 258; Secretary of Conference, 418; President, 443.

Wilkinson, Henry, teaching, iv. 128.

Wilkinson, John, short account of, iv. 292.

Will, John C., a supply, iv. 24.

Williams, John, some account of, iv. 359; his death, v. 240.

Williams, John A., his early history, iv. 483; Wilton, v. 202.

Williams, Richard, appointed to Montreal, i. 312; Quebec, 313; Montreal again, ii. 21; reference to, 75; Melbourne, 118; Chairman, 270; St. Armand's, 338; Kingston, 385, 436; Quebec, iii. 52.

Williams, Richard, a supply, iv. 389; Lake Simcoe, 427; Owen Sound, 451.

Williams, Thomas, introduced, iv. 321 ; on trial, 334 ; Glanford, v. 182.

Williams, Thomas G., his ancestors, i. 130.

Williams, William, a supply, v. 102 ; Aylmer, 184.

Williams, William H., his relationship, i. 130 ; his early life, &c., ii. 298 ; first Circuit, 306 ; L. Point, 356 ; a long move, 424 ; a great revival, 474 ; ord. Elder, iii. 3 ; Yonge St., 16 ; Toronto Circuit, 60 ; Perth, 137 ; Mississippi, 208 ; Cornwall, 247 ; Brockville, 299 ; Elizabethtown, 345 ; Richmond, 389, 416 ; Waterloo, iv. 339 ; Percy, v. 201.

Williston, John K., a short account of, iii. 385 ; Nelson, 414 ; Yonge Street, 455 ; letter from, iv. 280 ; Thames, 337 ; Strathroy, v. 187.

Willoughby, William, a desirable acquisition, iv. 119 ; in full connexion, 288 ; Elizabethtown, 340 ; a bachelor, 392 ; Newmarket, v. 197.

Willson, Hugh, an incident, i. 131 ; wise and well-informed, 303 ; E. Ryerson's home, iii. 8.

Willson, John V., a supply, v. 147 ; Nanticoke, 183.

Willson, Levi, his recollections of E. Ryerson's first sermon, iii. 8.

Wilson, John, M.A., appointed Professor in Vic. Coll., v. 131.

Wilson, Rev. James, his birth and early history, ii. 173 ; extract from his journal, 175 ; his portraiture, 177 ; Hallowell, 374 ; a power for good, 419 ; a further glimpse, iii. 33 ; sermon, 45 ; again effective, 69 ; Whitby, 108, 194 ; Trafalgar, 243 ; Ancaster, 264 ; Stamford, 290 ; Niagara, 329 ; superannuated, 365 ; death, v. 93.

Wilson, Rev. Shipley M., in deacon's orders, ii. 19 ; short account of, 20.

Wilson, Richard, his early history, v. 47 ; Lochabar, 155 ; Russeltown, v. 212.

Witted, John G., his visit to the Hamilton Conference, v. 50 ; leave to visit England, 106 ; his return, 129 ; Colborne, 199.

Wood, Anthony, death of, iii. 486.

Wood, Rev. Charles, recommended, ii. 329 ; conjectures, 327 ; doubts, 421 ; health fails, 483 ; on trial, iii. 210 ; Augusta, 246 ; Mississippi, 300 ; Richmond, 346 ; Elizabethtown, 388 ; A. Hurlburt his colleague, 416.

Wood, Rev. Enoch, D.D., his visit to Toronto Conference, v. 2 ; appointed Sup't. of Can. Meth. Missions, 8 ; his early history, 8-9 ; appointed President, 77 ; enters the Chair, 84 ; his Indian name, 131 ; visit to Canada East, 164.

Wood, William, a supply, iv. 348.

Woodstock, H. Byers there, iv. 375 ; a pleasant field, 436 ; zeal, 466 ; Fawcett and Cawthorne, v. 14 ; a new church opened, 162 ; McCullough and Dixon, 184.

Woodsworth, Richard, his arrival in York, iii. 364.

Woolsey, Rev. Elijah, Upper Circuit, i. 14 ; incident of, 44 ; history, 45 ; death, 46 ; correction and obituary, 328.

Woolsey, Rev. Thomas, a supply, v. 127 ; on trial, 141 ; short notice of, 142 ; Brighton, 201 ; Saskatchewan, 219.

Woolwich Township, first sermon in, ii. 458.

Wooster, Rev. Hezekiah C., app't. to Canada, i. 14 ; revival, 15 ; goes home to die, 15 ; a further account of, 46 ; his power in prayer, 48 ; death, 51.

Wright, Rev. Daniel, a supply, iv. 257 ; Bath and Isle of Tanti, 339 ; Vic. College, 394.

Wright, Rev. David, recommended, ii. 329 ; his early life, 330 ; conversion, 332 ; his first Circuit, 375 ; Belleville, 421 ; on trial, 441 ; Hallowell, 467 ; one hundred souls, iii. 37 ; in full connexion, 53 ; Augusta, 133 ; Matilda, 205 ; success, 245 ; Cobourg, 267, 295 ; revival, 332 ; Yonge Street, 381 ; Stamford, 413, 454 ; letter from, iv. 16 ; Credit, 339 ; Agent for Connexional Funds, 394 ; superannuated, v. 182.

Wyandot Indians, their first missionary, ii. 360 ; further notice of, 463 ; their numbers, iii. 54 ; at Amherstburg, iv. 86.

15*

Y.

Year of Wesley's death, the, i. 8.

Yellowhead Chief, exhorting, iii. 121.

Yellowhead Island, John S. Attwood, iii. 269; Allison and Currie, 296; change of name to Lake Simcoe Mission, 334.

Yeomans, Dr., a guide, iii. 71.

Yonge Street first in the station list, i. 19; Daniel Pickett there alone, 26; its extent, 111; a decrease, ii. 11; doubts, 42; another decrease, 130; exchange of ministers, 167; David Youmans, 227; increase, 311; Ryerson and Slater, 459; prosperity, iii. 60; Ryerson and Beatty, 109; Wilson, 194; division, 238; Norris, 268; Norris and Adams, 296; a revival, 328; large increase, 332; showers of blessings, 381; Corson and Stoney, 414; Stoney and Williston, 455; Beatty and Mulkins, iv. 23; Thomas Bevitt, 328.

York, first church erected in, ii. 131; opening of, and society formed, 140; Circuit organized, 165; its first class, 166; a remarkable case, 226; Brit. Wes. Society formed, 227; population of, in 1820, 320; the new settlements, 363; Rev. Fitch Reed's report, 265; increase, 416; supplied, 459; Wm. H. Williams, iii. 16; prosperity, 60; Ryerson and Beatty, 109; William R., 194; a happy pastorate, 239; a *Bokim*, 268; William Smith, 297; the seat of Conference, 309; Adelaide Street Church built, 332; George Street Church dedicated, 353; Alex. Irvine, 381, 414. (See Toronto City.)

York Conference of 1831, an account of, iii. 309; of 1833, 404.

York District, its. P. Elder, iii. 411; its stations and men, 455.

York "Gazette," the, published, i. 258.

Youmans, Rev. David, short account of, i. 291; ord. deacon, ii. 1; Ancaster, 10; Westminster, 130; supernumerary, 311; located, 391; re-admitted, iii. 147; Yonge Street,

238 ; Toronto Circuit, 268 ; Credit Mission, 297 ; Quar. Meeting, 303 ; his death, 313.

Youmans, Jay S., portraiture of, v. 175.

Young, Rev. George, a letter from, i. 266 ; some account of, iv. 359 ; a change unexpected, v. 68.

Young, Rev. William, licensed to exhort, iii. 268 ; Cavan, 339 ; letter from, 344 ; explanation, iv. 452.

Z.

Zeal, worthy of imitation, iv. 12 ; in the missionary cause, 446.

THE END.

POSTSCRIPT.

☞ OMISSIONS AND MISTAKES BROUGHT TO LIGHT IN PREPARING THE ALPHABETICAL INDEX :—(1) The admission of *Rev. J. G. Witted* into the Conference in 1850 is omitted. (2) We neglected to give *Rev. John Webster* any notice before his ordination, mentioned on page 85, vol. v. He was a member of the sturdy Webster family, Township of London, himself a good man and true. (3) On page 247, vol. v., I erroneously charged Mr. Cornish's Hand-Book with furnishing no account of the *Rev. H. H. Perdue*, for more information of whom see the Hand-Book. (4) It is thought that I have confused matters a little relative to the two younger *Armstrongs, John* and *John B.:* the latter began his labors on the *L'Orignal Circuit*, the former on the *Eaton;* and, (5), worse than all, I omitted our noble, zealous, soul-saving *Rev. John C. Ash* altogether. He was one of the *supplies* for 1855-56, a Devonshire man, who spent a year at Victoria College, and has labored faithfully the other twenty-one years. (6) There is no mention of the *Rev. Charles De Wolfe*, save in the stations from year to year. This is to be regretted, as he was one of the most amiable and accomplished ministers in the work, a native of Nova Scotia, who, I believe, had been designed for the law. (7) The name of the supply for Mud Lake, mentioned on page 126, vol. i., is omitted : it was dear *Orrin H. Ellsworth.* (8) On pages 174 and 178, vol. v., " *George L. Richardson* " should have been *G. T. R.*—a typographical error. (9) *Henry Tomkins,* Clarenceville, on page 212, vol. v., should be *Henry Lanton.*

A HUMBLE OVERTURE

FOR

METHODIST UNIFICATION

IN THE

DOMINION OF CANADA.

BY

JOHN CARROLL.

"A brother offended is harder to be won than a strong city; and their contentions are like the bars of a castle."—PROVERBS xviii. 19.

TORONTO:
PRINTED FOR THE AUTHOR, BY THE REV. S. ROSE.

Price 5 cents a copy; 50 cents a dozen; and $1 a quarter-hundred. To be had at the Book Rooms of the several Methodist bodies.

INTRODUCTION.

The dead-lock now existing to the further progress of unification among the Methodists of Canada, appears to be on the principle of "one is afraid, and the other dare not." Men of office have their good standing with their respective denominations to preserve, and they are afraid of committing the body to something which their backers will not approve. In which case, if some un-official man would propound a plan, which would embrace the concessions to be on all sides, in mere outline, it would be something to start from. This proposal few will be willing to make, for fear of losing prestige or something else.

Now, I have neither office nor prestige to lose; and feeling a profound interest in Canada Methodism, with the central body of which I have stood associated for more than fifty years,—eschewing the invitations of three successive generations of disruptionists. The present *brochure* will be considered venturesome by my friends, but I cheerfully take the venture. I have reason to know that former proposals did good to the cause of unity, though perhaps not to myself.

In the modifications of our own system proposed, I am sure I have the majority of members and ministers on my side, if they are not over-awed by the rigid conservatives, whose tenacity supply the place of numbers. But I implore them to consider the case with an enlightened consideration of all the circumstances, and to beware lest they prevent at this crisis the accomplishment of unification for ever. Some may think that my disapproval of some pet theories are rather bluntly expressed, but I think by this time they ought to be convinced that I am neither partial nor unkind.

I have mentioned several things as matters of personal preference, which may be relegated to the category of minor details, and accepted or not as in no wise vital to the general character of the scheme. Many things in the organization when first launched would doubtless be modified in the process of legislation from four years to four years.

Inviting the prayers of all the friends of unity, "that we all may be one," I remain, with love to all concerned,

THE AUTHOR.

A HUMBLE OVERTURE, &c.

METHODIST DIVISIONS A DISGRACE AND A CAUSE OF FEEBLENESS.

THE many divisions in Methodism are nothing to its credit, showing that those who bear the name have set too little store by unity, which they have so often severed for very trifling considerations. If this pettish tendency to interrupt communion on trivial grounds marked the infancy of our denomination, it is time that we had "put away childish things," in this particular; and that we now cultivate the dignity of denominational manhood. If we do not, we shall find ourselves outstripped by a sister denomination, which has recently composed the differences between almost as many sections of Presbyterianism as there are of Methodism.

NONE OF OUR ORIGINAL PRINCIPLES CONFLICT WITH COMPROMISE.

Looking back on the original testimony and character of Methodism, which all sections of it profess to revere, there is really no principle involved that need keep us apart. Methodism was not the result of declaring for or against Church establishments, for it pronounced an establishment from the first, "a merely human institution;" it did not declare for or against Presbyterianism, or Episcopacy, for its Presbyterial section in England holds fraternal relations with its Presbyterio-Episcopal Sister in the United States, and its ordinations and ministerial *status* are reciprocally regarded as on a par. *Connexionalism*, however, is a characteristic of Methodism under every name and aspect which its many sections have assumed, or preserved.

There are only three features essential to Methodism, and these three have been retained by all: namely, its *peculiar doctrines*, or its *manner* of emphasizing the doctrine of assurance, or the witness of the Spirit, and the possibility of "perfecting" of that "holiness," "without which no man shall see God;" certain *prudential means of grace of a social character*, such as the class and fellowship meeting, and the lovefeast; and the *itinerancy*, or the *united, rotating, itinerant pastorate*, including a central appointing power. Methodism is a *revival* —it means *conversion:* and the preaching of the above-mentioned doctrines, and the maintenance of a ministry detached from local ties, and the frequent assembling together above referred to, are necessary to conserve that revival and to promote conversions, or to the "spread of scriptural holiness over the land." If these essentials are preserved, other things may be modified according to circumstances; for it has been a principle in Methodism from the first, that no exact system of Church order is taught in the New Testament.

THE CHANGES PROPOSED ARE NO "CONCESSION."

To adopt a useful feature by one section from another, or in forming a union with another, cannot be called a "concession." And, after the experience of eighty-five years in Canada, and the experiments which have been tried, I believe we could compile a better system of Methodism than is exemplified in any one section of it now upon earth, a system which would give all reasonable consideration to the laity, combined with efficiency to the administration of the pastorate; and a system which would give all reasonable liberty to local courts, in all matters not infringing on connexional authority and unity, and yet would provide for a thorough central authority and supervision, which the exigencies and energy of a Connexion require.

LAY RIGHTS.

With these general principles laid down, I come to the details of their application. As to the *first* of these, a proper consideration to the laity, they should share in all the counsels of the Church, excepting what refers strictly to the work which is peculiarly a minister's, and to the character of ministers, which, so long as the laity are tried by a jury of their own peers, should be canvassed by ministers alone, not prohibiting charges to be preferred by laymen, of course. Personally, I do not attach so much importance to this particular as some, for I would be quite as willing to be tried by laymen as ministers, in expectation of quite as just or lenient a verdict; but the majority of all the ministers in all the older branches of Methodism do not feel as I do, and regard this point as vital. And it would be unjust and unreasonable to wrest the prerogative from them, so long as they continue to exercise it with the fidelity they have done in the past, especially as they only, in contradistinction from the laity, are subject to an annual examination of character. If all the lay-members of District Meetings and Conferences had the following questions asked about themselves, there would be some reason in making the inquiry reciprocal: namely, "Is there any thing against his moral and religious character? Does he believe our doctrines, and obey our discipline, especially in the matter of reading the Scriptures, maintaining family and private prayer, observing the Lord's Supper, and fasting or abstinence? Has he been punctual in attending all the society meetings, especially prayer and class-meetings? Is he equitable in all his business transactions?"

LAYMEN IN THE DISTRICT MEETINGS AND ANNUAL CONFERENCES.

But this one matter of character conceded, I think it is very unwise in the ministry, whether it be to further unify the body or not, to withstand the claim of a seat to laymen in the District Meeting and the Annual Conference, which is only the District Meeting on a larger scale, on all the questions propounded, [as to the District Meeting] from question "FIFTH," page 40 of the Discipline of the M. C. OF CANADA, to the end, on page 49, except such as may be construed to relate to the character and qualifications of ministers; and, [as to the Annual Conferences] all from question 3rd, Discipline, page 32, to question 19, on the following page, excepting questions 12, 13, and 14. I do not stop to argue the propriety of this, as it is a necessary concession from the largest body in order to the adhesion of nearly all the others; and I know of no reason from Scripture, or practical utility, against the lay participation indicated.

When I hear any such reasons urged, it will be time enough to answer them, which, I presume to say, will be no very difficult task. With these qualifications, I would most readily concur in the manifesto of the Primitive Methodist Conference, that "there shall be an equal number of Laymen to Ministers in all our Church courts."

But I do not think it would be wise or well to allow "all business meetings to elect their own chairmen." If it be simply some committee for a temporary object, that would follow of course; or if it were a connexional one and the disciplinary chairman unable to attend; but for District Meetings, Quarterly Official Meetings, Leaders and Stewards' Meetings, and Trustee Meetings, to be able to set aside the Chairman or Superintendent, is to empower them to sin against connexional unity, and to carry a district or circuit out of the body which it is the very design of connexionalism to prevent. Such an act is as much disrespectful to the *laymen* in the court above, which appointed the presiding officer, as it is to the *clergymen* in that body.

CHAIRMEN OF CHURCH BOARDS TO BE MINISTERS.

As to *secular* men being eligible to preside in Conferences, whether Annual or General, it is simply ridiculous. Can you expect a man to handle the deliberations of an ecclesiastical body and to decide questions of Church order, the bent of whose mind has been to the "study of things carnal and secular," in preference to one who has spent years in familiar intercourse with such matters? As well might you depute one of these clerics to go and conduct the commercial transactions of that secular candidate. Again, is it seemly that a gentleman, whose business posters are at that moment on the fence, should be presiding over the deliberations of a grave ecclesiastical body? Would it not shock the sense of propriety of ten thousand, where it would gratify the whim of one? It cannot be hoped that this will ever be conceded. I believe I would go farther than almost any other of the oldest body for organic unity, but I would never concur in that. It is suicidal to the Church itself, to wish to deprive ministers from performing the very functions for which they have been trained and are qualified.

NOMINATIONS IN THE QUARTERLY OFFICIAL MEETINGS.

As to "Circuit Quarterly Meetings nominating their own officials," I am free to admit that leading influences in the older Methodist bodies have pushed the claim of pastoral nomination so far and with a tenacity that has rather impaired pastoral influence, while it was hoped to add to pastoral authority. But then, both the clergy and the laity of the Church should be represented in these official appointments. And this is the ground for pastoral nomination: its advocates say, not without show of propriety, "I *nominate*, you *elect*." By this mutual veto on each other, they must be forced to accord in the end. It will not do to say, "The ministers may *vote* in the Quarterly or Circuit Meeting as well as the lay officials;" yes, but being outnumbered ten to one, they are sure to be out-voted. I think the principle of this joint action, or mutual veto, is correct, but we have unfortunately reversed the Scriptural order: the Apostles said (Acts vi. 3,) "*Look ye out* among you honest men, of good report, and full of the Holy Ghost and wisdom, whom *we may appoint.*" Our Discipline should first fix the standard of qualification, then let the laity choose men corresponding with this description, and let the pastorate have the right of finally authorizing, or vetoing, if they have cause to believe an individual unworthy; but, of course, at the same time being responsible as they are in all other respects to the judiciary of the Church.

I hold some peculiar opinions myself about the powers of these local or circuit courts, and the way they have exercised their powers in times past. Let the stickler for lay-suffrage remember that those quarterly meeting elections are no election by the general laity of the Church, but is the election of lay-officials of one another—the doing of a close corporation, answerable to no one, but often over-topping the ministry and rank and file of the Church at the same moment. Talk of priestly tyranny; I have seen more intolerable tyranny enacted by a few local courts that I could particularize than all the ministers I ever knew. I believe the true analogy would be, let the whole society elect the Stewards who handle their money once a year, and no Society "Representatives" would be needed; let the pastor appoint the Leaders, with the concurrence of their several classes; and let these, with the local preachers, exhorters, S. School Superintendents, and Representatives of Trustee Boards, as at the present appointed, constitute the Quarterly Official Meeting. The Stewards would represent the financial interests of the membership, and the Leaders would be at once the sharers of the ministers' pastoral work and authority, and yet the representatives of their several classes as well.

METHOD FOR CALLING AN ARBITRARY CHAIRMAN TO ACCOUNT.

I think that what the demanders for electing the chairmen of Church-meetings seek to prevent is the right of a clerical chairman to refuse putting a vote, or his adjourning a meeting at his own will. There is no doubt that some tyrannical things have been done by arbitrary men, (and all the enactments in the world will not prevent some men being arbitrary when they get into office—it is their nature) especially when goaded on by dangerous and turbulent levellers. These two extremes create all the trouble; but their conduct on both sides works the cure of the mischief: people get weary of it and put it down. Now this power of a chairman complained of is practically possessed by the chairmen of all bodies; but both theirs and ours are amenable for their acts, and they ought to be. If a chairman of a meeting sees that a resolution is unconstitutional, he should refuse to put it; but if his ruling is reported to be in conflict with the rights of the laity, there should be a court for trying the question, in which the laity should compose a moiety of the members. If a chairman refuse to put a motion which conflicts with connexional authority and unity, he deserves respect and commendation; but if he does it barely out of stupid adherence to his own preferences in matters unessential, he deserves to be arraigned and deprived of his office.

CONCESSIONS TO THE EPISCOPALS.

The preferences and wishes of the Episcopal type of Methodism deserve to be considered in a plan for unification, and the introduction of some of its characteristics would be not a concession merely, but real elements of strength, energy, and usefulness.

THE EPISCOPAL OFFICE.

First, then, as to the Episcopal office itself: The change in the original Canada Conference from a permanent Episcopacy to that of an annual Presidency arose from no dissatisfaction with the Episcopacy, but on the principle of compromise for peace sake, the same which is now being urged. All that remain of the ministers and members who were connected with the Church before 1832, have no prejudice, but pleasant memories of that form of Methodism. It is true, there is a large infusion in the present "Methodist Church of Canada" who either came from non-Episcopal Methodist bodies in England since 1832, or were brought into the Church during this period, and all of those bodies of that type in this country, contracting parties to the Union, can not be expected to have any proclivities for Episcopacy, and may even have prejudices against it, whose preferences will require concession. Besides, the views of the Eastern Conferences deserve to be considered, which have not been trained in notions at all leading to Episcopacy. Yet even these, I would venture to say, if they went to reside in the neighboring republic, would feel no scruples in uniting with the prominent Methodist body in that country because of its Episcopacy.

GENERAL SUPERINTENDENTS.

But even supposing our Episcopal friends will have to surrender something for union in that particular, the essentials of Episcopacy may be preserved and a real element of good secured. The very short experiment in the newly-united body of a President of General Conference, without any general supervision of an authoritative kind, should have convinced us that the contrivance is an anomaly and an instance of connexional weakness and incompleteness. A General Superintendency, presiding in the Annual Conferences, would give a homogeneity, a unity, and an energy to the united body, which we need not expect to have in our present disjointed mode of operation. But the General Superintendency may be secured without the form of a separate ordination, or a life-long incumbency of office. An election from General Conference to General Conference, or for the space of four years, provided successful administrators were eligible to re-election, would secure all the benefits of oversight, without the danger of confounding an *office* with an *order*. You could keep the efficient, or get rid of the inefficient, which you cannot do with a life-long Episcopacy. If our Episcopal brethren will yield the consecration, which is absurd in a mere presbyterial overseer, we shall be able, I hope, to secure the General Superintendency in the united body.

A MODIFIED PRESIDING ELDERSHIP.

If we have travelling General Overseers, we may get rid of the expense of Presiding Elders, or travelling Chairmen—unless in the case of missionary ground, where I would have the Annual Conferences empowered to relieve the chairmen of districts from the care of particular charges, and to instruct them to travel constantly throughout their respective districts; in which case, they might be called Presiding Elders,—indeed, in either case, in my humble opinion, it is a more expressive name than chairman.

THE DIACONATE, OR HALF-ORDINATION.

The restoration of the diaconate, or the giving of a probationer the half-ordination, empowering him to baptize and marry, and to assist the elder at the sacrament, at the end of two years well endured probation, with a seat in the Annual Conference, would, while it would seem like a concession to our Episcopal brethren, be a valuable administrative arrangement in itself, for which I could furnish something like Wesleyan precedents and many reasons for its probable usefulness.

A MERE OUTLINE.

Now all these proposals could be amplified, illustrated and argued or defended at much greater length, if I did not think that a mere outline exhibition of my plan, besides being simplest, is best at this stage of proceedings. When I find any part to be misunderstood or challenged, it will be time enough to explain or defend.

COMPROMISES ABOUT EQUAL.

According to the scheme which I have sketched above there would be concession and compromise about equally exercised on all sides : the present Methodist Church of Canada would be conceding lay-co-operation to a much greater extent than now in the District Meeting, and the same in the Annual Conference in lieu of its present mixed-committee system ; the Primitive Methodists would be giving up one-half of their lay-delegates ; and all those bodies which have full lay-delegation at present would be surrendering several things to pastoral authority and ministerial prerogative which ministers do not enjoy among them now. I do not say anything about our Episcopal brethren surrendering the matter of lay-delegation in the Annual as well as General Conference, for they have it under consideration ; but our brethren of the Evangelical Association, if they came into the measure, would be surrendering that which they have not yet conceded to the laity—a representation in Conference ; and the Episcopal Methodists would be surrendering their Bishops, proper, for General Superintendents, elected for a term of four years ; and they would be giving up their travelling Presiding Elders, unless in rare cases, as a temporary expedient for supervising the newer parts of the work, more likely to be supplied with a younger and less experienced ministry. The diaconate, perhaps, might not be much cared for one way or another on any side ; but all the other bodies besides themselves would be adopting what they have not been much—or lately—used to, a General Supervision instead of an Annual and Local Presidency.

*** If any considerable number of Methodists in any locality, upon the perusal of it, approve of this scheme, let them call an unofficial meeting and express their approval. This might be done in sections, by those of the several bodies apart ; or done by a mass meeting of all sorts of Methodists together. This will give impetus to the union movement, and show the state of public opinion.

www.ingramcontent.com/pod-product-compliance
Lightning Source LLC
Chambersburg PA
CBHW030401230426
43664CB00007BB/694